Man and Forest Series

No. 3

General Editors

Klaus Seeland
Franz Schmithüsen

A joint research venture of the

Council of Cultural Growth and Cultural Relations, Cuttack

and

Chair of Forest Policy and Forest Economics,
Swiss Federal Institute of Technology (ETH), Zurich

in co-operation with

Deutsche Gesellschaft für Technische Zusammenarbeit (GTZ)
Tropenökologisches Begleitprogramm (TOEB)
(Tropical Ecology Support Programme)

In Indonesia, the author was supported by the Promotion of Sustainable Forest Management Systems (SFMP) Project under the auspices of the Ministry of Forestry and the GTZ.

The German version of this study was submitted as a dissertation to Albert-Ludwigs-University of Freiburg in August 2000.

The supervision and the examination of the study was provided by
Professor Dr. Stefan Seitz
(Institute of Ethnology, Albert-Ludwigs-University, Freiburg),
as well as by
PD Dr. Klaus Seeland
(Forest Policy and Forest Economics,
Swiss Federal Institute of Technology, ETH, Zürich).

Financially, the study was enabled by a scholarship from the Tropical Ecology Support Programme (TÖB - PN 90.2136.1) of GTZ.

Man and Forest Series

General Editors: Klaus Seeland; Franz Schmithüsen

The Man and Forest Series consists of monographs and readers on the use and management of forests and an account of forest lifestyles in various regions of South Asia. It aims at providing the findings of an eight years research project (1992-99) to the public. The volumes in this series are the outcome of a cross-cultural research network between the Chair of Forest Policy and Forest Economics, Swiss Federal Institute of Technology (ETH), the Deutsche Gesellschaft für Technische Zusammenarbeit (GTZ) and Non-Government as well as Government Organisations in India, Nepal and Bhutan. The series welcomes contributions covering relevant issues in the man-forest interface.

A Forest Tribe of Borneo

Resource use among the Dayak Benuaq

For my grandfather
Bakot
and his little great-grandson
Timm Bakot

A Forest Tribe of Borneo

Resource use among the Dayak Benuaq

by
Christian Gönner

D.K. Printworld (P) Ltd.
New Delhi

Cataloging in Publication Data — DK

Gönner, Christian.

A forest tribe of Borneo.
(Man and forest series; no. 3).
Includes bibliographical references (p.)
Includes index.

1. Dayak (Indonesian people). 2. Benuaq (Indonesian people). 3. Ethnology — Borneo. 4. Natural resources — Borneo. I. Title. II. Series: Man and forest series; no. 3.

ISBN 81-246-0193-3

First published in India in 2002

Supported by: Tropical Ecology Support Programme (TOEB)
Deutsche Gesellschaft für Technische Zusammenarbeit (GTZ)

Published and printed by:
D.K. Printworld (P) Ltd.
Regd. office : '*Sri Kunj*', F-52, Bali Nagar
New Delhi - 110 015
Phones : (011) 545-3975; 546-6019
Fax : (011) 546-5926
E-mail: dkprintworld@vsnl.net

Foreword

SCIENTIFIC knowledge of local communities in developing countries with by and large sustainable management practises has a great ecological and political value for the global environmental protection agenda. The material Christian Gönner is providing and interpreting is a valuable contribution to understand an indigenous conceptualisation of local resource use and forest management. It shows a remarkable geographical range of marketing and trade that transcends the widespread common notion of locally bound subsistence economies. The highly flexible modes of subsistence and trade of the Dayak Benuaq who live in Borneo (East Kalimantan) under conditions of economic uncertainty have been discussed with the author and are partly reflected on the background of experiences which were made in a research-network on the indigenous use and management of forests in the wider Himalayan context over the last nine years. The research network was initiated and co-ordinated by the Chair of Forest Policy and Forest Economics at the Swiss Federal Institute of Technology. The book is the author's PhD dissertation, in which one of the editors of this series acted as co-guide. It is the result of true interdisciplinary research and reasoning taking methodologies from the natural and social sciences into account.

This analysis of the lifestyle of the Dayak Benuaq of Lempunah village is published in a phase of transition, a time when their traditional mode of production and resource management is challenged by new and powerful interventions from outside. Economic and political interests have ventured into the interior of Borneo's forests and change many conditions which have been essential to lead an almost independent tribal lifestyle over centuries. However, it is most interesting to gain a detailed insight into what a traditional tribal life-style was and, to a certain extend, still is and how it reflects the various adaptations to local environmental conditions.

The conditions that prevail in Indonesia today show the limitations of such communities as the Dayak Benuaq to survive in continuation of their traditional patterns of resource use. These and their social norms and cultural values related to them are not only threatened by the pervading power of an emerging nation state and economic penetration of remote areas due to international commercial interests. A tribal society which is at the cross-roads of various options of a modernised, or better to say, post-traditional way of life has nothing else to rely on but its age-old cultural identity and mode of production to make a living from. In the long run, and this can be seen from the rationale applied in the Dayak Benuaq's resource use patterns, their chance to adapt themselves to new socio-political conditions will largely depend on a timely transformation of their flexibility to react to environmental and any other changes.

Case studies such as the one presented in this book do not only contribute to the knowledge about a tribal life world which is fading away almost without being noticed. They are valuable because of their intricate knowledge of what is known by a forest dwelling culture who has appropriated the spirit and wealth of a world which was hitherto unknown to outsiders. They will always have their message to convey to the academic world and to political decision-makers who are trying to promote sustainability of resource use in the twenty-first century. Perhaps they can all learn from this forest tribe of Borneo.

Klaus Seeland

Franz Schmithüsen

Acknowledgements

FIRST of all I want to thank my wife, Susanne Schwarz, for all her invaluable support and the many inspiring discussions. Without her I might well have run wild. . . .

I am further indebted to the patience and co-operation of the people of Lempunah and Tanjung Isuy, who gave me and my wife the feeling of a second home. Special gratitude is owed to the family of my 'Benuaq-professor' and grandfather Kakah Abuk (Bakot); his wife Itaq Abuk (Jonen); my host father Kakah Seni (Teng); his wife Itaq Seni (Uteng); as well as to all their children and grandchildren. During my field studies, I learnt much about the Ohong forests from Taman Kadi (Acuy), Taman Tin (Asuy), Aling, Mexis, Ojot, Nyak, Tompo, Esmawati, Sandora, Maria Moy, Kaka and Taman Pikal (Sekot).

Constructive critical discussion partners, over many years, were my field assistant Benyamin and my wise 'lecturer' Akung. My grandfather Kakah Abuk and the late Kepala Adat of Tanjung Isuy, Dangud, generously allowed me a deep insight into the Benuaq's cosmovision.

It would lead too far to list all the Benuaq friends who helped us. None the less, a few must be mentioned by name, such as Sudirman, Suratno, Surni, Dah, Nomi, Sardi, Sehat, Mahlan, Ucun and Petrus. I cannot end this list, however, without special thanks to Tinan Lukas and Taman Lukas for saving my life, and the life of my wife, several times with delicious wild boar dishes and a cold beer.

I also wish to thank Nera and Aseng for their formal help, as well as our friends in Samarinda from Puti Jaji, Plasma, and SHK.

In Samarinda, we found a warm-hearted sanctuary with Hartmut Abberger, Anja Hoffmann and Michael Klingler, who joined us in many discussions and durian sessions. But also the other team members of the project on the Promotion of Sustainable Forest

Management Systems (SFMP) and the Integrated Forest Fire Management Project (IFFM), especially Hans Beukeboom, Gottfried and Michaela von Gemmingen, Dieter and Ingrid Haury, Alexander and Sabine Hinrichs, Rolf and Christa Ulbricht, Hans-Wilhelm and Ulrike von Haugwitz, as well as Sondra Wentzel, always made us feel welcome.

Paulus Matius identified the plant species, and Mustofa Agung Sardjono was always a patient help, as were his students Kori Basuki and Sunaryo. Doris Weidemann (GTZ-IFFM) provided me with the meteorological data.

Special acknowledgements should be made to Hadi Daryanto, project director of SFMP, and Hans-Wilhelm von Haugwitz, team leader of SFMP, who made my fieldwork possible. Apart from his support in formal issues, Mr. von Haugwitz and his wife also had a good eye for the deprivations of life 'in the field'. Johannes Huljus, successor of Hans-Wilhelm von Haugwitz, kindly helped me with the extension of my fieldwork.

Sondra Wentzel never tired of discussing my research problems. She also helped me with many valuable comments on my TÖB report. Other excellent discussion partners were Dietmar Stoian as well as Brian Belcher and Manuel Ruiz-Pérez from the Centre for International Forestry Research (CIFOR). Anja Hoffmann was a patient teacher regarding Geographical Information Systems.

I owe much gratitude to my supervisors Stefan Seitz and Klaus Seeland for numerous long discussions, for their constant help concerning formal aspects, as well as for the many constructive ideas. Klaus Seeland; Terence Hay-Edie; Herwig Zahorka; my wife, Susanne Schwarz and my father, Winfried Gönner proof-read my study. Special thanks are due to Günther Rietmacher, Richard Haep, Elisabeth Mausolf and Dorothea Otto of the Tropical Ecology Support Programme (GTZ), which sponsored and helped me to find my way through dense administrative jungles.

Finally, I would like to express my thanks to Franz Schmithüsen, the head of the Chair of forest policy and forest economics of ETH Zürich, for his valuable structural contributions, and for the uncomplicated publication of my research.

It would be presumptuous to believe that I have mentioned every person who helped me during the last five years in Indonesia or in

Europe. Thus, I want to thank all my friends and family for their letters, e-mails and thoughts that found their way to Lempunah.

Überlingen, March 2001 **Christian Gönner**

Das unbewusste oder halb-bewusste Bestreben, Ordnung in die Verwirrung der anthropologisch-ethnographischen Erscheinungen zu bringen, neigt sehr zur Annahme solcher grossen Ursachen, die, wenn sie thatsächlich als wirkende zu Grunde lägen, ungemein vereinfachende, klärende Erklärungen bieten würden.

The unconscious or half conscious endeavour to bring order into the confusion of anthropological-ethnological phenomena, tend to the assumption of causes so big that they would offer extremely simplifying, clarifying explanations, if they really were the effective causes.

— Friedrich Ratzel 1882:300

Summary

Keywords: *ethnology, cultural ecology, Borneo, South-East Asia, resources, forest use and management*

THE forests surrounding the Dayak Benuaq village of Lempunah (East-Kalimantan, Indonesia) have been used for more than 300 years in an extensive way. Today, these forests consist of hundreds of forest gardens (rattan, rubber and mixed fruit gardens), swidden fields and fallows.

The Dayak Benuaq cultivate more than 100 locally-differentiated rice varieties as well as 150 additional crops. Furthermore, at least 500 wild plant and animal species are extracted from the forest. This enormous reservoir enables the Benuaq to practice an extended subsistence economy including trade with various forest products.

Studying the local resource use over several years reveals substantial dynamics with frequent switching between different income sources, as well as a significant variation in the number and kind of swidden fields. These irregular temporal patterns are the result of general resource use strategies and individual decision-making rationales. The plausibility of the latter can be shown by analysing causal nets which integrate economic, ecological, social, religious, political, historical and emotional aspects.

The most relevant livelihood strategies are based on three principles: (1) food security through subsistence; (2) flexible use of diversified resources; and (3) use of natural dynamics. So far, most studies underestimated the high degree of individual flexibility, which allows farmers a fast and efficient response to unpredictable changes such as price fluctuations or natural calamities. Switching between different resources leads to times of intensive use and to other times without any extraction. As a consequence, this requires a thorough examination of the general concept of sustainability which is based on ecosystemic equilibria.

The preconditions of such a steadily-adapting and flexible resource use are: (1) local self-determination; (2) secure land and resource rights; (3) individual flexibility; (4) maintenance of a high level of biodiversity; as well as (5) a reliable social and religious cohesion. If these preconditions are met, the Benuaq's extended subsistence economy has a realistic chance to persist in an adaptive way. However, the recent political and economic changes in Indonesia do not permit any clear prediction of the future development of such local resource use systems.

Ringkasan

HUTAN-hutan di sekitar desa Lempunah (suku Dayak Benuaq di Kalimantan Timur, Indonesia) telah dimanfaatkan selama lebih dari 300 tahun secara ekstensif. Saat ini, hutan-hutan yang ada terdiri dari ratusan kebun-kebun hutan (rotan, karet, dan kebun buah campuran), daerah bekas ladang dan ladang-ladang.

Dayak Benuaq bercocok tanam dengan lebih dari 100 jenis varietas padi lokal serta 150 jenis tanaman pangan. Lebih jauh lagi, sekitar 500 spesies tumbuhan dan binatang dimanfaatkan dari hutan ini. Sumber daya yang besar ini memungkinkan rakyat Benuaq melakukan berbagai macam kegiatan ekonomi untuk kebutuhan pangan, termasuk kegiatan perdagangan berbagai macam hasil hutan ('extended subsistence').

Dengan mempelajari pemanfaatan sumber daya lokal selama beberapa tahun, terlihat adanya dinamika-dinamika mendasar dengan seringnya pergantian antara sumber pendapatan yang berbeda, demikian juga variasi yang jelas dalam jumlah dan jenis ladang. Pola-pola temporal yang tak berketentuan ini adalah sebagai akibat strategi-strategi pemanfaatan sumber daya secara umum dan pengambilan-pengambilan keputusan individu. Argumentasi yang terakhir ini dapat diperlihatkan dengan menganalisis jaring-jaring sebab-akibat ('causal nets') yang terpadu antara aspek-aspek ekonomi, ekologi, sosial, agama, politik, sejarah serta emosi.

Strategi-strategi yang paling relevan dalam kehidupan yang ada didasarkan pada tiga prinsip: (1) kecukupan pangan ('subsistence'), (2) pemanfaatan yang fleksibel dari sumber daya yang didiversifikasi, dan (3) pemanfaatan dinamika alam. Sejauh ini, hampir semua penelitian kurang mempertimbangkan tingginya tingkat fleksibilitas inidividu, yang memperbolehkan petani secara cepat dan efisien merespon perubahan-perubahan yang tak terkirakan seperti fluktuasi harga atau bencana alam. Pergantian pemanfaatan sumber daya mengarah pada saat pemanfaatan yang intensif dan saat tidak ada pemanfaatan sama sekali. Ini membutuhkan penelitian yang mendalam mengenai konsep umum suatu keberlanjutan ('sustainability') yang didasarkan pada keseimbangan-keseimbangan ekosistem.

Prekondisi dari pemanfaatan sumber daya yang secara terus menerus beradaptasi dan fleksibel adalah: (1) penentuan sendiri secara lokal, (2) hak-hak lahan dan sumber daya yang terjaga, (3) fleksibilitas individual, (4) pemeliharaan keanekaragaman hayati dengan tingkat yang tinggi, serta (5) kohesi agama dan sosial yang diandalkan. Jika prekondisi-prekondisi ini bertemu, berbagai kegiatan perekonomian untuk kebutuhan pangan dari suku Benuaq memiliki kesempatan yang realistis untuk tetap bertahan secara adaptif. Meskipun demikian, perubahan-perubahan politik dan ekonomi di Indonesia tidak memperbolehkan perkiraan yang jelas dari pengembangan sistem-sistem pemanfaatan sumber daya lokal di masa depan.

Contents

Abbreviations

a.r.	:	author's remark
a.t.	:	author's translation
app.	:	approximately
ASEAN	:	Association of South-East Asian Nations
BAPPEDA	:	*Badan Perencanaan Pembangunan Daerah* (Ind.), provincial planning board
c.f.	:	*cum fide*
DBH	:	diameter (of trees) in breast height
e.g.	:	for example
excl.	:	excluding
ff.	:	following pages
GPS	:	global positioning system
GTZ	;	Deutsche Gesellschaft für Technische Zusammenarbeit — German Agency for Technical Cooperation
HTI	:	*Hutan Tanaman Industri* (Ind.), timber plantation
i.e.	:	that is
i.g.	:	in general
ibid.	:	same citation
IDT	:	*Inpres Desa Tertinggal* (Ind.), national anti-poverty programme
IFFM	:	Integrated Forest Fire Management (GTZ project)
IHH	:	*Iuran Hasil Hutan* (Ind.), forest product tax
IMF	:	International Monetary Fund

incl.	:	including
Ind.	:	Indonesian
n	:	number
n.d.	:	no date
n.pl.	:	no place
NGO	:	non-governmental organisation
NRM	:	Natural Resource Management (USAID project)
p.	;	page
pers. comm.	:	personal communication
pl.	:	plural
ref.	:	referring to
Rp	:	Rupiah (during the research period, 1 $ US equalled 2.500-17.000 Rp)
RSD	:	relative standard deviation
RT	:	*Rukun Tetangga* (Ind.), neighbourhood association
s.	:	see
SD	:	standard deviation
SFMP	:	Promotion of Sustainable Forest Management Systems (GTZ project)
sg.	:	singular
sp.	:	species, not identified
spp.	:	species (pl.), several species of a genus
t	:	tonnes
TÖB	:	Tropenökologisches Begleitprogramm (GTZ, Tropical Ecology Support Programme)
units:	:	*g* gram, *kg* kilogram, *t* metric tonne, *m* metre, *km* kilometre, *l* litre, *h* hour, *d* day, *a* year
UNMUL	:	Universitas Mulawarman (in Samarinda)
USAID	:	United States Agency for International Development
yrs.	:	years

List of Illustrations

1

Research Context, Theoretical Frame and Methodology

Research context

THE use of natural resources always involves changes. These changes affect the environments of human actors as well as the people themselves. The result of these interacting relations between human beings and their environment is an interwoven net of causal chains, which are not comprehensible by mono-causal linearisations. Friedrich Ratzel (1844-1904) called this 'the old philosophical problem of interrelations between nature and humankind' (1882: 41, a.t.) which, to this day, has still not been solved.

Ratzel was one of the first ethnologists who dedicated himself to the study of 'interrelations between the earth and the life created and reproduced on it' (*ibid.*: 42, a.t.). His work was based on the earlier writings of Carl Ritter and Charles de Montesquieu (see *ibid.*: 43-4, 45-9). While searching for regularities in the interrelations between natural factors and cultural phenomena, Ratzel was always aware of the limited validity of such 'regularities'. In his work *Anthropo-Geographie oder die Grundzüge der Anwendung der Erdkunde auf die Geschichte (1882) he writes:*

> We have to console ourselves with the fact that what prevents us from discovering equally solid laws [like those of the natural sciences, a.r.] in this research area, is nothing else than the peak of creation, the free mind of man, to whom we owe on the other hand the most attractive and practically relevant aspects of our science. — *ibid.*: 52, a.t.

Ratzel reiterates elsewhere this general limitation of predictions of anthropo-geographical phenomena based on scientific laws (*ibid.*:

79-80), when he criticises the neglect of individual action in favour of a cultural level of examination ('Massenoperationen' of this chapter). With this remark, Ratzel anticipates a crucial theoretical problem of cultural ecology which re-occurred decades later (see section 'Theoretical Frame' of this chapter). In spite of these two references, which I chose deliberately in order to contrast the common interpretation of Ratzel's work (see Bennett 1976: 161-2, Bargatzky 1986: 24), Ratzel also states that human cultures depend on nature (*ibid*.: 86) to shape cultural phenomena including different ways of life (*ibid*.: 317) and national character (*ibid*.: 319).[1]

The possibilists around Franz Boas, and his students Clark Wissler (e.g., 1917, 1928) and Alfred Louis Kroeber (e.g., 1939), rejected such a deterministic point of view.[2] Instead, they emphasised the limiting character of natural settings restricting cultural phenomena. Within the framework of 'culture areas' (also 'cultural areas', see Kroeber 1939) the possibilists draw correlations between geographical[3] and cultural phenomena (mainly in North America). However, these descriptive correlations show only limited explanatory power (see also critique in Ellen 1982: 5,9,17-20).

Julian Steward tried to explain the origin of certain cultural phenomena by applying his concept of cultural ecology (1955: 30,36). The theoretical base of his work is provided by the biological concept of environmental adaptation (*ibid*.: 39), which he integrates into a theory of a multi-linear cultural evolution (*ibid*.: 18-29). By using a holistic research approach which emphasises the interdependency of cultural aspects (*ibid*.: 37), Steward anticipates certain systematic ideas of later years.[4]

Methodologically, Steward required cultural-ecology studies to display: (1) the analysis of the interrelationship of exploitative or

---

1. This opinion is called environmental determinism (Bargatzky 1986: 24).
2. However, Kroeber's opinion is not too far from Ratzel's when he says (1939: 205): 'No culture is wholly intelligible without reference to the non-cultural or so-called environmental factors with which it is in relation and which *condition* it.' (my emphasis)
3. Among these are according to Kroeber (1939: 205-17): 'physiography', 'natural vegetation', 'climate', 'water' and 'drainage'.
4. These systematic aspects also include feedback effects. Steward says in his major work *Theory of Culture Change* (*ibid*.: 31): 'He [man] introduces the super-organic factor of culture, which also affects and is affected by the total web of life.'

productive technology and the environment; (2) the analysis of behaviour patterns involved in the exploitation of a particular area; as well as (3) the analysis of further effects of such patterns on other cultural aspects (*ibid*.: 40-2). It is to show in case studies *how* the adaptation of a culture to its environment happens, and whether the adaptation process is similar for similar environments (*ibid*.: 42). However, it remains unclear, what Steward means by 'similar', and how these similarities can be measured in a comparable way (see critique in Vayda & Rappaport 1968: 485). Steward's definition of the 'cultural core'[5] also remains vague. This cultural core contains social, political and religious patterns, which are closely related to subsistence activities and economic arrangements, and which are shaped by the environment (*ibid*.: 37). The other, so-called 'secondary features' are defined (in contrast to the 'cultural core') as mere cultural-historical factors including random innovations and diffuse achievements (*ibid*.). The segregation of adaptive and culturally-relevant parts (i.e., the 'cultural core') from the cultural rest has been criticised by Geertz (1963: 7-8,10-11), by Harris (1968: 661) and by Ellen (1982: 61-2), as the theoretical base for such a segregation as well as possible interrelations between cultural core and the rest remain unclear.

Steward's critics express further doubts whether ecological adaptations are really of causal, and not merely of correlative, nature (see Ellen 1982: 63, Vayda & Rappaport 1968: 483-7). According to Vayda and Rappaport (*ibid*.: 485), Steward's theory lacks sufficiently large intercultural data sets. Additional critiques refer to Steward's combined terms 'culture' and 'ecology'. In their plea for applying an ecological research paradigm that includes 'cultural and non-cultural ecology', Vayda and Rappaport (1968) state that it is not cultures that interact with ecosystems but populations (see also Rappaport 1968: 381-2).[6]

The major achievements of the concept of cultural ecology were on practical, rather than theoretical, terrain. Still influenced by a possibilistic view, precise and detailed data were gathered within the

5. Steward defines the cultural core as 'the constellation of features which are most closely related to subsistence activities and economic arrangements' (*ibid*.: 37).
6. For a detailed critique of 'cultural ecology' see Ellen (1982: 61-5), Bennett (1976: 222-8) and Vayda & Rappaport (1968: 485-9).

framework of large-scale ethnographic field studies. These data covered geographic aspects such as rain-fall, soil structure, topography, cultivated crops, labour chronology, as well as aerial pictures of culturally-manipulated landscapes (e.g., Conklin 1957). Furthermore, several studies used data provided by other specialists, which enlarged the research beyond any single discipline.

The problem of finding a theoretical frame for integrating ecological and cultural parameters led to a more biological research perspective in ethnology. In 1963 Clifford Geertz introduces the 'ecosystem' in his book *Agricultural Involution* (1963: 3):

> The ecological approach attempts to achieve a more exact specification of the relation between selected human activities, biological transactions and physical processes by including them within a single analytical system, an *ecosystem*.

This biological approach, which regards human populations as part of wider ecosystems, was adopted by Andrew Vayda and Roy Rappaport, and became known as 'new ecology' or 'human ecology'.[7] In this context, Rappaport's work *Pigs for the Ancestors* (1968) is probably the most far-reaching attempt to interpret the behavioural patterns of an indigenous group of people[8] as a cybernetic system which remains in an equilibrium controlled by regulating forces. This interpretation attracted massive critique (e.g.,Bennett 1976: 181,182; Ellen 1982: 177-203,226-7; Vayda 1996: 9-14) of Rappaport's data and his evaluation (mainly regarding flows of energy; see critique in Rambo 1984: 48-9); as well as related to the rather general aspects of systems theory, such as the definition of boundaries and system units (see Vayda 1996: 10 and the following chapter); and the development of regulating mechanisms (e.g., Ellen 1982: 266 on the neglect of individual action; see also Ratzel's remark above).

In a modified version, the systems approach was further developed by Roy Ellen (1982) and by Terry Rambo (1984). A detailed critique will be given in the following chapter.

At the same time, Esther Boserup (1965) examined the

7. In fact, the term 'human ecology' was introduced much earlier by Park & Burgess (1924: 559).

8. The Tsembaga Maring in New Guinea.

development of agronomic systems from an economic and demographic angle. Although her idea that an increase of population density leads to a change of land use systems (1965: 117-18) has often been criticised, it remains a permanent stimulant for further investigations. Boserup's chain of argumentation focuses on the decline of soil fertility caused by an increasing population, which can only be coped with through a transition to more intensive cultivation methods. Boserup admits, however, the difficulty of how to decide whether the demographic change is the cause or rather the effect of other phenomena (*ibid*.: 117). Despite the often observed validity of this hypothesis at a general level, it displays a certain notion of technological determinism (Bennett 1976: 230). Further criticism is directed against the scant consideration of environmental factors and of locally-specific historical developments, which proved to be of great relevance in detailed case studies (e.g., Waddell 1972: 218, Padoch 1985: 287).

Another attempt to explain the interrelations between people and environment was propagated by John Bennett (1976), who also criticised the rigidness of systems theory, as well as the disregard towards individual decision-making strategies (e.g., 1976: 178-93). Instead, Bennett suggests a concept of 'adaptive dynamics', which he defines as follows (*ibid*.: 270): 'Adaptive dynamics refers to behavior designed to attain goals and satisfy needs and wants, and the consequences of this behavior for the individual, the society, and the environment.' Key-factors for analysing individual social adaptation are, according to Bennett: (1) 'adaptive behavior'; (2) 'strategic action'; and (3) the combination of both — 'adaptive strategy'. In contrast to the rather passive and deterministic character of systematic self-regulation, Bennett's emphasis is put on the active role of decision-making and individuals actors.

A similar approach that stresses the individual as *the* decision-making and acting unit is suggested by Vayda. His concept of 'progressive contextualisation' (Vayda 1983) was applied in the UNESCO Man and Biosphere (MAB) programme in East-Kalimantan, Indonesia,[9] in order to understand the causal relations between people and forest. This approach will be discussed in the next chapter.

9. The East-Kalimantan project started in the late 1970s under the leadership of Vayda (see King 1999: 148-50).

Embedded into this research framework were also the studies of Carol Colfer, who described and analysed local resource use patterns from a comprehensive perspective (1997, and undated reports). Apart from these investigations, there is (not only in Borneo) a striking lack of transdisciplinary long-term studies of dynamics and strategies of local resource use systems. This said, single aspects of indigenous resource use have been studied in detail. The following list contains the most relevant studies about land use of various Dayak groups in Borneo:

swidden agriculture:	Dove 1985a, Freeman 1992, Inoue & Lahjie 1990, Lahjie 1996, Sutlive 1992
other kinds of rice cultivation:	Padoch 1985, Padoch *et al.* 1998
rattan:	Fried & Sardjono 1992, Godoy 1990, Kraienhorst 1989, Peluso 1992, Sasaki 1997, Weinstock 1983b
rubber:	Dove 1993b, Dove 1994, Lawrence 1996
forest gardens:	Lawrence *et al.* 1995, Padoch & Peters 1993, Salafsky 1994, Sardjono 1990, Sardjono 1996
hunting:	Langup 1993, Salafsky 1993
Illipe nuts:	Blicher-Mathiesen 1994, Peters 1996
pepper:	Dove 1997
timber:	Peluso 1995a
medicinal plants:	Leaman 1995, Leaman *et al.* 1996
honey:	Lahjie & Seibert 1990
general NTFPs:	Grossmann 2000, Jessup & Peluso 1986, van Valkenburg 1997

However, none of these studies depict the respective local resource system as a whole. Rather, the focus is put specifically on a single kind of resource or a certain way of subsistence. This restriction has the advantage that such sub-systems are relatively good to examine, but the analytical isolation of single aspects neglects the dimension of the whole causal net. Hence, we have to deal with a trade-off between quantitative precision and transdisciplinary completeness. As both sides are complementary they would complement one another within a larger research team, such as in the MAB project. Yet, if personnel and funds are restricted (like for a PhD study) the two approaches in fact exclude each other and require a clear decision.

In this case study, the major questions refer to general livelihood strategies and their dependency on social, religious, economic, political, historical and emotional factors (see Ellis 1998: 16, Barlett 1980: 550-3). Thus, a holistic and comprehensive research approach appeared to be nessesary. The first methodological framework was provided by systems theory in order to consider the interwoven structure of ecological and cultural aspects of resource use. Because of severe theoretical objections against the ecosystem concept (see the following chapter), the approach was later modified before starting the field studies.

Some aspects such as a special focus on interrelations between different elements were included, others, such as fixed system boundaries or constant framework assumptions were discarded. The result is a structure supplementing Vayda's 'progressive contextualisation', in which causal chains are interwoven to open and dynamically-changing causal nets. As regards contents, a special emphasis is put on the causal analysis of individual decision-making processes.

A substantial advantage of causal nets is the fact that it is, in principle, irrelevant from where to start an investigation. Theoretically, the study of rattan use could be started from a world market perspective as well as from the perspective of an individual rattan collector. It was because of rather pragmatic reasons that I started my own investigation in a Dayak Benuaq village that I knew well since 1988. On the one hand, I already had excellent and warm personal relations with several families based on four earlier visits covering eight months between 1988 and 1993. On the other, Lempunah with its 350 inhabitants was just the right size to allow a level of descriptive completeness with sufficient analytical depth. These advantages were contrasted with the problem of transferring results to other sites, which might have been easier with a comparative study covering a larger area.[10] Since my focus was put on the analysis of decision-making patterns and strategies, which could also be done in other cases, the decision appears justifiable. The spatial restriction to a single village as the starting point of an analysis that reached well into the structures of world markets, allowed a rather long-term (in terms of a dissertation) collection of socio-economic data at a household level over four years (intensively between 1996 and 1999, plus qualitative data from 1988 until 1993, and from 2000).

Most of the Bornean resource studies listed above were limited to research periods less than two years (an exception was the MAB programme), some only referred to rather brief visits of several weeks (e.g., Godoy 1990). Under such circumstances, the impression a researcher perceives resembles a momentary picture that only allows a meaningful interpretation within its temporal context. Thus it is most doubtful whether some resource systems are indeed as constant as often suggested (e.g., Weinstock 1983b).

The main objectives of this study were the description of local resource use (as comprehensively as possible) and the multi-causal analysis of resource use patterns and strategies based on locally-given rationalities, as well as and on interpreted, partially statistically-tested plausibilities.

The following research questions guided this case study:

- What do the Benuaq perceive as 'resources'?
- How are resources used in Lempunah?
- What temporal and spatial patterns of resource use occur?
- Which resource use strategies are applied?
- What are the rationales behind these strategies?
- How are livelihoods secured in Lempunah?
- Which factors influence the local resource use?
- What are the prospects for resource use in Lempunah?

After introducing the theoretical frame, field methods — including some methodological experiences — are explained. The study area and the ethnography of the Dayak Benuaq are next described, before

10. Even a comparative study would, however, have only been representative for a certain area (e.g., East-Kalimantan).

a comprehensive description and analysis of the various resource use patterns, covering swidden agriculture, mixed forest gardens, rattan gardens, rubber gardens, and the non-cultivated forest 'in-between' is given. Resource use is then analysed considering socio-economic, temporal and spatial aspects, as well as strategies regarding the impact of external factors, persistence and dynamic change. Finally, some epistemological thoughts are reflected upon in a self-critical way.

Theoretical frame

THE ECOSYSTEM CONCEPT

The British phytologist Arthur George Tansley (1871-1955) introduced the ecosystem as a technical expression in an article on vegetational terms and concepts in 1935. The article was a response to a series of papers written by John Phillips (1931, 1934, 1935a, 1935b), who related the concept of plant communities of Frederic Clements (1874-1945) to the holistic philosophy of Jan Christian Smuts (1870-1950, see Golley 1993: 11).

The concept of communities consisting of plants *and* animals, however, goes back to Karl August Möbius (1825-1908), who speaks of 'Biozönose' or 'Lebensgemeinschaft' (Möbius 1877). It was later called 'biotic association' by Vestal (1913), while Shelford (1915) stated that plant and animal succession go hand-in-hand. In 1916 Clements developed the concept of the 'biome' or 'biotic community', which was further propagated by Phillips himself (see Phillips 1931: 4-5).

In his articles, Phillips describes the succession, development and climax of 'biotic communities' which he regarded as 'complex organisms' (Phillips 1931: 20).

The organismic nature of the 'biotic community' already appears in his first treatise, where he says: 'In accordance with the holistic concept of Smuts (1926), the biotic community is something more than the mere sum of its parts; it possesses a special identity — it is indeed a mass-entity with a destiny peculiar to itself.' (*ibid.*). This statement is repeated in the fourth paper: 'Communities are not mere summations of individual organisms, but are integrated wholes with particular emergents' (Phillips 1935b: 490).

Tansley, who is quoted by Phillips as a supporter of a systematic unit of plants, animals and inorganic factors (Phillips 1931: 3), fears, however, the loss of scientific clarity as well as Phillips' tendency towards 'religious or philosophical' dogmatism (Tansley 1935: 285). In order to clarify the terminology, he discusses the ecological *termini technici* used by Phillips.

His major critique of Phillips (and Clements) is directed against the concepts of 'biotic communities' and the 'complex organism'. Tansley rejects the term 'biotic *community*' mainly for linguistic reasons, as communities are made up by members, which should have more in common than plants and animals.[11] He also adds a spatial argument, when he says: 'Some of the animals belonging to these various animal communities have very restricted habitats, others much wider ones, while others again such as the larger and more active predaceous birds and mammals range freely not only through an entire plant community but far outside its limits' (*ibid*.: 296). This argument is even more important, as it was later used in a slightly different way against the ecosystem concept, developed by Tansley himself (see sub-section 'The Problem of Units and Boundaries' in this chapter).

Referring to Phillips' use of the term 'organism', Tansley says: 'We need a word for the peculiarly definite, sharply limited and unique type of organisation embodied in the individual animal or plant, and "organism" is the accepted term.' (*ibid*.: 291). He agrees that 'any piece of vegetation . . . has the character of an entity' (*ibid*.: 289) and that 'mature well-integrated plant communities . . . had enough of the characters of organisms to be considered as *quasi-organisms*, in the same way that human societies are habitually so considered' (*ibid*. 289-90). The consideration of an 'organic entity', which shows its own 'development' appears to be necessary due to the 'mass action' and an 'often delicate interlocking of the functions of the constituent organisms' (*ibid*.: 291). Tansley even compares the species of a plant community to the genes of an organism, but he vehemently rejects the idea of Clements and Phillips that the plant community *is* an organism (*ibid*.: 290).[12]

---

11. All the same, Tansley has no objections to speak of 'plant communities' and 'animal communities'. It is merely the mixing of both that is not accepted.

12. Especially in nineteenth-century America, the ecological organismic →

Despite his agreement on analogies with organisms, Tansley does not share the point of view that the 'complex organism' of Clements and Phillips shows emergent properties that are more than a mere summation of their parts (see Phillips 1935b: 490). He denies that those emergent properties are theoretically predictable from a thorough examination of the interacting parts. They are only unpredictable 'with our present knowledge' (*ibid*.: 297-8), as he then continues that, 'it is important to remember that these activities of the community are *in analysis* nothing but the synthesised actions of the components in association.' (*ibid*.: 299). Again, this is an argument which was later directed against his own ecosystem concept (see sub-section 'The Reification Problem' in this chapter).

While Tansley has major objections against Phillips' vague terminology and his 'extreme philosophizing' (Golley 1993: 15), he clearly accepts the existence of complex interactions between living beings and their environment. He states:

> This refusal [of the 'biotic community'] is however far from meaning that I do not realise that various "biomes," the whole webs of life adjusted to particular complexes of environmental factors, are real "wholes," often highly integrated wholes, which are the living nuclei of *systems* in the sense of the physicist. Only I do not think they are properly described as "organisms" (except in the "organicist" sense[13]). I prefer to regard them, together with the whole of the effective physical factors involved, simply as "systems". — *ibid*.: 297

Then he sets out:

> But the more fundamental conception is, as it seems to me, the whole *system* (in the sense of physics), including not only the organism-complex, but also the whole complex of physical factors forming what we call the environment of the biome

---

→ concept was historically influenced by Herbert Spencer, who tried to explain society in biological and ultimatively in physical terms (Hagen 1992: 4). Nevertheless, Spencer warned against analogies between society and an organism (*ibid*.: 5).

13. 'Organicist' means according to the organicist philosophy (e.g. Whitehead) that all organised 'wholes' can be regarded as 'organisms'. 'But then he [Phillips] must also call the universe an organism, and the solar system, and the sugar molecule and the ion or free atom' (Tansley 1935: 297).

> —the habitat factors in the widest sense. Though the organisms may claim our primary interest, when we are trying to think fundamentally we cannot separate them from their special environment, with which they form one physical system.
>
> It is the systems so formed which, from the point of view of the ecologist, are the basic units of nature on the face of the earth. Our natural human prejudices force us to consider the organisms (in the sense of the biologist) as the most important parts of these systems, but certainly the inorganic "factors" are also parts — there could be no systems without them, and there is constant interchange of the most various kinds within each system, not only between the organisms but between the organic and the inorganic. These *ecosystems*, as we may call them, are of the most various kinds and sizes. They form one category of the multitudinous physical systems of the universe, which range from the universe as a whole down to the atom. —Tansley 1935: 299

In contrast to Phillips, Tansley favours a less dogmatic but mechanistic and reductionistic way of science (Golley 1993: 15-16), preferring thus to present the ecosystem concept with a special emphasis on its physical character. He describes the temporal dynamics of ecosystems developing towards a dynamic equilibrium, to which the 'climax' is the nearest approximation: 'The more relatively separate and autonomous the system, the more highly integrated it is, and the greater the stability of its dynamic equilibrium.' (*ibid.*). There is even an evolutionary aspect, as 'there is in fact a kind of natural selection of incipient systems, and those which can attain the most stable equilibrium survive the longest.' (*ibid.*). Although Tansley feels that most ecosystems are moving towards an equilibrium (and maybe never reaching it), the system's property of an equilibrium has been frequently criticised by later authors.

According to Golley (1993: 34), Tansley did not explicitly clarify the nature of ecosystems. On the one hand, Tansley portrays the ecosystem as an analytical construction when he says:

> Actually the systems we isolate mentally are not only included as parts of larger ones, but they also overlap, interlock and

interact with one another. The isolation is partly artificial, but is the only possible way in which we can proceed'.

— Tansley 1935: 300[14]

But, on the other hand, he describes it as a natural object, closely related to Clements' communities. This definitory vagueness might have contributed to future interpretation debates. The lack of clarity is probably due to the concept's origin from a theoretical debate never tested empirically by Tansley himself (Golley 1993: 34).

THE APPLICATION OF THE ECOSYSTEM CONCEPT

Although others had investigated trophic interrelations before, mainly in aquatic surroundings (for bibliographic examples see Golley 1993: 50), it was Raymond Laurel Lindeman (1915-42) who first applied Tansley's concept in his effort to describe a lake ecosystem[15] (Lindeman 1941, see Golley 1993: 35-60). His concept of a food cycle was based on earlier work by the German limnologist August Thienemann (1882-1960), while Lindeman's studies of energy flows between different trophic levels were partially anticipated by Lotka, Haskell and Juday (see Golley 1993: 61). These quantitative studies linked ecology to thermodynamics, and eventually to the cybernetics of Norbert Wiener and the mathematical information theory of Shannon and Weaver (*ibid*.: 62).

The structural resemblance of biological, physical and engineering systems led to a single, unified holistic perspective, a general systems theory (e.g., von Bertalanffy 1950, 1968),[16] while its ecological version gained much popularity after Eugene Odum published his

---

14. Again we find the awareness of a problem (the problem of units and boundaries) which was used decades later as a major point of critique against the ecosystem concept.

15. Earlier limnological work by Forbes already emphasised ecological interrelations between plants and animals of a lake, but Forbes' terminology remained on a rather metaphoric level in order to explain these new and poorly-understood findings (see Hagen 1992: 7-8,12).

16. The origin of a systems concept is traced back by von Bertalanffy to Leibnitz, Nicholas of Cusa, Paracelsus, Vico and Ibn-Kaldun (von Bertalanffy 1968: 11). Von Bertalanffy himself combines information theory, the theory of automata, game theory and queuing theory in his general systems theory, which allow the mathematical analysis of systems (*ibid*.: 22-3).

textbook *Fundamentals of Ecology* (1953).[17] Odum gives the following definition of an ecosystem (1971: 8):

> Living organisms and their nonliving (abiotic) environments are inseparably interrelated and interact upon each other. Any unit that includes all of the organisms (i.e. the "community") in a given area interacting with the physical environment so that a flow of energy leads to clearly defined trophic structure, biotic diversity, and material cycles (i.e., exchange of materials between living and nonliving parts) within the system is an ecological system or *ecosystem*.[18]

During the following period, ecosystem studies focussed mainly on energy flow pathways, limiting factors, biogeochemical cycling, productivity, trophic transfer and species diversity (Golley 1993: 80-93, 117). Fitting into a modernist and technical worldview (see *ibid*.: 2, 106-7), large-scale projects like the biome studies of the International Biological Programme (IBP) (*ibid*.: 109-40), the UNESCO Man and the Biosphere (MAB) programme (*ibid*.: 161-6), and several smaller long-term studies (e.g., Hubbard Brook, see Golley 1993: 143-51), were launched under the paradigm of the ecosystem approach. Research questions dealt with system properties, such as the structure, equilibrium levels, stabilising mechanisms and persistence of systems (see Ellen 1982: 94). Models were built based on increasingly quantitative data assisted by sophisticated computer programmes, and expectations to understand, and eventually predict, systematic structures and behaviour rose high (see Moran 1990a: 7; Golley 1993: 109-10). However, despite the enormous financial and personnel resources involved in the IBP (the IBP biome programmes involved over 1,800 scientists, see Golley 1993: 139), the impact on ecosystem theory was marginal. Golley (*ibid*.: 189) concludes:

> It was not until the ecosystem modeling approach failed to provide adequate whole system descriptions and testable

17. In 1956, Evans proposed the ecosystem as the basic unit in ecology (Evans 1956: 1127-8), which could be applied on every level 'on which life is examined' (*ibid*.: 1127). Evans stresses the open nature of ecosystems, through which quantities of matter and energy are passed.

18. More recent definitions add information as an essential component that is exchanged between the system's elements or passed through (see Ellen 1982: 74).

> predictions that most ecosystem ecologists adopted reductionist methods in ecosystem studies. The ecosystem model continued to be employed, especially by the generation that developed the concept, but it was no longer the dominant method used for structuring research questions. Instead, models became tools used for organizing data and generating questions.

Another critical aspect was the rather abstract character of an ecosystem, in which the close links to engineering sciences detracted from the 'biological reality encompassed in the species' (*ibid*.: 106-7). Ethological questions related to evolution theory, especially, led to studies concerning individual behaviour and strategies, rather than abstract levels such as systems. Nowadays, it appears that the ecosystem concept has its own niche in a field which was partly responsible for its origin: in ecological philosophy and environmental ethics (Golley 1993: 205). Although it sounds ironic regarding Tansley's rejections of philosophical dogma, the public awareness of an environmental crisis has led to an increased interrelation of scientific concepts and socio-political questions about ecosystems.

THE ECOSYSTEM CONCEPT IN ANTHROPOLOGY

Beyond its application in ecology, the ecosystem has a history of its own in anthropology. It was Tansley himself, who suggested integrating human activity into ecology. In his 1935 article he writes:

> But it would be difficult, not to say impossible, to draw a natural line between the activities of the human tribes which presumably fitted into and formed parts of "biotic communities" and the destructive human activities of the modern world. . . . Regarded as an exceptionally powerful biotic factor . . . human activity finds its proper place in ecology.
>
> —Tansley 1935: 303

In 1963, Clifford Geertz proposed the ecosystem concept as a useful unit of analysis for anthroplogical studies (1963: 3). Five years later, Vayda and Rappaport (1968: 494) also suggested applying ecological units such as individual organisms, populations, communities, and ecosystems. By adopting an ecological perspective, human populations become commensurable with other units, enabling quantitative studies of energy and material flows (*ibid*.: 494). Other authors soon followed, and several seminal studies were published during the first decade (e.g., Rappaport 1967, Clarke 1971, Kemp 1971, Waddell 1972 or Nietschmann 1973).

The holistic nature of the approach made it especially attractive to anthropologists. The use of ecosystems allowed the study of small, rural communities (Moran 1990a: 13; Netting 1990: 229) with a focus on 'flow of energy, health and nutrition status of populations, relative efficiency rates of various forms of labor organization and cropping practices, and into social organizational aspects of subsistence strategies' (Moran 1990a: 14). Moran (*ibid.*) concludes:

> The ecosystem approach provided greater context and holism to the study of human society by its emphasis on the biological basis of productivity and served as a needed complement to the cultural ecology approach.

Among the added merits of the concept are: a broad framework for description and analysis provided by systems theory that emphasised the internal dynamics, development and change of systems (Moran 1990a: 11; Ellen 1990: 192); the structural and functional similarities between natural and social systems (Winterhalder 1984: 302); a stress on holism, while maintaining the focus on special relationships (Ellen 1990: 191); a shift from the gross correlations of earlier approaches towards more specific and integrated studies regarding 'networks of mutual causality' (*ibid.*: 192).

Empirically, the ecosystem approach led to new techniques (Ellen 1978: 290; Ellen 1982: 93) which allowed the close analysis of interdependencies and interactions between human populations and their environments based on quantified data. Apart from the mere scientific advantages, Rappaport states that 'the ecosystem provides a framework within which humans can think well about their general relations to the world' (Rappaport 1990: 45). The system concept is simply 'good to think' (*ibid.*). Although the popular understanding of ecosystems and the scientific view were not always the same, the concept had a strong impact on the environmental movement starting in the 1960s with a certain revival in the 1990s (see Moran 1990a: 11; Rappaport 1990: 45; Golley 1993: 3, 205).

After its enthusiastic initial phase during the first decade, the ecosystem approach was critically reviewed in social anthropology. The major points of critique were similar in both anthropology as well as in ecology. As these objections are crucial for understanding my own reserach approach, I will briefly discuss the major issues which I want to address as: (1) the reification problem; (2) the problem of self-regulation and change; (3) the problem of units and boundaries; and (4) the explanatory problem.[19]

THE REIFICATION PROBLEM: IS THE ECOSYSTEM AN ACTING ENTITY?

Harking back to the concept of a 'complex organism' or 'superorganism',[20] the ecosystem was sometimes treated as an entity with its own properties and survival strategies, showing a high degree of self-regulation (see Moran 1990a: 16). An important question is whether the ecosystem (or any system) has emergent properties that the summation of its elements does not provide? Tansley (1935: 297-8, see above) denied this vehemently, referring to a lack of knowledge at the time, which was, however, not the same as the theoretical impossibility of predicting systematic properties by analysing the parts of a system. He critisises the use of the expression 'summation' (*ibid.*), as it is unclear what the summation of the parts of an ecosystem should actually mean.

This point is also stressed by the systems theorist Ludwig von Bertalanffy (1968: 55):

> The meaning of the somewhat mystical expression, "the whole is more than the sum of parts" is simply that constitutive characteristics are not explainable from the characteristics of isolated parts. The characteristics of the complex, therefore, compared to those of the elements, appear as "new" or "emergent". If, however, we know the total of parts contained in a system *and* the relations between them [italics by me], the behavior of the system may be derived from the behavior of the parts.

The problem, however, is not only a practical one, referring to limited knowledge. In most cases a scientist (or any other person) will not be

---

19. Another critique refers to the overemphasis of quantitative data and an obsession with measurement (Gross 1990: 310), and too much focus on energy budgets and material flows (see Vayda & McCay 1975: 295-6).
20. This view is similar to the super-organic concepts of Kroeber (1917) and White (1949) cited in Moran (1990a: 16).

able to predict a system's behaviour based on an analysis of the elements and their interrelations. A limiting factor is the degree of coupling, which blurs the nature of cause and effect. If an element affects another one, which might re-affect the first in a feedback-loop, and if these interacting elements are connected with others, the complexity of the system might also *theoretically* exclude an exact mathematical analysis. Such unpredictable states are called 'deterministic chaos' (see Küppers 1987: 18). This does not mean, however, that these systems do not show any regularity. In fact, they can develop well-ordered patterns (Küppers 1987).

Hence, we can say that a system's behaviour is caused by the interactions of its elements, but we must admit, that in cases of high complexity, this behaviour is not predictable, if this prediction is based on an analysis of the system's elements. While still being somehow the sum of its parts, the system behaves like an entity with emergent properties. This does not mean that an ecosystem *is* an acting entity. Yet, its activity can be understood with Tansley's words quoted above:

> But it is important to remember that these activities of the community are in analysis nothing but the synthesised actions of the components in association. We have simply shifted our point of view and are contemplating a new entity, so that we now, quite properly, regard the totality of actions as the activity of a higher unit. —Tansley 1935: 299

We find this problem again on a sociological level. Can the behaviour of a group be constituted by the sum of individual actions[21]? Feeling that the systems approach was too abstract a concept, several critics claimed that the decision-making role of the 'individuum' was neglected in the approach (see Vayda & McCay 1975: 300; McCay 1978: 409; Orlove 1980: 246-8; Vayda 1983: 270; Moran 1990a: 21; Lees & Bates 1990: 249, 253-4; Vayda 1996: 16-17). Von Bertalanffy is also well aware of this problem, when he says (1968: 52-3):

> Man is not only a political animal; he is, before and above all, an individual. The real values of humanity are not those which it shares with biological entities, the function of an

---

21. A supporter of such an individualistic view in ecology was Henry Allan Gleason (1926), who described the biological community as a coincidental assemblage of independent species sharing an area arbitrarily defined by the ecologist (cited in Hagen 1992: 29).

> organism or a community of animals, but those which stem from the individual mind. Human society is not a community of ants or termites, governed by inherited instinct and controlled by the laws of the superordinate whole; it is based upon the achievements of the individual and is doomed if the individual is made a cog in the social machine.

Interactions between people and their environments were now seen as more process-oriented, where individual persons made their decisions, not necessarily acting for the group's or population's benefit. Even Roy Rappaport, whose *Pigs for the Ancestors* (1968) was criticised on this ground, admitted that his analysis would have been 'richer' had he included individual choices and actions (Rappaport 1990: 62).[22] This new focus on individuals is paralleled by a similar development in evolutionary biology, where the individual organism (in a more extreme version, even single genes of that organism[23]) is regarded as the actual level for selection (see Orlove 1980: 248). The success or 'fitness' of a species or an individual strategy, defined by its survival or persistence, is often related to its degree of 'adaptation', a somewhat controversial expression. It suggests an active process of adapting, which might be the case for human populations, but obviously not for asocial, genetically-evolving species.

According to Darwinist evolutionary theory, adaptation (to certain environmental conditions) leads to *ex post* observed advantages regarding natural selection. The conditions for this advantage are, however, randomly caused by mutations, and genetically inherited (Dawkins 1989). Hence, for human populations, 'adaptation' (not meant as a physiological adaptation) can only be used in an analogous way as a criterion for the (again interpreted *ex post*) persistence of a cultural trait. Whether this is of much explanatory value or not, remains to be questioned. An *ex post* perspective only describes a certain function, its adaptive quality is ascribed based on certain *assumptions* rather than on demonstrations (see Friedman 1974: 457); but it does not explain why things came about and why they persist (Ellen 1982: 193).[24]

---

22. He still stresses that he had mainly studied rituals and warfare, two forms of social activity, which are among the highest aggregated ones (Rappaport 1990: 62).
23. See the theory of the selfish gene by Richard Dawkins (1989).
24. This is sometimes referred to as the 'fallacy of functionalism' (Ellen 1982: 193).

If adaptation processes do occur, however, they are caused by individuals 'through social structures', not by the structures themselves (Ellen 1978: 298). It is individuals or households that have to cope with problems, not the system. This individual-oriented approach is also proposed by Vayda & McCay (1975: 299-302), as well as by McCay (1978: 409) in order to understand group processes and interactions in complex systems. The relevance of an individual-level is further supported by the broad literature on rational acting (e.g., Nash 1967, Görlich 1993, Campos & Root 1995, Rubin 1998). Events on a macro-scale might be analysed by tracing back causality to an individual micro-scale, but it seems impossible to predict the behaviour of complex systems vice versa.

THE PROBLEM OF SELF-REGULATION AND CHANGE

A common point of critique is the strong emphasis on functional integration, stability and regulatory mechanisms in ecosystem research (see Netting 1990: 229). Originating from Tansley's article, equilibrium and stability are closely linked to the ecosystem concept. According to Tansley, an ecosystem is constantly developing towards a dynamic equilibrium, which cannot be perfectly reached but is only approachable to a degree that depends on the 'given conditions and with the available components' (Tansley 1935: 300). This 'highest stage of integration' and nearest approach to a perfect dynamic equilibrium is called 'climax' (*ibid.*). The closer a system is to this equilibrium, the more likely it is to survive (*ibid.*). Its stability further depends on its autonomy and integration: 'The more relatively separate and autonomous the system, the more highly integrated it is, and the greater the stability of its dynamic equilibrium is' (*ibid.*).

However, both for practical and for theoretical reasons, this concept is of little use, as the relative distance of a 'system' from such an unattainable equilibrium, as well as the very existence of the assumed equilibrium, cannot be determined. Nevertheless, fitting well into the physiological (Eugene Odum), and into the mechanistic (Howard Odum), analogies of ecosystems, the idea of equilibria or homeostases intrinsic to systems, influenced ecosystem research for many years (see Hagen 1992: 128-30).

Today, the relation between the complexity of a system and its stability is all but clear (see Ellen 1982: 189). While studies of linear models show that the probability of stability decreases with an increase in complexity (i.e., the degree of connectedness among the system's elements; see May 1973), more recent network analysis indicates that functional diversity appears to be related to stability (Van Voris *et al.* 1980). Golley (1993: 100) states: 'Simple systems may be stable, and species-rich communities may be unstable. No universal pattern holds.' Long-term studies from tropical rainforests suggest, however, that instability and dynamics might even be a major cause for species richness (Colinvaux 1986: 682-3; Primack & Hall 1992). Hence, the causal direction between stability and diversity could, in fact, be inverted.

Even though many systems show a certain persistence ('resilience')[25] over a longer period of time (e.g. Ellen 1982: 189), they might be all but stable (see Vayda & McCay 1975: 298). These often-observed dynamic changes challenged the acceptance of the ecosystem concept. According to Tansley and his successors, equilibria were an essential property of ecosystems. But do these equilibria (or 'homeostatic states' as some authors prefer to call them) exist *in reality*? In biology, this is seriously questioned (see Holling 1973: 2), and Ellen also believes that 'nature is not, then, in a state of balance but is subject to periodic upsets due to climatic and other geographical processes' (1982: 187). This critique of an over-emphasis on equilibria is also shared by other anthropologists such as Moran (1990a: 15), Netting (1990: 229) or Vayda & McCay (1975: 293).

Theoretically-speaking, equilibria are intrinsic aspects of certain complex models,[26] but they only occur if cybernetic means of self-regulation function in a specific way (see von Bertalanffy 1968: 161).[27]

---

25. Stability means in this sense 'the ability' (qualitative stability) and the 'rate of return' (quantitative stability) 'of a population to return to equilibrium from a disturbance' (Foin & Davis 1987: 9). Holling adds the term 'resilience', which he defines as the property of the system to absorb changes of its variables and still persist (1973: 17). According to Foin and Davis (*ibid.*) 'resilience' or 'persistence' means 'recovery of a disturbed population to some, not necessarily the same, equilibrium point'.
26. There are, in fact, only a few possible ways in which a dynamic system can behave: towards unstable equilibrium, towards neutrally-stable cycles, towards stable equilibria, towards a domain of attraction, towards a stable limit cycle, and towards a stable node (see Holling 1973: 4; see Bossel 1989: 142-3).
27. This is well documented for systems in engineering sciences or simplified cases of theoretical biology (see von Bertalanffy 1968, Bossel 1989).

Divergence from homeostasis[28] leads to impacts within the system that are compensated in negative feedback relations. Engelberg and Boyarsky (1979: 319-23) have claimed that ecosystems are not cybernetic, as they lack an information network which could transmit the information of measured differences to the compensating parts of the system. This critique, however, depends on the definition of 'cybernetic' as Patten and Odum show in their reply (1981: 888), which is supported by Golley (1993: 203-4): 'It does not seem useful to divide systems into cybernetic and noncybernetic systems. . . . The question is, how is control mediated in ecosystems?'

This seems to be the crucial question: how is control mediated, and who or what is controlling? Rappaport gives an almost trivial answer: 'Because a Maring local group is a component of the ecosystem which it regulates . . . the ecosystem is by definition self-regulating' (1990: 43).

Indeed, when people are part of an ecosystem, the question of regulation reaches a new dimension, when dynamic processes such as learning, adaptation, communication, or technological innovation are involved (see Ellen 1982: 191; Lees & Bates 1990: 249). It does not appear to conform to the ways of human decision-making, if responses to environmental change are only perceived as systematic answers, rather than individual 'adaptation strategies' (see McCay 1978: 403-4 and above).

So, how are ecosystems regulated? Are these regulating processes goal-oriented or mere reactions to intra-systematic disturbances? In fact, speaking of 'regulation' only makes sense if a certain kind of state is maintained or shifted in a controlled way. Whether this state is determined by a purposive goal, or whether it is the result of non-guided interactions, is essential. It appears that many studies had a notion of the first, purposive interpretation. The goal was generally seen in 'the survival or adequate functioning of the system' (Ellen 1982: 181), which was ensured by regulating the flow of energy and material within an ecosystem through homeostasis. The most prominent example of a system regulated in such a homeostatic way is again Rappaport's *Pigs for the Ancestors* (1968). A detailed critique of this model is given in Ellen (1982: e.g.,104-6, 182-3, 226-7).[29]

28. Another expression is 'steady state' or 'Fließgleichgewicht' (von Bertalanffy 1968: 158). This expression is also used for open dynamic systems.

29. Another teleological version is the systematic development towards an →

The regulating processes are, in this case, negative feedback loops. These feedback loops are at least cybernetic parts of systems, whether they are considered as cybernetic systems or not. Regulative forces, however, do not necessarily mean that a system always develops towards stability. In fact, most systems are not in a homeostatic state at all (see Holling 1973: 2; Foin & Davis 1987: 26-8; Ellen 1990: 196). This does not necessarily mean they are close to collapse, but it is obvious that a simple homeostatic model would be far too simple to explain the interactions within ecosystems (see Ellen 1982: 191). Furthermore, they cannot explain temporal and structural change (see *ibid*.: 195; Netting 1990: 229; Lees & Bates 1990: 249). Ellen notes that positive feedback, which is often neglected in the analysis (of usually closed systems) can lead to substantial change (Ellen 1982: 196). These changes can be as severe as to lead to a new system structure including new properties and behaviour (see Bossel 1989: 161-2).

Hence, it seems inappropriate to speak of 'regulation' in the analysis of systematic behaviour. 'Regulation' implies too much of a mechanistic and purposive perspective. In the case of dominant system elements, such as people, parts of the system will be regulated in Rappaport's sense (see above), but the effects of their actions are not always controlled in a way we could properly call 'regulatory'. Indeed, most ecosystems with human participation are far too complex to allow this kind of far-sightedness.

The idea of homeostatic, stable systems was probably induced by the observation of apparently persisting systems. However, it is unclear in most cases whether the same system has persisted or whether it has changed into a new system. Even Tansley was aware of this point, when he wrote: 'Many systems . . . which appear to be stable during the period for which they have been under accurate observation may in reality have been slowly changing all the time, because the changes effected have been too slight to be noted by observers.' Nevertheless, his major conviction was a stable one: 'But there may clearly be minor changes within a system which do not bring about the destruction of the system as such.' (Tansley 1935: 302). This statement leads us to several crucial questions: What is a 'system as such'? Where are its boundaries? When does it change into a new system?

→ increasing complexity (see Golley 1993: 99). As the relation between complexity, stability and evolutionary processes are still unclear (see above), this hypothesis will not be discussed here.

THE PROBLEM OF UNITS AND BOUNDARIES

As Golley has stated (1993: 34), the nature of Tansley's ecosystem concept was still somewhat vague. Tansley was aware of the analytical constructiveness of an isolated ecosystem, despite its overlap and interaction with other systems (see Tansley 1935: 300), but the interpretation as a biological (and spatial) entity, was more readily seen and adopted.

Today, most biologists and anthropologists reject the idea of an ecosystem as a biological unit. Colinvaux (1973: 549) states that ecosystems with the self-organising properties of a climax society are found nowhere, and Vayda & McCay (1975: 300) conclude that: 'The ecosystem is an analytic, not a biological, entity.' System boundaries are generally demarcated following practical reasons and the respective research question (McCay 1978: 403; Moran 1990b: 284; Netting 1990: 229; Ellen 1982: 78, 192; Rappaport 1990: 43), although it is widely accepted that ecosystems, and especially those with human involvement, are not isolated entities. Even remote communities have some kind of economic or political interaction with others, and thus allow flows of material, energy and information (see Netting 1990; Ellen 1982: 192). Systematic closure was assumed mainly for the sake of precise and efficient data-gathering and analysis (Moran 1990b: 285-6). This arbitrary cutting out of a system implies serious doubts about the relevance of its analysis to the real problem. In a similar vein, Taylor and García-Barrios (1995: 15) argue that case-studies suitable for systematic research do not necessarily reflect the 'natural situation'.

On the other hand, there are different degrees of autonomy and integrity like spatial, social or cultural units such as watersheds, islands, households or ethnic groups (see Ellen 1990: 217 and critique in Vayda 1996: 15). However, the unit discussions within the Man and Biosphere programme (MAB) revealed that these gradual differences were not sufficient to solve the demarcation problem. Di Castri (1976: 245 cited in Vayda 1983: 267) summarises:

> Human uses of the environment are not confined within ecosystems. Economic systems are specifically organised around the exchange of material, of energy, and even of people between ecosystems; they cut across ecosystems in order to take advantage of the complementarities and contrasts of different ecological zones.

An even more serious objection against system boundaries was perhaps brought forward by Vayda, when he argued that 'boundaries are already demarcated before the research actually begins'. (1996: 9; see also 1983: 267). Although this might be analytically convenient, it restricts the results in an unnecessarily limited way. As Ellen (1982: 89) says, 'because boundaries are often arbitrary and drawn for convenience, they may become a source of artifacts which distort rather than facilitate analysis'. Nevertheless, not all authors give up the concept of boundaries. While Rappaport embeds local ecosystems within so-called 'regional systems', Ellen proposes a concept of graded boundaries according to different degrees of closure regarding geomorphologic, biogeographic and cultural criteria (1990: 196-203).

THE EXPLANATORY PROBLEM

Is the ecosystem concept a theory at all? Rigler (1975: 15) says: 'When ecologists use the word "concept" they use it, not as a synonym for "theory", but as a substitute for it' (cited in Winterhalder 1984: 303). But is this sufficient?

Expectations during the 1960s and 1970s about the theoretical power of the ecosystem approach were high. Quantitative data were collected, organised and arranged into models, that could be (partially) simulated on computers. However, the descriptions of the investigated systems remained incomplete, mainly due to the vast dimension of interactions and a practical problem in assessing them (see Ellen 1982: 89-93). Besides, computer-aided analysis did not result in many valid predictions.[30] The enormous complexity of interactions (see Ellen 1982: 87 and comments above) seems to limit the degree of predictability of any realistic model.

Does it then make sense to link ecosystem research to a general theory of systems as Ellen suggests (1978: 300), or is it better to apply other theoretical concepts lent from neo-Darwinian evolution theory, neo-Ricardian economic theory or Marxism, as Winterhalder proposes (1984: 311)? How can processes in complex settings be described, analysed and understood? Is it enough to be content with Rappaport's modest statement that 'we can do little more than outline the general structure of such systems, try to measure a few important

30. Golley (1993: 189) concludes that this theoretical failure brought many ecologists back to reductionist methods in the investigation of ecosystem processes.

interactions, and attempt to locate the species with which we are concerned in the web' (1990: 51)? Or should we be more optimistic?

A frequently criticised shortcoming of the ecosystem concept was its lack of testable hypotheses (e.g., Gross 1990: 310-11). Ecosystemic descriptions and explanations still remind of the 'functionalist fallacy', which demonstrates that certain practices have effects, which in return are assumed to be their purpose (see Ellen 1982: 193). However, it should be possible, even in complex systems, to test hypotheses of causal relationships with the help of multivariate statistics (see Godoy *et al.* 1998b; Ruiz Pérez & Byron 1998, Homer-Dixon 1996). This does not substitute for overall quantitative predictions of a system's behaviour, but that may simply be too demanding.

If the behaviour of the whole system is of interest, we should restrict ourselves to a qualitative understanding. This partially refers to Rappaport's statement but also focusses on questions in a possibilist sense: What are the limits of systematic behaviour? Which are the main factors that are responsible for change? What are the possible directions of the systems development under the known circumstances? Before we address these questions, we should briefly re-assess the critique of the ecosystem approach.

Despite its merits, the limitation and the artificiality of a discrete system have become obvious. *A priori* demarcated boundaries cut a system out of its interrelative network, temporal changes are neglected by a focus on stability and equilibria, and systematic behaviour veils individual actions, which are integrated into a kind of 'superorganismic' entity. On the other hand, the ecosystem concept, or more generally-speaking, systems theory in von Bertalanffy's sense, was the first approach to take the holistic nature of complex, inter-relative settings into account. To retreat to the field of reductionist monodisciplinary research questions can hardly be an alternative.

An approach that considers causal interactions of intersecting processes without committing the artificial lopping-off of a systematic concept, is 'progressive contextualisation' as proposed by Andrew P. Vayda (1983, 1996). The research focus is set on significant human activities or people-environment interactions 'by placing them within progressively wider or denser contexts' (Vayda 1983: 265). Boundaries are not demarcated, and no assumptions are made about pre-defined systems or stability (*ibid.*: 267-8). Instead, the causal links related to the research problem are followed 'sometimes far beyond the boundaries of a nation-state or island' (*ibid.*: 268). The approach is further based on the premise of rationally-acting individuals (*ibid.*: 266, 270) in the sense that what might appear as a systematic behaviour can be explained by the summation of individual actions. Progressive contextualisation was applied during the MAB project in East Kalimantan (see Kartawinata & Vayda 1984; Kartawinata *et al.* 1984; King 1999: 148-50), where the causality of forest conversion was investigated.

At that time, not only the research procedure and its theoretical frame, but also the relevance of such studies came increasingly into the critique of the ecosystem concept. In many cases ecosystems were chosen out of convenience, but with little regard to actual, often 'life-threatening problems' of the investigated people (see Taylor & García-Barrios 1995: 15; Vayda & McCay 1975: 296-7; Lees & Bates 1990: 254-62). Instead, Vayda and McCay suggested to focus studies on human responses to 'natural hazards' (*ibid.*). This direction was picked up by Lees and Bates, who prefer, however, to speak of 'events' rather than 'hazards' (1990: 255), a term that is later also adopted by Vayda (1996).[31] An advantage of studying events is the connection to decision theory, which might allow generalisations about 'response hierarchies and the ordering of human behavior in terms of costs and risks' (Lees & Bates 1990: 255; see also Vayda & McCay 1975: 300).

Examples are droughts, pest infestation, toxic contamination, natural disasters, events generated by the human environment, such as market instability or a land-reform law (*ibid.*). Lees and Bates stress further that the selection of 'events' depends on the subjective interest of the researcher (*ibid.*: 269). They prefer the term instead of 'perturbation' because it is more neutral. In fact, events, in a wider sense and with varying intensity, occur all the time. Thus, an event is just a starting point, from where the causal interaction network is unfolded, including everyday behaviour as well as specific responses to strong impacts. A similar approach studying intersecting processes, rather than systems in the social analysis of ecological change, is suggested by Taylor and García-Barrios (1995).

If we leave the systematic concept and adopt the study of 'intersecting processes' or 'events' by 'progressive contextualisation',

31. The expression 'event' seems to be used in these articles in a colloquial sense, as it is nowhere explicitly defined.

what is gained and what is lost? With regard to the extensively discussed shortcomings of the ecosystem concept, we must acknowledge that much fewer assumptions are made that distort the local situation in a too abstract and artificial way. On the other hand, the formulation of quantitative models has become more difficult. However, since simulated models have so far only been of limited value in ecosystems with human participation, we can postpone this objection until better analytical means are available.

Following 'causal chains', (Vayda 1996) allows the analyst to draw a more proportional image of a complex setting, without the arbitrary cutting out of a part that is regarded as an analytical unit. This set of causal chains constitutes a temporal configuration of interrelated elements, which can still be called a 'system' in the sense of von Bertalanffy's general definition (1968: 38), as 'a set of elements standing in interaction'. Yet, if we apply von Bertalanffy's definition, the question is what then is not a 'system' (see Engelberg & Boyarsky 1979: 323)? It appears that we only have to follow the causal chains far enough to find at least some kinds of remote interaction between anything. Hence, I will only refer to the term 'system' in a colloquial sense throughout this study rather than in an analytical one.[32] Trapped between the practical necessity to limit one's research perspective to certain spatial and temporal configurations of elements, and the fact that these configurations are never isolated and will change in time, the analysis of causal chains related to the respective research question offers a trade-off without unnecessarily rigid assumptions.

CAUSAL NETS

A major problem of studying networks of any sort is their intrinsic complexity. A mere linear analysis by following causal chains is unlikely to provide adequate explanations. Feedback loops interfere and too many interactions occur simultaneously. Indeed, simple mathematical calculus is already at its limit when a simple system of a few coupled differential equations has to be solved. For these kinds of mathematically-describable systems, numeric simulations can lead to a sufficient understanding. Real networks of people-environment interactions, however, are far more complex and generally do not

32. Taylor and García-Barrios (1995: 7) speak of systems 'in the strong sense of having clearly defined boundaries and coherent internal dynamics governing their development, structure and stability, and their adaptation to external influences'.

translate into fixed mathematical equations. And with Simberloff (1980: 26), 'we must agree that we will not, in the near future, have sufficient information or insight to produce equations as predictive as those of most physicists and engineers' . So what are the alternatives? We have concluded that simple linearisations of networks can hardly be a good approximation, while the dynamic (and pseudo-simultaneous) numeric analysis is confined to a few special cases of rather physical quality.

If we retreat from the field of prediction and keep to the mere analysis of what had happened in the investigated context (e.g., responses to 'events' or a certain ways of decision-making), it should be possible to identify the relevant elements including the quality of their interrelations. It is important to stress that, depending on the significance of interactions, not everything is linked to everything else (see Simberloff's critique of holistic concepts, 1980: 29). For a limited observation period, at least, only a portion of all possible interrelations is manifested. This limited number of identified interrelations, complex as they still are, reduces the dimension of the 'causal space': not every development is possible. Hence, a qualitative multicausal explanatory interpretation of an event or an observed pattern should be possible by reconstructing[33] the interaction pattern that has led to the respective state.

Nevertheless, a complete, quantitative reconstruction is impossible, and it remains uncertain whether *all* relevant elements will be found. An understanding of such a network's behaviour is only feasible by approximating the set of relevant elements and their interdependencies step by step. By proceeding in this way, many 'unfalse explanations' might be possible, depending on the depth of the analysis (Vayda 1996: 23). However, while several explanations will be rejected 'because of evidence against them' (*ibid.*), others could

33. This partially refers to Ellen's 'generative analysis' (1982: 226-33), where he suggests to concentrate on 'end-states of behavioural processes', which are the outcome of decisions made at different times. Ellen's approach is also backwards-oriented, as he says: 'Observed patterns at any one point in time may be seen as end-states of the cumulative interaction of social and ecological processes and scheduling sequences' (*ibid.*: 227). However, the use of the expression 'end-state' is misleading itself, since these so-called end-states are in fact transient states, as most of these processes will not stop at the time of their observation.

compete in an evolutionary sense leading to an increasingly shared understanding among those who are interested in the case.[34]

The web-like quality of the causal links can be depicted and visualised in a network diagram (see Vester 1999: 56-7), consisting of the identified elements (people, plants, animals, objects, categories, concepts, ideas, etc.) and their interrelations (see chapter 5, 'Conclusions'). For any instance, this diagram will only be a representation of the reality that is perceived by the researcher.[35] In order to avoid too much arbitrary interpretation,[36] the causal quality of the noted interdependencies has to be tested or at least to be proposed in a convincing, although still hypothetical way.

The analysis of causal networks is still theoretically weak. Networks consisting of more specific interrelations, such as kinship, descent, social contacts, or trade relations, allow a mathematical approach based on graph theory (Schweizer 1996: 111-204).[37] Such a structural analysis, however, will not lead towards causal understanding in complex people-environment settings, as the interrelations observed here are too heterogeneous, ranging from material flow, to religious

---

34. A similar approach is described in Vester (1999), where an iterative process is chosen in planing complex projects. As many different stakeholder groups participate in this process, the 'solution' is found in an evolutionary way leading towards consensus.

35. Ellen (1982: 206-7) differentiates two kinds of models: the interpretative and the cognitive one. While the first represents the world as described and understood from the point of the researcher, the second one is confined to the world as it is described and understood by the informant. This differentiation, however, is only of limited use in such a study, since the informant's view has to be translated into a report written by the researcher. Hence, the 'emic' version passes a subjective filter and becomes another sort of an 'etic' point of view (also see 'Final Reflections').

    Vester describes a way to cover the most relevant fields with a criteria matrix referring to 7 areas of life (1999: 188-92). This approach resembles the cultural ecological checklist developed by Seeland (unpublished), which is briefly described in the following chapter.

36. This refers to Ellen's remark (1982: 202): 'While it is a relatively simple exercise to draw double-headed arrows for reciprocal causation and insert arrows feeding back to the original independent variable, it is another matter to test these theories in a definitive way.'

37. In these cases, properties such as density, structural holes, bridges, cutpoints, centrality, closeness-centrality, or betweenness-centrality, characterise the structure of a network and allow comparisons between different networks.

and cognitive aspects. All the same, certain structural features such as closed loops, causal by-passes, or relative isolation, might help to understand the network in a qualitative way. Additionally, certain elements can be left out, or highlighted in order to emphasise their relative importance.

In cases of sufficient data quality, the strength of causal relations can be estimated in order to differentiate between weaker and stronger interdependencies. Thought experiments are possible regarding more specified questions about the direct interdependencies of certain parts. This would even allow testable hypotheses to be set-up. The actual validity of these thought experiments, however, depends on the structural invariance of the model. As only explicitly-known interrelations can be included, the model's predictable power remains limited. But in contrast to conventional systems analysis, new insights can easily be incorporated into the model, as it is not confined to certain boundaries or categories. Even temporal changes in the network's structure, or in the quality of interrelations can be included, and in due course the network structure becomes more realistic.

An approach reaching beyond classical systems analysis is Frederic Vester's 'sensitivity model' (1999: 157-233), which includes a comprehensive description and visualisation of complex relations, an impact analysis, a structural analysis (e.g., feedback loops), and an optional simulation of 'system' parts and scenarios based on fuzzy logic.[38] While the descriptive parts of this approach are suitable for assessing the dimension of a causal net, it depends on the specific research question, whether a simulation is useful. Although the 'sensitivity model' allows the incorporation of qualitative data, a simulation is always based on more-or-less fixed assumptions as well as on the same analytical level, despite causal chains that intersect different levels (e.g., from world markets to individual decision-making) at different time scales.

CLOSING REMARKS

The discussion of systematic concepts in studying people-environment interactions shows that a linear, mono-causal approach is not suited to cope with the complexity observed. Ellen (1982: 89) addresses

38. Although Vester's book (including the sensitivity model) was published after I had finished my data analysis, my own approach was influenced by Vester's earlier work (e.g., Vester 1984).

this point, when he says: 'It has been suggested (Woodwell 1970: 26) that ecosystem complexity is so great as to preclude any single-factor analysis that is both accurate and satisfying.' Yet, once we skip mono-causal approaches, there is little left. Systems theory provides a wide range of techniques, but all of them are restricted by the objections discussed above.[39] Thus, on the one hand, we have to consider the enormous complexity required for a somewhat holistic concept; but on the other, we are in search of analytical instruments to dissect this dense web of interactions. Both aspects exclude each other to some extent. The closer we get to the details, the further we get from an integrative point of view.

The approach applied in this study is a deconstructive multicausal analysis of resource use patterns along causal chains following Vayda's 'progressive contextualisation'. The complexity of a certain, always temporally-restricted, context is represented as comprehensively as possible by applying elements of Vester's 'sensitivity model', while the observed causal links are investigated in as a reductionist a way as possible, based on an iterative field approach discussed in the following chapter. This approach is suited to analyse observed strategies and responses regarding their past rationale, but it is not designed to predict future developments. However, given the great variation of human behaviour and the high degree of complexity in ecological-cultural settings, such predictions would be on very shaky ground anyway.

Field approach and data analysis

The causal network approach described earlier section provided the methodological framework for this study. Hence, the first step was to identify the relevant elements of the Benuaq's resource use patterns and their interrelations. As the analytical depth of the approach is limited by practical constraints such as funding, time and personnel (see Vayda 1983: 271-5), only parts of the actual web can be unfolded. Yet, an arbitrary starting-point of the analysis bears the danger that one gets lost or trapped in a rather insignificant part of the network

39. Vester's approach does not explicitly require clearly demarcated system boundaries, as his 'sensitivity model' is open to additional elements and relations. Nevertheless, its predictive power is limited due to the very nature of complex systems (see Vester 1999: 226-7,233).

while overlooking others.[40] In order to avoid such an *a priori* focussed perspective, a preliminary phase was carried out, during which a general and broad overview was achieved. This research phase included extensive literature studies and several preparatory field visits.[41] A cultural-ecological checklist compiled by Seeland (n.d.) was adopted to the specific local conditions. This checklist covered arrays, which were identified as generally relevant to people-environment interactions, such as the social field, cultural values, and geographic elements referring to a cultural-ecological perspective.

Based on my former investigations, I applied mainly ethnological field methods for collecting data, such as participant observation, semi-structured interviews and interviews of key-informants (for these methods see Spradley 1979 and 1980, Fischer 1985, and 1992) to gain a preliminary fuzzy but rather comprehensive overview.[42]

---

40. During my preparation phase in 1993 I got temporarily carried away by focussing too much on the use of medicinal plants while neglecting other, more relevant aspects of resource use in Lempunah. In a similar vein, Vayda accuses Rappaport for having only found, what he already had in mind, before he actually started his field research among the Maring. 'And I know from having been in the field with him [Rappaport] that he assumed from the start that the ritual actions he was observing had roles in ecosystemic self-regulation. Indeed he became interested in the ritual actions precisely because of this assumption.' (Vayda 1996: 10).

    This remark refers indirectly to a general problem of working with a hypothesis-oriented approach.

41. Three prior visits of four months between 1988 and 1991 had a special focus on religious ceremonies and the regional ecology, while a fourth visit to the field site in 1993 (five months) was explicitly meant as a broad preparational survey. During this time, I also improved my knowledge of the local language (Benuaq). In addition, the first nine months of 1996 were used to maintain the broad but fuzzy perspective, until my understanding was comprehensive enough to start with more focussed research questions (for another 26 months between 1996 and 2000).

42. The length of such a preliminary phase depends on the researcher and his or her research situation but might take up to several months. A subjective test could be to cross-check one's explanations of cultural traits with different informants or to carry out thought experiments. However, it is unlikely that during this phase a researcher can get as far as being able to respond culturally appropriate in a given social and ecological context (see Frake 1962, cited in Ellen 1982: 224).

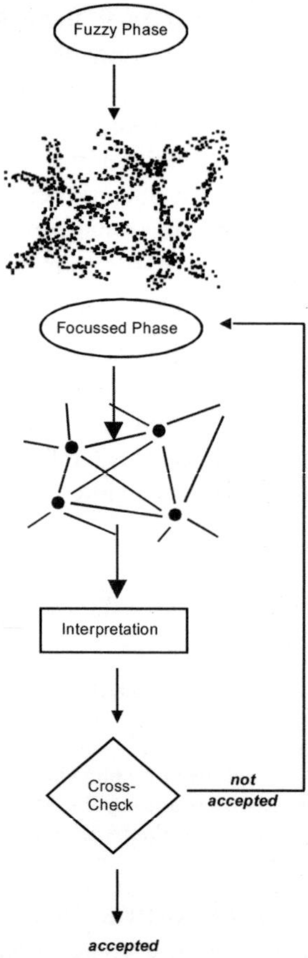

Fig.1.1: Research process

Once the structure of the local resource use system became clearer, I continued with more focussed research on the interactions between people and their environment in order to understand the observed spatial, temporal and strategic patterns. This second phase included analytical methods derived from geography, cultural anthropology and biology. Quantitative data were gathered and tested statistically, wherever it seemed suitable and possible.[43]

Preliminary results and interpretations of the focussed phase were cross-checked with my key-informants. In cases of discrepancy, the respective research question was again investigated, before the conclusions were accepted. This iterative research process is illustrated in *fig*. 1.

As in most ethnological fieldwork, a crucial part was played by my informants. Most of them had been known to me for several years, and some were already personal friends when my main research started in 1996. While I had a few general consultants from Lempunah, Mancong, Tanjung Isuy and Muara Tae, who helped me especially during the fuzzy phase and the cross-checking process of my study (n=8), special key-informants (n=10) explained the more detailed interrelations between the various elements of the local resource use,

---

43. Statistical tests included Mann-Whitney U-tests in lieu of a t-test (Sokal & Rohlf 1973: 217-20), Chi-square and goodness of fit (G) tests (*ibid*.: 286-94) as well as a 2×2 test (G-test) of independence including Yates' correction for small sample sizes (*ibid*.: 296-303). Generally, non-parametric tests were preferred as normal distribution of data could not be assured.

such as management techniques, criteria for decision-making, social interactions or religious aspects. During the preliminary phase, one informant was asked to conduct a comprehensive study of the local resource use in his own village (Mancong, a neighbouring village of Lempunah). The qualitative results of this study were used as a reference for my own studies in order to assure their relative completeness. Hence, the descriptive part of my work mainly originates from the knowledge of my informants, and has thus to be regarded as local or indigenous knowledge, although every part of it was finally filtered through my own perspective.[44] Wherever possible, I tried to compare the local knowledge with 'hard' statistic tests. Examples are given for dependencies between environmental factors, such as forest age, soil type, and rice yield, for the accuracy of cognitive forest maps, and for the cause of structural patterns in forest gardens.

In general, only information was included in the pattern analysis which was provided by at least two informants. In addition, individual cases, even if contradicting other opinions, were added if I observed them myself, or if I had good reasons to believe them.

The collected information was aggregated according to the locally-defined resource sub-systems and integrated in the respective causal nets. For each causal link an explanation is provided, either based on the local knowledge, on my own observations, on physical measurements including statistical tests, and — in very few cases — on literature.[45]

---

44. The interpretative character of ethnographic studies was extensively discussed during the post-modern critique of ethnology (see Marcus & Fischer 1986, Stellrecht 1993). It shows what cognitive ethnologists often neglect: it is impossible to represent someone else's reality without interpreting it. Even if so-called 'emic' approaches are chosen (i.e., approaches claiming to investigate the inside view), the results always reflect the researcher's interpretations. However, this does not mean that intersubjective studies are useless. Results are always shaped by several intersubjective and intercultural filters and interpretations. The findings and their interpretation have to be questioned in a critical way like any other research results. Yet, they will remain valid until better interpretations replace them.

45. Literature about the Dayak Benuaq is still very limited, and studies about their resource use hardly exists at all.

Methodology

MAPPING OF SWIDDENS AND FOREST GARDENS

The position of every swidden in the village area between 1995-6 and 1998-9 was determined with a GPS[46] (global positioning system). The size of 20 swiddens was measured in 1996 by using a compass and tape measure.[47] About 1,000 forest gardens (rattan, rubber and *simpukng* gardens[48]) were cognitively-mapped by villagers.[49] The gardens were entered into a 1: 50,000 river map, obtained from the provincial planning board (BAPPEDA), and amplified by photo-copying to 1: 10,000. Rivers and creeks were identified and marked by a small group of informants, who also put forest trails on the map, while GPS-positions of recent swidden fields were marked for further orientation. During an initial meeting, the purpose of the mapping programme and its methodology was explained, and land right issues were discussed in details.

Gardens were usually mapped by small groups of neighbouring farmers during evening hours. The scale (1 square = 1×1 km) was explained, referential questions (e.g.: 'How many minutes from river *x*?' or 'How far from farmer *y*?') were repeatedly asked.

Different kinds of locally-defined forest gardens, but also former longhouse places, graveyards and sacred rocks were marked with different symbols and different colours.[50] All gardens were coded

---

46. GPS measurements showed a standard deviation (n=3 × 20) of 26 to 111 m. On average the accuracy of the instrument is between 50 and 100 m.
47. The actual field size was calculated trigonometrically by using an estimated polygon projection of the fields. The regression coefficient for seed amount versus swidden sise was 0.967 (n=19). As this correlation was sufficiently precise, the area of rice fields was not measured in the following years.
48. *Simpukng* gardens are mixed forest gardens containing mainly fruit trees.
49. Due to an increasing number of land rights conflicts, (participatory) community mapping has recently become a major task for local NGOs. The methods usually include sketch mapping, combined with GPS surveying (see Sirait *et al.* 1994, Momberg *et al.* (undated)). A critical review is given by Peluso (1995b).
50. The villagers were asked to use the map as a draft, as some people did not dare to mark their gardens out of the fear to make mistakes. Corrections were made with tippex.

and filed in a database with their exact geographic position. The codification was necessary to reduce the risk of abuse in the course of the on-going land rights conflict (see sub-section 'Chronology of Events' under chapter 2, and Gönner 1999c).[51]

Some methodological and application experiences

An attempt to work with bigger groups failed, as many people felt too shy (Ind. *malu*) to speak up, and the whole discussion was dominated by a few men. Women also participated in the mapping but to a lesser extent (there were no explicit restrictions or preferences). Some people, however, never showed up due to personal animosities with the village chief, who initiated the mapping. These households were later visited by me, and finally all but two families joined the programme.

Participants showed big differences in their ability to transfer their spatial knowledge to a two-dimensional map with a rather unusual scale. The major reference points were swiddens mapped themselves with GPS, and rivers that were derived from aerial pictures. In some cases people did not agree with the official river map, and cross-checking in the field showed that the map contained some misinterpretations, which we subsequently corrected according to the villagers' knowledge.

A colour code for the different garden types was later replaced by a combined symbol and colour code, as the local co-ordinator turned out to be colour-blind.[52]

A major problem of the mapping project was that the political opponents of the village chief did not trust him (and me) in the

---

51. As all gardens were mapped individually, the traditional *adat* system might be eroded when it comes to individual negotiations between a company and garden owners instead of the whole community. Therefore no names were included in the map, only code numbers (a code list remained in the village). Another problem is that many men filled in gardens on behalf of their wives, brothers, sisters, etc. However, by using only one representing name, the Benuaq's inheritance system is not properly reflected.

52. In fact, we had already used a combination of different colours and symbols, but rubber and fruit gardens only differed in their colour. Because of his uncertainty, the co-ordinator did not continue with the mapping when I was absent. Only when we had changed the codes did he feel secure to carry on alone.

beginning. Rumours spread that the whole mapping was only preparing a new German business after a GTZ rattan team had visited the site, and it took us quite some time to convince the villagers, that the mapping was in their own interest to gain a better position for land rights discussions with companies and government officials.

Apart from its importance as a documentation of spatial resource patterns, the map is used as a means for discussing land rights issues with conflicting parties, such as a nearby oil palm plantation company (see Gönner 1999a,1999c). The political dimension of this mapping project became dramatically apparent in May 1999, when military forces searched the house of Lempunah's village chief for the map. Anticipating such a step, the village chief had, however, hidden the map in a secure place. At that time the land rights conflict between several Benuaq villages and an oil palm company had escalated, and the company was supported by police and military forces. A few months later it became public that the company had operated without proper permits. However, at that time, several houses were already devastated, and several villagers (not from Lempunah) had spent months in prison.[53]

The participatory mapping of resource units was finished after more than 80 per cent of all remembered gardens had been marked. The remaining (estimated) 20 per cent were difficult to cover due to absent owners, and a few people who still had second thoughts. Yet, the disastrous forest fires of September/October 1997 and February/March 1998 made the continuing of the mapping rather obsolete, as more than 90 per cent of all gardens were destroyed, or severely damaged. In April 1998, a final map was drawn, and four copies of the map (1: 10,000) were handed over to the villagers. The accuracy of the mapped gardens was cross-checked along two 3,000 m transects by using a compass and a 50 m tape measure. Table 1.1 shows the result of this test for gardens along two transects for a distance of 500-3,000 m from Lempunah (T_1) and Kangkang Puya (T_2). Gardens closer to the village were less accurate, since the drawing space on the map was limited.

---

53. The arrested villagers were all proved not guilty by a public court in Tenggarong in October 1999. A comprehensive description of this land rights conflict is given on the internet website http: //members.xoom.com/Oilpalm/Lonsum.html.

Out of 27 gardens along T_1, 18 were mapped correctly (67per cent), 5 were missing (forgotten), and 4 were mapped too close to the trail. Out of 35 gardens along T_2, 23 were mapped correctly (66 per cent), 8 were missing (6 were actually forgotten, 2 not yet mapped), and 1 was mapped too close to the trail. The average difference between measured and cognitively-mapped garden positions was found to be less than 50 m, which is below the GPS's accuracy. However, there might be an untested bias against remote gardens, which had not been visited for a long time. At least in a few cases, villagers had problems in locating those far-away gardens. In addition to the location and the estimated size of forest gardens, fallow forests were also mapped along these two transects in order to analyse spatial patterns.

Table 1.1: Difference of garden location between cognitive-mapping and measuring

No.	*map*	T_1	*± m*	*No.*	*map*	T_2	*± m*
No. 1	500 m	550 m	50 m	No. 1	600 m	600 m	0 m
No. 2	650 m	650 m	0 m	No. 2	650 m	650 m	0 m
No. 3	750 m	750 m	0 m	No. 3	1100 m	1100 m	0 m
No. 4	850 m	850 m	0 m	No. 4	1100 m	1150 m	50 m
No. 5	1600 m	1600 m	0 m	No. 5	1150 m	1300 m	150 m
No. 6	1750 m	1650 m	100 m	No. 6	1250 m	1350 m	100 m
No. 7	2200 m	2100 m	100 m	No. 7	1650 m	1650 m	0 m
No. 8	2450 m	2400 m	50 m	No. 8	1750 m	1750 m	0 m
No. 9	2650 m	2650 m	0 m	No. 9	1800 m	1800 m	0 m
No. 10	2700 m	2650 m	50 m	No. 10	1950 m	1900 m	50 m
No. 11	2850 m	2750 m	100 m	No. 11	2200 m	2150 m	50 m
				No. 12	2250 m	2200 m	50 m
				No. 13	2350 m	2350 m	0 m
				No. 14	2450 m	2450 m	0 m
				No. 15	2500 m	2500 m	0 m
				No. 16	2650 m	2650 m	0 m
Mean:			41 m				28 m

Individual *simpukng* gardens were mapped regarding the positions of the trees within four 50× 50 m sample plots. One *simpukng* was mapped by myself, three were mapped by two field students from Mulawarman University in Samarinda, supervised by me. Local names of plant species were provided by key-informants. The scientific identification was kindly provided by Paulus Matius, a dendrologist of

Mulawarman University based on local names[54] and one field visit for confirming unclear species. Mammals, reptiles and birds were identified by myself using different field guides.[55]

HOUSEHOLD INTERVIEWS AND SOCIO-ECONOMIC SURVEY

Semi-structured household interviews were carried out between 1996 and 1999, covering four years of resource use in Lempunah (1995-8). In 1996, 95-100 per cent of Lempunah's households were interviewed regarding their subsistence strategies, their sources of income and their expenses. In 1997, 1998 and 1999 a representative part (approximately 95 per cent of RT III and 35 per cent of RT I/II, each sample consisting of 18 households) was re-studied to document temporal changes. The selection of the 35 per cent sample was a weighted random selection among different houses. Initially, 35 per cent of all houses were selected randomly. The result was then de-biased regarding family relations and wealth.[56] The representativity of the sample was cross-checked with the 100 per cent sample of 1996, and showed no significant differences for all tested variates.[57] The semi-structured interviews covered the following aspects:

Rice cultivation: amount of seeds; rice varieties; amount of previous harvest; rice availability during the last 12 months; number of rice fields during the last five years; field location; type of soil and forest; forest age; field ownership; labour sharing; use of chainsaws; problems and pests.

---

54. Mr. Matius is a Dayak Benuaq himself.

55. A detailed comparison between the avian diversity of an old forest and a patchwork of forest gardens and swidden fallows, as well as a study on wetland birds, was carried out by me and reported elsewhere (Gönner 1999b, 1999c, 2000). The applied field guides included Davison & Chew 1990, King *et al.* 1975, Smythies 1981, MacKinnon & Phillipps 1993, Payne *et al.* 1985, and Liat & Das (1999).

56. Five households with close family relations and similar resource strategies had been in the random sample; three of them were replaced by other randomly selected households.

57. *G*-tests for goodness of fit and Mann-Whitney *U*-tests for sample variances revealed no differences between the 35 per cent and the 100 per cent sample regarding the following variates: daily expenses (t=1.576, n_1=45, n_2=16); income sources (G=7.199, υ=14); field size (t=0.083, n_1=45, n_2=16); field position (within village area or outside, G=0.588, υ=2); ownership status (G=0.157, υ=2); fallow age (G=2.847, υ=4); and soil type (G=1.540, υ=2).

Other crops: grown vegetable and fruit varieties; cultivated rattans; new planted rubber trees rubber trees.

Sources of income: ranked sources of financial income with examples (ranks from 1-4; 1 = most important).

Daily expenses: estimated daily expenses for rice, sugar, cigarettes, cooking oil, onions, salt, gas, soap, tooth paste.

Top expenses: annual top expenses, such as new motor bikes, chainsaws, rituals, etc.

In addition, more detailed information was collected by interviewing key-informants (1996-2000) concerning resource management strategies. Wherever possible, quantitative data from previous visits were added to gain a better picture of the temporal patterns.

Some methodological experiences

A major initial problem was the definition of a household. The administrative Indonesian definition of a married couple and their children (counted as as KK — *kepala keluarga* — 'head of the family') seemed to be too narrow to suit the situation in Lempunah, where generally several 'households' of this kind live under one roof and share at least substantial parts of their economy. Hence, the selection of the interviewed households focussed on different houses first ('domestic units'). In the 1996 sample, all houses in Lempunah were visited and the present people were interviewed. Several people, however, were overlooked, as they were temporarily absent from the village during the interview period. Following the classification of Wilk & Miller (1997: 67-8) I only included 'full-time residents' in my survey, while part-time residents, absent members and temporary visitors were not regarded during these repeated interview series.

Most interviews lasted between 30 minutes and one hour, as I felt it was too intrusive to demand more time. The purpose of the study was explained,[58] and during the last two series (1998

58. I referred mainly to the necessity of explaining the rationality of the local resource use systems to official authorities such as the Ministry of Forestry and Estate Crops, which hosted the GTZ project I was attached to. The villagers were also used to 'the necessity' of data gathering from earlier visits of Indonesian field students.

and 1999) 5,000 Rp[59] were paid for each interview. In the first year (1996), I was assisted by an interpreter for Benuaq-Indonesian. The following interview series were conducted in Benuaq by myself. In general, whoever was present at the time of the interview was included, although individual dominance varied greatly. No special gender-oriented interviews were carried out, although I frequently consulted my female key-informants (n=2) on issues such as medicinal plants or weaving. Generally-speaking, Benuaq women openly participate in discussions, which they occasionally also dominate.

In order to avoid a pressure on quantitative, 'hard' data,[60] I mainly applied a semi-quantitative, ranked approach, derived from the toolbox of participatory rural appraisal (PRA) and rapid rural appraisal (RRA, see Schönhuth & Kievelitz 1994). While this worked excellently in assessing the relative importance of income sources, it did not work for gathering data of financial expenses. The interviewees generally calculated the exact numeric figure first, and translated it then into a rank. Hence, I changed the approach in cases of financial expenses to a quantitative one. However, despite the exact appearance of these figures, there was much uncertainty about the accuracy of the answers. Many people responded hesitatingly to questions like: 'How many pieces of soap do you need in a month?' In order to reflect this blurredness, I re-translated the quantitative data into ranked categories by dividing the 'exact' figures by 10.000 and rounding the results up to the category boundaries (i.e., a value of 17,800 Rp became 1.78, which fell into the category 2 between 1.5 and 2.4).

59. This equalled 1-2 kg of rice or about 70 per cent of the daily wage on the oil palm plantation.

60. The effects of this pressure can be seen in many studies, where exact interview figures with two or three decimals are given for categories, which are often unknown in the respective culture (e.g., hectare or hours, see also critical comments in Gönner 1999c).

2

Research Area and Ethnography

Research area

THIS case study was carried out in Lempunah, a Dayak Benuaq village in East-Kalimantan, Indonesia. Some additional data were included from the neighbouring villages of Tanjung Isuy, Mancong, Muara Tae and Perigiq. Lempunah's geographical position is about 200 km west of the province capital Samarinda at: 0° 34.433' S and 116° 5.112' E. The village area covers 9,200 ha of managed secondary forest. It is situated on the small Ohong river, which flows into Lake Jempang, the largest lake of the Middle Mahakam Basin (Suyardiputra *et al*. 2000: 1). The area is flat (between 40 m and 100 m above sea level) and dominated by tropical lowland evergreen rain forests, as well as by alluvial freshwater swamp forests.[1]

Alluvial lowland soils are found along the Ohong river, while Ultisols and Inceptisols are probably dominant in the drier parts of the area (Ansyahari *et al*. 1984: 14-19). Spondosols were found in the vicinity of Lempunah (*ibid*.) and are likely to occur also in the village area.[2] The Middle Mahakam Basin receives an average annual rain-fall of 2,100-2,400 mm.[3] There are no clearly distinguished rain-fall seasons, but normally July, August and September are the driest months, while March, April, November and December are wetter. The temperature ranges between 21°C and 38°C with a daily mean of

1. For forest types see Whitmore (1990: 12-15, 22-3).
2. The soil references given in Ansyahari *et al*. (1984) are from several localities around Lempunah with similar vegetation and landuse patterns. However, no additional soil samples were taken for this study.
3. 1995 was a year of rather extreme rain-fall with 4,212 mm measured in Melak (Weidemann, pers. comm.).

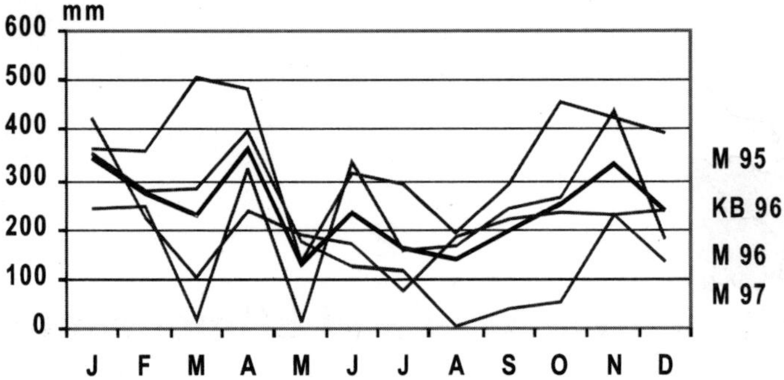

The bold line indicates the average of the four data sets. Meteorological data were kindly provided by Doris Weidemann (GTZ-IFFM)

***Fig.* 2.1: Rain-fall distribution between 1995 and 1997 at two locations, each approximately 70 km from Lempunah (Melak, north-west of Lempunah: M95, M96, M97; Kota Bangun, south-east of Lempunah: KB95)**

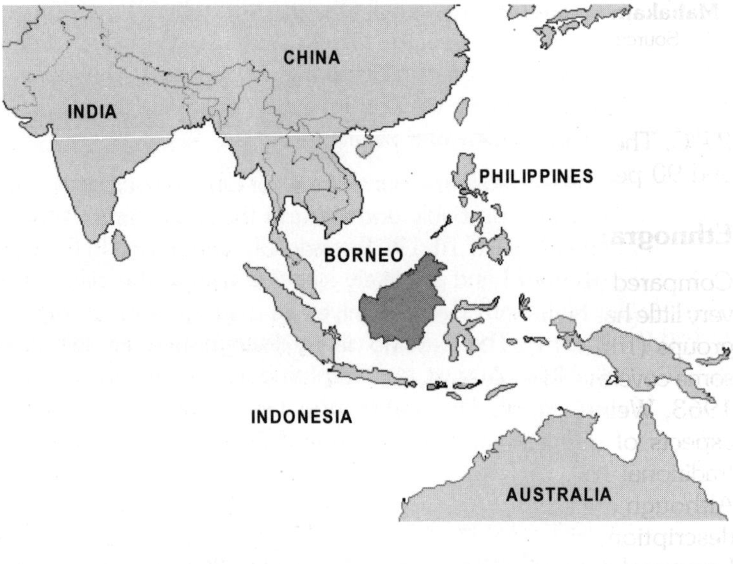

Map 1: South-East Asia with Borneo (dark grey)
Source: GIS-version of a digital map compiled for GTZ, modified by the author, Samarinda 1999

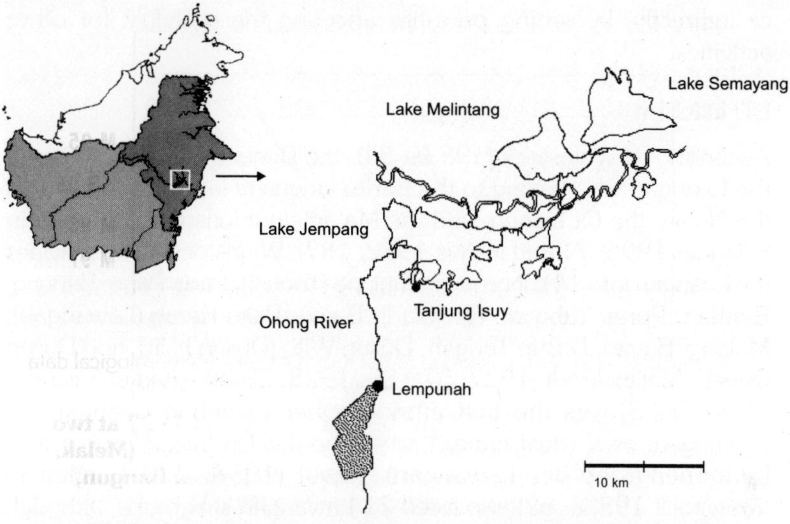

Map 2: Borneo [Indonesian provinces with East Kalimantan (dark grey); Sarawak, Sabah (Malyasia) and Brunei (white); and the Middle Mahakam Basin with the village area of Lempunah (mottled grey)]
Source: GIS-version of a digital map compiled for GTZ, modified by the author, Samarinda 1999

27°C. The average relative humidity fluctuates between 72 per cent and 90 per cent (Ansyahari *et al.* 1984: 6-7).

Ethnography of the Benuaq

Compared with the rich literature about the Iban, Kenyah, or Kayan, very little has been published about the Benuaq and their neighbouring groups (Tonyoi, Bentian). While their ritual life has recently found some coverage (Bonoh 1985a, 1985b, Massing 1981, 1982, Sarwoto 1963, Weinstock 1983a, Hopes *et al.* 1997, Hopes 1997), other aspects of the Benuaq's ethnography, including social structure, traditional law, or land use, remain so far almost undocumented. Although this chapter cannot provide a full, monography-like description, it is meant to embed the issues of resource use in Lempunah into a more comprehensive cultural framework. A special emphasis is given to religious aspects, as rituals and ceremonies are essential elements of daily life in Lempunah that often interact with resource activities, either directly, in rituals referring to agriculture, or indirectly, by setting priorities affecting the schedule for other activities.

ETHNICITY

According to Weinstock (1983a: 84), the Benuaq are a subgroup of the Luangan who belong to the Barito language family together with the Ngaju, the Ot Danum and the Ma'anyan (Hudson 1967 cited in Sillander 1995: 71 and in Avé 1972: 187). Weinstock further divides the Luangan into 14 subgroups: Tunjung (Tonyoi), Pasir, Pahu, Benuaq, Bentian, Purei, Taboyan (Tiwoian), Bawo, Paku-Kerau (Lawangan), Malang, Bayan, Dusun Tengah, Dusun Wito (Dusun Hilir), and Dusun Dayeh. Mallinckrodt (1927: 579-85, 1928: 28-30, cited in Sillander 1995: 72-3) was the first ethnographer to define Luangan (or Lawangan) as a tribal entity,[4] which he divided into 21 subgroups (Stammengroep der Lawangan). Riwut (1958: 220-1, cited in Weinstock 1983a: 82) also listed 21 Lawangan subgroups, although his system differs from Mallinckrodt's, including 'different names for the same people and ethnic names that don't exist or are questionable' (Weinstock 1983a: 82). The difference between Weinstock's and Mallinckrodt's classification is mainly the 'Stammengroep der Dusun', in which Mallinckrodt had put 8 subgroups, that Weinstock included in his concept of Luangan (Weinstock 1983a: 82-4). Sillander points out that the Dusun are different from the Luangan in terms of self-identification, but resemble each other culturally (1995: 74).

As in many other areas of Borneo, ethnicity and the concept of belonging to a specific tribal group (above village or river level) is quite low among the Luangan. Similar to the ethnonyms Iban, Land Dayak, or Ngaju, the name Luangan was never used locally in the sense ethnographers use it today (see Sillander 1995: 72, 76). It is therefore more a concept ordering indigenous groups along a cultural and linguistic scale in order to stress socio-cultural differences (although there is always some kind of overlap). The total population of Luangan referring to Weinstock's terminology is estimated at 50,000-100,000 (Sillander 1995: 71; Weinstock 1983a: 198-228).

---

4. According to Sillander (1995: 73-4) Weinstock's rejection of the term Lawangan as an ethnonym for several subgroups is justified, as Lawangan (or Lowangan) refers to a specific local subgroup already mentioned by Schwaner (1853) and Grabowsky (1888), which Weinstock prefers to call Paku-Kerau (1983: 214, 216).

The term 'Luangan' appears to be only used rarely as an ethnonym among the Benuaq. Most Benuaq perceive themselves as being Dayak (distinguishing them from Muslims), Benuaq (distinguishing from other Dayak groups), and more precisely as Orang Isuy (people from Tanjung Isuy), or as Orang Lempunah or *Akas*[5] (for people from Lempunah). Sometimes an identity derived from a river branch is used (Benuaq Ohookng — all Benuaq living along Ohong river). Common identity in daily life usually refers only to the village level. The main reason to include the Benuaq within the Luangan group is, besides linguistic similarities, the belief system, which is called *kaharingan* in Central Kalimantan, is yet another term that Benuaq along the Ohong do not use or even know.

Kaharingan was accepted as an official religion (Ind. *agama*) in 1980 by the Indonesian government (Weinstock 1981), now called *hindu-kaharingan*, since it had to be officially[6] linked to one of the major world religions. Before that, it was only regarded as a belief (Ind. *kepercayaan*), although religious reasons had a strong impact to separate the (Dayak) province Central Kalimantan in May 1957 from predominantly Muslim South Kalimantan (Weinstock 1983a: 11,12). But even if the expression *kaharingan* is not used in Lempunah, the major features of this religion, including secondary mortuary rites and shamanistic curing rituals, are found among all of the Barito-speaking Dayak groups of South-East Borneo.[7]

THE BENUAQ: HISTORY, SETTLEMENT AREA AND LANGUAGE

According to the oral history of the Ohong villages, their common origin is traced back to Mount Lumut listing 23 different locations.[8] This genealogy resembles Weinstock's findings, who also mentions

---

5. The name *Akas* refers to a former longhouse which was probably the first one after a fission between Lempunah and Muara Nayan, a neighbouring village.
6. The Indonesian states *pancasila* philosophy requires that every citizen believes in one of the world religions.
7. The expression *kaharingan* is also found among Dayak groups of northern Borneo, but not in this rather strict sense of a belief system. The male supreme deity of the Tempasuk Dusun of Sabah is called *kenharingan*, thus suggesting old etymological and cultural roots (Weinstock 1983: 19).
8. This version was reported by an informant from Muara Tae.

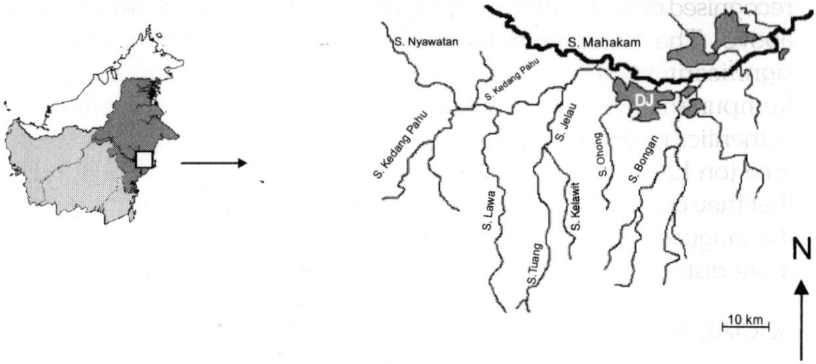

Map 3: Settlement area of Dayak Benuaq in the Pahu watershed and south of Lake Jempang (Danau Jempang — DJ), based on Massing's data (1982:58)

the mythological origin of the Luangan from Gunung (Mount) Lumut (1983a: 72-3). Today, the settlement area of the Benuaq stretches from Bongan in the east, to Lake Jempang and the Ohong river in the north, and the Kedang Pahu watershed (including the Jelau, Kelawit, Tuang, Lawa, Pahu and Nyawatan rivers, see Massing 1981: 85) towards the tributaries of the Teweh river in Central Kalimantan. In many areas the Benuaq overlap with other groups such as the Tonyoi (Tunjung) in the north-west, the Bentian in the west, or Kutai Malays in the east.

According to Massing (1981: 86), the Benuaq distinguish six subgroups (plus the Bentian, which are included in this classification) on a purely geographical basis:

(1) Benuaq of the Bongan river; (2) Benuaq of the Ohong river and Lake Jempang; (3) Benuaq of the Kelawit, Tuang and Jelau river; (4) Benuaq of the lower Lawa river; (5) Benuaq of the upper Pahu and Nyawatan rivers; and (6) Benuaq of the Idan river. Massing reports 23,400 based on provincial statistics (1981: 86), while Weinstock estimates their total number at 20,000 (1983: 205).

The Benuaq language is regarded as a Luangan isolect within the Barito language family (Hudson 1967), although explicit linguistic studies have so far not been carried out. A word list based on Swadesh's (1971: 283) is given in Annex A1.[9] There are several locally-

9. Benuaq orthography is also explained there.

recognised dialects, referring mainly to Massing's classification quoted above. The Benuaq of Tanjung Isuy speak a dialect that shows significant influence from Kutai Malay, while the dialect from Lempunah and the other Ohong villages is regarded as more authentic, resembling dialects spoken in the west of the settlement area (on Lawa, Pahu, Nyawatan rivers). Most of my informants said that they could understand much of the Bentian isolect, while Tonyoi, the language of their neighbours to the north-west, appears to be more distant and is not understood by Benuaq.[10]

SOCIAL STRATIFICATION AND STATUS

Similar to Dayak groups like the Kenyah (see Whittier 1973, Whittier 1994: 142-4), the Kayan (see Rousseau 1990: 163-87, Rousseau 1994: 111-13), or the Maloh (King 1985), Benuaq society is stratified, although compared to these other groups, in a less rigid way.[11] According to the *kepala adat* in Lempunah, transitions between different strata and marriages across them were not uncommon.[12]

The highest stratum refers to community leaders and their families, who are called *mantiiq*. In contrast to Kayan *maren* (Rousseau 1990: 172) and Maloh *samagat* chiefs (King 1985: 127), Benuaq *mantiiq* had to prepare their own fields (similar to Kenyah *paran*, see Whittier 1978: 102), but were assisted materially by the other villagers (shares of rice harvest, game, etc.) and with labour. In Lempunah, this tradition lasted until the 1960s. Nowadays, Lempunah's *mantiiq* enjoy only little help from others, and although their descent is still remembered, the strata play very little role in the local elections. The former prestige of a *mantiiq* might also have been eroded by the political division of village leadership into a

10. Although the Tonyoi share many cultural aspects with the Benuaq (including their mythology and many rites), they are linguistically and historically quite distinct from other Luangan groups (Weinstock 1983: 198); while the Bentian were also included under the Benuaq sub-groups by Massing's informants (1981: 86), as well as by Knappert (1905: 592, cited in Massing 1981: 85).

11. Besides stratified societies, there are also so-called egalitarian Dayak groups such as the Iban and the Bidayuh (see King 1993: 197-207), although these classifications are not absolute as Iban also recognise status differences (King 1993: 198).

12. Strata transitions were also possible among the Kayan (Rousseau 1990: 175-8) and among the Kenyah (Whittier 1978: 110-11), but they obviously occurred much rarer.

traditional chief (*kepala adat*) and an administrative leader (*kepala desa*),[13] the abolishment of slavery, and the introduction of a monetary economy which brought new opportunities and status symbols, not necessarily held by the old leaders.[14]

The intermediate stratum, to which the vast majority belongs, is called *merentika*,[15] while the *ripatn* 'slaves' make up the lowest stratum. In cases of (often temporary) indebtedness, a *merentika* could decline in rank and become a *ripatn* (also called *olui belangui tabaas*). Other *ripatn* were bought or caught in warfare (then called *batakn ulutn*, see also Massing 1981: 89), including people from other ethnic groups such as Javanese or Buginese. According to the *kepala adat*, *ripatn* were sacrificed in large *guguq* or *kwangkai* rituals, especially when a *mantiiq* was sick or had deceased. This former tradition is also reported for Kayan slaves (*dipen*), who were ritually killed in cases of sickness or death of a *maren* aristocrat, or for the construction of a new longhouse (Rousseau 1990: 176), as well as for Maloh *pangkam* (King 1985: 127).[16]

Ripatn could rise to the *merentika* stratum by buying their freedom. Theoretically, this was also possible for Kayan (Rousseau 1990: 178) and Maloh slaves (King 1985: 101), although it rarely happened due to the slaves' usually limited possessions (Rousseau

13. Stratification also became less relevant in the social life of Kayan and Kenyah (see Armstrong 1992: 203), although it is still found in ritual and symbolic aspects (*ibid.*).

14. In some areas, however, the aristocratic strata had better access to cash crops and education, and managed to reconfirm their supremacy (see Alexander 1992: 219 for Kenyah *maren*). In Lempunah, the *mantiiq* family of the present village chief also belongs to the families that are better off, although two non-*mantiiq* families are much richer due to their success in trading.

15. Massing (1981: 89) calls this stratum *merendika*, while Hopes (Hopes *et al*. 1997: 16) calls it *marantika*. It is likely that the expression is influenced by the Indonesian *merdeka* — independent.

16. The rationale for killing a slave in a mortuary rite is to give the deceased an assistant for his life after death. The *ripatn* sacrifice during a curing rite (e.g., *nalitn rotatn*) is most probably meant as a substitute for the sick *mantiiq*. In a similar way, exchange souls (*silih*) are offered during *belian* rites, while the *ripatn* sacrifice has been replaced by that of a water buffalo. The human sacrifice is symbolically still alive in the *melas tautn* ceremony (e.g., Tanjung Isuy, May 1996), where a human-like statue that is made from a banana trunk, is shot by a blowpipe and decapitated with a *mandau*.

ibid.). Among the Benuaq, a free *ripatn* could eventually even come into a leading position.[17] The children (at least the daughters) of *ripatn* were allowed to marry *merentika*, while *mantiiq* could marry *ripatn*.

In contrast to Kenyah, Kayan and Maloh, no buffer stratum between *mantiiq* and *merentika* was mentioned in Lempunah.[18] Massing (1981: 89) and Hopes *et al.* (1997: 15-17) also do not report any other stratum, although Massing speaks of *pengawa*, members of lineages related with *mantiiq* (*ibid.*). This term is known as *pengkawar* in Lempunah. It refers to a high-ranked secretary-like[19] position under the *mantiiq*. However, in Lempunah this position is certainly not a social stratum.[20]

Today, the stratification of Benuaq society is practically invisible (see also Massing 1981: 86), although the respective descent of a family is well-remembered. Yet, this stratum membership plays only a minor role in daily life (see above). According to my informants, recent status is earned with a well-respected life according to the *adat* (i.e., intact family and social life, no economic problems, to have a 'good heart', friendly and generous behaviour, hospitality, readiness to help). Wealth and purely economic status symbols such as TV sets, chainsaws, boat engines or motorbikes, were not mentioned but rather denied, although they do play a major role among the younger generation. Apart from the *mantiiq*, people like blacksmiths, *pembeliatn* shamans, successful hunters and war heroes, also traditionally enjoyed a high status.

---

17. Kayan *dipen* could also gain their freedom when they had successfully fought as war leaders (Rousseau 1990: 175-8).
18. Such ritually-important buffer strata are known from the Kayan (*hipuy ok* for relegated *maren* aristocrats and for risen *panyin* commoners, see Rousseau 1990: 166), the Kenyah (Whittier 1978: 110-11), and from the Maloh (King 1985: 98-9). However, the respective prestige of each of these strata appears to be different. While Kayan *hipuy ok* (Rousseau 1990: 165) and Maloh *pabiring* (King 1985: 98-9) belong ritually to the upper class, Kenyah *panyin tiga* are ritually regarded as members of the middle class (Whittier 1978: 110-11). These buffer strata are believed to have stabilised the stratification which might have been questioned in cases of more direct transitions (see Rousseau 1990: 179-80).
19. This comparison was given by the *kepala adat* of Lempunah.
20. Other organisational positions were *kepala pokaatn* (respected villagers) and *let* (leader of a village part).

KINSHIP AND MARRIAGE

Like all other Dayak groups studied so far (see Leach 1950: 81, King 1994: 6), the Benuaq are a cognatic society, in which the kinship nomenclature is bilaterally symmetrical between the father's and the mother's side (see Freeman 1992: 66; for kinship terms see Annex A1). Inheritance is bilineal from mothers to daughters, and from fathers to sons in the case of special, often ritual personal belongings; and ambilineal in the case of land, to which all descendants, male and female, have the same rights. Status, as in the case of *mantiiq* descent, can be ascribed through both the maternal and the paternal side (see Murdock 1960: 2-6).

In general, an individual person perceives his or her kinship in a kindred-like way, although the Benuaq have no equivalent expression for 'kindred'.[21] Lateral family bounds are counted up to third cousins: *warsinai/warsineq* (first cousins), *warduaq* (second cousins), *wartolu* (third cousins). Fourth cousins are usually not regarded as family in cases of shame or conflicts.

Traditionally, young married couples had to live 3-7 years in the place of the bride's parents, depending on the parents' demand for assistance. After this period, the couple had to return to the husband's family for the same period, before it was allowed to choose a domestic location of its own. If the couple did not return to the husband's family, they had to pay an *adat* fine. None the less, I never found any evidence for this second part of the rule (i.e., the return to the virilocal place). In fact, even Lempunah's *kepala adat* himself twice followed his subsequent wives to their villages without returning to his parents' place. Due to this *de facto* uxorilocal pattern, the parents-in-law of a man play an important social role. In Lempunah, the most predominant pattern in collective swiddens was the combination of sons-in-law with their wives' families, and the authority of a father-in-law which has to be respected more than that of a man's own father.

Although marriage prescriptions are nowadays less strict, in 13 out of 15 recent cases the husband still followed his wife, while there

---

21. Nor do Kayan, Kenyah and other Dayak groups have such an expression (King 1994: 12). Kindred is here understood following Freeman (1992: 67) as an extensive bilateral grouping. Freeman further defines the kindred as 'a cognatic category which embraces all of an individual's father's kin, and all of his (or her) mother's kin' (*ibid.*).

was a 3: 1 ratio of village exogamy against endogamy. In 13 cases the respective spouse (12 men, 1 woman) married into Lempunah, in 19 cases they married away from Lempunah (11 men, 8 women), and in 10 cases couples married within the village. Traditionally, marriages between cross-cousins (marriage of the mother-brother's daughter) of any degree were regarded as favourable, while parallel cousin (marriage of the father-sister's daughter) marriages were regarded as *sahu* (taboo).[22]

An even more severe *adat* offence is a marriage of partners from different genealogical levels. Counting from a common ancestor, one partner might belong to a different generation although both are of similar age. Such a case would be regarded as an incestuous marriage like between father (mother) and daughter (son) or uncle (aunt) and niece (nephew) and has to be purified with a *melas tautn* ceremony (see above). The mythological rationale for this cultural trait is given in the *Temputn Sahuq Sumakng* (Hopes *et al.* 1997: 160-7).

HOUSEHOLDS AND OTHER SOCIAL GROUPS

According to King (1994: 17), in most Bornean societies the largest percentage of households can be categorised as nuclear or stem families. This definition also fits the Indonesian administrative one, which regards married couples with their children as families (*keluarga*) and households (counted as *kepala keluarga*, see above). However, the 'houshold' is not necessarily synonymous with the domestic unit, as 110 households shared 76 domestic units (individual houses or longhouse apartments) in Lempunah. In several cases, the domestic unit was inhabited by an extended family generally including three generations and, thus, constituting several households. While food is often shared between the households of a domestic unit, financial income is usually managed individually by each nuclear family.

Hence, the household appears to be the relevant unit in terms of resource and capital allocation, although there is a close co-operation[23] that extends floatingly along kinship relations. On a larger

22. According to some informants, in the case of a parallel cousin marriage, a purifying *melas tautn* ceremony including the sacrifice of a water buffalo has to be performed in order to appease the angered spirits. Others stated that marriages of parallel cousins were allowed.
23. In my guest family, the head of the extended family helped his married children with investments such as a new chainsaw.

scale, the predominant social organisation in Lempunah is through kinship with a strong relation between a woman's parents and her own core family (see above), including other close family members. If only relations between parents and their children as well as between brothers and sisters are regarded, the nuclear families of Lempunah configure as a net shown in *fig.* 2.2.

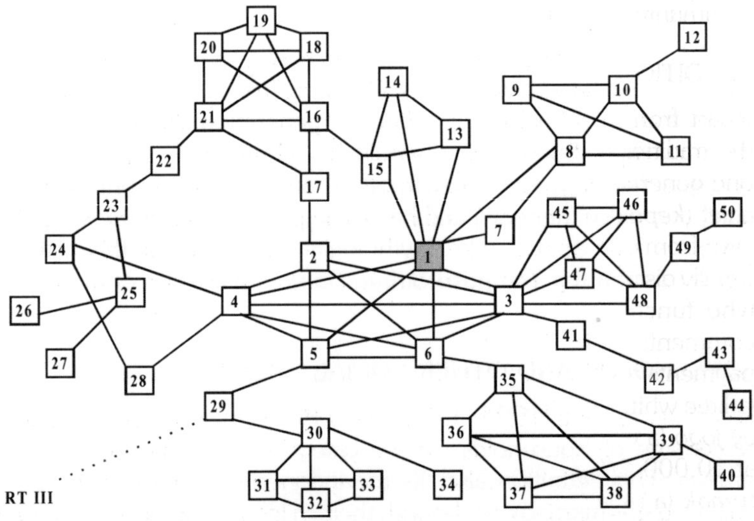

The grey box indicates the village chief's household

***Fig.* 2.2: Direct family ties through parental and sibling connections**

This net links 50 nuclear families directly to one another. With the exception of five families new to Lempunah, only 10 other nuclear families are not directly linked to the net. However, they are included at the second order (*warsinai*). In this net, the village chief (dark grey in *fig.*2.2) and one of his step brothers occupy the most central position with 10 direct links to other households. This number rises to 20, when the subsequent links originating from the direct ones are included. The consequence of this affiliation can be seen in rituals and conflicts, when the organising core is set-up by close family members.[24]

24. An instructive example of alliances during a conflict is given in a later chapter sub-section, 'Socially and Religiously-Embedded Strategies' under chapter 4). Yet, besides the immediate family members some friends of rather distant family ties also joined the alliance.

Although intra-village conflicts are said to be motivated individually, or by cross-family ties, even at the *warsinai* level, the core of a fluctuating group that usually opposes the village chief and his followers is constituted by four households without direct links to the net of *fig.*2.2. These observations stress the significant importance of close family members, who are usually relied on, while the kindred, defined locally up to *wartolu* level, would cover almost the whole community of Lempunah due to the dense web created by marriages.

TRADITIONAL *ADAT* LAW AND LAND TENURE

Apart from marriages, many other social aspects are regulated by the traditional *adat* law.[25] This unwritten law is handed down from one generation to the next and supervised by the traditional village chief (*kepala adat* — 'head of *adat*'), and by acknowledged elders (also from other villages). Cases of violations against the *adat* law are usually discussed in a meeting (*berinuq*), often including many people who function as witnesses (Ind. *saksi*), or contribute with their comments until a consensus is found.[26] Financial fines and ritual payments are imposed in terms of the *adat* currency with *lampakng* (a little white pot) as the smallest unit[27] valued at 2,500 Rp; followed by *jogo* (a white plate) valued at 5,000 Rp; *gusiq* (a small jar) valued at 10,000 Rp; *antaakng* (a large Chinese jar) valued at 20,000 Rp; *tumak* (a ritual spear) valued at 25,000 Rp; and *genikng* (a bronze gong) valued at 50,000 Rp.

Land tenure is also regulated under the *adat* law. According to Appell (1986: 119-20) there are two modes of land tenure among swidden agriculturalists: (1) circulating usufruct systems, and (2) devolvable usufruct systems. In the first case, no permanent usufruct

25. The term *adat* is known all over Indonesia and usually applied for traditional customs and traits. *Adat* law is 'the indigenous normative system of various Indonesian societies and communities' which varies within the nineteen law areas identified for the Indonesian archipelago (Löffler 1996: 28).

26. This can last for a whole night.

27. The *adat* fine claimed from the oil palm company was also calculated in terms of this *adat* currency. Hence, 1 *lampakng* was claimed per square metre of cleared land, which ran up to several billion Rupiah (that were never paid). Other fines were set at: 10 *antaakng* for a knife fight in 1989, 1 *antaakng* for defamation, 5 *antaakng* for theft of rattan from forest gardens, and 5-10 *antaakng* in cases of divorce.

is acquired by the clearing of primary forest, and everyone has the same right to use a fallow forest originally cleared by others. Examples of this mode are found among the Rungus and the Bulusu. The second, more common mode in Borneo refers to permanent rights derived from the first clearing of a primary forest. These rights can be transferred to other legal parties such as other individuals, or groups of people. Examples for this kind are the Iban, Bidayuh, Kenyah, and the Benuaq.

This mode can be further differentiated into partionable usufruct (e.g., among the Iban), where the usufruct remains with the domestic unit (*bilek*) and is not segregated with inheritance, while the divisionable usufruct is divided among the descendants (*ibid*.: 120-2). The latter kind is found among the Benuaq, although in some cases where children never contributed to the maintenance of forest gardens, their usufruct was partially restricted. The tenure rights (*ngempotn*) are derived from the clearing of a piece of primary forest and extended to the further use of the subsequent fallow, including the establishing of forest gardens.[28] These gardens are later divided[29] among the children including those who have permanently left the village. If other people establish gardens on the respective fallow, land tenure (Ind. *hak milik*) remains with the primary owner, while the usufruct (Ind. *hak pakai*) of the planted crops belongs to the new farmer.

During the land clearing activities of a nearby oil palm company, these combined cases frequently resulted in internal conflicts, as the company would not compensate for the land, but only for standing crops such as rattan, fruit trees or rubber. Hence, the original owners came away empty-handed, while others sometimes received substantial sums of compensation money.[30] Similarly, the disposal of forest gardens also became increasingly problematic. Traditionally, all family members involved have to be consulted when someone wants to sell a forest garden. However, during the negotiations with the oil palm company, many people sold gardens for which they claimed rights, without the agreement of their co-heirs. These conflicts then had to

---

28. Usually the person who cleared the forest also established the forest gardens.
29. i.e., the total number of gardens is divided, not the garden itself.
30. In fact, the financial compensation for planted tree crops was rather marginal, but due to the often large number of trees and gardens it could add up to several million Rupiah.

be solved in line with the *adat* law, although this often conflicted with state law, which only partially accepts *adat* law (see Löffler 1996: 29-36).

Wild-growing resources can usually be harvested by everyone, and fruits from *simpukng* forest gardens are considered as open access resources, as long as they are collected for personal consumption alone.

COSMOVISION

The origin of the world, of humankind, of the spirits, of animals, plants, longhouses, sickness and death, war and the social order, everything is explained in the vast mythological complex of the *temputn*. *Temputn* are myths recited during the major ceremonies of life and death,[31] such as *guguq* and *kwangkai*. These myths belong to the special knowledge of *pembeliatn* healers (especially those of the *belian turaatn* complex) and of *pengewara*, ritual specialists for the secondary mortuary rites. The common knowledge of *temputn* is only fragmentary, and refers to the narrative core of the myths omitting the often very detailed genealogies of spirits and cultural heroes.

An excellent collection of Benuaq *temputn* was compiled by Michael Hopes, Madrah and Karaakng (Hopes *et al.* 1997) based on Indonesian transcriptions of Karaakng, who is, according to Hopes, one of the most experienced Benuaq *pengewara*. This collection will be the major reference for my own interpretations of Benuaq cosmovision and rituals, enriched with my own data based on interviews of local *pembeliatn* and *pengewara*, as well as on detailed notes of dozens of *belian* and *kwangkai* ceremonies from the period between 1988 and 2000. As ritual life is also of significant social importance in Lempunah, influencing many aspects of decision-making in the use of natural resources, this chapter is given more weight than other ethnographic issues.

According to the *Temputn Langit Tana* (Hopes *et al.* 1997: 20-8), the origin of the heavens and the earth, the primordial world was based on the shoulders of Wook Ngesok, a spirit who stood on the back of Beniak Lajang Langit, the 'Wild Eagle of the Skies'.

---

31. The large body of legends and folk tales is called *intootn*. The knowledge of *intootn* is widespread among the population, and not confined to ritual specialists.

While Lolakng Kintang ('Beautiful Kintang') and her ancestors (eight generations) lived on the left shoulder, Imang Mengkelayakng and his ancestors (also eight generations) lived on the right one. After both had suffered for a long time ('Imang Mengkelayakng had been seven times married and seven times a widower, seven times a father and seven times left childless; Lolakng Kintang had had seven husbands and been left a widow seven times, seven times a mother and seven times left childless.', *ibid*.21) they decided to kill themselves by jumping off the rock where they lived into endless darkness. So both went to the edge of their respective sides, when they met at the gap. They spoke to each other, telling their stories of ill-fortune. Then Imang Mengkelayakng suggested to live on and marry instead of killing themselves. And so they built a house spanning the gap between their rocks, uniting their two families.

In due course many children were born, who are known as the Seniang, spirits of the sun (Seniang Olo), the moon (Seniang Bulatn), and the stars (Seniang Bintakng). Finally, there were so many of them, all crying and longing for more space, as the world was still very small, and Imang Mengkelayakng sought the advice of the two families. Then, Perjadiiq Bantikng Langit ordered Tataau Junyukng Ayus and Ayakng Siluuq Urai[32] to supervise the widening of the heavens and the earth until there were eight levels of skies and eight levels of the earth,[33] including many different locations for the Seniang spirits. However, once the Seniang had left, the earth was an empty place, and so Ayus and Siluuq gave Ayakng Komakng Lolang and Petek Telose Sie the order to form a figure out of the remainder of the primordial material from which earth and skies were made. This figure became known as Taman Rikukng. Feeling lonely he created a female companion, called Ape Bunga(n) Tana,

32. Ayus and Siluuq later also appear in folk and fairy tales. However, most informants claim that these tale heroes are different from the deities, despite having the same names.

33. According to some informants, there are 8 levels of skies, but only 7 levels of earth. However, the number is not to be seen in a mathematical sense, as there are many more locations, both in the skies and in the earth.

> out of a rib from his left side.[34] After three incestuous relations with Ape Bunga(n) Tana and her female descendants, more Seniang spirits were born, becoming the ancestors of wild boars, monkeys, snakes, bees, wasps, fish, and many spirits such as Tonoi earth spirits, Juata water spirits, Nyahuq omen spirits, forest spirits (Jin, Wook), Nayuq and Timang spirits, as well as of humankind.
>
> The attitude of these spirits towards human beings is based on the erroneous killing of one Seniang by her siblings. When Taman Rikukng — now known as Tatau Lisatn Tunyukng[35] and his wife left for their rice field they said to their children '*pekate piak bura*'[36] — kill the white hen — in case the little ones would become hungry and quarrelsome. However, the children only heard 'kill . . . bura'. So when they became hungry they killed and ate their little sister named Bura despite the protest of the oldest siblings, who were limbless and could thus not intervene.
>
> After they had eaten her sister, all became invisible and turned into spirits. Those who had not eaten from Bura became Seniang spirits living in the skies and watching over the humans' morals. Those who had eaten the raw flesh of Bura turned into malignant Papaiq spirits harming humans through sickness and death, while those who had eaten cooked meat became Tangkai spirits, including Nayuq and Timang spirits, who can be relied on as familiars of the humankind.
>
> — Hopes *et al*. 1997: 40

However, the youngest sister, Narik, who was still in the cradle during the massacre, later had a daughter called Sia, who had a son, named Punen, the forefather of humankind. With Punen, the first real human being, the primordial time ended.

---

34. This biblical motif was not reported in Lempunah, where the female companion is made from soil. In another version Taman Rikukng gives his sperm into the soil, and his companion grows.

35. Taman Rikukng changed his name each time he married in order to have the same level of descendency as his wife. To marry someone of a different level would be regarded as marrying his daughter or grandchild and hence be *sahu* (taboo).

36. In Lempunah it is not a hen but a white catfish (*baukng bura*).

THE BENUAQ PANTHEON

Although there appears to be much local variation of deity and spirit names, some rather general systematics seem possible following the creation myths reported by Hopes *et al.* (1997), as well as by my own unpublished data (Gönner 1990), and the information provided by Massing (1982).

Kayangan and Perjadiiq Bantikng Langit (*Lantalah*)

According to the *temputn* myths (Hopes *et al.* 1997), there is a group of very old spirits dwelling on the shoulders of Wook Ngesok including the 8-generation lineages of Lolakng Kintang and Imang Mengkelayakng, as well as Tataau Junyukng Ayus, Ayakng Siluuq Urai, and Perjadiiq Bantikng Langit (see above). These primordial spirits are possibly identical with the Kayangan reported by my Lempunah informants, although this was never positively confirmed.[37] These deities which are also referred to as Kayangan Walo, the eight Kayangan,[38] are said to be older than all other spirits, and already dwelt in the skies when heaven and earth were still close to each other.

Among these primordial deities is also Perjadiiq Bantikng Langit (see also Hopes *et al.* 1997: 5,188, Perejadig in Massing 1982: 61, or Lantalah). Sometimes Perjadiiq Bantikng Langit is referred to as a celestial creator, although in the *Temputn Langit Tana* (Hopes *et al.* 1997: 20-8) he is only a primus inter pares (although one who gives orders). It seems likely that the role of Perjadiiq Bantikng Langit changed over time into a creator god, influenced by monotheistic religions like Islam or Christianity. His mythological role appears to be rather limited, and he is rarely invoked in rituals.[39]

---

37. The expression Kayangan is not mentioned by Hopes or Massing, while my informants did not explicitly give the individual names of the Kayangan deities, only their 'colours'. One informant stated that they now live on Mount Meratus, which is well-known among the Benuaq Ohookng as a spirits' place.
38. The extension *walo* (8) is often applied for spirits, such as Luikng Walo, Siluuq Walo, Seniang Walo. The number is not meant literally, but rather in the meaning of 'all' or 'many'.
39. I only heard *pembeliatn* healers calling his name during a *belian* once or twice.

Seniang spirits

In the direct descent of the deities described above are the Seniang spirits. According to the myths there are primary Seniang, the children of Lolakng Kintang and Imang Mengkelayakng; as well as secondary Seniang, those children of Taman Rikukng, known at that time as Tatau Lisatn Tunyukng; and his third wife, Ayakng Dilakng Tunyukng, who had not eaten the meat of their sister Bura (see above). Seniang are spirits of the elementary forces (see Massing 1982: 61) including the annual cycles (Seniang Tautn), the sun (S. Olo), the moon (S. Bulatn), the stars (S. Bintakng), the rain (S. Osaq), the wind (S. Dolaq), and the drought (S. Koren); as well as spirits watching over taboos (S. Sahu). The Seniang live in the different skies above Tenung Tenangkai and might only be invoked in great rituals, including *belian turaatn* rites.

If the traditional *adat* law or a taboo (especially regarding incest) is broken, the temper of the Seniang becomes hot, causing severe droughts and disasters. These disasters can only be prevented or redressed with adequate offerings that cool down the earth and skies such as in *nular* or *melas tautn* ceremonies. According to the *temputn* about the origin of human beings, there are two more groups of spirits, descending from Taman Rikukng and his wife: the Tangkai, spirits originating from those children who ate cooked meat of Bura, and the Papaiq, spirits originating from those who ate the raw flesh of their sister.[40] Although the myth does not recall the detailed origin of all spirits invoked in recent rituals, I will ascribe the most relevant spirits, reported by Hopes *et al.* (1997: 13-16,186-90), by Massing (1982: 61-2), and by my own informants to these two lineages.

Tangkai spirits

Tangkai spirits are generally benevolent, and assist humans against disease and other crises for the reward of adequate offerings. Although the generic expression Tangkai is not explicitly mentioned in Lempunah or by Massing (1982: 62), it appears that several sub-groups, known in Lempunah and in Massing's paper (*ibid.*) as Mulukng (Molukng, Ntuh) belong to this group, relating to their mythological

---

40. Besides the Papaiq spirits, the animals of the forest also originate from those children who ate the raw flesh of Bura, while human beings descend from Narik who was still too little to commit this crime.

origin and dwelling location in a heaven called Tenung Tenangkai.[41] The Mulukng include: Kenyong [Dewa],[42] an important assistant spirit in the *belian* curing rites; Ton(d)oi, earth spirits also dwelling in jars, spears, gongs, plates and the eight earth-levels, who guard the (long)house, the field and the village, symbolised as snakes; Juata water spirits, especially important during pregnancy and after birth, often symbolised as crocodiles or fish; as well as Sentiu, Jamu, Bisu Walo, and Gaib Wali, all invoked in *belian*.

Massing (*ibid.*) questions whether Nayukn (Nayuq), Jiwata (Juata) and Ntonoi (Tonoi) should also be classed as Ntuh (Mulukng) or Seniang, 'as they are invoked directly and also requested to intervene at higher levels'. The creation myth is not clear about this issue either, speaking first about the origins of Tonoi, Juata, Nyahuq, Nayuq and some forest spirits, but referring later to the generic term of Tangkai for benevolent spirits differentiating them from Papaiq and Seniang. If these three classes are regarded, the Mulukng must be included among the Tangkai together with the Nayuq, the Timang, Juata and Tonoi spirits.

The Nayuq spirits are associated with blood, warfare and head-hunting. They are of great importance in the larger *belians* such as *bekeleeu* and *guguq* ceremonies. The Nayuq live in the skies as well as in powerful places on earth. In Lempunah they are generally distinguished from the Mulukng or included in the more pragmatic group of Pengirikng (see below).

The Timang are powerful spirits usually symbolised as tigers,[43] although they may take a human form (see Hopes *et al.* 1997: 189). Similar to the Nayuq, the Timang spirits are included among the Pengirikng in Lempunah, but not among the Mulukng. Another Tangkai group are the Nyahuq spirits. After having eaten the cooked meat of their sister Bura, the Nyahuq first kept their human shape.

41. Some Mulukng are also believed to live on Mount Meratus, about 100 km south of Lempunah, as well as in waters and other powerful earthen places.

42. The Sanskrit expressions *deva* (= god, goddess) and *rajah* (= king; e.g. *Rajah Kenyong*), which are also used in the Indonesian language, are often added to Mulukng spirits as honorary titles. However, some informants stated that Dewa is a helpful spirit itself.

43. Tigers have never actually occurred in Borneo (see Payne *et al.* 1985). Hence, the Timang symbols probably originate from Kutai's Hindu past (fourth-fifth to sixteenth century, see Boyce 1986: C1-C6).

However, later, when Apen Peningir, another cultural hero, gave them 'old *tuak*' to eat — uncooked rice mixed with blood — they unwittingly violated the taboo imposed by their father Taman Rikukng not to eat raw flesh or blood. So they became accursed and changed their shape to birds (see Hopes 1997: 15-24). From then on, the Nyahuq spirits helped humans (especially in the cultivation of rice) for adequate offerings in return.

These offerings, traditionally given at the start of the agricultural year, are known as *pakatn nyahuq*. However, I never witnessed a *pakatn nyahuq* in Lempunah, although the rites were still known. Nevertheless, the Nyahuq spirits are respected in the consideration of omens, indicating good or ill fortune associated with rice cultivation and other aspects of daily life (i.e., journeys, former head-hunting expeditions).

Papaiq spirits

This generic expression also appears to be unknown in Lempunah.[44] According to the respective *temputn* (Hopes *et al.* 1997: 39,188), the Papaiq are a group of spirits who can cause sickness and ill fortune to human beings. It is not clear whether this group also includes the great variety of forest or mountain spirits called Wook, Blih and Jin. Wook are mobile spirits, often associated with strange sounds or calls in the forest. The most prominent figure is Banci, a spirit probably of Hindu origin, often taking the form of a wild, furry black-haired woman with long claws. Although Banci can cause dangerous fevers, she might be benevolent if treated correctly.

Other examples of Wook are Mulaakng forest spirits, or Merwaaq spirits of the undead. Blih (from Ind. *iblis* = devil), are generally believed to enter people and cause sickness; while Jin (Ind. = genie, evil spirit) are associated with special locations, such as trees (especially strangling figs), rocks, caves or wells. The Papaiq spirits are believed to cause sickness by abducting the vital souls of human beings, the *juus* (see below), or by entering humans.

Crop spirits

An important group of spirits, whose mythological origin remains

44. The name Papaq exists, however, as an expression for unspecified evil spirits.

rather unclear are the crop spirits,[45] such as Lolakng Luikng[46] (rice spirit), Lolakng Legikng (cassava spirit), Lolakng Leok (banana spirit), Lolakng Lebukng (maize spirit), Lolakng Rejeh (sweet potato spirit), and Lolakng Lueh (ginger and curcuma spirits). Of these spirits, Lolakng Luikng (also referred to as Luikng Walo — the eight Luikng, see Hopes *et al.* 1997: 187) is by far the most important. Lolakng Luikng is perceived as the soul of rice, who has to be brought back before the harvest from her temporary domicile at Siluuq's place in the centre of water (Ind. *pusat air*).[47] This journey is accompanied by the *ngeluikng* rite explained below. Lolakng Luikng is also invoked in *belian* curing rites, where she transmits messages between the *pembeliatn* healers and the Mulukng spirits.[48] If the harvest is threatened by drought, the crop spirits are called during the *belian turaatn* part of a *nular*, or of a *guguq* (*melas tautn*) ceremony. According to a *temputn* from Mancong,[49] Lolakng Luikng is the only daughter of Beritutn tautn, son of Seniang Penitah, and Diaakng Serunaai.

> As predicted by Seniang Penitah, the couple suffers despite great efforts against severe problems. Droughts and pests torment the family, and Beritutn tautn is at his wits' end until an old woman (believed to be the mother of Siluuq and Ayus, see above) appears in his dream and tells him to sacrifice his daughter Lolakng Luikng. Beritutn Tautn does as he was told and the hardship has an end. However, life is not as it used to be, and Beritutn Tautn and his wive suffer from their sorrow. Then they decide to visit Seniang Penitah at his celestial domicile. When they arrive, they see a young girl

---

45. These spirits are not mentioned explicitly by Massing (1982), or in the *temputn* compiled by Hopes *et al.* (1997), although Hopes (*ibid.*: 187) names Luikng as the spirit of the rice plant without referring to her mythological origin.

46. *Lolakng* means beautiful [woman].

47. This subject which resembles the Greek Demeter-Kore (Persephone) myth was not reported by all informants. The respective *temputn* is also not clear about this matter, but suggests rather that Lolakng Luikng stays temporarily with a Seniang spirit in the heavens. Hence, the version referring to the centre of water might be a local variation of the same motif.

48. This information transmission is symbolised by casting yellow rice.

49. Noted by my field assistant in April 2000 (Benyamin 2000).

> threshing rice, who looks just like Lolakng Luikng. In fact, it is Lolakng Luikng, who was exchanged with Lolakng Tepukng, a replicate made by Seniang Penitah from flour, before the sacrifice. When the parents learn about this, their sorrow is gone and they live together with their daughter in Seniang Penitah's place for some time, before they return to their own place, leaving Lolakng Luikng in the spiritual world, where she becomes a mediator invoked in rituals.

Besides these deities and spirits, a number of cultural heroes and heroines exist, occasionally referred to as *nabi* (Ind. [Islamic] prophets). These include Taman Rikukng, Punen, Aji, Datu, Monaq, and Kilip, who brought humankind all sorts of knowledge, including the use of water, fire, rice, the construction of longhouses, traditional *adat* law and the various rites necessary in life and death. In many myths and legends, Ayus and Siluuq also play the role of *nabi* who already occurred in the creation myths as primordial (probably Kayangan) deities (see Hopes *et al.* 1997: 22,31). If invoked in rituals, sacred names must be applied (e.g., Waatn for Siluuq).

A last category is formed by the Pengirikng spirits. This group refers to the direct aides of the *pembeliatn* healers. They include the Nayuq and the Timang spirits, as well as personal sahabat (Ind. = friends), often ancestors, and the Kelelungan Kelangun, the immortal head souls of the deceased (also known as Kelelungan, see Massing 1982: 61, Hopes *et al.* 1997: 187).

RITUALS

Ritual life among the Benuaq and Tonyoi[50] shows a dual pattern differentiating rituals of the living world (*belian*) from those related to death (*kwangkai*).[51] This dichotomy is also reported by my informants, although a third ritual complex associated with agricultural activities does not fit entirely into the *belian-kwangkai* dualism despite its clear affiliation to aspects of life. Hence, I will first describe the rituals of the *belian* type, then those belonging to *kwangkai*, and finally rites related to other aspects of life such as birth, marriage and agricultural activities.

---

50. It is widely believed that the Dayak Tonyoi (Tunjung) adopted Benuaq rituals (see Weinstock 1983a: 82,85-7,198; Sillander 1995: 76).

Life rituals

According to Weinstock (1983a: 38), there are three major types of life rituals among the Luangan: (1) curing *balian* (*belian*); (2) thanksgiving *balian*; and (3) family rituals. I will not follow this classification, as there is no evidence among the Benuaq that they hold 'thanksgiving' rituals, while some of the family rituals will be discussed under agricultural rites. Instead, I prefer to describe the general features of these life rituals first, before exploring the respective fields of application.

All Benuaq life rituals involve the assistance of *pembeliatn*.[52] *Pembeliatn* are mediators (male or female) between the human and the spiritual sphere. In cases of sickness he or she is the one to look for the cause of the disease, and to conduct the rites in order to bring back the vital souls (*juus*) abducted by Papaiq spirits, or to exorcise them in cases of possession. *Pembeliatn* either learn their skills, or they derive them in their dreams. Usually a person who wants to become a *pembeliatn* has to absolve a long and expensive apprenticeship. Due to the vast amount of essential ritual knowledge and the effort for acquiring them, most *pembeliatn* are specialised in one kind of *belian* (see below).[53] In larger ceremonies (e.g. *bekeleeu* or *guguq*), these different *belian* kinds are frequently combined, and

---

51. There are several symbolic differences including the basic figures (8 for *belian* rites, 7 for *kwangkai* rites); gender (there are male and female *pembeliatn* healers, but only male *pengewara* specialists in *kwangkai*); or the payment of ritual specialists (the right half of sacrificed animals in *belian*, the left half in *kwangkai*).

52. Pembeliatn are the Benuaq's equivalent to the Iban's *manang*. Graham (1987: 1-2) calls the *manang* 'shamans' following Mircea Eliade (e.g., 1991). Her key argument is the *manang's* wandering shamanistic character in contrast to 'spirit possession' and 'spirit mediumship'. In a similar way, Benuaq *pembeliatn* apply elements of wandering shamanism, although in combination with spirit possession as well as mediumship. According to Thiel's (1984: 133-7) definition of shamanism (ecstasy, protection-spirit, vocation, social and formal integration) Benuaq *pembeliatn* can, indeed, be regarded as 'true shamans'.

53. In Lempunah there are seven recent specialists for *belian sentiu*, two for *belian turaatn*, one for *belian bawe* (women's *belian*) and two *pengewara* specialists for the *kwangkai* rites. The already mentioned *melas tautn* ceremony in Tanjung Isuy (1996) was conducted by an external *pembeliatn*, who knew the *sentiu* as well as the *turaatn* rites, and even worked as a *pengewara*. However, nowadays, this extensive ritual knowledge appears to be extremely rare.

up to a dozen *pembeliatn* can co-operate towards the end of such a ceremony. *Pembeliatn* have to fulfill their tasks whenever they are required.[54] They receive relatively little payment,[55] and have to work as farmers like everyone else in the village.

Belian: While sickness and disease (*rotatn*) is the major daily cause for *belian rituals*, these ceremonies are also required in the case of broken taboos (*sahu*), or as preventions to prepare for a good new year.[56] In most cases, the larger *belians* (*bekeleeu*, *guguq*) are held for several combined purposes.[57] Theoretically, a complete *belian* should last 8 nights or multiples of 8. However, as a *belian* night is not necessarily congruent with a physical night,[58] almost no *belian* fits this rule, while small curing *belian* are also possible for 1 or 2 nights including the sacrifice of chickens, although generally not of pigs.[59]

The most common curing *belian* in Lempunah is *belian sentiu* (*senteo*, see Massing 1982: 73), a ceremony that is said to be relatively

---

54. When one *pembeliatn* returned to Lempunah after having joined me in the forest for several days, he had to conduct a *belian* in the same night, despite his fatigue.
55. The payment includes a part of the sacrificed animals, rice, fabrics, plates, and (not always) some money. The amount of the payment is not prescribed, but 'something' has to be given.
56. As these *melas tautn* (*guguq*) rituals are often held after the rice harvest, they were misinterpreted as thanksgiving rituals (e.g., Weinstock 1983a: 44-7, Massing 1982: 67). Explicit interviews of knowledgeable *pembeliatn* from several areas, however, revealed that the purpose of a *melas tautn* ritual is always directed towards the future. An expression for 'thank' does not even exist in Benuaq language.
57. A large *guguq* ceremony held in Tanjung Isuy in 1996 for more than 3 months had the major purpose to purify the *sahu* of four marriages of forbidden descent constellations, as well as the cleaning (*melas*) of the whole area for the coming year. During this so-called *melas tautn* (=*nalitn tautn*) ceremony, sick people were also ritually healed, although healing is the major purpose of the more specific *nalitn rotatn* ceremonies.
58. As the various ritual phases belonging to one *belian* night often last too long due to unpredictable circumstances (e.g., new diseases, incomplete ritual equipment), the last parts of such a night are often postponed to the next day.
59. An exception of the rule that a *belian* with a pig sacrifice must last four or eight nights is the *belian menengal*. It is held in cases where evil spirits demand the blood of a human being, for which the blood of a sacrificed pig is offered *in lieu*.

new. According to Lempunah's traditional chief (Ind. *kepala adat* = traditional head), *belian sentiu* originates from the Bongan river (see Map 3), where it was introduced by two shamans at the beginning of the twentieth century. *Belian sentiu* is a curing rite combining elements of mediumship, wandering shamanism and possession shamanism. Although the amount of ritual equipment increases from night to night, each night shows three distinct parts consisting of various elements (see also Massing 1982: 71):

The opening: *Luaq* (*Dianella* sp.) incense is burnt, while the pembeliatn get into contact with the spiritual world. They treat themselves with a paste from rice flour and tawar water, cast yellow rice in order to invoke Lolakng Luikng as a mediator with the Mulukng spirits, and invoke their spirit aides, communicating via the *awiir*, coloured-cloths hanging from a wooden cross (*kota batuq* — 'stony town').[60] The invocation is then continued with different dances accompanied by fast drum-beating and gong — playing (performed on six small gongs). During these dynamic dances, the pembeliatn's juus travels into the spiritual world looking for the cause of the disease.[61] This first part is finished with the hearing of a family member who explains the situation via the pembeliatn to the spirits.

The curing part: After the hearing of the family member(s), the pembeliatn start singing and invoking again followed by more dancing and the (spiritual) treatment of the sick persons, which includes purification rites from belian turaatn and the sacrifices of the final night.[62]

The closing part: After a break, the *eboq* is brought, a stick or rope with several ritual items and offerings hanging from it. The eboq is the place, where the abduced juus of the patients are exchanged against payment or exchange souls (*silih*). Here, the pembeliatn also

---

60. The *kota batuq* is only used for larger *belians* including the sacrifice of pigs. In smaller ceremonies the flower of the *Sepootn* palm (*Areca catechu*) — *mayang* — is used instead.

61. An important place to collect the relevant information is Sencangan Walo — the crossing of the Eight Paths (see Hopes *et al*. 1997: 188). From here, it is possible to get access to the different spiritual realms.

62. Only domestic animals such as chickens, pigs and — in the case of a *guguq* — also water buffalos are sacrificed. These animals are rarely killed for food consumption, and if this is done, they are generally killed in a way that no blood is spilled (e.g., by drowning), as this could anger the spirits.

take back their own juus, which travels to the spiritual world before they finish the ceremony.

Afterwards, the respective house is *tuhing*, i.e., it is forbidden for those who did not participate in the ritual to enter for a certain time, depending on the length of the ceremony.

Within the *belian sentiu,* several sub-types are employed, such as *belian kenyong*, *b. dewa*, *b. joget*, *b. kuyakng*, *b. jamu*, *b. ruang*, *b. dari*, *b. pantun*, *b. semur*, *b. timuuq*, or *b. semuan*. These sub-types are required for the invocation of different benevolent spirits (e.g., 'Kenyong, Joget, Pantun, Jamu', etc.). For the invocation, different equipment, dances, rhythms and melodies (gongs, or bamboo flutes in the case of *b. jamu*) are required. A more comprehensive description of several *belian sentiu*, as well as the ritual elements is given in Gönner (1990).

The second *belian* performed in Lempunah is *belian turaatn* (also called *belian timeeq* or *belian beneeq* — 'common *belian*'). *Belian turaatn* is believed to be much older than *belian sentiu*, and the ritual specialists are also knowledgeable of the *temputn* myths.[63] In contrast to *belian sentiu*, the *pembeliatn* do not dance but invoke spirits and Kelelungan souls accompanied by slow drum-beating. Usually, both *belian* types are mediated by different specialists.

A third kind of *belian*, *belian bawo*, is not performed in Lempunah, although it is widespread in other Benuaq areas (see Bonoh 1985, Massing 1982: 71-2, Weinstock 1983a: 39). However, *belian bawo* resembles *belian sentiu* in many respects, with the latter probably replacing it in the eastern parts of the Benuaq settlement area (see also Massing 1982: 73).

In their pure form, these *belian* kinds are only applied for small curing rituals of one or two nights.[64] While *belian sentiu* is used for most kinds of diseases, *belian turaatn* is more associated with *juus* souls of the head. More serious diseases, the purification of broken taboos, or the preparation of the new year require larger ceremonies involving combinations of *belian sentiu*, *belian turaatn*, as well as *belian bawe* (performed by female *pembeliatn*).

63. The *temputn* are recited during large *belian* ceremonies involving *turaatn* parts, but not in *belian sentiu*.

64. There are some more small curing rituals, such as *nyemur* and *memang*, which require much less ritual equipment and no animal sacrifices. These rites are, however, only a first attempt to treat a disease.

Naraja, Nerajaah, Toraja: A curing ceremony combining *belian sentiu* and *b. turaatn*. It lasts four nights including the sacrifice of at least one pig. *Naraja* ceremonies were rather common in the two dwellings of RT III.

Bekeleeu: This ceremony resembles a *naraja*, but lasts at least eight nights, including the sacrifice of several pigs. *Bekeleeu* ceremonies were held in Lempunah every year, organised by different families. They were usually celebrated in order to fulfil promises given to the spirits during earlier diseases in the respective family, or in cases of very serious sickness, which required the combination of different *belian* types and the invocation of Nayuq spirits (see *temputn* reported in Hopes *et al.* 1997: 141-50).

Seniang: In cases where a *bekeleeu* ceremony was not successful, the Seniang spirits are directly invoked applying *belian turaatn* elements. For this rare ceremony two pigs have to be sacrified.

Nular: The *nular* ceremony is held especially for appeasing the Seniang spirits in cases of droughts or broken taboos. Further, the crop spirits as well as Kelelungan souls and Timang spirits are invoked for a successful agricultural year. *Nular* ceremonies mainly consist of *belian turaatn* elements. Although their major purpose is a purifying one, they can also be combined with *belian sentiu* curing rites.

Guguq: The *guguq* is the highest *belian* ceremony lasting a minimum of sixteen nights,[65] although it often takes up to several months in order to complete all the different rites. The *guguq* requires the sacrifice of at least one water buffalo.[66] It can be held for different, often combined purposes:

- *Curing*, in cases of very serious diseases that could not be healed with smaller ceremonies. These ceremonies are called *nalitn rotatn* ('curing the disease').
- *Purification*, in cases of broken taboos (*sahu*), e.g., marriages between partners of forbidden genealogies (*nalitn tautn* — 'curing the year').

---

65. The *guguq* celebrated in Tanjung Isuy in 1996 consisted of sixteen parts. However, as most parts took up to several days and nights, the whole ceremony lasted much longer.

66. In former times *ripatn* slaves were sacrificed.

- <u>Preparation</u> for the new agricultural year with advance offerings to the spirits (*melas tautn* or *nyolukng tautn*- 'cleaning the year', 'finishing the year').

The *guguq* usually includes many ritual elements, such as those of the *bekeleeu* or the *nular*, as well as combinations of curing rites (*belian sentiu*, *belian turaatn*). *Guguq* involving several villages are called *ngompokng* or *nuaq* (the highest form).

The ritual equipment depends on the length of a *belian* and might include several hundred items (see Gönner 1990, Massing 1982: 67-74), as well as many ritual plants (see section 'Forest Medicine' under chapter 3). The more serious a disease, the longer a *belian* should be, invoking as many useful spirits as possible. During the final stages of the great *melas tautn* in Tanjung Isuy (1996) even Islamic prophets were invited to attend the sacrifice of the water buffalo. This comprehensiveness is attempted in order to prevent the neglect of spirits that might take revenge on the *pembeliatn* himself.

Death rituals

Like other Barito-speaking Dayak groups, the Benuaq perform secondary mortuary ceremonies (see Weinstock 1983a: 49-57, Sillander 1995: 71), the so-called *kwangkai* (*kuangkai* or *gombok*). These ceremonies are described explicitly by Massing (1981), Weinstock (1983a), Bonoh (1985b), as well as by Gönner (1990).

Immediately after death, a gong is beaten to inform the village (*titi*). The corpse is then guarded while a coffin is built. On the second day, the deceased is buried in the forest close to the dwelling, and the house is purified with a *tota timui* ritual.[67] Seven[68] days later, a ceremony called *took* (Ind. *beroah*) is held in the house, where the *pengewara*[69] present food and clothes to the souls of the deceased

67. In a *tota timui*, elements of *belian turaatn*, and occasionally also of *belian sentiu*, are applied.

68. Seven and its multiples are the numbers related to death.

69. In contrast to the *pembeliatn*, only men are allowed as *pengewara*, while among the Ma'anyan the mortuary rites are an exclusively female domain (see Weinstock 1983a: 52, Hudson 1966: 359).

singing the *sentangih* songs.[70] According to Benuaq belief, the *juus* souls of the living body (see also Hopes *et al.* 1997: 187, Massing 1982: 61) are transformed by death into two immortal souls: Liau (Liaaw), associated with the body (corpse), and Kelelungan Kelangun (often referred to as Kelelungan), associated with the intellect (skull). Both immortal souls are also known as *roh* (Ind. = soul).

In a second ceremony (*ngelangkakng*), food, cigarettes, sweets and drinks are offered to Liau and Kelelungan. According to Massing (1981: 90), this ceremony is performed 100 days after the death. However, in Lempunah the only *ngelangkakng* I witnessed was held at the beginning of the harvest for the souls of 64 persons who had died during the last decades. The ritual was also accompanied by *pengewara* who sang *sentangih* songs and presented young rice (*keloq*) to the souls of the deceased.

The final ceremony is held after several years,[71] when the family has gathered enough money and resources to carry out a *kwangkai*. The *kwangkai* consists of different stages,[72] until a water buffalo is

70. This procedure is different from what Massing observed in other Benuaq areas (1981: 89), were the corpse was placed in a carved coffin after seven days. According to Weinstock (1983a: 52), the Dutch, and later the Indonesian administration, had ordered the burial to be carried out within 24 hours after death for health reasons. However, this regulation is not always followed.

71. Although the *kwangkai* should ideally be held after seven years, it usually takes longer. However, in one case in Mancong, a *kwangkai* was already carried out not even one year after the death of a young woman.

72. The late *kepala adat* of Tanjung Isuy, who was one of the most prominent Benuaq *pengewara*, named 14 different stages in the *kwangkai*: (1) *domaq ampa* — preparation phase; (2) *sentangih* — exhumation, purification and transfer of the skeleton to the longhouse, as well as singing of *temputn* and *intootn*; (3) *ngerankau* — a dance, where at first seven or a multiple number of men and later also of women dance in a row seven times (or multiples) through the longhouse; (4) *noong banukng oree* — sacrifice of pigs; (5) *beriputn batur mesatn* — marriage between the ironwood tree (male) and the *bengeris* tree (female); (6) *beriputn belontakng* — marriage of the ironwood pole (male) and the rattan rope (female) to which the water buffalo is tied, (7) *ngencoor* — accompanying the pole to the sacrifice place; (8) *belontakng* — erecting the pole; (9) *malapm kendoyakng* — the night before the sacrifice; (10) *noong banukng solukng* — sacrifice of a water buffalo; (11) *numpuq kelungan* — bringing the Kelelungan soul to Tenung Tenangkai; (12) *ncoi liau* — accompanying the Liau soul to Mount Lumut; (13) *nulaq banukng* — second burial of the bones; (14) *tapung tawar* — ritual purification of the longhouse.

sacrificed and the immortal souls are led to their final destinations. While the Kelelungan souls dwell in Tenung Tenangkai together with the Nayuq spirits (see Hopes *et al.* 1997: 187), where they can be called for help in *belian* ceremonies, Liau is not invoked but lives in a parallel world in a mythical longhouse on Saikng (Mount) Lumut. This 'journey to paradise' (Massing 1981) passes many existing locations back to the headwaters of the Mea and Tewe rivers, where the Luangan (in the sense of Weinstock 1983a: 72,73) locate their origin. A *kwangkai* should last a multiple of seven days, although, like in the case of *belian* rites, this rule does not necessarily refer to astronomic days. The final sacrifice, especially, is often delayed until all rites are complete and the time is found to be right.[73]

Apart from their religious meaning, a *kwangkai*, as well as a *guguq*, also bear important social aspects. The organising family[74] of such a big and expensive ceremony gains or reconfirms their status while assuring the aide of the Kelelungan souls and benevolent spirits. However, towards the end of the ceremony, the religious rites are of almost secondary relevance compared to the accompanying festival-like activities. Gambling (*tongkok*[75])' cockfights (*saukng piaq*), traditional sport competitions (blowpipe shooting, *behempas* fighting, climbing), competitions in poetry (*pentangin*), and a fair with food and sales stalls attract thousands of regional visitors; while for young people the final events of a *kwangkai* or a *guguq* are a welcome chance to find their spouses.

These fair activities are also essential to cover at least a part of the expenses.[76] Traders and stall owners have to pay concession

---

73. This also depends on the financial returns from gambling, as these earnings contribute substantially to the funds of the ceremony.

74. Most rituals are carried out by extended families (see the social net in *fig.* 2.2), although, friends are also occasionally involved. An exception are small agricultural or individual curing rites (see above).

75. After a dice with one red side is set under a cover by the owner of the bank, the players set their money on the four different fields of a playing board. The cover is then lifted and those players win whose money faces the red side of the dice. It is also possible to combine different sides for reduced winnings. Beside *tongkok*, several card games are played.

76. The *guguq* in Tanjung Isuy (1996) costed 16 Million Rupiah (at that time approximately US $ 6,000 or the equivalent of the average daily expenses (per family) of more than 11 years!). *Kwangkai* ceremonies are in the same order of magnitude (see Massing 1981: 101-3).

fees, and a certain part of the gambling profits is contributed to the ceremony's costs.[77] Occasionally, small subsidies are contributed from the district government. The organisation of a *kwangkai* or a *guguq* includes dozens of family members and village elders, who are responsible for advice, performance, fund-raising, traditional law, decoration, mutual help, security, accomodation, transportation, welcoming of guests and consumption.

Other rituals

Supplementary to these two large ritual complexes, there are several additional rites, usually of a smaller scale.

Rites during pregnancy and after birth: After the third month of pregnancy, a ritual called *nyamatn butukng* is held, where a white pot is wrapped in a *sarung* cloth and placed on a white plate (symbolising the embryo in the womb). The *sarung* is opened after birth, and on the fourth day a *tota timui* purification rite (including elements of *belian sentiu* and *belian turaatn*) is carried out, while food is offered to the assisting spirits of the midwife in the *luran pujut* ritual. During pregnancy, several *buyatn* food taboos must also be followed (see sub-section 'Conservation of Resources' under chapter 4).

Wedding rites: The wedding (*beriputn*) is performed by a belian *turaatn pembeliatn*, or by the *kepala adat*, and generally witnessed by the village elders and noblemen (*mantiiq*). Wedding rites include the repeated ritual purification of bride and bridegroom, who sit on two gongs, with chickens, leaves and clothes waved over the couple's heads. The purification is completed with a *tota timui* ritual, including blessings with *tawar* water and rice paste, and a bath in water with *Ngeraseh* and *mayang* (the flower of *Areca catechu*). The ritual price for the bride (*pengalaq*) is 10 *antaakng* (Chinese jars valued at 20,000 Rp each[78]); 1 *genikng* (gong valued 50,000 Rp); and 1 *tumak* (spear valued at 25,000 Rp); adding up to 275,000 Rp which

77. Ten per cent of all profits (both of the bank's as well as of the winners' profits) are subtracted and divided by three. One-third goes to the police, as gambling is illegal; one-third is for the owner of the gambling set; and one third is contributed to the *kwangkai* organiser.

78. This valuation is only of symbolic meaning. Real jars are currently traded at prices of several million Rupiah. The symbolic value for jars was recently increased as it used to be only 12,000 Rp in 1988-9.

have to be paid to the bride's parents, while 5 *antaakng* (= 100,000 Rp) have to be paid to the bridegroom's parents.

Agricultural rites: Agricultural rites include *pakatn nyahuq*, the feeding of the Nyahuq spirits, *ngeluikng*, the bringing back of the rice spirit, Lolakng Luikng, as well as several small redressing rites against pests. In cases of droughts, *nular* ceremonies or even *melas tautn* ceremonies can be held (see above). Most of the rituals and ceremonies described are still common in Lempunah and the neighbouring Benuaq villages. Belian curing rites are found almost every night in one of the villages, and larger ceremonies such as *bekeleeu*, *guguq* or *kwangkai* are held almost every year in the subdistrict. A sample of 36 housholds interviewed between 1996 and 1998 revealed the following number of ritual activities:

Table 2.1: Compilation of rituals held in 36 households (RT I/II, RT III) between 1996 and 1998

As different families may have joined the same ceremonies, these figures are not equivalent to the total number of rituals held in Lempunah

	1996	*1997*	*1998*
kwangkai	1	0	3
guguq	0	1	0
bekeleeu	30	10	20
naraja	3	2	2
seniang	3	0	0
belian sentiu	23	25	19
belian turaatn	2	4	2
tota timui	1	0	2
total	63	42	48

During the study period, most families (86 per cent) joined at least one *bekeleeu* ceremony,[79] while *belian* rituals were held almost every year (69 per cent - 92 per cent of all households). The success

79. 86 per cent of the households joined at least one *bekeleeu* between 1996 and 1998, 45 per cent joined at least two, and 14 per cent joined three *bekeleeu* in the three years.

rate of these curing rites was between 68 per cent and 79 per cent.[80] Given the fact that in many cases *belian* rites are only held when modern health care (provided by a doctor in Tanjung Isuy and his staff) could not help,[81] this rate stresses the continuing need for these rituals. The financial aspects of rituals are discussed later (see section 'Socio-economy' under chapter 4). However, it is safe to say, that ritual expenses rank high in most families' budgets despite much mutual help. Regarding health aspects, as well as the social factors discussed above, rituals still play an important role in Lempunah, although most villagers have officially converted either to Catholicism or to Protestant churches. In contrast to most other parts of Borneo, the traditional religion of the Benuaq is still alive despite missions and public health care (see also Massing 1981: 85, 1982: 58,59). This religious persistence might be mainly due to two factors:

(1) The Benuaq area is situated between the influence spheres of Islam (coastal areas and Lower Mahakam) and Christianity (Apo Kayan and Upper Mahakam). Thus, the first permanent missionary (from Nusa Tenggara Timur, East Indonesia) came to Tanjung Isuy only in 1978,[82] more than 70 years after the Catholic Church had started its mission in Laham (1906-7) on the Upper Mahakam.

(2) The Benuaq seem to have a rather adaptable belief system frequently incorporating exogenous elements. A good example is *belian sentiu*, which probably originates from Bongan. This popular curing ritual replaced the older *belian bawo* rites among the eastern Benuaq.[83] There is also evidence (see Weinstock 1983a: 24-5, Massing 1982: 61) that the (usually not worshipped) supreme deity of the Benuaq, Lantalah (Latala, Lahatala, Mahatala, Mahatara, Hatala or Alatala in other Luangan areas, see Weinstock *ibid.*), is an exogenous concept most likely influenced by

80. A *belian* was counted as successful when the respective patient(s) had recovered afterwards. The cases counted as unsuccessful include chronical diseases (e.g., blindness, rheumatism) as well as cases which could only be cured by a later more complete *belian* rite.

81. Occasionally, sick persons were brought to better equipped hospitals in Muara Muntai, Tenggarong, and Samarinda.

82. Protestant missionaries had already arrived in the 1950s. However, they found no followers as they were perceived as too restrictive.

83. It even includes phrases from the Koran.

Islam ('Allah Ta'ala') and Hinduism (*maha* = great).[84]

This relatively soft encounter with other religions has probably allowed a transient change of the traditional Benuaq belief system, which has survived so far, as its socio-religious and medical advantages still prevail. Where this demand ceases to exist, rituals (like those formerly held during the rice cycle) also vanish among the Benuaq.

Lempunah — the village, the people and relevant events

DESCRIPTION OF LEMPUNAH

According to the oral history of Lempunah, all Benuaq villages along the Ohong river originate from the Kelawit area in the west.[85] From here, the ancestors moved downriver building new longhouses until they reached the area of Lempunah, where they have lived for 'hundreds of years'. Two rock formations are known as the first mythical longhouses of Lempunah: Batuq Baliq and Batuq Nontoy. They were followed by at least ten other longhouses,[86] until the village reached its present location at the beginning of the twentieth century. The first non-mythical longhouses, Rawa Opotn and Naroy, are also known as predecessor longhouses of Muara Nayan, a village not far from Lempunah. The next longhouse appears to be the sole precursor of Lempunah, while the Muara Nayan line departed at this stage. This longhouse gave the inhabitants of Lempunah their specific name: *Akas*. Another longhouse fission probably occurred at Perau (presumably in the nineteenth century), when one part moved back to the Kelawit area, while the other stayed behind.

---

84. The open nature of Benuaq belief also became apparent when the ceremonial leader of the *guguq* in Tanjung Isuy (1996) invited 14 Islamic prophets to the final sacrifice.

85. This information, which was reported by Lempunah's *kepala adat*, is further supported by the names of the first two longhouse chiefs in Lempunah's oral history, Impotn Unguq (chief of Rawa Opotn) and Impotn Mahaan (chief of Naroy), as *impotn* is the expression for grandfather in the language of the Dayak Tonyoi (or Tunjung), who live not far from the Kelawit area. The respective Benuaq word would have been *kakah*.

86. According to the administrative village chief (Ind. *kepala desa*), these longhouses did not co-exist but were built subsequently. All of them are situated within the present village boundaries (see Map 6), where their remains can still be seen. Their temporal order was only known by one old man (a former *kepala adat*), but was alluded to partially by other informants.

As each longhouse probably lasted one generation (30 to 40 years), Lempunah's settlement history covers at least 300-400 years within the same settlement area. This estimation is, however, only based on oral history and rough calculations. A more thorough analysis could be possible by assessing the $^{14}C/^{12}C$ ratio in old ironwood poles, although the application of this method would be restricted by the relatively fast degradation of organic matter under tropical conditions. Nevertheless, it could provide a more reliable estimation of the age of individual longhouses.

Today, Lempunah belongs politically to the subdistrict (Ind. *kecamatan*) of Jempang and the district (Ind. *kabupaten*) of West-Kutai.[87] The boundaries of the village area are shared with Pentat to both the east (Ohong river), and to the south (Tola river); with Muara Nayan to the north (Nayan river and Merayo river); and with Muara Tae and Muara Pahu subdistrict to the west (watershed between the Ohong river system and the Kelawit river system). The village consists of three administrative parts. Two form the main village (RT I, RT II[88]), while two small and remote dwellings (Kangkang Puya and M(u)ara Gusiq) configure the third part (RT III), situated six kilometres away (see Map 4).

The population of Lempunah is predominantly Dayak Benuaq with a minority of only two Dayak Tonyoi (Tunjung), two Javanese and one Banjarese. According to village statistics, 54 per cent of the inhabitants are Catholic, 43 per cent are members of Protestant churches, and 3 per cent are Muslims.[89] In 1998, Lempunah's population was counted at 117 households including 347 persons (51 per cent men, 49 per cent women), consisting of 57 households in RT I, 27 households in RT II, 26 households in RT III, and 7 households of unclear localisation. Hence, the population density within the official village area is 3.77 people per square kilometre. According to two former village chiefs, the overall population remained rather constant between 1940 and 1998, although a few people had migrated to Tenggarong (the former district capital), and to the provincial capital of Samarinda. Between 1996 and 1998, the local population increased by four persons.

---

87. The former district of Kutai was divided in 1999 into three new districts in line with the Indonesian decentralisation programme.

88. RT means *rukun tetangga* (neighbourhood association).

89. A Catholic church was constructed between 1993 and 1996; a Protestant church was finished in 1999.

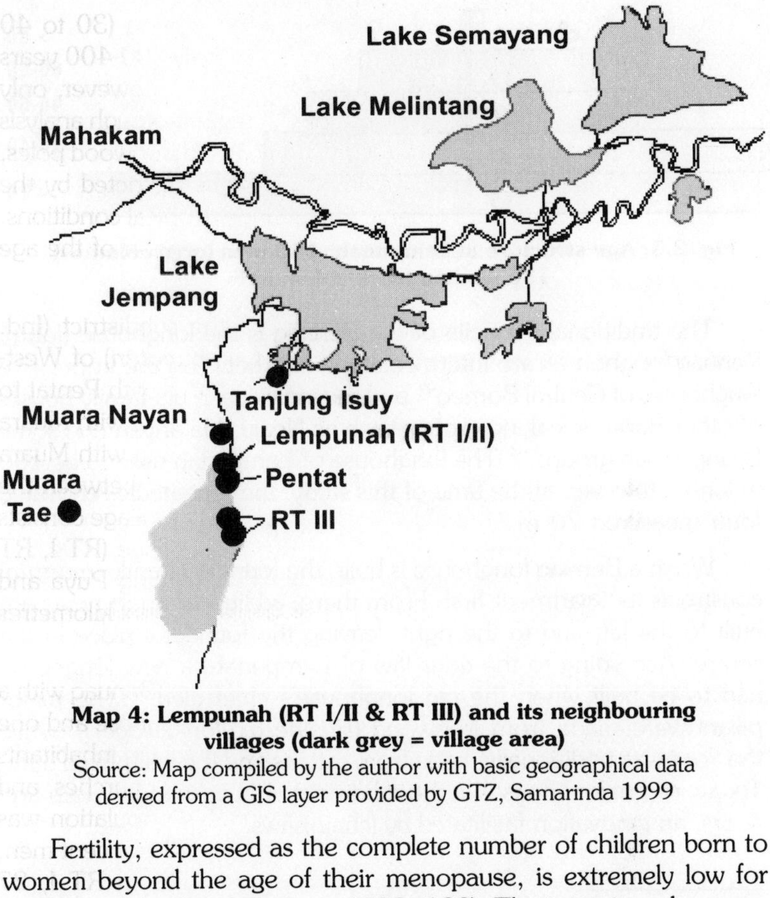

Map 4: Lempunah (RT I/II & RT III) and its neighbouring villages (dark grey = village area)

Source: Map compiled by the author with basic geographical data derived from a GIS layer provided by GTZ, Samarinda 1999

Fertility, expressed as the complete number of children born to women beyond the age of their menopause, is extremely low for traditional societies (see Lang 1993: 128). The interviewed women (*n*=17) had given birth to 3-4 children on average (2-3 surviving babyhood, 1 death, not including miscarriages and stillbirths). The number of sisters and brothers of these women who survived their babyhood, was about 4-5 (*n*=30),[90] indicating a significant decrease in family size over just one generation.[91]

The present age structure (1999) is shown in *fig*. 2.3.

---

90. The number of deceased siblings was impossible to reconstruct. Hence, the total number of children might have been much higher.

91. One reason for the decreased number of children is the regular use of contraceptives (mainly the pill) from the 1970s onwards.

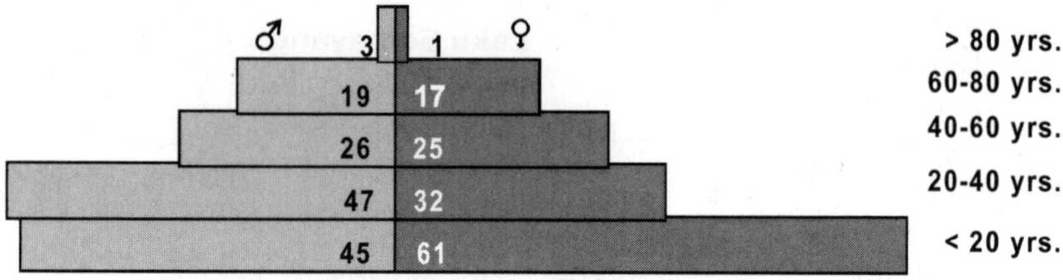

***Fig.* 2.3: Age structure in Lempunah: 140 men (grey columns), 136 women (dark columns)**[92]

The traditional domicile of the Benuaq is the longhouse (*louu*). Benuaq longhouses are intermediate in size between the impressive longhouses of Central Borneo[93] and the individual multi-family houses of other Barito-speaking groups such as Ngaju, Ma'anyan and some Luangan sub-groups.[94] The longhouse of Lempunah used to be 100 m long. However, at the time of this study, the repeatedly-renovated *louu* measured 70 m.[95]

When a Benuaq longhouse is built, the founding family (*mantiiq*) constructs its apartment first. From there, additional apartments are built to the left and to the right, leaving the founder's place in the centre. According to the *adat* law of Lempunah, a new longhouse had to be built when the old longhouse's chief died.[97] The major pillars were made from ironwood (*Eusideroxylon zwageri*), while the floor was traditionally made from rattans and the walls from bark. Today, recent longhouses in the subdistrict all have wooden walls and floors, an innovation facilitated by (chain)saws.

---

92. Age figures for adults are taken from official village statistics. In a few cases, where the age was obviously wrong, I estimated the respective category. Figures for children were assessed by household interviews.

93. In the 1950s, the longhouse of Long Laput was 700 metres long (Southwell 1959: 49, cited in Rousseau 1990: 104), although the average length is generally between 75 and 150 m (Rousseau 1990: 104).

94. In Loksado (South Kalimantan) the local Dayak live in so-called *rumah besar* (i.e. large house), large, almost square, houses with appartments arranged outside, leaving a large-roofed commual terrace inside.

95. Old stilts were seen along another 30 meters.

96. Not all kitchens are that clearly separated from the main house; some are included in the *orooq*.

97. It is unclear, whether this *adat* instruction was always obeyed.

Since the 1960s, most families in Lempunah and the surrounding villages moved to individual houses.[98] Nowadays, only a few families live permanently in the longhouse, although it is frequently used for the performance of large rituals (*kwangkai*, *guguq*, *bekeleeu*) and village assemblies (*berinuq*). According to the village chief, several families are thinking of moving back to the longhouse, once its government-sponsored reconstruction (scheduled for 2000-3) will be finished.

Prior to the education system and commercial opportunities which encouraged a more permanent village life, most families spent the major part of the year in farm houses (*ukop* — annual farm house, *balai* — permanent farm house), often far from the longhouse. Generally, several (5-20) households of an extended family had adjacent swiddens, assisting each other during work in the fields and in cases of sickness or against attacks.[99] It was mainly after the rice harvest that the farmers moved back to the longhouse, when the festivities generally took place. The longhouse and other permanent settlements, such as Kangkang Puya and Muara Gusiq, were also visited on the arrival of traders who sold or bartered iron, salt and fabrics against forest products and rice.

Today, the village consists of individual wooden stilt houses, built on both sides of the Ohong.[100] The children of three villages[101] are educated in Lempunah's elementary school, which covers the first six years. The next secondary school is located at Tanjung Isuy, 13 km away, the closest high-school is in Muara Muntai, a two-hour boat ride from Tanjung Isuy.[102] Three small shops provide the villagers

---

98. According to the village chief most families moved to individual houses as the old longhouse became dilapidated, and due to a general process of individualisation. Additionally, this trend was supported, if not enforced, by Indonesian government policy of the late 1960s (see also Rousseau 1990: 124).

99. Occasionally, individual households also preferred to settle alone. During the research period, one couple still lived far upriver, visiting the village only rarely to sell some pieces of wrought-iron work made by the husband.

100. Dwellings along rivers are the predominant settlement pattern in Borneo (Rousseau 1990: 103).

101. The school is attended by children from Lempunah, Pentat and Muara Nayan. Depending on the water level, children have to walk twenty to forty minutes from Muara Nayan to the school.

102. A new high-school was being set-up in Tanjung Isuy in 2000.

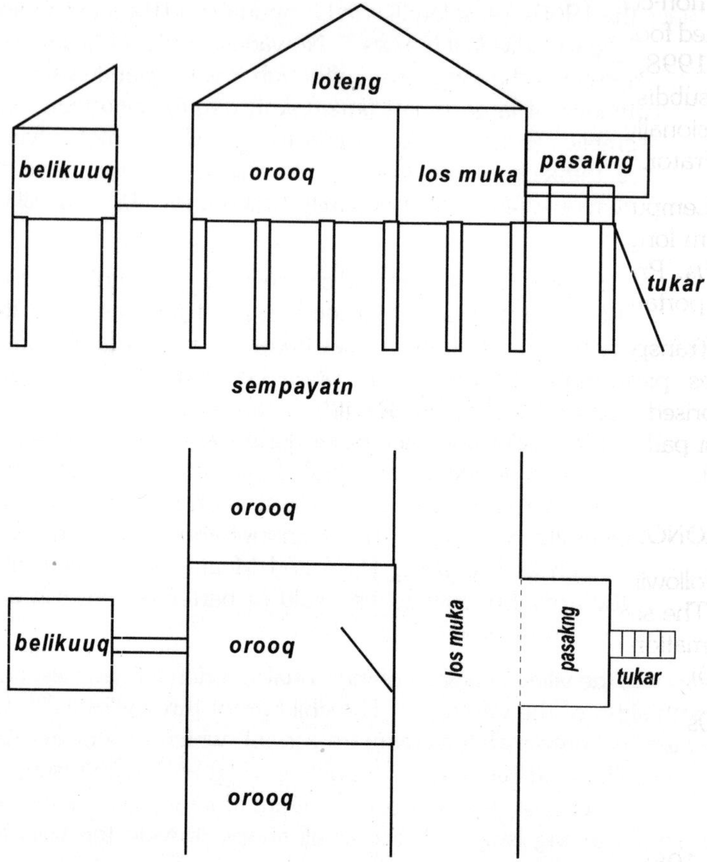

Legend:

orooq	apartment
los muka	inner veranda
pasakng	resting place
tukar	ladder
sempayatn	posts
loteng	second floor (mainly for storage)
belikuuq	kitchen[96]

***Fig. 2.4*: Cross-section and ground plan of the longhouse in Lempunah**

with non-cultivated necessities such as soap, toothpaste and brushes, canned food, sugar, cooking oil, bottled drinks, spices, onions, etc. In late 1998, a few relatively wealthy households were connected to the subdistrict's electric grid. Before that, electricity was only occasionally available during the evening hours, provided by a single generator.[103]

Lempunah is linked to the subdistrict capital of Tanjung Isuy by a 13 km long weatherproof road, which was constructed in the early 1990s. Prior to the road, the small Ohong river was the major transportation route, while visitors used a small footpath.

Transportation is nowadays mainly arranged by trucks, mini-busses, pick-ups, motorbikes[104] and, depending on the waterlevel, motorised canoes. The remote RT III is only accessible via a small forest path (1.5 hours) and — during the rainy season — by river (1 hour).

CHRONOLOGY OF EVENTS IN LEMPUNAH

The following events had major impacts on village life and local resource use. The selection, however, is a subjective one, based on weighted information provided by villagers and on my own observations (1988-2000).

1970s	A logging company selectively cuts timber in the forests around Lempunah. Conflicts are rather small, as the local people are allowed to use the logged-over areas for swidden agriculture.
June 1988	Excellent rattan prices bring substantial wealth to Lempunah. Many families own generators, TV sets, and boat engines.
late 1989	Rattan prices drop off; several families sell their TVs and generators.
March 1991	Rattan prices are still low. A wooden boardwalk is built due to the annual floodings.

103. Electricity is now provided from 5 p.m. until 7 a.m.

104. Irregular car transports are provided by private entrepreneurs mainly from Tanjung Isuy. In addition, trucks of nearby companies (coal, oil palm plantation, logging) also pick up passengers. Motorbike taxis operate at request for 5,000 Rp (1996) to 10.000 Rp (1999). The ride takes about 20 minutes.

July-Nov.1993 A mechanical water pump is installed, and the construction work for a Catholic church has started. A road has been built between Lempunah and Tanjung Isuy. A tree plantation (HTI[105]) and an associated transmigration project clear-cuts several dozen hectares, including burial sites and forest gardens, triggering a serious landrights conflict. Local NGOs and private legal consultants try to intervene.

1994 The land clearances have stopped, although the issue of financial compensation is not yet solved. A tree bark (*Kayu Lem*) is intensively collected due to its good price. The natural stock is soon depleted.

1995 Still the same situation as in 1994. Excellent rubber prices provide substantial income, while the rice harvest is only marginal.

1996 The old road is repaired and made weatherproof. The HTI has virtually stopped its activities, and most transmigrants have left the settlement. However, the destroyed gardens and graves have not been compensated for. While the ongoing conflict with the HTI is not yet solved, a new conflict arises between an oil palm company and several Benuaq villages. About 30 per cent of Lempunah's inhabitants are in favour of the company, which promises high income and modernisation, while approximately 70 per cent reject the project. Resource prices are generally low, the rice harvest is good. Many people find work in the oil palm estate's nursery, and during land clearance activities. The first 20 million Rupiah of IDT[106] credits are distributed among the villagers.

---

105. HTI means *Hutan Tanaman Industri* (industrially planted forest).

106. The government-run IDT project (*Inpres Desa Tertinggal* — 'presidential decree for backward villages') was originally intended as a credit free of interests. Villages below the official poverty-line received an annual credit of 20 million Rupiah for three years. The individual share of each family depended on family size as well as on personal contacts to the budget's administrator (not the *kepala desa*). The credit was intended to be used →

1997 16,500 ha of former forest gardens and swidden fallows have been cleared by the oil palm company in the immediate vicinity of Lempunah. The rice harvest was average. Resource prices are still low. Wage work for the oil palm company is the major source of income. Forest fires start in September. Large parts of Lempunah's forests burn in October.

1998 Forest fires rage again from February to April, destroying most rattan gardens as well as many rubber and *simpukng* gardens. The rice harvest is completely lost. Prices for freshwater turtles rise high, which leads to an intensive extraction from dry swamps. Most field activities of the oil palm company are stopped due to the drought and the Asian financial crisis. During the second half of the year, rubber and rattan prices increase substantially. In November and December, two of the company's three base camps are occupied by demonstrators from nine villages, who demand a just financial compensation as well as an end to a further expansion of the estate.

1999 Again, a poor rice harvest due to a lack of suitable seeds. The two base camps are held until the end of April, when police forces take the camps back by force. Several villagers are arrested. They are released in October, and the company is found to hold no valid operation documents. Rubber prices decrease again. Several households are connected to the electric grid.

2000 Rats and mice reduced the rice harvest. Most households collect rattan, which is processed in the village. A government programme to renovate the longhouse starts. Although the oil palm company has stopped its field activities, the legal issues of the conflict are not yet solved. A documentary film about daily life in Lempunah is shot by a German TV team.

→ for small-scale business investments, such as chicken farming, etc. However, because of poor information policies as well as an often urgent demand for immediate cash, many of these projects failed.

3

Description and Analysis of Resource Use

Land use categories and succession cycles

THE combination of swidden agriculture and the use of extracted and cultivated forest products is the basis of the livelihood in Lempunah. This basis also provides the understanding of the term 'resources' which I use in this study. Although there is the Indonesian expression *sumber daya alam* for natural resources (literally meaning 'energy sources of nature'), the Benuaq do not use a generic term for 'resources'. Without explicitly distinguishing 'resources' from 'non-resources', I will call plant and animal species used by the people of Lempunah 'resources'. This rather utilitarian perception is generally shared by the Benuaq, as in daily life, the practical use of a resource appears to be more important than its relations to Benuaq cosmovision. Of course, natural materials such as water or minerals, human labour, individual or collective knowledge, capital or available information can also be regarded as 'resources', but wherever these aspects are considered in this study, they are *expressis verbis* named.

By opening annual swiddens and establishing subsequent forest gardens, the forest landscape has been kept in a permanently-changing state of manipulated parts (swiddens and forest gardens) and natural succession of swidden fallows. Local expressions for these forest and cultivation stages are given in Table 3.1.

Table 3.1: Locally-defined land use categories

umaq	swidded for 1 year
babar	1 year fallow, used again for rice cultivation
kwakoq	2-10 year-old fallow, used for rice cultivation

uraaq	general expression for swidden fallows regarding individual ownership; also used for 10-30 year-old fallow forest
kerengkakng	fallow older than 30 years
bengkar	primary forest, or at least very old *kerengkakng*
payaq	swamp (also swamp forest)
jaras	*kerangas* (heath forest)
dempaq	flat area (no swamp and no hill)
saikng	hill or mountain
roboot	forest (in contrast to village, *umaq* or forest gardens)
kayuq	wood, also woods
kebotn	garden
simpukng	mixed forest garden
kebotn ue	rattan garden
kebotn getah	rubber garden

These expressions are not sharply defined, but overlap. While some people would call a 25-year-old fallow forest *uraaq*, others would regard it as *kerengkakng*.[1] On top of the actual age of a fallow forest, relative tree size (diameter), present tree species, and the general appearance, are also taken into account for the respective typology.

The base for most forest gardens and the different fallow types is the *umaq* (Ind. *ladang*), an annual swidden on which rain-fed upland rice is cultivated along with a wide range of vegetables and other crops. The swidden, which is cleared from old or fallow forest, is the starting-point of two possible future developments: it is either left to

1. Occasionally, *kerengkakng* is further differentiated in *kerengkakng tia* (young *kerengkakng*) and *kerengkakng tuha* (old *kerengkakng*). The expressions *babar* and *kwakoq* are only used if a fallow of the respective age is used again for rice cultivation. Hence, the use of these terms depends on an actual conversion to a swidden, not to a certain fallow forest stage. A general expression for a swidden fallow would be *uraaq*, especially if the ownership is emphasised ('*Ohoq uraaq aap*.' — 'This is my swidden fallow.'). Besides, *uraaq* has a second meaning as a more specific fallow stage, 10-30 years after the rice cultivation.

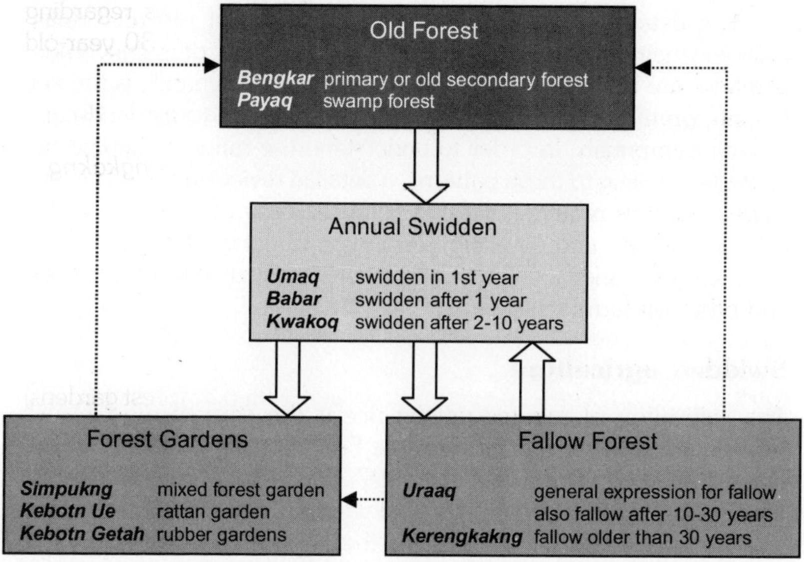

The arrows indicate the transitions between these units.
Dotted arrows represent rare but possible transitions

***Fig. 3.1*: Locally-defined landuse units**

fallow, to be re-used after a certain period; or parts of it are enriched with rubber, rattan or fruit trees, transforming the site into permanent forest gardens. This latter pathway is initiated by adding desired crop species to the site. However, the growth of these forest gardens depends mainly on self-reproducing dynamics resembling natural succession, while additional human labour input is kept to a minimum.

According to the local definition, all categories are interrelated in a closed cyclical network with transitions of different likelihoods. Hence, the swidden system of Lempunah should not be called 'shifting cultivation', but rather 'cyclical cultivation'. Even pristine-looking *bengkar* or *payaq* forests are possible results of long, undisturbed fallow periods, although this succession is not very common, at least not nowadays. A rigid segregation between cultivated and natural forest is also not suitable for describing the forest environment in Lempunah, as all parts of the forest are influenced by the local people. Hence, the term of an 'amalgamation' of nature and culture (Seeland 1997: 1) seems to be more appropriate.

The detailed transitions between the different resource units, including their self-dynamic growth due to succession, or to enrichment planting, are illustrated in *fig*.3.2. This temporal dynamic is the key for interpreting the spatial patterns of the patchy forest landscape around Lempunah. In order to understand the rationale behind the strategies leading to these patterns, a detailed review of the respective landuse units is required, starting from the base of subsistence, the annual swidden; and covering permanent forest gardens, as well as more irregular and flexible use of resources, including forest products and other off-farm activities.

Swidden agriculture

The cultivation of rain-fed upland rice is the core of most Dayak subsistence strategies in Borneo (see Freeman 1992: 152 for Iban, Dove 1985a for Kantu', Colfer 1997: 46-51 for Kenyah). Despite the partial introduction of high-yield varieties and irrigation in some areas, swidden agriculture remains the basic means for securing a livelihood.[2] In addition to its nutritional importance, rice is also of religious relevance. The various steps of the agricultural cycle are traditionally accompanied by corresponding rituals (see Freeman 1992: 154, 173, 179, 189, 203, 205, 209, 214, 217, 238; Dove 1985a: 163-4, 174, 185, 266, 281, 288, 290, 304-5, 329, 341; Sumual 1998: 52-5), although nowadays only few farmers perform them in Lempunah. But rice and its soul or spirit, Lolakng Luikng, is still of great ritual importance, with rice being offered to please spirits, or even functioning as a means for communication with the spiritual world.

The annual agricultural cycle dominates life in Lempunah and sets the frame for additional income-generating activities. Despite a substantial cash demand (for additional food, cigarettes, medication, education fees, clothes, chainsaws, TVs, boat engines, motor bikes, etc.), most labour is allocated for securing subsistence.[3] Generally, this also holds for the few specialists in Lempunah (teachers, carpenters, blacksmiths, shop owners), who cannot rely solely on their business, but have to grow rice and vegetables as well.

2. A survey among villagers of their most important goal in life revealed the successful management of a swidden and securing food supply as the general answers.

3. No exact labour allocation studies were carried out, but the temporal dominance of swidden activities was apparent during the field study.

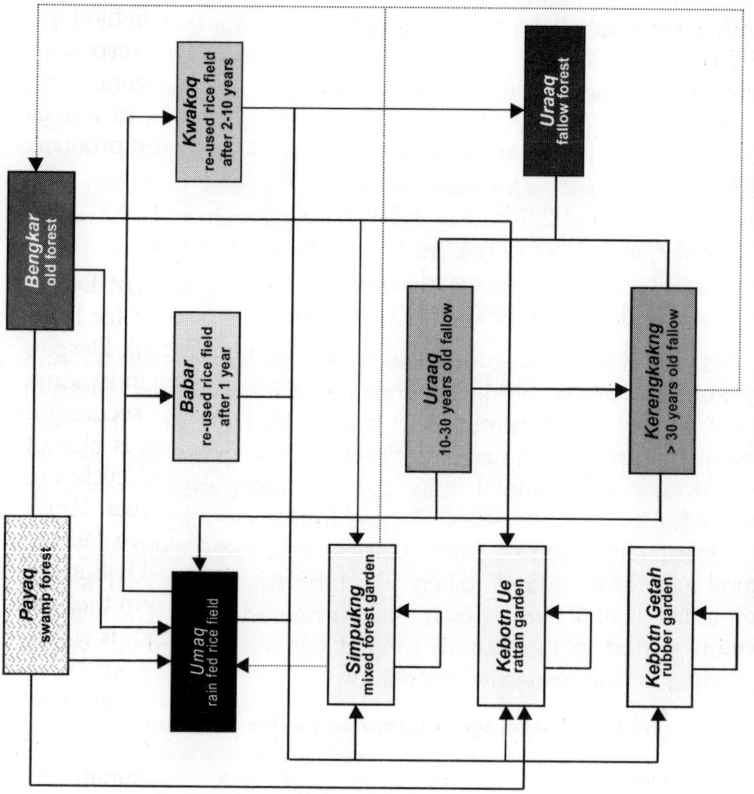

The weight of the lines expresses the likelihood for the respective transition.

***Fig.* 3.2: Fallow succession and temporal interrelation between local resource units**

Most families prepare one swidden or *umaq* [*tautn*] per year[4] with an average size of 1.58 ha per core family, ranging between 0.5 ha to 2.9 ha (*n*=19, 1995-6). As several members of the extended family sometimes share the same field, the average field size was slightly larger with 2.15 ha, ranging from 0.5 ha to 5 ha (*n*=19, 1995-6). These figures are in the same range as those for East Kalimantan Kenyah farmers with average field sizes between 1.36 ha and 2.38 ha (Colfer 1991: 70-1); for Kantu' farmers in West Kalimantan with field sizes ranging from 0.03 ha to 7.95 ha (Dove 1985a: 91); as well as for Iban farmers in Sarawak with field sizes between 0.6 ha and 2.7 ha per (*bilek*) family (Freeman 1992: 248). On average, in 6.4 out of the last 8 years between 1991 and 1998, each family had at least one swidden per year (RT I/II: *n*=11, RSD=19 per cent; RT III: *n*=15, RSD=11.5 per cent).

A swidden is generally only used one year for rice cultivation. It might occasionally be used a second year (it is called then *babar*), if the soil fertility is still estimated as sufficiently high, or if there are constraints to prepare a new site. Swiddens which are also used for the cultivation of perennial fruits and vegetables are often kept as gardens for a few more years. Planted fruit trees, rubber or rattans can subsequently become forest gardens that grow along with the natural succession, and are taken out of the swidden cycle. The field is left to fallow until the regrown forest is cleared again. The average rotation period in Lempunah ranged between 5 and 30 years, depending on the respective conditions.[5]

Table 3.2: Average rotation period for swiddens

	1995-6	*1996-7*	*1997-8*	*1998-9*
RT I/II	25-30 years	15-20 years	-	5-10 years
RT III	25-30 years	25-30 years	-	5-10 years

4. This is different from several other Dayak groups who maintain two or three swiddens per year (e.g., Dove 1985a: 69, Colfer 1991: 75, and Jessup 1983, cited in Colfer 1991: 71).

5. Young fallow forest was preferred in 1998-9 as old grown forest was severely damaged by forest fires, and the danger of getting hit by dead falling trees was estimated as too high to clear older forest. Besides, young forest was close to the village, and the burning by forest fires was almost complete. Hence, much less labour was necessary to prepare a swidden.

Primary, or at least old secondary forest (regarded as *bengkar*), was in 13 per cent of total cases (RT I/II),[6] or 0 per cent respectively (in RT III), used for swidden cultivation. Table 3.3 summarises the number of swiddens and the percentage of households/domestic units which had a swidden between 1995 and 1998. Map 7 illustrates the spatial distribution of all swidden localities.

Table 3.3: Number of swiddens, number of swidden locations, percentage of households with swiddens, and average number of swiddens per domestic unit (house)

	RT I/II				*RT III*			
	1995	*1996*	*1997*	*1998*	*1995*	*1996*	*1997*	*1998*
n swiddens	62	41	13	74	18	24	7	21
n locations	52	36	13	66	18	24	6	19
households with fields	76.5%	54.7%	14.9%	81.0%	70.8%	87.5%	29.1%	79.2%
fields per domestic unit	1.1	0.8	0.2	1.4	0.9	1.1	0.3	1.0

The agricultural cycle generally starts in June with the decisions as to whether and where to prepare a new swidden, and ends in April with the end of the harvest. In-between there are many steps, which illustrate general patterns of individual decision-making and strategies to cope with constraints of various kinds. *Fig*.3.2 shows the temporal order of these steps during the cycle, which are briefly summarised in Table 3.4. Each step is further described in detail and analysed regarding the decision-making processes and the respective strategies.

Table 3.4: Locally-defined steps in the swidden year, including approximate labour demand and labour division regarding sexes

Eraakng	marking of a new swidden site in order to claim the place; June-August; 1 day, men/women
Nokap	slashing of scrubs and small trees with a *mandau* (bush knife); June-September; up to 1 month, men/women
Noong	felling of bigger trees with axe or chainsaw; July-September; some days to several weeks, men

6. *Bengkar* forest can only be found in a distance of more than 15 km from the main village. Most fields were made in the vicinity of a transmigration settlement which had road access.

Oikng Joa	the slash is left to dry; September; 10 days to 1 month
Nyuru	burning; September/October; 1 day, men/women
Mongkakng	in cases of incomplete burning, unburnt wood is piled up, dried and burnt again; September/October; some days to several weeks, men/women
Ngasaq & Moyaas	a few days after the burning, holes are stabbed into the soil by men (*ngasaq*), rice seeds are inseminated by women (*moyaas*), and other cultigens are also planted; October; 3-10 days, men/women
Ngejikut	weeding; November-January; 2-3 months, men/women
Durukng Umaq	guarding and protecting the field against animals; January/February; 1-2 months, men/women
Ngotapm	harvest; February-April; several weeks, men/women

The swidden activities listed above are highly dependent on weather conditions and should be carried out at certain times known by star constellations. However, the reality is less fixed. There is substantial flexibility for the different steps as the annual rain-fall distribution is rather unpredictable, despite a long-term pattern that fits the agricultural cycle. The different steps therefore overlap, which is shown in *fig.* 3.3.

DECISION-MAKING PROCESSES BEFORE ESTABLISHING A SWIDDEN

Before the agricultural cycle can start, however, a most relevant question must first be answered:

Should a swidden be established at all?

This question depends on the weighing up of several factors. Their direct interactions are depicted in *fig.* 3.4, from where further causal relations are subsequently traced.[7] The annually varying figures in Table 3.3 reflect the summation of individual decisions. Nevertheless, certain events, like the drought of 1997-8, may have such a strong impact that the decision-making pattern looks more uniform than in other years.

7. The influential factors were assessed mainly through key-informant interviews.

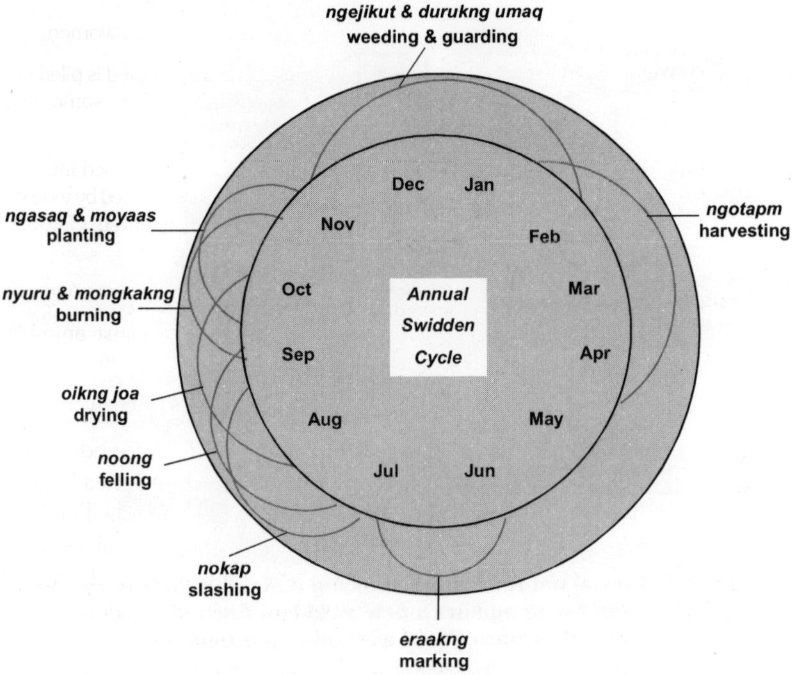

***Fig. 3.3*: The agricultural cycle in Lempunah with temporally-overlapping activities**

Despite the great variation between different individual decisions, there are some general patterns in constraints and coping strategies.

- Sufficient rice supply allows alternative occupations instead of having a swidden.

  A lack of rice supply can be coped with by buying rice with income from off-swidden activities, by supplementing rice with fast-growing cassava, or by borrowing rice from relatives.

- Important rituals, sickness, or political affairs such as conflicts, can delay swidden activities beyond the point of no return.

  Delays can be coped with by the use of chainsaws, hired labourers, labour exchange, shared fields, younger fallow forests, or fast-maturing rice varieties.

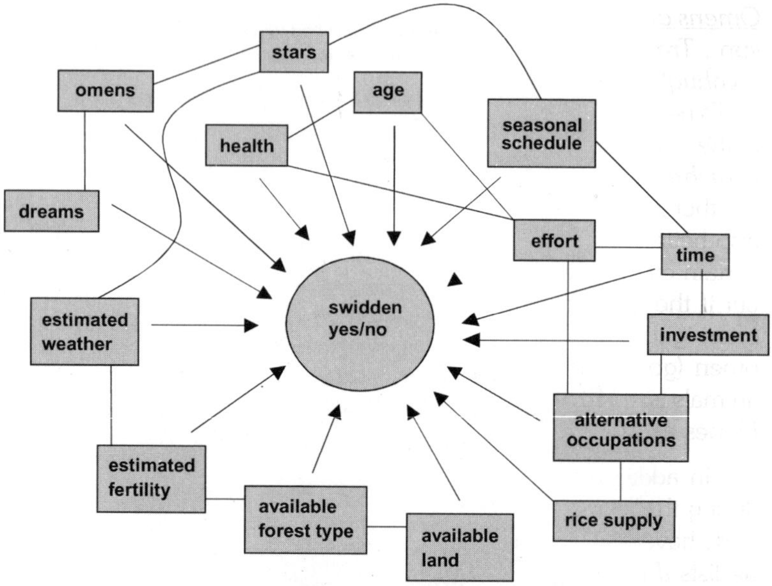

***Fig.* 3.4: Causal net for factors showing a direct influence on the decision for or against a new swidden. Each of these factors is interrelated with other parameters**

- Suitable land is scarce for some families.

  A lack of suitable land can be coped with by borrowing a field from other people (*usually relatives*) *including people from neighbouring villages.*

- Bad dreams and omens can prevent the cultivation of a swidden.

  Some bad omens can be ritually purified.

- Negative weather forecasts can prevent people from preparing a swidden (e.g., during the drought of 1997-8).

  Bad weather is generally coped with ritually. In cases of extreme rain-fall (*too much or too little*), *different soil types and rice varieties may partially reduce the risk of crop failures.*

For making the final decision whether to prepare a swidden or not, the following interrelated parameters (see *fig*.3.4) have to be considered and weighed up:

<u>Omens and dreams</u>: Dead animals, especially dead deer (*Muntiacus* spp., *Tragulus* spp.), and yellow leaves are regarded as bad omens (*nyahuq*) for a chosen swidden site, while the opening of the *Laliaq* bird's nest (unidentified) indicates the direction for a good field position. If the 'ne-ne-ne-ne . . .' call of the Little Spiderhunter or *Seset* (*Arachnothera longirostra*, although *Seset* is also a term used for another *Arachnothera* species) is heard during the slash phase, it is also better to choose a new site. Bad omens can be redressed, to a certain extent, with specific rituals (*petawai betentau*, *nempalah*[8]), but if the agricultural cycle has already proceeded too far, they are often ignored.[9] The *nyahuq* are in fact a group of spirits that bring omen (good and bad) in the shape of birds and sometimes other animals (see Hopes 1997: 166). Their mythical origin is reported in Hopes *et al*. (1997: 23-4).

In addition to the omens mentioned above, Hopes states that during the felling period of rice cultivation, the calls of several omen birds have to be regarded. Besides the *Seset* (*Arachnothera* spp.), he lists *Juruh* (Crested Jay — *Platylophus galericulatus*[10]); *Apou* or *Papo* (Trogons — *Harpactes* spp.); *Bumut* (Greater Coucal — *Centropus sinensis*); various woodpeckers; *Belakotok* (Malkoha — *Phaenicophaeus* spp.); and *Selebumatn* (White-rumped Shama — *Copsychus malabaricus*); as relevant omen birds of the Benuaq and Tunjung (*Tonyoi*) from Eheng (approximately 80 km north-west of Lempunah).[11] Other bird species that function as omen and indicator

---

8. *Petawai betentau* is the lowest form of redressing the influence of bad omens. It is performed on the way by praying and offering seven or eight small wooden *Pesaq* (*Fordia* sp.) figures, or at home with a small ritual including the offering of plates with fabrics, rice and wooden figures (made from *Pesaq* and *Toouq Tawai* — *Costus* sp.). A higher level of these rituals is *nempalah*, which is also carried out at home and includes the sacrifice of a chicken.
9. One farmer, however, related his inobservance of bad omens to the later death of his wife and his lost harvest. In another year, he ignored the *nyahuq* three times, then his youngest son died.
10. This species is not known in Lempunah.
11. Hopes argues that omen birds are distinctive mainly because of their calls, and that several are 'physically quite unremarkable'. This is definitely not true for the magnificent trogons. When I saw one specimen from close distance together with one of my key-informants, who was a well-known hunter, he did not recognise the bird by its appearance. It seems that many birds are known by their calls, but only sometimes recognised when they are seen. →

birds in Lempunah are: *Kangkang Kapot* (Indian Cuckoo — *Cuculus micropterus*) for hinting a good fruiting season; *Sentapit* (Plaintive Cuckoo — *Cacomantis merulinus*) indicating death; *Mentit* (Flowerpeckers — *Diceidae*) and *Beniang* (Brahminy Kite — *Haliastur indus*). The function of the two latter species was not known by my informants.[12]

While most people know a few omen birds, the detailed knowledge is kept by the *belian turaatn* shamans, who have to deal with the Nyahuq spirits in rituals like *nular* or *melas tautn*. Dreams (*umpiiq*) are interpreted in a way similar to the omens, referring to decisions that must soon be made. Thus, bad dreams (*umpiiq daat*) can substantially delay the departure for a journey, or make a farmer look for a new swidden location.

<u>*Star constellations*</u>: The agricultural cycle is linked to an astral calendar. The different constellations indicate different steps in the preparation of a swidden as summarised in Table 3.5. The relative position of the star constellations is watched around 5 a.m.[13] It seems that *Potiiq* is not entirely the same as Orion but refers only to the belt plus a few stars on the right side, resembling a spear-trap. *Beapm* is

---

→ Dove mentions the Rufous Piculet (*Sasia abnormis*), White-rumped Shama (*Copsychus malabaricus*), Scarlet-rumped Trogon (*Harpactes duvaucelii*), Diard's Trogon (*Harpactes diardii*), Banded Kingfisher (*Lacedo pulchella*), Crested Jay (*Platylophus galericulatus*) and the Maroon Woodpecker (*Blythipicus rubiginosus*) as omen birds known among the Kantu' (1985a: 86). Freeman (1999: 107) lists the same species for the Iban.

12. It is a striking fact that all omen bird species are abundant. It is impossible to walk in the forest for less than two hours without being crossed by a Little Spiderhunter, and the death call of the Plaintive Cuckoo is heard daily close to Lempunah. Hence, it might be that omen are perceived mainly and interpreted in undecided situations, where different alternatives appear to be equivalent. Thus, unconscious decision-making processes might be enhanced by the now conscious perception of an omen bird, that is usually overlooked due to its common presence. As the most relevant phase for the interpretation of omens is the risky felling stage, during which just a little bit of extra caution might save one's life, we almost find a rational explanation for the relatively high abundance of omen birds.

13. My own identification of these constellations became a problem as stars were invisible between August 1997 and April 1998 due to the haze caused by the forest fires. It was not until September 1998 that I could watch and discuss star constellations with a few informants on just one occation.

not a constellation known to Western astronomy, but a bow of stars resembling a pig's jaw beginning with Bellatrix, a star in Orion, while the heap of stars in the Pleiades could be taken for a pool. The name of *Beramanuq* is also used for a medicinal plant (*Eurycoma longifolia* Jack.), which has a star-like shape if looked at from above.

Table 3.5: Locally-relevant star constellations

Identification partially by Hopes (1997: 39), partially by my informants

Local Name	*Meaning*	*Constellation*	*Zenith*	*Agricultural activity*
Piuluuq		unidentified	August	rise of *Piuluuq*: felling zenith: burning; sowing on *babar* fields
Sempuatn	wild boar's wallow pool	Pleiades	9.9.	sowing
Beapm	lower jaw of a wild boar	a bow of stars starting with Bellatrix (Orion)	29.9.	sowing
Potiiq	spear trap for wild boars	belt of Orion	1.10.	sowing
Beramanuq		Sirius	24.10.	too late for sowing

The same constellations are also known among the Iban. According to Freeman (1992: 171), the first appearance of the Pleiades at dawn marks the beginning of the cycle with the taking of omens and the clearing of the undergrowth (June). The time between their appearance and zenith, or Orion's arrival and zenith, is regarded as optimal for sowing (end of August until end of September). Among the Benuaq, equally, it is believed that once Sirius has passed the zenith, it is too late for sowing rice, as it will no longer mature.

Although most activities show substantial temporal overlap, the rise of *Beramanuq* (Sirius) is the deadline for sowing rice. If rice is planted later, the average rain-fall pattern does not fit with the maturing process. A last alternative is to use *Sanukng* rice varieties, which mature faster than normal ones, and allow late sowing. While the star constellations are still known as seasonal indicators,[14] modern

14. Although some people differentiate up to nine constellations (additionally *Malikng*, *Nyui Jongkokng*, *Breoo* and *Belentookng*), most people only recognise those listed in Table 3.2. Even for these well-known constellations, I found much disagreement in identification, meaning and temporal order among different informants.

calendars, or simply following other people's activities, appears to be a far more common practice in scheduling swidden activities.

Health, age and effort: The decision to prepare a swidden or not also depends on the physical state of a person. An old or a sick person might decide more easily to do without a swidden than a young and healthy farmer, at least, if there are viable alternatives. In several cases, swiddens were not been prepared due to sick family members who required help, and often ritual assistance. A criterion that has also to be regarded is the expected effort. In the case of physically-easier alternatives, a decision might be made in order to reduce the effort for making a living.

Time, seasonal schedule and assistance: Between June and the rise of *Beramanuq*, there is much room for flexibility to keep to the agricultural schedule. If delays occur, time can be made up by asking for help (*konookng* for wage work, *plou* for exchange labour). On average, 33 per cent (RT I/II) to 60 per cent (RT III) of households are temporarily engaged in *plou* systems (usually for sowing and harvesting). If the respective working steps take several days, the *plou* groups alternate between the different fields in order to treat every swidden equally. In other less frequent cases, workers are paid for *konookng* help.

During the harvest, the daily wage is one *beleq* of rice (Ind. *kaleng*, app. 11 kg of unhusked rice), or the equivalent in Rupiah. For weeding, the workers are paid by plots of approximately 100 m^2 (1996-7: 5,000 Rp), and for felling the price is negotiated. Another possibility for making up lost time is to use a younger fallow forest, as this means less effort during the felling step. If an older fallow is preferred because of a higher expected soil fertility, the use of a chainsaw[15] can significantly accelerate the process. In many cases, chainsaws were borrowed, or *konookng* workers were paid.

The higher percentage of borrowed chainsaws in RT III is directly linked to the poorer economic situation in RT III compared to RT I/II.

Investments: One case where the decision for or against a swidden was left undecided until the very last moment was observed in 1997. As the official weather forecast predicted a prolonged drought, most

15. Chainsaws were introduced to the people of Lempunah in the 1970s when a logging company operated in the village area.

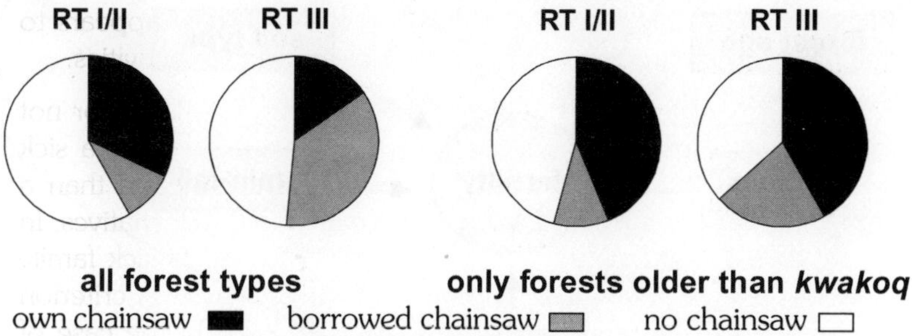

***Fig.* 3.5: Use of chainsaws for preparing a Swidden (1995-98); RT I/II *n*=81, RT III *n*=53**

people in Lempunah decided not to prepare a swidden, but to look for alternative sources of income to supplement their rice stocks. One of my key-informants argued in this vein, and decided to wait and see how the rice planted by a few others would grow. However, he had already paid 110,000 Rp for getting his site cleared, and when he went there for a last visit (after the zenith of *Beramanuq*), he spontaneously planted three *beleq* (app. 33 kg) in order to get at least a part of his investment rewarded. Nevertheless, the harvest failed completely, as it did for every other household.

Expected fertility: The fertility of a site is believed to depend on the condition of the forest, as well as on the relation between rain-fall, planted seed varieties and soil type. It can also be further influenced by ritual means.

Forest age: The fertility of a swidden depends on the fallow period. A Mann-Whitney U-test shows significant differences between the average yield of swiddens made on *babar* and *kwakoq* fallows (e.g., less than 10 years); those of medium age such as *uraaq* and *kerengkakng* (10-50 years); and old secondary or primary *bengkar* forest (older than 100 years).[16] However, the older a fallow, the further it is away from the village. The same test reveals significant differences between these three fallow categories regarding the average distance of swiddens from the settlements.[17]

16. *Babar/kwakoq* vs. *uraaq/kerengkakng*: $t=1.755$ ($p<0.05$); *babar/kwakoq* vs. *bengkar*: $U=31$ ($p<0.01$); *uraaq/kerengkakng* vs. *bengkar*: $t=2.625$ ($p<0.01$).

17. *Babar/kwakoq* vs. *uraaq/kerengkakng*: $t=2.064$ ($p<0.05$); *uraaq/kerengkakng* vs. *bengkar*: $t=4.192$ ($p<0.001$).

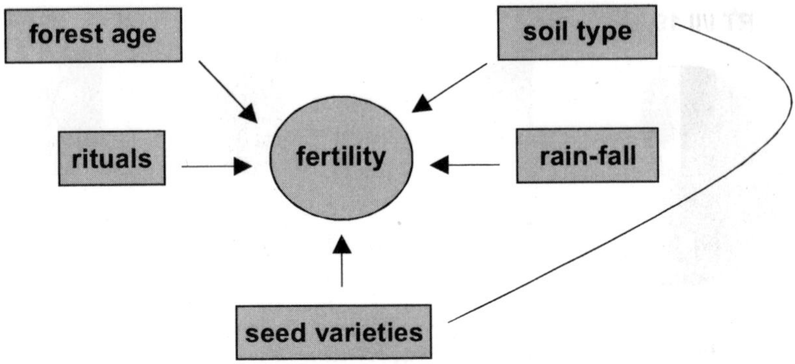

***Fig.* 3.6: Locally-perceived model of interdependency regarding fertility**

Table 3.6: Average yield (kg of unhusked harvest per 1 kg seeds) and distance of swiddens regarding different fallow periods

Forest Type	*fallow age*	*mean yield*	*n*	*mean distance*	*n*
babar & kwakoq	1-10 years	22.3	8	2.9 km	13
uraaq & kerengkakng	10-50 years	34.8	54	3.6 km	41
bengkar	> 100 years	75.0	4	17.0 km	7

The distribution of forest types is shown in *fig*. 3.7.

As an older fallow does not only mean a higher fertility but also greater walking distances and more labour during the felling period (but less weeding!), a trade-off has to be made in selecting a new site. This trade-off is biased towards older forests by the use of chainsaws, which substantially facilitate the felling.

Soil type and rice varieties: The tests for checking soil fertility reported in Poffenberger & McGean (1993: 16-17), was not found for Benuaq farmers in Lempunah. None of my informants knew about the method to stab a *mandau* into the soil and to estimate fertility and moisture from deposits on the blade, or to bury the stem of wild ginger and to watch its shooting. Two types of soil are known as suitable for swidden cultivation: black sandy soil (*oneeq metapm*, not identified, rich in organic matter), and yellow soil (*tana lemit*, e.g., alluvial soils). White sandy soils (*oneeq bura*), which are found under kerangas (heath) forest, are of less value.

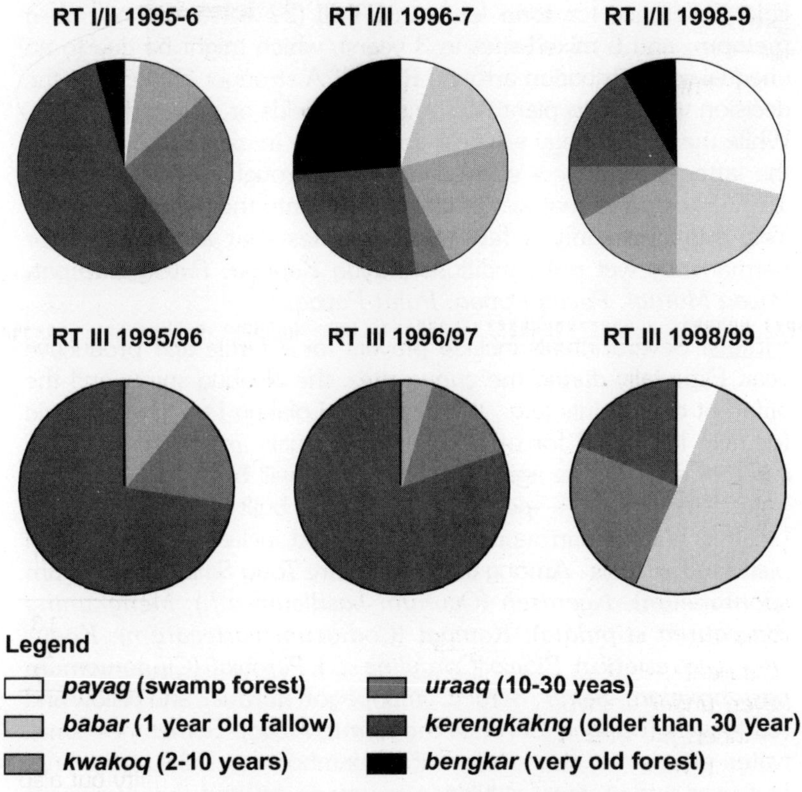

***Fig.* 3.7: Distribution of forest types**

The rice yield did not show any significant difference between these two locally-defined soil types. Swiddens on *oneeq metapm* on average yielded 36.5 times the amount of seed sown (*n*=24), while those on *tana lemit* yielded 36.3 times (*n*=25). Fields with mixed soils (*n*=13) yielded slightly more with 39.8 times (not significant, all data pooled from 1995 and 1996). All informants stated that *oneeq metapm* is more suitable in dry years, while *tana lemit* is only useful in averagely wet years. My data do not allow this hypothesis to be tested, as *all* swiddens failed in the extreme dry season of 1997-8.

However, since rain-fall patterns are perceived as unpredictable, no common preferences are generally made for either of the two soil types. The distribution shows no difference for RT I/II (21 *tana lemit* versus 20 *oneeq metapm,* and 9 mixed sites in 3 years), and only a little preference for *tana lemit* in RT III (27 versus 20 of *oneeq metapm,* and 6 mixed sites in 3 years), which might be due to an unequal soil distribution arround RT III.[18] A stronger impact was the decision whether to plant rice on swamp fields or on rain-fed fields. While the first strategy will be a good choice in extremely dry years, the latter requires less effort. During the droughts of 1982-3 and 1997-8, only rice that was planted directly into the swamp matured. Yet, there are only a few local varieties that are suitable for permanently wet soil conditions (*Payaq Kepoyu*, *Payaq Kumpat*, *Payaq Muntai*, *Payaq Popoq*, *Pulut Payaq*).

<u>Rituals</u>: Several rituals include prayers for a fertile and productive year. Especially during the *guguq* rites, the Nyahuq spirits and the different crop spirits (e.g., the rice spirit Lolakng Luikng) are asked for help in reward for offerings. Other rituals are confined to the different steps of the agricultural cycle and will be described at that point. Traditionally, a special place has to be built on the swidden for Lolakng Luikng, surrounded by a vine and including several ritual plants as her 'toys'. Among these plants are *Touq Salah* (*Saccharum spontaneum*); *Ngeraseh* (*Ocimum basilicum c.f.*); *Mengkuning* (*Baccaurea stipulata*); *Komaat* (*Codiacum variegatum*); *Koyur* (*Tetracera asiatica*); *Biowo* (*Cordyline* sp.); *Perowali* (*Cinnamomum partenoxylon*); *Sekur*, *Serai* (*Cymbopogon nardus*); and yellow and red flowers (*Bungaq Gerungakng Lemit/Meaq*). Sometimes, small water places are also made out of bamboo for Lolakng Luikng. However, today, most swiddens are made without these religious elements, and the respective rituals are rarely carried out.

<u>Expected weather</u>: The annual rain-fall pattern is rather unpredictable and shows only some regularity if averaged over many years (see *fig.* 2.1). This unpredictability was often stated by my informants, and preventive adaptations are generally regarded as prone to fate. Despite this acknowledged unpredictability, some people try to predict rain-fall with regard to the previous year, (i.e., if the last year was dry, the new one might be wet).

Several rituals such as *nular* or *melas tautn* are partly meant to pray for suitable weather conditions and a good harvest. In addition, *sahu* — broken taboos — (especially incest, and offences against

18. Neither soils, nor their distributions in the field, were studied during my research.

marriage rules) are purified by these expensive and long-lasting rites. It is believed that *sahu* offenses cause the anger of celestial spirits. If their anger becomes serious, the heavens will heat up, until a drought comes and destroys the rice harvest. Hence, it is the shamans' major task to cool down the heavens and earth. This can be done with the sprinkling of *tawar* water, and with the blood of sacrificed animals (see sub-section 'Rituals' under chapter 2). *Nular* rites can be carried out in the field (generally the ritual is shared by several families), or in difficult cases, also in the village.

> A *nular* was held at Pentat, the neighbouring village of Lempunah, in October 1993, after it had not rained for almost three months, and the suitable time for planting crops was almost over. The ceremony lasted about two weeks (16 ritual nights) and included the sacrifice of several pigs. Towards the end of the ceremony, rain came. However, *nular* rituals did not work during the drought of 1997/98, although I twice witnessed that a little rain fell on the day of sacrifice.[19]

Although there are no clear strategies for predicting rain-fall for a whole season, it is common knowledge, that different soils, as well as different rice varieties, have different properties regarding rain-fall. Nevertheless, as shown above, the distribution of selected soil types does not reveal distinct preferences. As rain-fall is perceived to be quite unpredictable, strategies tend to diversify rather than be monospecific. This was also observed by Dove (1993: 145-59) among the Kantu' of West-Kalimantan. He stresses that a randomised selection has the advantage that at least some fields might fit the actual weather conditions, whilst a decision based on pre-determined weather predictions might bear a higher risk of failing. *Ex post*, differences in the yield are often linked to a causal relation between soils, seed varieties and the actual rain-fall pattern.

<u>*Available land and forest*</u>: In most cases, land owned by a family is chosen for swidden cultivation. In cases of open access (*hutan bebas* — 'free forest' or *hutan adat* — 'forest according to the traditional

19. A physical explanation for these ritually-fitting rainfalls could be that the ritual masters waited for a change of the wind direction (from south-east to north-west) before they decided on the exact date for the final sacrifice. Such a change was usually followed by some rain within the next 24 hours (I observed this pattern several times during the drought).

law'), the village chief has to be informed.[20] However, as most parts of the forests around Lempunah belong to someone, there are restrictions on where to prepare a swidden. If no suitable localities are available of one's own (e.g., too far away), land has to be borrowed (*opeekng*, usually from relatives). In general, only annual crops are permitted on these borrowed fields in order to avoid later conflicts about resource ownership.[21]

Several families also own land outside the official village area due to their descent or a former conversion of *bengkar* forest. Others borrowed fields outside of Lempunah when the locations were significantly closer to the village than an alternative site within the village area. In 1995, when more than 50 per cent of the swiddens of RT I/II were situated externally, these 'outside' swiddens were also significantly closer to the village than those within (2.9 km *vs*. 4.1 km).[22] About half of them were borrowed, while only one in six was borrowed within the village area.[23] In RT III, the proportion of external fields was much smaller, probably because of an abundance of close alternatives within the village area.[24]

<u>*Rice supply and swidden size*</u>: Rice supply is a major criterion in the decision-making process for having a swidden or not. If rice stocks are big enough to last for some more months in the new year, alternative occupations might be favoured against the preparation of

20. Only *bengkar* forest allows open access. However, this might be restricted by the village chief. When one farmer wanted to prepare a swidden in a remote *bengkar*, this was forbidden by the village chief in favour of a small-scale ecotourism project. The village chief, who initiated the project, emphasised that it was his right to prohibit forest conversion in this case.
21. In fact, cases in which borrowed land is planted with perennials are common. This has turned out to be a major problem in the recent conflict with the oil palm company regarding financial compensation, as only planted resources were compensated, but not the land.
22. $p<0.05$ for a two-tailed Mann-Whitney *U*-test ($t=2.217$).
23. This difference is significant: $\chi^2=5.457$ (for $p=0.05$, $\chi^2=3.841$), hence the hypothesis that borrowed fields are distributed in the same way as owned fields has to be rejected. On the other hand, a 2 × 2 test for independence (with Yates' correction) showed that the ownership status is independent of the position within or outside the village area ($G=2.42$).
24. The proportion of external fields in RT I/II was: 53 per cent (1995), 52 per cent (1996), 29 per cent (1998); in RT III: 17 per cent (1995, 1996), 13 per cent (1998). If the population density within a radius of 5 km is compared between RT I/II and RT III, it becomes obvious that available sites are more abundant around RT III.

a new swidden. In cases with increasing rice supply, there is a tendency for farmers to reduce the size of a new field. In 8 out of 12 individual cases studied between 1995 and 1998, the new field size was smaller than the old if the rice supply had increased (2 were the same, and only 2 increased the size of their fields with increasing rice supply).

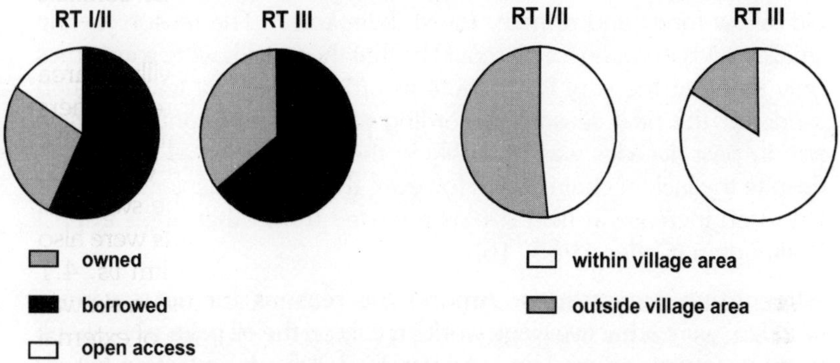

***Fig.* 3.8: Distribution of swidden sites regarding tenure and location**

Table 3.7: Rice supply from the last harvest (in months) versus seed amount and field size[25]

	RT I/II			*RT III*		
	rice supply	seeds	field size	rice supply	seeds	field size
1995	5.4 mo	43 kg	1.9 ha	9.0 mo	37 kg	1.6 ha
1996	10.5 mo	26 kg	1.1 ha	11.0 mo	30 kg	1.3 ha
1998	0 mo	34 kg	1.5 ha	1.7 mo	20 kg	0.9 ha

The rather small field size in 1998, despite the poor supply for that year (the 1997-8 harvest failed completely) was influenced by the lack of seeds after the drought. As the productive capacity decreases rapidly after one year,[26] and no new seeds were gained in early 1998, people had to purchase seeds from traders, friends or relatives who lived in areas who at least had a marginal harvest in 1998. Prices for seeds increased up to 1,000 per cent in 1998, and many families did not find as many seeds as they wanted to plant.[27]

25. The correlation coefficient between seed amount and cleared field size is 0.967 (n=19). 1 *beleq* (app. 11 kg) equals 0.48 ha.

26. At least this is the local perception.

27. The provincial government sent seeds to several villages. All of these seeds failed, however, as they would have required irrigation which is unknown in Lempunah.

The size of swiddens is further influenced by family size;[28] the number of available workers; and the demand of subsistence crops depending on alternative sources of income. A highly-significant difference of field size was observed between young fallow forest (*babar*, *kwakoq*: 0.9 ha on average, n=11) and old fallows (*uraaq*, *kerengkakng*: 1.5 ha, n=43), while no difference was found between old fallow forest and primary forest (*bengkar*).[29] The reason for the smaller fields in young forests could be that these fields were sometimes only made at the very last minute in order to yield at least enough seeds for the next season. According to most informants, the field size in past decades was probably in the same range as it is today, despite the lack of chainsaws. However, the use of chainsaws has not led to an increase in field size as reported from other areas in East Kalimantan (Colfer 1983: 16).

Alternative occupations: Among the reasons for not having a swidden, were attractive wage work (mainly on the oil palm plantation); good resource prices (e.g., rubber in 1995); long-lasting rituals (*kwangkai*, *bekeleeu*); and the political activities related to land rights conflicts between the village and various companies. Rituals like the *kwangkai* funerary rites can last up to three months. The organisation and the hosting of sometimes dozens of guests does not usually allow a proper swidden cultivation at the same time. For small families or bachelors, looking for financial income is often a better option than the labour intensive swidden. Young villagers are often also more independent from local social obligations and can, thus, react more flexibly to new opportunities.

Eraakng — Where should a swidden be prepared?

The selection and the marking of a new swidden site is usually done between June and July. In many cases, the new site is chosen close to the last one. About 50 per cent of the farmers who had swiddens, chose a site in the two subsequent years less than 500 m from the

28. The correlation coefficient between field size and the number of consumers (children younger than 11, and people older than 70 were counted as 0.5 only) was only 0.59.

29. Mann-Whitney *U*-test $p<0.001$ (t=3.110) for *babar/kwakoq* vs. *uraaq/kerengkakng*; not significant for *uraaq/kerengkakng* vs. *bengkar* (t=1.177).

previous site (RT I/II: 49 per cent in 1996, 52 per cent in 1998; RT III: 65 per cent in 1996, 29 per cent in 1998).[30] Only in a very few cases (RT I/II 4 cases, RT III no case), was the same field used again. A considerable advantage of choosing a nearby site was that the same fieldhut can be used again from the very beginning of the new cycle. Travel time, and time spent constructing a new field house, can be saved by using the old one. Since the Benuaq usually store rice under the field house, and only carry it to the main settlement according to the actual demand, further labour can be saved if these exhaustive carrying walks are not necessary.

Another important factor is the availability of fruit and vegetables grown in the old swiddens, which are still available during much of the new cultivation period.[31] A similar preference is shown for proximate forest gardens, which can be used during the rice cultivation period, and later enlarged by new plantings on the swidden.[32]

When asked how they choose a new swidden site, many farmers said '*kaitn neyau kayuq*' — 'we look at the woods'. It appears that this answer is an expression for a holistic perception of the forest and its probable soil fertility. The farmer 'knows' intuitively whether a certain forest part is suitable for swidden cultivation or not.[33] However, since it is impossible to fully transfer a farmer's intuition to my own or a reader's perception, I tried to analyse this intuitive judgement by breaking it down into decision-making criteria. Yet, I cannot explicitly say *how* these criteria are considered during the decision-making for selecting a new swidden site. All I can give are correlations between rational criteria and the actual decisions, which look plausible in retrospect. The decision-making process itself remains somehow vague, and varies among different individuals. Some people obviously

---

30. A similar preference is mentioned by Dove (1985: 63) for the Kantu', who also like to prepare swiddens close to past, or other current fields, as well as close to rubber groves. About a third of the households studied by him made swiddens adjecent to those of the previous year.
31. These advantages are also described by Dove for the Kantu' (1985: 64).
32. This was reported by one farmer who tried to combine several scattered rubber gardens by preparing subsequent swiddens in-between.
33. Padoch (1986: 279) mentions that examining the standing vegetation regarding its age and composition is a commonly observed way to select a field site among swidden cultivators.

consider the criteria depicted in *fig.* 3.9 in a rational way,[34] while others might rely on their intuition based on experience and acquired knowledge, or simply imitate the decisions of more experienced farmers. Especially among young farmers, the latter appears to be a common strategy used for other decisions during the agricultural cycle.

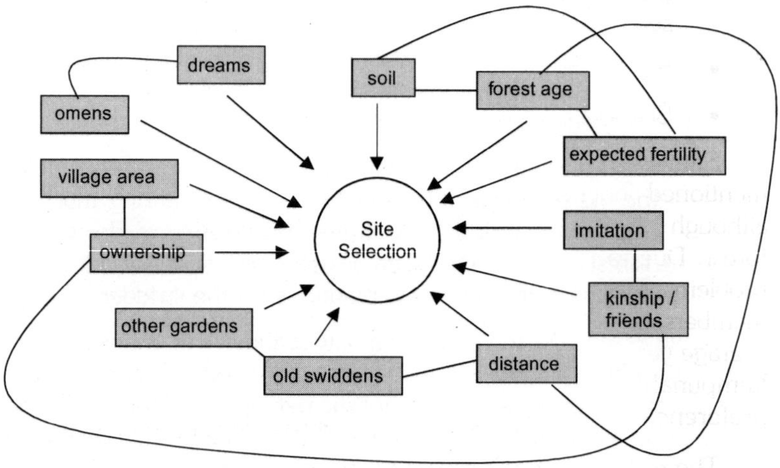

***Fig.* 3.9: Identified criteria for selecting a new swidden site**

The following patterns were observed:

- Older fallow forests promise higher yields.
- Older fallow forests are situated further from the village than younger ones.
- Older fallow forests mean more effort during felling, but less weeding.
- The use of chainsaws reduces labour demand during felling.
- A short distance to the village is favoured.
- Different soils show different adaptation to drought or floods.
- Flat terrain is preferred against steep slopes.

---

34. I.e., they weigh up the criteria against one another and try to optimise their decisions regarding individual preferences. At least, many of my informants verified the relevance of the identified criteria.

- Omens and dreams impose certain restrictions on site selection.
- One's own sites and locations within the village area are generally preferred.
- In many cases, a site close to that of the previous year is selected.
- Sites close to forest gardens are often favoured.
- Site selection is influenced by social groups (kinship or friends).

Site selection is an individual trade-off between the criteria mentioned above. Hence, an old farmer might choose a nearby site, although the expected fertility is lower than in an old but remote forest. Due to the younger fallow, he also has to cope with weed problems. This might be done by asking for help from younger family members. Similarly, every household makes its own decision, and in average years there is a rather scattered pattern of swiddens around Lempunah and RT III, reflecting the great variation in individual preferences.[35]

> The extraordinary event of the drought and the forest fires of 1997/98, however, shaped this spatial distribution in a specific way. The fires had devastated much of Lempunah's forest in late 1997 and early 1998. Old growth forests, such as *kerengkakng* or *bengkar* were no longer suitable for swidden cultivation. Many trees were dead, but had not yet fallen down. Hence, the hazard of these potentially dangerous trees was estimated as too high to work in such forests.[36] Furthermore, the burning was incomplete, and in order to assure a sufficient nutrient supply, a second burning with high labour input (for piling up the unburnt wood) would have been necessary. Thus, most farmers showed no preference for these otherwise favourite forest sites. Instead,

35. In contrast to the Kantu' studied by Dove (1985: 63), other Benuaq groups (Poffenberger & McGean 1993: 19), and Kenyah in Ritan Baru (my own observations in 1998), there is no clear preference for sites close to rivers or roads. Most swiddens were accessed on foot, while only a few remote fields by truck or motorbike.
36. Even walking through these dead forests was dangerous. On one walk, three trees crashed down not far from me.

the weeds of young, often completely burnt fallows were burnt again, and many swiddens were prepared close to the village without too much labour demand.

In addition to the already discussed criteria, a few more aspects have to be explained to understand the rationale behind the farmers' site selections.

Indicator plants: Despite the more holistic examination of a possible swidden site based on the farmer's experience, several plant species were reported as indicators for good soil fertility:

Bekalukng (unidentified)

Bemaatn (*Donax caniformis*, Maranthaceae)

Beramboyut (*Macropanax dispermus*)

Beteteq (unidentified)

Butootn (*Stachypterinum jagorianum*, Maranthaceae)

Isaaq Ngkookng (*Cominsia gigantea*, Maranthaceae)

Ngkuukng (*Macaranga* sp., Euphorbiaceae)

Tempuro (*Dillenia* sp., Dilleniaceae)

Maranthaceae are also reported by Poffenberger & McGean (1993: 19) as common indicator species known by Benuaq farmers from Damai (more than 100 km north-west of Lempunah). In addition, they mention Musaceae, Arecaceae, Myrtaceae and Zingiberaceae. Two other species are known for indicating sandy soils (*Nagaaq* — *Schima wallichii*), and yellow soil (*Pipit* — *Lithocarpus elegans*).

Distance: Between 1995 and 1998, the average distance of swiddens was 2.8 km (RT I/II) and 2.0 km (RT III), which is less than an hour's walk through the forest.[37] The slightly greater distances in RT I/II reflect the smaller area of close and available forests, owing to the shape of Lempunah's village boundaries. A greater distance between settlement and swidden bears several disadvantages, such as more walking time; more physical effort (especially for carrying rice, but

37. This does not include several fields close to a remote transmigration settlement which was accessible by road. The average distances (as the crow flies) resemble those given by Dove for the Kantu' (1985: 412), which range between 1.6 and 2.7 km depending on the forest type.

even daily return trips can be exhausting for elderly or sick persons); limited accessibility during periods of pest predation and theft; and reduced security (in former times). The optimal choice would therefore be a field location as close as possible to the domestic unit.[38]

This is in contrast to the spatial distribution of old (and thus more fertile) forests, which are generally further away from the village than younger fallows (see above, Forest age). In several cases, a great distance led finally to a neglect of the fields. This could be due to limited access because of slippery roads, as the very remote fields were visited mainly by motor bike or by truck, health problems, or incidents that required the farmer's presence in the village (e.g., conflicts, rituals, and political or financial issues). While a closer swidden might still have been visited from time to time, this becomes more difficult with increasing distance. Hence, even in years characterised by good harvests, some remote fields failed because of neglect. The strategy described by Lawrence *et al.* (1997: 11), where Dayak farmers in West Kalimantan increased the size of remote fields to mitigate crop losses, was not observed in Lempunah.[39]

The distance of fields within the village area of Lempunah in 1995 was significantly greater than for those fields outside the village's boundaries.[40] Hence, a short distance might have been appreciated more than secure long-term land tenure. This difference was not found in other years. Regarding ownership status, the distance showed no significant difference, although there was a clear correlation between external fields and borrowed status in 1995.

Kin and friendship: A criterion for site selection is kinship. In 19 cases (RT I/II between 1995 and 1998), a son-in-law followed his wife's parents. This pattern was the most common one among kinship groups who had neighbouring, or even shared, swiddens. In 10 cases, adult (usually unmarried) children followed their parents. While swidden groups consisting of siblings were rare (5 cases), further family relations or friendship were more common. Neighbouring swiddens offer the

---

38. In very few cases, people chose to live permanently on their fields.

39. The correlation coefficient for field size *vs*. distance was 0.017 for RT I/II (n=61) and 0.044 for RT III (n=51).

40. Average distance from RT I/II: 4.1 km for 'within', 2.9 km for 'outside' (two-tailed Mann-Whitney *U*-test, $t=2.217$, $p<0.05$, 21 fields 'within', 24 'outside').

advantage of labour exchange as well as solidarity in cases of sickness and other problems.[41]

Another aspect mentioned by farmers was a 'dilution effect' in respect to pest predation. As the activities on neighbouring fields are usually synchronised, crops mature at a similar time (also depending on the varieties), and pests may have difficulties in destroying all crops at once.[42] For instance, if a party of macaques (*Macaca* spp.) predates a field it can destroy a harvest within a few days. However, if there are several fields, the proportion eaten might be smaller. There is also additional attention from neighbours, and not every field has to be guarded all the time whilst it matures, which allows for other occupations, such as rubber tapping. In 1996, one farmer gave up his field (after felling), as no one joined him. He said that, alone, he had no chance against the monkeys.

After a site has been chosen, the *pakatn nyahuq* ritual was traditionally held for appeasing the Nyahuq spirits. This ritual, which is described by Sumual (1998: 53-5), is also known in Lempunah, although I never saw farmers carrying it out. Nevertheless, certain religious prescriptions such as the reading of omens are still found, while some farmers purify their fields by sprinkling *tawar* water, or the blood of a sacrified chicken, in order to cool down the land and keep it fertile.

WORKING STEPS DURING THE SWIDDEN CYCLE

Once a site is selected, it is marked by slashing some parts of the undergrowth.

Nokap — *Slashing*

The slashing of small trees and scrubs is done by men and women between June and September with a *mandau* (bush knife). The rise of *Piuluuq* and the fruiting of *Pesaaq* (*Fordia* sp.) indicate the optimal starting time. *Nokap* takes up to one month for an average field. In

---

41. In several cases, curing rites (*belian*) were carried out in the field with the assistence of neighbouring farmers. A serious problem in the past were attacks, against which swidden groups offered some help.

42. This strategy only works partially in cases of extreme pest breakouts, such as in 1999 and in 2000 when locusts, rats and mice appeared in large numbers and destroyed more than half of the harvest.

cases of young fallows (*babar* or *kwakoq*), this step is sufficient and needs no further felling, as large trees are still absent (see also Dove 1985a: 103-4).

By slashing, the undergrowth is killed and can then dry until the burning. Dove (1985: 101) also mentions that slashing enhances the safety of farmers so that they can better escape falling trees. Furthermore, it is far from easy to work in, or even walk through, fallow forests, as rattans and other undergrowth plants constitute spiny obstacles. Hence, their removal facilitates the next step, the felling of big trees. Labour input ranges between 4 and 9 person days per hectare, which is comparable to the figures reported for Kantu' (7-8 working days per ha, in Dove 1985a: 106), and Kenyah (1-30 person days per ha, in Lahjie 1996: 153). It depends above all on the fallow stage, as younger fallows contain more undergrowth than old forests (see also detailed data in Lahjie 1996: 153). If slashing was incomplete, this is called *bemas*.

Noong — *Felling*

Between July and September, trees which were not slashed during *nokap* are felled. The *noong* phase can overlap with *nokap*, although Dove is right when he says that slashing should be finished well ahead of felling, as the slashed vegetation might not dry well when it is too soon covered by felled trees (1985: 110).[43] Trees are felled to increase the input of sunlight into the swidden and to provide nutrients by burning the felled trees later on (see Dove 1985a: 115).[44] Felling is traditionally done at breast height with an axe called *wase*, made by the farmer out of a blade (obtained from the village's blacksmith and weighing about 1-1.5 kg) and a wooden shaft (60-80 cm long), at which the blade is fastened with rattan. The shaft is rather flexible giving the axe additional swing.

Noong is generally performed by notching up to 30 or more

43. In a case I observed in detail, the farmer's wife was still slashing the undergrowth on about 20 per cent of the swidden area, while her husband and her son already felled big trees. However, later on, the slashed vegetation did not burn well (1996 was also a rainy year) and the family suffered a complete harvest failure. A greater temporal distance between slashing and felling might indeed have improved the drying.

44. If the problem was only to increase sunshine input, trees might also be girdled as it is done in rattan gardens.

smaller trees, and then by felling a big one which triggers a chain reaction. The big tree tears down several smaller trees, which have overlapping canopies, or hit other trees when they fall. The same technique is also described for the Kantu' (see Dove 1985a: 119-20). By applying this self-enhancing method, working time can be substantially reduced, as the notching rate is about 75 per cent faster than the felling rate (*ibid.*). This domino-like cascade of falling trees bears a severe danger, however, that the workers might get hit.[45] Where vines or liana disturb the felling direction, as they link trees to one another, they are cut with the *mandau*.

Trees with large buttresses, or extraordinary hard trunk bases, are felled from *santukar* ladders at a height of 2-4 metres. A detailed description of Kantu' ladder and platform models, which are also used among the Benuaq, is given in Dove (1985: 116). However, I never saw a tree being felled from a ladder or a platform, and high tree stumps were rare on the swiddens around Lempunah. This might be related to Dove's findings that felling platforms are seldom used in secondary forest[46] (1985: 117). Fruit or rubber trees (often planted during the previous swidden cycle), as well as potential 'honey trees', are spared.

Felling is perceived as hard work. It can be facilitated by labour exchange and by the more recent use of chainsaws. Today, more than 50 per cent of all fallow forests older than 10 years (i.e., *uraaq*, *kerengkakng* and *bengkar*) are felled with chainsaws.[47] In cases where no chainsaws are available, paid workers can be hired (1996: 35,000 Rp per day; 1997: 110,000 Rp for slashing and felling of about 2 ha). However, it is interesting that the size of fields prepared with or without chainsaws is the same (both 3.0 *beleq* or 1.44 ha for *uraaq*, *kerengkakng* and *bengkar*), which contrasts with the impact of chainsaws in Kenyah villages, where the saws led to an increase in field size (Colfer 1983: 16).

45. When I joined a farmer once for two days of felling, we made a narrow escape from trees which fell too early because of a breeze. In two other cases the same year, farmers got hit. While one suffered a hip dislocation, the other received a fractured skull. Both survived, but they still suffer from their accidents.

46. Dove gives no reason for this pattern, but it must be related to a smaller abundance of big buttresses in fallow forests.

47. In order to reduce the danger of getting hurt, the chainsaw of my host family was blessed with *tawar* water during the *ngeluikng* rite.

The time demand for felling was not measured. According to my informants it was between two days (using chainsaws) and 21 days for an average field of about 1.5 ha. This is in the same range as the figures given by Dove for the Kantu' (44 working days for cleared forests ranging between 1.1 to 10.4 ha per household; Dove 1985a: 94, 128), and those reported by Lahjie for Kenyah (between 8 and 40 days for 1 ha; Lahjie 1996: 153-4). The actual number of person days, however, varies greatly depending on the forest type and field size. If the felling stage was done improperly, it was called *kuhu*.

Oikng Joa — *Drying*

Once the undergrowth is slashed and the trees are felled, the vegetation is left to dry for at least four weeks. The optimal time for *oikng joa* is August and September, the driest months in Lempunah. In general, the older a fallow, the longer the drying takes, with primary forest requiring the longest period. If *oikng joa* is incomplete, the burning will be incomplete as well, and a disproportionate amount of time is necessary to prepare a second burning.

Nyuru — *Burning*

Burning the dry vegetation releases nutrients from the slashed trees and undergrowth, as well as from the humus layer.[48] Furthermore, plants competing with rice for nutrients and light are removed (at least for a while), and the cleared swidden is made easier to work in (see also Dove 1985a: 131). Once the wood is dry enough, the swidden is burnt within a few hours (by men and women). Traditionally, it should be done when *Piuluuq*, *Beapm*, *Sempuatn* and *Potiiq* 'unite' at their zenith.[49] The burning usually starts at noon, when the

48. According to Whitmore (1990: 136-137), 40 per cent — 90 per cent of the nutrients are found above ground, depending on the respective kinds of nutrient (e.g., 60 per cent — 90 per cent of nitrogen is found below ground) and the forest type. About 10 per cent of the nutrients below ground are contained in the root system (*ibid.*). Whitmore emphasises that the widespread opinion that most of the nutrients are in the biomass is 'seldom true' (*ibid.*).

49. With the exception of *Piuluuq* (which is earlier) the other star constellations pass their zenith between 9.9. and 1.10. The Kantu' say similarly: 'Once we [the three stars of Orion's belt] have passed the center of the sky, you stop planting.' As planting follows only a few days after burning, it is the same constellation that indicates these steps.

temperature is at its highest and vegetation moisture is low. Fire is set with a petrol-torch (made from hollow bamboo) every 10-20 m. The burning patterns vary from burning from the outside inwards, to meandering through the field, following the wind direction.

In dry years, a firebreak (1-2 m wide) is made around the field (*ladakng*), to prevent the fire from escaping into forest gardens, other fields and the forest itself. All vegetation in the break is removed and the soil surface is cleaned with a broom-like stick. In the rainy year of 1996 this precaution was unnecessary.[50] These *ladakng* are also made around protected trees or forest gardens. During the drought of 1997, *ladakng* were frequently made for small gardens. However, swidden sites were not burnt until rain had started in early November.[51]

The early rain-fall in 1996, (the first week of October) let many farmers repeatedly postpone the burning of their swiddens until they could not wait any longer and burnt despite the humid vegetation. Thus, many locations burnt incompletely (*bangkakng*), which required additional but often futile work (see below). As a result, many swiddens only achieved marginal yields or failed completely.[52] The deadline for burning is the rise of *Beramanuq* in the second half of October, when it starts to rain. An alternative that I never observed, but which is reported by Dove (1985: 141-2), is to postpone the burning until the next year. Farmers in Lempunah were, however, forced to burn even under unfavourable circumstances, as they only prepare one swidden per year, while the Kantu' studied by Dove generally have two or three.

Mongkakng — *Second Burning*

If the first burning was not complete, the unburnt wood is piled up

---

50. One informant stated that *ladakng* had become rare since mutual assistance is declining, which limits the time for work in the fields.

51. No forest fires originated in 1997-8 from the swiddens around Lempunah, as no one dared to burn due to the extreme drought and the high risk of an escaping fire. The damage such a fire could cause would lead to severe adat fines, as it would be clear, from which field the fire had started.

52. The field I studied most intensively had no significant yield (less than 50 kg of rice), and its owner said: '*Api beau maan.*' — 'The fire has not eaten'.

and dried again.[53] This labour intensive step depends on the weather and might take another few weeks. As this second burning might coincide with the beginning of the rainy season, it often only improves the conditions marginally. Another method of redress is reported by Dove for the Kantu' (1985: 154-6): the unburnt vegetation of parts of a swidden is burnt again without prior collecting. Afterwards, the remaining unburnt vegetation is 'cleared away' by carrying it out of the swidden in order to facilitate future working steps and to increase the input of sunlight. This technique, however, was not observed in Lempunah. Once a site is burnt, it has to be planted as well. Otherwise, the nutrients released will be partially lost until the following year.

Ngasaq/Moyaas — *Dibbling and Sowing*

Some days after the final burning, the sowing begins. Depending on the field size and the available help, this phase can last up to three weeks. Usually, families co-operate in *plou* groups. In RT I/II, 33 per cent of all rice-growing households were involved in *plou* groups during the planting phase (on average 3 additional persons; in 1999 one group consisted of more than 60 people!). In RT III, the proportion was clearly higher at 60 per cent (6-7 additional persons; the largest group was reported to have consisted of 20 people).[54] These labour exchange groups alternate between different fields everyday in order to distribute chances and effort equally.

Additionally, labour can also be hired for a wage (*konookng*). In one case, a household paid 30,000 Rp per sown *beleq* (app. 11 kg) in 1996, as all family members were busy with rubber tapping at the same time. Theoretically, the labour of the planting phase is shared strictly between men and women: men dibble holes into the soil (*ngasaq*), into which women give the rice seeds (*moyaas*).[55] However, if there is a lack of help, both steps are done by both sexes.[56] The

53. It is difficult to re-burn the swidden without first heaping up the unburnt vegetation, as the already burnt parts of the swidden will function as firebreaks (see also Dove 1985a: 154, but see below).

54. The difference between RT I/II and RT III is related to the much closer distances of swiddens in RT III compared with the scattered pattern in RT I/II. Farmers in RT I/II appear to be more individualistic than those in RT III.

55. This kind of labour-sharing is found all over Borneo (see Sutlive 1992: 75 for the Iban, Dove 1985a: 175-9 for the Kantu').

56. This is also reported by Dove for the Kantu' (1985: 179).

planting parties proceed downhill in rows. The whole phase is usually called *ngasaq*, referring to the male part only,[57] or *ngasaq-moyaas*. *Ngasaq* is done with a stick (about 2 m long) with an attached ironwood tip (*asaq*). Traditionally, percussion-tips could be used, but are nowadays only produced for sale as handicrafts. The seeds are stored in small rattan baskets (*bisaatn*) which are tied to the woman's hip.

Planting distance, or the number of seeds per hole, are not consciously varied. Whenever I asked farmers (while planting rice) they said that the planting distance and the number of seeds per hole are not dependent on the soil type, the forest age, or the inclination of a slope. Some people mentioned that those differences were more relevant in the past, when the distance between two holes was larger in old forests (an arm's length, app. 50-75 cm in *kerengkakng*, *bengkar*) compared to young fallows (a hand plus a cubit's length, app. 20-50 cm in *babar*, *kwakoq*, *uraaq*). This difference was explained by the greater fertility of old fallows which makes the rice grow bigger and demand more space, while the distance in young fallows has to be kept smaller because of competing weeds.[58] As the importance of rice has decreased slightly over the last decades, mainly due to new means of income, some formerly known adaptation techniques might have been lost.[59]

After the forest fires and the drought, rice was also planted in the swamps (1998-9). The technique was that used for irrigated *sawah* fields: seedlings were cultivated for two months in nurseries, and then transplanted into shallow water (app. 15 cm deep). Before they were planted into the swamp field, large seedlings were divided into 2-4 parts. These swamp fields were made in addition to rain-fed swiddens, and were intended to become permanent fields.

---

57. The expression is also used in a sexual sense: *ngasaq sobot* = 'to stab [in the] mosquito net' = to make love.

58. Similar differences in planting distances regarding different forest ages were reported by Colfer for Kenyah farmers (1991: 71) with 80 cm for fields cut from primary forest, and 50 cm for those cut from secondary forest.

59. This is also reflected by the relatively small number of swiddens per household (per annum as well as over several years) if compared with other Dayak groups.

Rice varieties: Between 1995 and 1999, 106 different, locally-identified rice varieties (71 common, non-glutinous varieties, 35 glutinous varieties) were cultivated in Lempunah.[60]

Apart from their segregation referring to glutination,[61] these varieties are differentiated by their origin, by the physical appearance of the plant or the seeds, and by their taste. The names can be arranged by the following categories:[62]

- place of origin (e.g., *Bogor*, *Jawa Bali*, *Payaq Muntai*, *Samarinda*)
- group of origin (e.g., other Dayak groups such as *Bentiatn*, *Kenyah*, or the government — *pemerintah*)
- other origins (*bawiiq*, rice found in the stomach of a wild boar)
- size (e.g., *isip* — 'small as the cutting knife', *sabuuq* — 'small as ash', *kediq* = 'small')
- colour (*meaq* = 'red', *bura* = 'white', *metapm* = 'black', *bulaau* = 'golden')
- animals (*bitiq* = 'ant', *kelawat* = 'gibbon', *ngkotiq* = insect species, *lais* = fish species, *uraakng* = 'fresh water prawn', *ureeq* = fish species, *pelanuq* = 'mouse deer')
- fruits (e.g., *lempukat*, *lisaat*, *mayang*)
- plants (*jangkau* = tree species, *niwokng* = palm species, *ngono* = rattan species, *serai* = 'citronella grass')

---

60. As not all varieties were known to my key-informants, there might be some duplication through different names. In Mancong, 139 different rice varieties have been planted by 25 farmers during their lifetime (most of them are still active farmers). The average number of varieties was 7, ranging from 2 (probably young farmers) to 19. Since the average number per field is 5-7, turnover in Mancong seems to be rather small.
61. Glutinous varieties contain 3.7-5 per cent Dextrine as well as a higher amount of amylopectine (Rehm & Espig 1984: 20).
62. Similar categories (place, group and manner of origin, size, shape) are given by Dove for the Kantu' classification (1985: 161).

Pare (non-glutinous rice varieties, male character)

Abong
Ampung
Bau Beneeq
Bawiiq
Bekapm
Bentiatn
Beramaakng
Bidai
Bogor
Boyut
Bura
Busaakng Bura
Busaakng Mea
Daliiq
Isip
Jangkau
Jawa Bali
Jeluakng
Jemiaq
Jempaka
Jerai
Kalang Niwokng
Beleq Bitiq
Kalukng Kelawat
Kalukng Niukng
Kaluq
Kempal
Kenyah
Keriyat
Kumpat Bura
Kumpat Metapm
Lempukat
Lempunyau/Tahai
Lisaat
Loh
Lunkot
Majaat
Mayang Liukng
Mayang Ukor
Mayas
Ngkotiq
Ngono
Nyium
Payaq Kepoyu
Payaq Kumpat
Payaq Muntai
Payaq Popoq
Pemerintah
Penawar
Piraaq
Sabuuq
Sahai
Sanukng Beneeq
Sanukng Sinang Pariq
Sasaq Jalan
Serai Bau/Gunung
Sinang Boyus/Buyut
Sirep Lais
Sului
Titus
Tokookng Bujur
Tokookng Bulaau
Tokookng Guntul
Tokookng Jarum
Tokookng Kantur
Tokookng Pelanuq
Tokookng Sebet
Uraakng
Ureeq
Uway
Waatn

Pulut (glutinous rice varieties, female character)

Ajaatn
Berempet
Beteteq
Buaq
Bujaq
Gusiq
Jaring
Jomit
Jue
Kelingkap
Keramuuq
Kesuma
Kumpir
Langooq
Mayang
Meaq Kediq
Meaq Sarukng
Mening
Mit
Ngeraseh
Pariq
Payaq
Pelet
Petutn
Rau/Metapm
Samarinda
Sanukng
Saruuq Kediq
Saruuq Solai
Seloping Kediq
Seluakng
Seset
Tiwaq/Tiwakng
Tongau
Wakaai

Not all of the names could be interpreted by my informants, and it often remained vague whether the name of an animal or a plant was being used because of physical resemblance (e.g., *Sirep Lais* = 'flipper of the *Lais* fish'), or because of a story related to the origin of the respective variety (e.g., *Bawiiq*).

Apart from the personal harvest, seeds are mainly acquired by exchange, gift, financial payment, re-payment,[63] and probably also by theft (see Dove 1985a: 165-9). Since seeds can only be stored for up to one year without loosing their productive capacity, it is of great importance to maintain the diversity *in situ*.[64] Hence, droughts such as in 1982-3 and in 1997-8 have severe impacts on crop diversity.

63. Borrowed seeds have to be re-paid after a good harvest with 50-100 per cent interests, while borrowed rice is free of interests.

64. It is commonly stated that after just one year, only one in three seeds will germinate. Hence, the harvest of 1997 was no longer suitable as seeds for 1998-9. Besides, most seeds were eaten during the drought and economic crisis.

Due to a lack of available rice seeds, the overall number of varieties cultivated in 1998 was reduced by 24 per cent for non-glutinous, and 49 per cent for glutinous varieties, compared with the same households in 1995 (*n*=24).[65] The search for seeds was extended downriver to the district centre of Tenggarong, where some families had relatives, and upriver, to areas which had received some rain during the drought, and thus harvested at least some rice.[66] The price for seeds had, however, increased up to more than ten times the price of the previous year (40-60,000 Rp per *beleq*), due to a reduced supply and a general price increase of about 300 per cent because of the Indonesian financial crisis.

In all years, the overall diversity of cultivated rice varieties showed a significant difference between RT I/II and RT III.

Table 3.8: Number of cultivated rice varieties in 12 households

RT	*Σ 1995* *pare + pulut*	*Σ 1996* *pare + pulut*	*Σ 1998* *pare + pulut*	*Σ 1995-8* *pare + pulut*
RT I/II (*n*=12)	25 + 16	21 + 8	17 + 5	43 + 17
RT III (*n*=12)	15 + 7	15 + 8	11 + 2	23 + 10

While there is partial overlapping, only a few varieties are exclusively cultivated in RT III:

The big observed differences in the overall diversity between parts of the village cannot be explained by a difference in the numbers of varieties per household, which is only slightly larger in RT I/II (see Table 3.10).

---

65. Both years resembled each other as the previous harvest was marginal (1995), or even lost (1998). If the numbers of varieties are compared between 1998 and 1996, the loss is slightly smaller (21 per cent for *pare*, 36 per cent for *pulut*). A short visit in 2000 revealed that only the number of *pulut* varieties had slightly recovered (13 in 12 households of RT I/II), while the *pare* diversity remained at a low level (16 varieties in 12 households).

66. Only a few varieties were sold in the village. There was some supply of high yield varities from the government (announced as 'padi gunung' — 'hill rice', which, however, was not the case).

Table 3.9: Distribution of rice varieties: RT I/II *vs.* RT III

	only in RT I/II	*only in RT III*	*in both*
Pare 1995	14	4	11
Pare 1996	13	7	8
Pare 1998	11	5	6
Pulut 1995	10	1	6
Pulut 1996	3	3	5
Pulut 1998	5	2	0
Pare 1995-8	23	3	20
Pulut 1995-8	10	3	7

Table 3.10: Average number of rice varieties per household

	RT I/II	*(n=12)*	*RT III*	*(n=14)*
	pare	*pulut*	*pare*	*pulut*
1995	4.1	2.6	2.9	1.4
1996	2.8	1.5	2.6	1.6
1998	2.8	0.5	1.9	0.2
mean	3.2	1.5	2.5	1.1

As the turnover rates of varieties from one year to the next are also at a similar level in both parts of the village (see Table 3.11), the difference must be caused by a greater individual variation in the main village. This greater variation probably reflects a larger pool of varieties in RT I/II due to the larger number of households and the better access to neighbouring villages for seed acquisition.

Table 3.11: Sørensen indices (see Krebs 1985: 447-450) for similarities of rice varieties between different years[67]

	RT I/II		*RT III*	
	Pare	*Pulut*	*Pare*	*Pulut*
1996 *vs.* 1995	60.9%	66.7%	93.3%	80.0%
1998 *vs.* 1996	31.6%	50.0%	30.8%	20.0%
1998 *vs.* 1995	28.6%	30.0%	23.1%	22.2%

67. Sørensen index = $100\% - \frac{\sum_{i=1}^{n}|x_i - y_i|}{\sum_{i=1}^{n}(x_i + y_i)} \cdot 100\%$ *xi*, *yi*: =1 if variety *i* is present in year *x* or *y*.

The similarities between 1995 and 1996 in RT III might be estimated to be too high due to a methodological problem. Rice varieties planted in 1995 were only assessed in early 1997. Hence, some answers could be mixed up with the varieties of 1996. The decrease of overlapping from 1996 to 1998 is mainly explained by a loss of varieties due to the long drought of 1997-8. Since all swiddens failed in 1997-8, no new local seeds were available for the season of 1998-9.

If the diversity of rice varieties of neighbouring swiddens is compared to that of a combination of any other two fields, no significant difference is found (see Table 3.12).

Table 3.12: Average number of rice varieties on two neighbouring *vs.* two non-neighbouring swiddens in 1995 (*n*=5 pairs, only RT I/II)

	neighbouring	*non-neighbouring*
Pare	5.0	5.2
Pulut	3.4	3.6

This is surprising as neighbouring fields are generally owned by the same extended family, often constituting 'parents and daughter plus son-in-law' constellations. However, these close kinship relations did not increase the sharing of rice varieties. The underlying rationale is that the success of different varieties depends on the personality of the respective farmer. Not every variety fits everyone. Hence, there are personal preferences. In addition, new varieties are tested, and the risk appears to be divided among several family members. Similarly, Setyawati (n.d.) reports that Apau Ping farmers in East Kalimantan laughed at her question as to whether different rice varieties matched different soil conditions. Whilst also cultivating 4-5 varieties on average per household and year (*n*=44), the reason for this diversification seems to have been taste and the need for different varieties to match different kinds of consumption.[68]

This is also the case in Lempunah, where individual taste preferences were mentioned, as well as the need for different varieties used in daily life and rituals (especially *pulut* varieties). Several varieties are known for their specific properties, such as a limited tolerance to water-stress (*Tokookng Bujur*, *Lisaat*); suitability for cultivation in swamps (e.g., *Payaaq* varieties, *Jemiaq*, *Kempal*, *Lempunyau*, *Mayas*); fast-maturing properties (*Sanukng*); suitability for large families (*Lisaat*, *Kalang Niwokng*, because of their large corn size); or their growing height (*Jawa Bali*). However, the idea that different varieties are suitable for different soil types or even different slopes or elevations (see *ibid.*: 163), could not be verified in Lempunah.

68. A difference between Apau Ping and Lempunah is that Apau Ping farmers already make their decision which varieties to plant after the harvest (i.e., several months in advance), whereas there is much trade and exchange in Lempunah until the planting starts.

A great diversity is not an explicitly-stated objective in itself, like what is ritually prescribed among the Kantu' in order to reduce risk (Dove 1985a: 163-5). Nevertheless, a high level of diversity is maintained, whether based on a forgotten environmental rationale or on habituation.[69] On average, 20 to 43 kg of seeds are sown annually on a swidden (i.e., a mean of 5.6 to 8.6 kg per variety; *pulut*: *pare* app. 1: 3, equalling 14 to 29 kg/ha), depending on the field size and seed availability. Data from Kenyah farmers in the Apo Kayan are in the same range between 22 and 33 kg per ha, however, using fewer varieties (on average 3.2 per family, Colfer 1991: 71).

<u>*Maturing stages of the rice plant*</u>: The different stages of the maturing rice are compared to a woman's pregnancy and the birth of a child.

Beramaq	'wants to become pregnant'
Nyeloi	'starts to be pregnant'
Untukng Maiiq	'slim pregnancy' (*maiiq* = thin/slim; *untukng* = pregnant)
Untukng	'pregnant'
Meet	'starts appearing'
Mentir Uraakng	'appears here and there', like prawns (*uraakng* = prawn)
Tompoq Olukng	'appears like islands' (*tompoq* = island)
Belampar	'starts bearing contents'; this step is also called 'the beauty' — *Lolakng*
Jehas	'all have appeared and are filled with contents'
Luai	young rice (luai = 'soft')

<u>*Other crops*</u>: In addition to rice, at least 150 other crop varieties are planted on the swiddens of Lempunah. These include 20 cassava varieties (*Manihot esculenta* Crantz); 15 kinds of sweet potatoes (*Ipomoea batatas* (L.) Poir.); 26 banana varieties (*Musa x paradisiaca*

69. As said before, the importance of rice cultivation might have decreased over the last decades due to additional sources of financial income. Like in Apau Ping, where Setyawati no longer found augury (*ibid.*), some well-adapted cultivation strategies might have shed the common knowledge of their underlying rationale. My informants also stated that more time was spent on the swiddens in the past.

L.); 17 sugar-cane varieties (*Saccharum* spp.); 9 cucumber varieties (*Cucumis sativus* L.); 11 chilli varieties (*Capsicum* spp.); 4 ginger varieties (*Zingiber officinale* Rosc.); and 48 other kinds of vegetables (see Annex 3).

In 1995 and 1996, 76.7 per cent of 40 households cultivated crops other than rice. On average, 31.3 varieties (standard deviation = 22.6) were grown, ranging from only one additional crop, to 106 varieties per household per year. Compared to rice, less effort is put into the cultivation of these additional cultigens, which are often eaten up by monkeys, deer or wild boars before they can be harvested. After the harvest failed in 1998, many families intensified the cultivation of cassava in extra gardens which were often fenced against pest predation. While in average years cassava is regarded as a relish of second choice, it becomes very important in years of low rice supply, as it grows fast, even on exploited soils.[70]

Several crops, like sugar-cane or bananas, are also used in subsequent years, and perennials such as fruit trees or sugar palms (*Arenga pinnata* (Wurmb.) Merr.) are used for even longer, and eventually become a *simpukng* garden over the period of fallow succession. These additional cultigens are generally planted together with rice on the newly burnt swidden (some are already planted before the burning, e.g. bananas). But in principle, many of them can be planted throughout the year, depending on seed supply and the demand of supplementing food.

Ngejikut — Weeding

Weeding is necessary in all swiddens made in fallow forests and fallow bushland, as grasses and other weeds compete with the maturing rice for nutrients, water and light. Especially if the burning was incomplete, weeds can become a major problem. Weeding is not necessary in *bengkar* forests. Generally, a swidden is only weeded once between November and January. The *ngejikut* phase can last up to six weeks and involves men and women.[71] Better-off families frequently employ *konookng* workers who are paid per weeded area (app. 100 m^2 for 5,000 Rp in 1996-7; total amount spent for *konookng* weeding 40,000 to 125,000 Rp).

70. This strategy is also known among the Kantu' (see Dove 1985a: 345).

As weeding is a labour intensive stage, it often coincides with other occupations. In contrast to the Iban (Sutlive 1992: 77), weeding is not done exclusively by women, and men also participate. Hence, in years of increased cash demand (e.g., after a failed harvest) there is a conflict of interest between creating income (e.g., by tapping rubber or collecting rattan), and increasing the chances of a good harvest through weeding. This conflict might even lead into a vicious circle, as poor weeding (*kejomooq*) will lead to another poor harvest, which will again increase the demand for financial income in the following year.

Durukng Umaq — Guarding

Weeds are not the only problems that endanger a sufficient harvest. *Fig.* 3.10 illustrates locally-ranked pest problems for different years.

These problems are redressed by several means. Some swiddens are fenced in order to keep large mammals such as wild boar (*Sus barbatus*) or deer (*Cervus unicolor*, *Muntiacus* spp., *Tragulus* spp.) out of the field. Spear traps (*potiiq*) are installed around the field.[72] If no fence is made, small trees and forest undergrowth are slashed in a way that twigs and branches reach out of the swidden in order to prevent deer from entering the swidden. This defense is called *bentiakng* (see the *perimpah* bush fence of the Kantu', Dove 1985a: 252-3).

---

71. Dove (1985: 231) gives an average 49 working days per hectare for the Kantu'.

72. Dove reports that 62 per cent of all deer and pig taken in hunting were caught in or near the swiddens of the Kantu' (1985: 239). No data are available for Lempunah, but pigs were frequently killed close to swiddens.

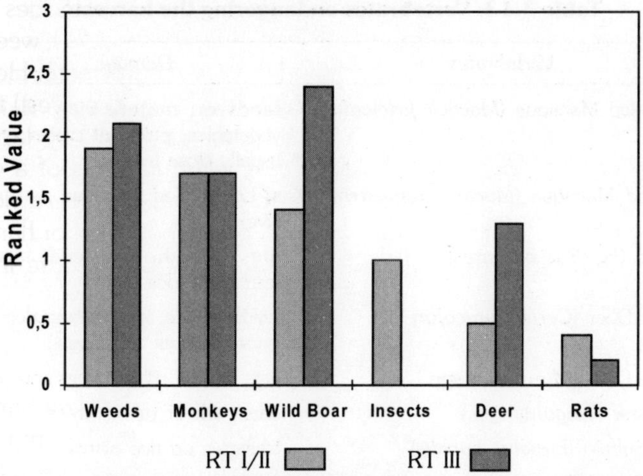

***Fig.* 3.10: Average of locally ranked (0-3, 3 = strong impact) pest problems in 1995-6**

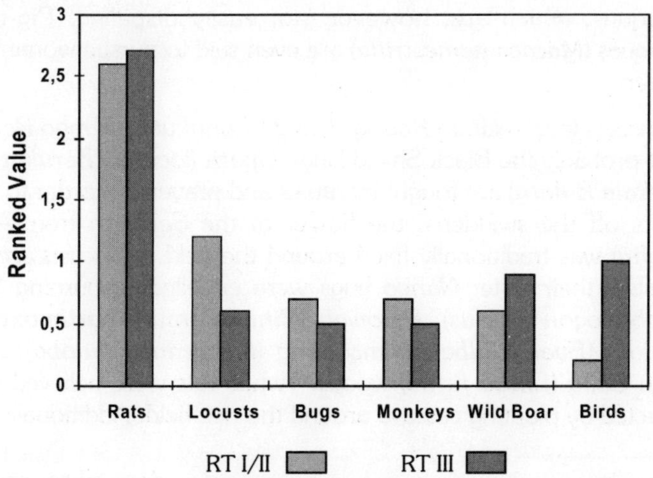

***Fig.* 3.11: Average of locally ranked (0-3, 3 = strong impact) pest problems in 1998-9**

Table 3.13: Vertebrates endangering the harvest[73]

Vertebrates	*Damage*
Long-tailed Macaque (*Macaca fascicularis*)	feeds on mature rice, fruit and vegetables, pulls out cassava tubers, usually close to rivers
Pig-tailed Macaque (*Macaca nemestrina*)	s. Long-tailed Macaque, away from rivers
Bearded Pig (*Sus barbatus*)	digs out shoots, feeds also on immature rice
Sambar Deer (*Cervus unicolor*)	feeds on rice; knocks over rice plants (more difficult to harvest)
Barking Deer (*Muntiacus* spp.)	eats bark of rubber trees and cassava
Mousedeer (*Tragulus* spp.)	eats bark of rubber trees
Water Buffalo (*Bubalus bubalis*)	tramples on rice plants
Munia (*Lonchura* spp.)	feeds on rice grains
Tree Sparrow (*Passer montanus*)	feeds on rice grains
Mice (*Mus* spp.)	feeds on harvest and roots
Rats (*Rattus* sp.)	feeds on harvest and roots

In addition, the swiddens are guarded by people, dogs and cats. In cases of associated fields, neighbours also keep an eye on each other's swiddens. Rodent poison is occasionally used to fight macaques, which are, however, not easily dispelled. Pig-tailed Macaques (*Macaca nemestrina*) are even said to pursue women and children.

Insects (e.g., *Nango Kodoq*; *Nango Longkueh*; *Nango Rangau* (most probably the Black Shield Bug); *Upatn* (locusts); *Berukat*; and *Tengkala Bulatn*) are fought by rituals and prayers. In order to keep locusts off the swiddens, the flower of the *Sepootn* tree (*Areca catechu*) was traditionally fixed around the field, as locusts are said to dislike their taste. *Nango* bugs were expelled by burning *Serai* (*Cymbopogon nardus*), *Perowali* (*Cinnamomum partenoxylon*), *Potukng* (*Evodia alba*), *Nancaakng* (*Macaranga triloba*), *Ayau Bulau Baliq* (*Litsea firma*) woods,[74] while rats were believed to be distracted by planting cassava around the rice field. Additionally, rice

73. Pigs, monkeys and deer were also reported by Colfer (1997: 120-3) as major predators for cultigens in Kenyah villages.

74. *Serai* and *Perowali* are woods with a strong fragrance, while *Potukng* and *Nancaakng* are of general ritual importance.

for the *meruaq* souls (= *liau* souls) was ritually offered up to three times a year in order to keep pests (mainly rodents) away.

However, nothing helped in early 1998, when a substantial part of the harvest was destroyed by locusts and rodents.[75] Sutlive also reports from the Iban (1992: 79-80) that: 'Despite the rituals and techniques aimed at guarding the fields, some of each year's crops is inevitably lost to insects, animals, and birds'. Similarly, Dove (1985: 243) states: 'The poisoning of insect pests is never more than partially successful in the swamp swiddens and is even less effective in the dryland swiddens.'

Although there is a certain acceptance of pest predation among the Benuaq of Lempunah, which is mythically linked to man's leadership among the living beings,[76] I was frequently asked whether I knew of a strong poison to help them kill the pests. It is important to mention that even the most diverse fields containing up to 11 rice varieties was no better off than swiddens with only one rice variety. A diversification of varieties could not reduce the pest damage (see also Brown & Marten 1986: 252-9). Even the temporal synchronisation of the swidden work, also reported by Dove (1985: 244-5) and by Sutlive (1992: 71), did not help in 1998 and 1999. In less extreme years, this strategy might however dilute pest pressure on individual fields. Yet, after the forest fires, many predators like snakes or civets, were still rare. Hence, there was little to prevent the rodent populations from increasing.

Ngotapm — Harvest

The harvest starts depending on the maturity of the cultivated varieties in February and lasts until April. However, before the actual harvest

75. In 1999-2000, the swiddens were again severely damaged by rodents. Most farmers estimated their loss at more than 75 per cent, which would only be sufficient to provide new seeds, but no food.

76. According to the *kepala adat* of Lempunah, man was declared 'King of the Animals' by the celestial deity Lantalah (Perjadiiq Bantikng Langit). However, as the King he has the obligation to share his yields with mice, monkeys, wild boar, deers and birds. In a similar way, the Iban say: 'One for the rat, one for the sparrow, one for the pig, and one for us', when they sow (Sutlive 1992: 75). Brown & Marten (1986: 242) also state: 'They [subsistence farmers in South-East Asia] often regard the animals that feed on their crops as fellow creatures with a legitimate claim to some of the produce, as long as the animals do not destroy more than 'their fair share'.

begins, immature *pulut* rice is harvested and brought to the village. Here it is fried in a pan, and later unhusked with *alu* ironwood pestles (2-2.5 m long) that are rhythmically pounded (*tempaq*, mainly done by women) into an ironwood mortar (*losukng*). The unhusked *pulut* rice is then mixed with red palm sugar (from the *Arenga pinnata* palm) and desiccated coconuts to make a delicious dish (*keloq*). This meal is part of the *ngeluikng* ritual, the bringing back of Lolakng Luikng, the rice spirit. This ritual is carried out in the individual house for the swiddens owned by the family.

After planting, the beautiful (= *lolakng*) Luikng, as well as the spirits of the other crops, move downriver where they dwell until they are called back to their respective fields. On its way back, Lolakng Luikng is accompanied by the *kelelungan* souls of the deceased. The way is described in detail to the rice spirit, including the names of all involved family members, so that it will not be mistaken by a different field (and hence bring fortune to other people). Besides, all other relevant spirits (e.g., Timang, Juata, Nayuq, Mulaakng, Tonoi, as well as the belian spirits Rajah Kenjong, Rajah Dewa, Bisu Walo, Gaib Wali, Pantung and others) have to be informed that the forest was hurt and large trees were felled in order to make a living. If they are not addressed, they would get angry and cause sickness and death.

The prayers are carried to the spiritual world by *pulut* rice (for the celestial spirits, the *pulut* is cast into the air; for the Tonoi earth spirits, it is dropped through the floor gaps; and in both cases, Lolakng Luikng mediates these prayers to the spirits). Working tools such as an axe, the *mandau* bush knife, other knives, as well as the grindstone, are symbolically fed with new rice, for having worked well and not caused harm to anyone.[77] *Keloq* and the husks of the new rice are given to the old rice to make them acquainted.[78] In the swidden, eight panicles of each rice variety (still immature) are cut and brought to the *ukop* farm house, where they are hung on the wall. These bundles are called *ayapm Luikng* — '*Luikng*'s Pangolin' and are meant to delight Luikng as toys (Ind. *mainan*).

---

77. While it was stated earlier that the Benuaq do not know thanksgiving rituals, this ritual is an exception (as well as the songs for Lolakng Luikng).

78. This ritual is also reported by Weinstock (1983: 45) for the Luangan, where it is called *kerwaiyu*.

Although harvesting is perceived as exhausting labour,[79] it is done in a cheerful way with much teasing and the singing of funny songs (mainly by women), as well as thanksgiving songs for Lolakng Luikng. Labour exchange (*plou*) and wage work (*konookng*[80]) are common. Both men and women work together moving downhill. The rice ears are cut with a special finger knife (*isip*) and collected in a rattan basket (*gamaq*), which is tied to the hip. When the *gamaq* is full, the ears are given into a bigger rattan basket (*amoq*), in which it is transported to the farm house (*ukop*). Here it is stored separately for each swidden member, and later threshed (*neek pare*, by stepping on the panicles that are spread on a plaited rattan mat), and winnowed (*nyoet/niyau*, empty husks are blown away when the rice is thrown up on a round *lewakng* plate made of rattan). Afterwards, the threshed and winnowed rice (*oikng*) is sun-dried (*moing*), and stored in the *ukop* until it is required in the village. In order to protect it from monkeys or human thieves, it is closed in wooden walls under the *ukop* (*kelengkikng* or *lasaq*), or in a round bark container (*ancooq* or *ongkaq*, made from the bark of an old *Bekalukng* tree).

This habit is different from many other Dayak groups (e.g., Bahau, Iban, Kantu', see Sutlive 1992: 81, Freeman 1992: 216-18, Dove 1985a: 323), who carry the whole harvest to the longhouse, where it is husked and weighted.[81] It is believed that the harvest can still be diminished by spirits,[82] theft or by pests, so several further redressings are made. If a farmer owns a magical stone (generally very round and smooth), it can be stored together with the harvest in order to protect it. In addition, several often fragrant plants such as *Berowali*

79. According to a myth, in the days of Puteri Siluuq, it was sufficient that the heroine cooked rice leaves which came by themselves to the *ukop* hut following rattan strings. However, Olooq, the wife of Siluuq's brother Ayus, once looked into the cooking pot, although she was forbidden to do so. After this offence, Siluuq transformed Olooq into a dog and left her downstream where she brought wisdom to the town people, while the people of the interior were left with the crude knowledge of Ayus. Since then, harvesting rice is much more exhausting than it used to be.

80. Generally, one *beleq* (app. 11 kg) of unhusked rice, or its equal in Rupiah, is paid per working day.

81. Thus, accurately quantifying the harvest was not possible for farmers in Lempunah. Estimates were made by the farmers some months later after hulling.

82. The possibility that rice can be diminished after the harvest is also reported by Sutlive for the Iban (1992: 83).

(*Cinnamomum partenoxylon*), *Koyur* (*Tetracera asiatica*), *Sekur*, *Longaq*, *Penyempur* (*Ilex* sp.), *Serai* (*Cymbopogon nardus*) and *Bekakakng* (*Melastoma malabathricum*) are given to the rice store to keep insect pests away.

Later, when there is demand for rice, parts of the harvest are carried to the village in plaited *lanjukng* rattan baskets or, more commonly nowadays, in 25 kg rice sacks. In the parties I joined, 20-55 kg of unhusked rice were carried per person (men and women, sometimes twice a day). In cases where the swiddens were very remote but accessible by road, the whole harvest was sometimes brought to the village by truck. In the village, the *oikng* rice is husked by pounding (*tempaq*) or, more often, mechanically. It is then referred to as *boyas* and ready for cooking.

YIELD AND RICE SUPPLY

The following yields of threshed, but unhusked, rice were reached on average per family[83]:

Table 3.14: Average yield in *beleq* (b, app. 11 kg) based on the amount of seeds of the same families between 1996 and 1999 (RT I/II: *n*=10, RT III: *n*=14)

	RT I/II		RT III	
1996	101 b (std = 77)	33 × seeds (std = 21)	116 b (std = 97)	37 × seeds (std = 21)
1997	67 b (std = 88)	36 × seeds (std = 27)	96 b (std = 50)	36 × seeds (std = 20)
1998	failed		failed	
1999	< 50 b	< 20 x seeds	< 50 b	< 30 x seeds

The average yield is estimated at 650-700 kg of unhusked rice per hectare per year. This is in the same range as figures given by Dove for the Kantu' (1985: 409), which range between 293 kg/ha[84] and 606 kg; and those given by Lahjie for Kenyah farmers (1996: 157), ranging between 442 kg and 2,600 kg/ha. The Kenyah data of Colfer (1997: 50-1) are a little bit larger with 783 kg/ha for young secondary forest, and up to 1,392 kg/ha in other places; while Freeman's figures (1992: 252-3) suggest that Iban farmers

83. The figures of 1996 and 1997 are estimates of the farmers, the 1999 figures are gross estimates by myself.

84. Per hectare of cleared forest.

harvest on average 20.6 times their seed amount,[85] which is also in the same order of magnitude.

All authors emphasise, however, the great variation of the yield, depending on experience, working skills (including appropriate timing), distraction by other occupations, assistance, health condition, ill-suited weather, pests, or soil fertility. The impact of these factors has been partially tested for swiddens in Lempunah, revealing a statistically-significant positive impact of forest age, probably due to a greater soil fertility and less weed problems; and a moderately positive correlation between seed amount (or as an equivalent, field size) and yield.[86] No difference in the yields was found for different soils. The whole net impact of these partially interrelated parameters affecting the rice yield of swiddens is illustrated in *fig.* 3.12.

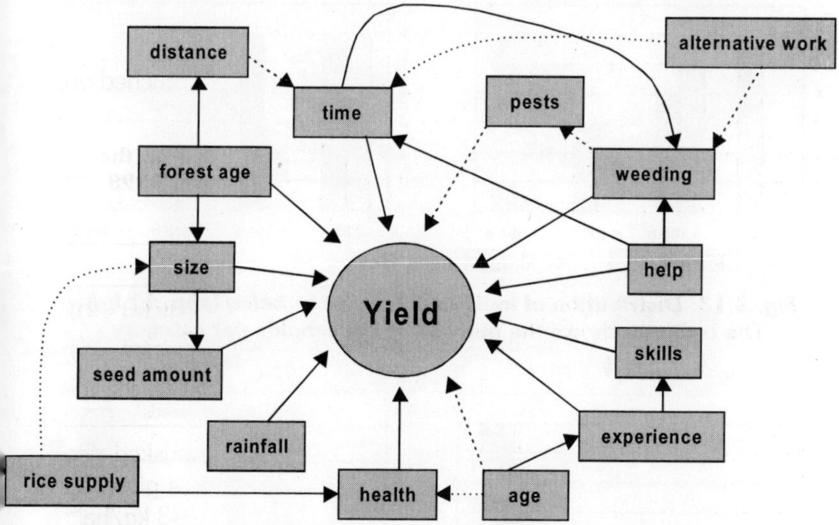

Full lines symbolise positive impacts, dotted lines symbolise negative impacts

***Fig.* 3.12: Set of partially interrelated impact parameters influencing the yield**

---

85. This figure is calculated by comparing the 343 gallons (1 gallon = 4.546 l), which equal 60 times the planted seeds (*ibid*.: 252) as a too optimistic estimate, with the average yield of 118 gallons per acre (1 acre = 0.405 ha, see page 253).

86. Although this appears to be trivial, no correlation was found by Colfer (1991: 71) for Kenyah fields in Long Ampung and Long Segar. The correlation coefficient in Lempunah was also only 0.56 for RT I/II (*n*=20) and 0.53 for RT III (*n*=28), but the correlation becomes apparent in the scatter diagram.

The most important question is whether the yield is sufficient to cover the demand for rice for another year. Interviews (n=74) revealed an average annual demand of 635 kg of husked rice for food per family. This equals to about 900 kg of unhusked rice (app. 80-5 *beleq*). Contributions to rituals and festivals require another 10 *beleq* on average,[87] plus 3 *beleq* for seeds. Hence, about 95 *beleq* or 1,045 kg of unhusked rice are required annually for an average core family. In RT I/II this objective (as a total village mean) was reached only in 1996, while RT III succeeded in 1996 and 1997. At the individual household level, only 33 per cent (RT I/II 1997) to 75 per cent (RT III 1996) of all families reached a full self-sufficiency with the new harvest.

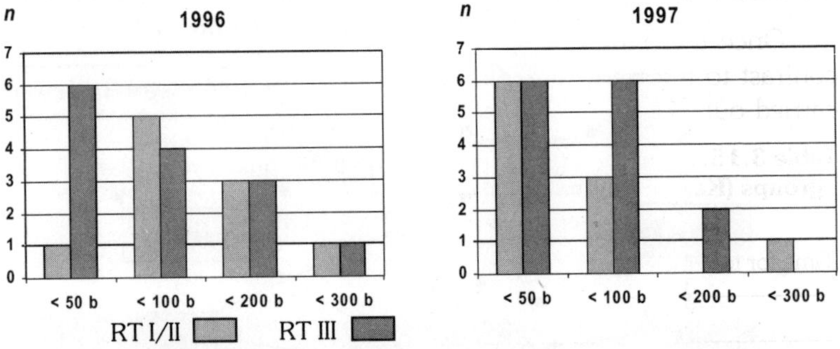

***Fig.* 3.13: Distribution of individual harvest in *beleq* (app. 11 kg). The ordinate shows the number of households per category**

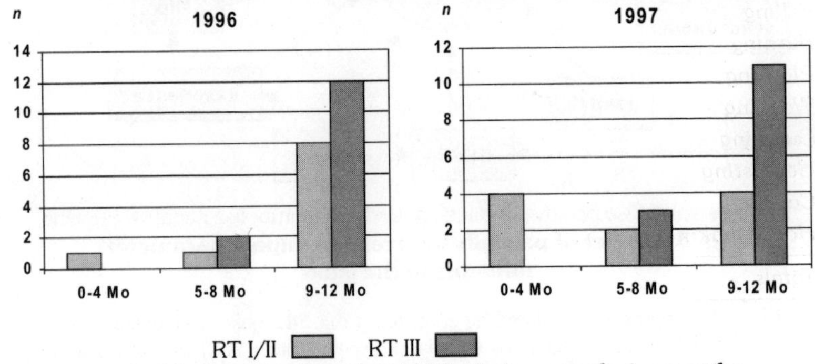

***Fig.* 3.14: Distribution of individual rice supply in months. The ordinate shows the number of households per category**

87. *Bekeleeu* and *kwangkai* rites demanded an average of 142 kg per household over a period of two years. Additionally, about 30 kg are needed for smaller healing rituals (*belian*).

Rice supply (in months starting with the previous harvest) was estimated by the farmers as illustrated in *fig.* 3.14. The high supply in RT III for 1997 is caused by rice stocks remaining from previous years.

Until the drought in 1997-8, the overall rice supply in Lempunah was secured (an average of 95 *beleq* per household for RT I/II and RT III 1996-7). The situation changed dramatically in 1998 when the harvest failed completely. Rice had to be bought at increasing prices,[88] and seeds were lost for the following season. Pests (mainly locusts and rodents) diminished the harvest in 1999, as well as in 2000. Similar pest problems, following droughts and forest fires were also reported after the drought of 1982/83 (Mayer 1989: 32).

Once the harvest is over, the year is regarded as finished.[89] In contrast to the Kenyah (Colfer 1997: 51), no thanksgiving ritual is carried out, but the period between the end of the harvest and the

Table 3.15: Estimated workdays for 1 ha, compared with other Dayak groups (Kantu' see Dove 1985: 377; Iban see Freeman 1992: 245; Kenyah see Lahjie 1996: 153-4)

Time for tool-making is not included, as figures are only provided by Dove (*ibid.*)

	Benuaq	*Kantu'*	*Iban*	*Kenyah*
Selecting	1	1	no data	no data
Slashing	6-8	8-9	12-14	1-30
Felling	2-14	4-12	10-34	1-40
Burning	1-6	1-4	1	1-3
Planting	10-12	13-15	22	9-16
Weeding	0-40	0-49	29-48	0-82
Guarding	2-10	1-4	no data	no data
Harvesting	25-45	30-49	34-48	46-105
Carrying	6-12	4-5	2-3	no data
House-making	4-36	3-4	no data	no data
Totals	*57-184*	*73-143*	*> 110-170*	*>50-165*

88. Due to the shortage and the Indonesian financial crisis, the price of rice increased four-fold. In the end of 1999 it was still three times higher than before the crisis.

89. Similarly, the Kantu' also change the name of a swidden from *umai* to *memudai* after the harvest is completed (Dove 1985a: 265).

start of a new agricultural cycle is frequently used for other religious festivities, such as a *guguq tautn*, which includes prayers and offerings for a successful *new* year. Although workdays were not measured exactly, estimates of several informants are summarised and compared with Kantu', Iban and Kenyah data in Table 3.15.[90]

CLOSING REMARKS

The interdependencies of aspects in the swidden-related decision-making processes are summarised in *fig*. 3.15. This complex web is an overlay of many individual cases, which remains open to future additions.

Each connecting line in *fig*. 3.15 represents a causal relation described earlier. Those lines with an arrowhead are unilinear cause-effect relations (mainly positive, some negative), while the plain lines indicate a causal relation that is not necessarily directed. The purpose of this web is to visualise the complex character of the decision-making processes. Every decision is an individual trade-off between many aspects, which cannot be understood by a simplistic decision-making chain, as preferences and priorities depend on too many different factors. Nevertheless, there are certain common patterns despite the great individual variation. These patterns, also including other off-farm resource activities will be discussed later (see sub-section. 'Temporal Patterns' under chapter 4).

The illustration does not show preferences,[91] but is meant to sketch out the dimension of causal relations within decision-making in swidden agriculture. Starting from this comprehensive level, a researcher can easily identify the major factors related to more specific problems, for which this web provides the frame of a contextualised analysis. The deeper an analysis will get, the more details and causal links can be added to the web. However, the degree of interconnectivity

---

90. The estimate of guarding time was made by myself. However, this figure is somewhat vague as there is much overlap with other occupations such as tool-making, weeding, or harvesting.

91. This could be done by weighting the connecting lines. However, in this study, such a weighting would have had a certain 'expert' quality that is not based on quantitative parameters, but on mere subjective estimations. All the same, the existence of causal connections can be derived directly from qualitative and semi-quantitative data.

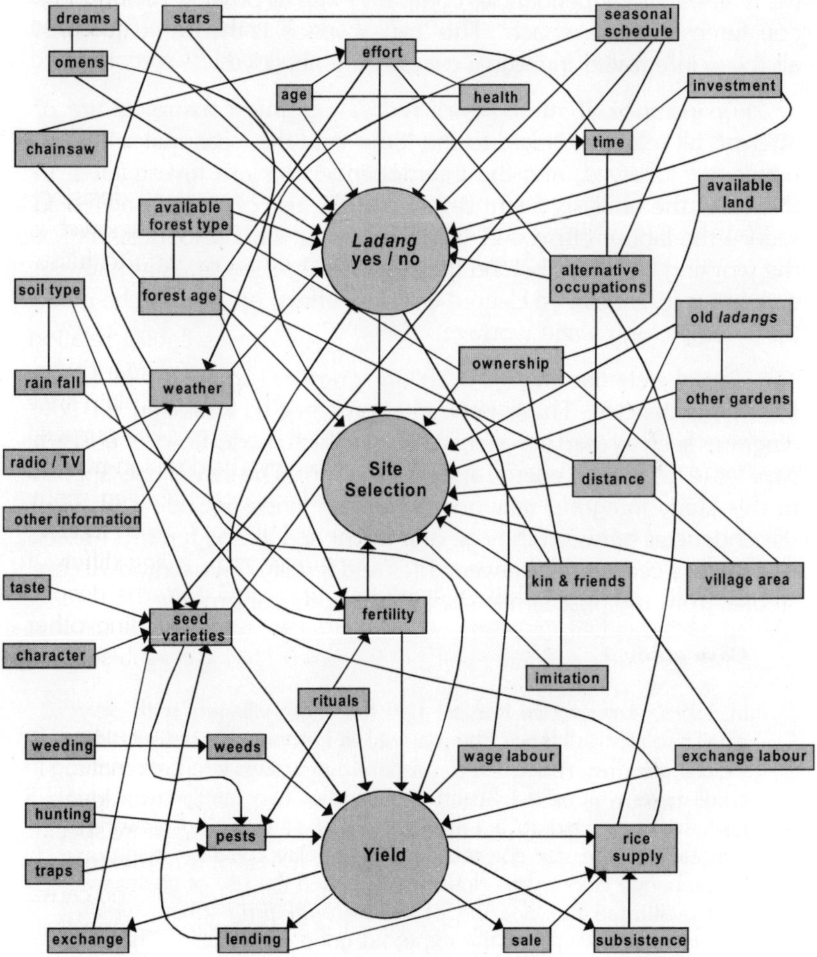

***Fig.* 3.15: Interdependencies in the decision-making processes of a swidden cycle**

is limited. Not everything is related to everything else. The fraction of the realised interdependencies compared with all possible connections constitutes a 'causal space'. This 'causal space' is the frame in which all these integrated individual cases are embedded.

For instance, if strategies of redressing time constraints are of interest, all relations linked to the 'time' and the 'seasonal schedule' boxes are followed, and the interdependencies are investigated. In this case, the analysis might reveal that the use of a chainsaw could reduce the labour effort and save time, if the stars also indicate that the working steps are behind the prescribed schedule. Alternatively, a younger forest can be cleared with less effort, or time can be made up by employing wage workers.

Causal nets like in *fig.* 3.15 are graphic summaries of causal interdependencies. These networks must not be mistaken for flow diagrams such as used in systems theory, which model flows of uniform variates (e.g., matter, energy and information). The causal nets applied in this study integrate relations of various kinds, including physical dependencies between the age of a forest and its soil fertility, as well as cognitive connetions between rites and fertility. Two individual case studies from my host family shall illustrate this approach:

Case study 1

In 1995, a poor rice harvest had left most villagers with only small rice stocks. Hence, the majority of Lempunah's households, including farmer *A* decided to prepare a new swidden. Land right conflicts as well as the health problems of two family members had, however, led to a temporal delay of the land clearing, indicated by the star constellation. This delay could be made up by exchange labour with close relatives, and the use of chainsaws that facilitated the clearing of old *kerengkakng* forest, which was chosen because of the expected good soil fertility. The site was further selected considering a reasonable walking distance (app. 1.5 hours) and the ownership. As the area belonged to *A*'s family, it was possible to enrich the swidden with rattan, fruit and rubber in order to establish permanent forest gardens. Indeed, the relatively good soil fertility and sufficient rain-fall resulted in a good harvest, which filled the empty rice stocks. Pests and weeds diminished the harvest only slightly as they were redressed with guarding, traps, and weeding.

Case study 2

In October 1997, everything indicated a serious drought. It had not rained since June, and the mass media news that reached Lempunah spoke of a strong El Niño event which was believed to last well into 1998. Hence, most households in Lempunah had decided not to prepare swiddens as they feared that the crops would not grow. Farmer *A* had also hesitated to continue with his field preparations. However, as he already had paid for the clearing of his site he was undecided how to continue. The site was located close to a transmigration site, approximately 20 km from Lempunah. Farmer *A* had a swidden there the year before, together with several of his close relatives, who also joined him in 1998. Although access to this site was difficult (7 hours of walking, or irregular transports by truck or motorbike), the old *bengkar* forest promised high yields. Then, in early November, farmer *A* visited his site a last time to take back some equipment. But when he saw the cleared site, he remembered the amount of money he had already invested. So finally, he decided to plant rice despite all the bad weather prognoses. His intention was to harvest at least the seeds for 1998. Yet, the drought continued, and farmer *A*, as well as the few other farmers who tried their luck, suffered a complete crop failure.

Simpukng forest gardens

Simpukng or *lembo* (Ind.) forest gardens are a traditional and important part of the Benuaq's resource system (see Sardjono 1990). In Lempunah, their size is on average 0.1 ha (*n*=26).[92] They consist of wild-growing, semi-cultivated or planted, useful trees (e.g., fruit trees, or *tanyut* [*luatn*] 'honey trees'[93]). Other plants such as herbal, medicinal or ritual plants, and animals are used as well (see Sardjono 1990: 47), although their use is not confined to forest gardens, but occurs across the whole forest.

Simpukng can be established in two different ways. Fruit trees

92. In Barong Tongkok (Dayak Benuaq and Tonyoi/Tunjung), an area approximately 70 km north-west of Lempunah, the average size ranges between 0.1 ha and 2 ha (Sardjono 1990: 65).

93. Several tall-growing tree species, such as *Koompassia excelsa*, are used by bees for attaching their combs. These trees are owned individually and the usufruct is restricted to the owner.

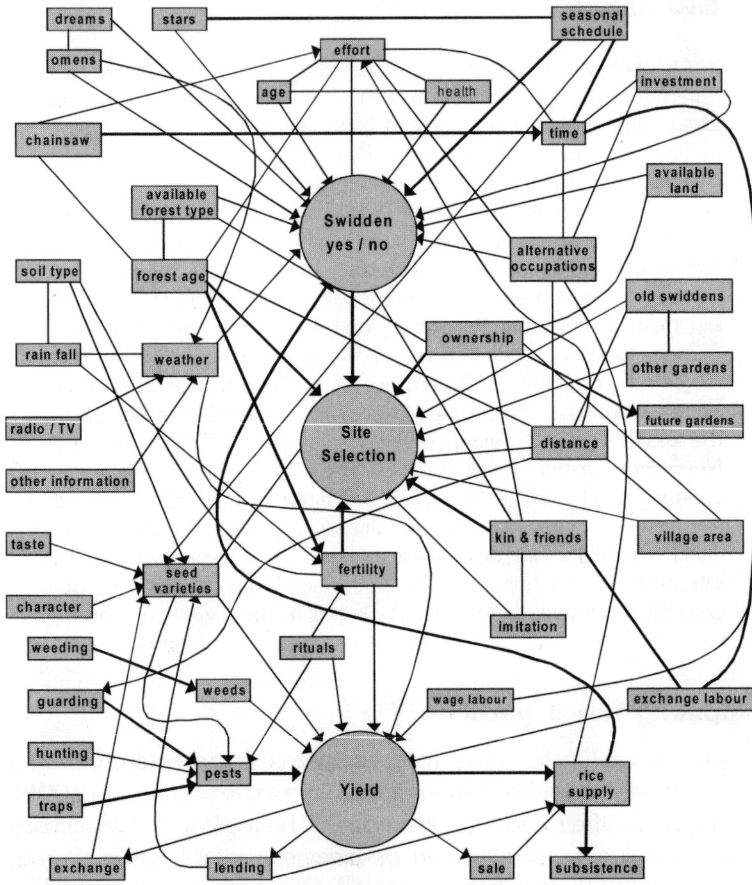

***Fig.* 3.16: Causal links relevant in case study 1 (1995-6) are indicated by bold lines**

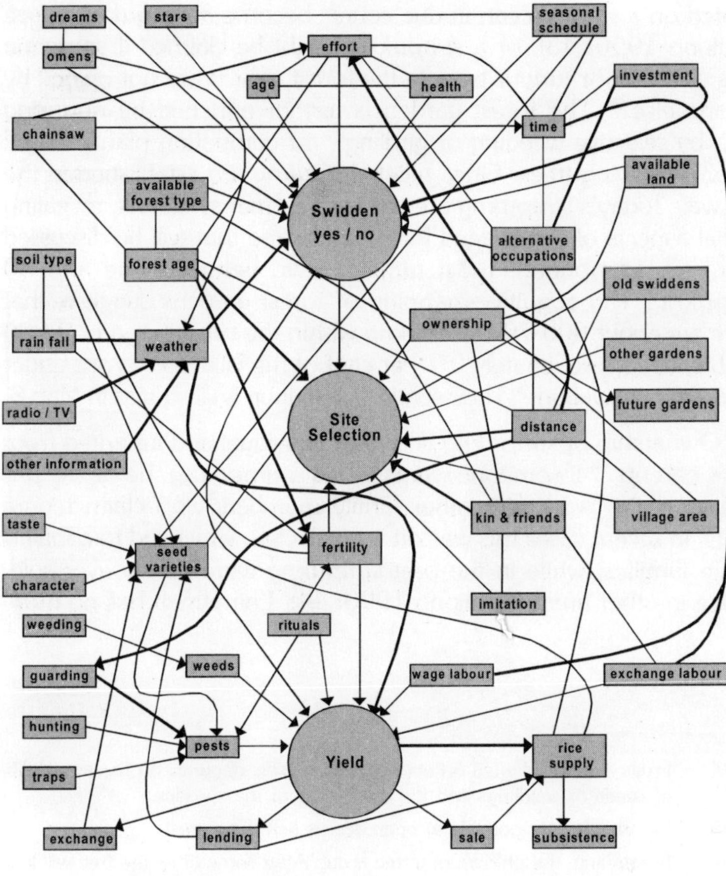

***Fig.* 3.17: Causal links relevant in case study 2 (1997-8) are indicated by bold lines**

planted on a swidden can in due course become a *simpukng*[94] (see Sardjono 1990: 43), or a *simpukng* might be claimed if someone finds wild fruit or *tanyut* trees in the forest, which are not owned by anyone else.[95] The forest garden is further enriched by nurturing (e.g., by selective weeding or girdling[96] of competing plants) useful but wild-growing trees. Since most *simpukng* are established in the first way, today's *simpukng* are traces of former swiddens, revealing spatial aspects of a managed forest landscape that will be discussed later.[97] In Lempunah, most families own between one and 30 *simpukng*. The cognitive-mapping of forest gardens suggests that there are about 600-700 *simpukng* within the village area of 9,200 ha. Hence, approximately 0.7 per cent of the village area are under *simpukng* cultivation.[98] Their spatial distribution is illustrated in Map 8.

Ownership of *simpukng* is usually individual and inherited from one's parents.[99] If someone wants to sell a *simpukng*, he or she has to discuss the issue with other family members who claim tenure rights. In recent cases this was often neglected, which led to conflicts within families, while in the past *simpukng* were hardly ever sold. Unlike in other areas (Sardjono 1990: 44), Lempunah has no more

94. Fruits are not planted on every swidden. This depends on the availability of seeds or seedlings and the ownership of the swidden.

95. I.e., this is only possible in open access *bengkar* forest.

96. By girdling, the phloem of a tree is cut. After some time, the tree will lose its leaves and sunlight is increased on the forest floor.

97. A similar landscape dotted with forest gardens called *mawa'n* that mark 'where dwellings were located many decades or even a century or so ago' was reported by Pinedo-Vasquez & Padoch (1996: 335) for the Balai subdistrict in West Kalimantan. Like among the Benuaq, these forest gardens also originate from fruit gardens that surrounded permanent or temporary settlements (e.g., field huts).

98. If the immediate area close to the village is regarded, the area under fruit gardens is in the same range as in a Dayak village in West Kalimantan, where 4 per cent of the managed forests (1,800 ha studied, i.e., within 3.3 km around the village) are used in a similar way (Lawrence 1997: Figure 2).

99. All inherited *simpukng* should be equally divided among the children. In cases of divorce, gardens of the first marriage are divided among the children of the first marriage, and gardens of the second among the children of the second.

community *simpukng.*[100] *Simpukng* are mainly used in mast-fruiting years, when they become open access areas with usufruct for anyone who wants to eat fruits. However, it is prohibited to collect fruits in someone else's garden for commercial purposes.

It is also during these high-yielding years that *simpukng* are tended. The undergrowth is slashed and vines are cut in order to support desired trees and to facilitate the harvest of fruits. Occasionally, new trees are planted. A similar management is reported by Pinedo-Vasquez & Padoch (1996: 335) for *mawa'n* forest gardens in West Kalimantan, where weeding in gardens rich in durian (*Durio zibethinus*) also coincides with fruit harvests, while *mawa'n* with commercially-important illipe nut trees (not cultivated in Lempunah) are cleared with controlled burning. However, during most of the time, *simpukng* are left to their own dynamics, following the succession. This limited labour input results in a spatial structure resembling the natural succession of a swidden fallow.

Tree and species numbers are summarised in Table 3.16.

Table 3.16: Comparison of 4 sample plots (each 250 m²). In plot A, only species within the *simpukng* were assessed with DBH > 5 cm; species with DBH > 10 cm were assessed for the whole plot

	Plot A	*Plot B*	*Plot C*	*Plot D*
age	40 yrs	10 yrs	50 yrs	15 yrs
planted trees				
DBH >10 cm	40	64	83	91
DBH > 5 cm	45	122	128	154
wild trees				
DBH >10 cm	136	24	17	18
DBH > 5 cm	>198	116	47	29
planted species				
DBH >10 cm	4	4	17	1
DBH > 5 cm	9	11	20	2
wild species				
DBH >10 cm	37	12	10	9
DBH > 5 cm	>51	18	23	14

100. A former longhouse *simpukng* burned many years ago.

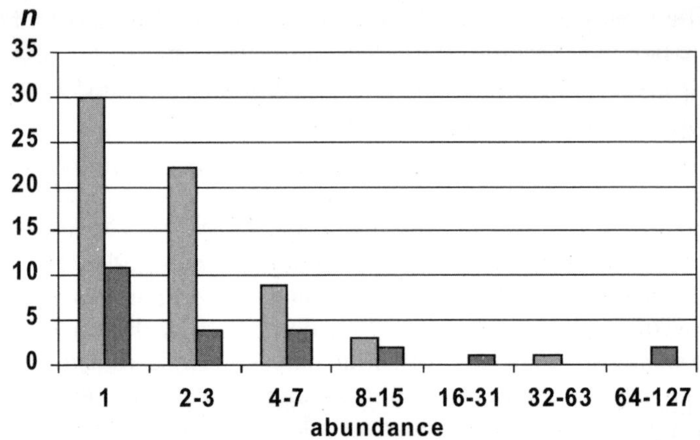

***Fig.* 3.18: Abundance distribution of planted (dark) and wild (grey) tree species (DBH > 10 cm) in 4 *simpukng* covering one ha**

With the exception of the two most dominant cultivated species, rubber (*Hevea brasiliensis*) and *Kelapapa* (*Vitex pinnata*),[101] the abundance distribution of planted species is not significantly different from the distribution of wild species. Most species are rare and only occur once or twice in the four sample plots. This reflects a permanent competition between planted and wild-growing trees, unless some of the latter are removed during a temporarily intensified management period. Superficially, a *simpukng* looks like the surrounding forest with boundaries blurred by the dense undergrowth of herbs and seedlings. It forms an undistinct, slightly manipulated island, regarding its species composition within the fallow forest succession.

101. In *simpukng A*, *B* and *C*, rubber trees (*Hevea brasiliensis*) are the most dominant species (*A*: 33 per cent of all planted trees, *B*: 71 per cent and *C*: 39 per cent), while *Kelapapa* (*Vitex pinnata*) was planted as a monoculture in *simpukng D* (99 per cent). Despite the dominance of rubber trees, these forest gardens are called *simpukng*, even though a *kebotn getah* (a real rubber garden) would only contain rubber trees as planted species. The integration of rubber trees into mixed forest gardens is also known from *mawa'n* in West Kalimantan (Pinedo-Vasquez & Padoch 1996: 336). Generally, monospecific rubber gardens have only existed for a few decades in Kalimantan, while mixed forest gardens are much older.

The spatial distribution of planted and wild trees of these four sample plots is shown in *fig*. 3.19.

Of 402 locally-differentiated plant taxa (76 plant families) that are extracted from Lempunah's forests, a minimum of 34 families with 163 species or variations are found in the *simpukng.*[102] This is comparable to the more than 100 fruit species reported by Pinedo-Vasquez & Padoch (1996: 337) for *mawa'n* forest gardens in West Kalimantan, and to Sardjono's findings from Barong Tongkok with 35 plant families and 127 woody plant species, of which 55 per cent were wild, 23 per cent semi-cultivated and 22 per cent planted (Sardjono 1990: 67).

Although most of these plant species can be used, a great diversity is not the major purpose of a *simpukng*, but rather a result of the low labour input. In fact, many *simpukng* (e.g., plot D) only consist of a few cultivated species, which are added and left to the natural succession of the swidden fallow. Yet, by limiting their labour input to the initial planting, the Benuaq (as well as other Dayak groups) have developed a very efficient way of generating desired resources by using the dynamic forces of nature. More management input could possibly enhance the yield per *simpukng*, but so far, there has been no necessity to intensify the system, as long as the mere number of these low-labour-input forest gardens is sufficiently high to cover the local demands.

Since the wild-growing species of a *simpukng* also occur elsewhere in the forest, a farmer will not necessarily go to one of his own *simpukng* to look for a certain medicinal plant, if he can find it closer to the village. *Simpukng* are integrated parts of the forest, and there is no use to differentiate between resources within or outside a *simpukng*, as long as the usufruct is the same.[103] The situation in this

---

102. Data drawn from the four sample plots (at least 25 planted and 75 wild-growing tree species (DBH > 5 cm), 8 rattan and 1 bamboo species), as well as from interviews.

103. According to the traditional *adat* law, swidden fallows (including *simpukng*) belong to the person who first cleared the respective primary forest (or his descendents). Hence, there is no legal difference between a simpukng and the surrounding fallow. However, in due course, a difference can occur, when the fallow is lent to someone else, and claims to the usufruct are later made by both parties. In general, it appears that the ownership of simpukng is more easily recognised (also by companies and governmental institutions) than that of a swidden fallow.

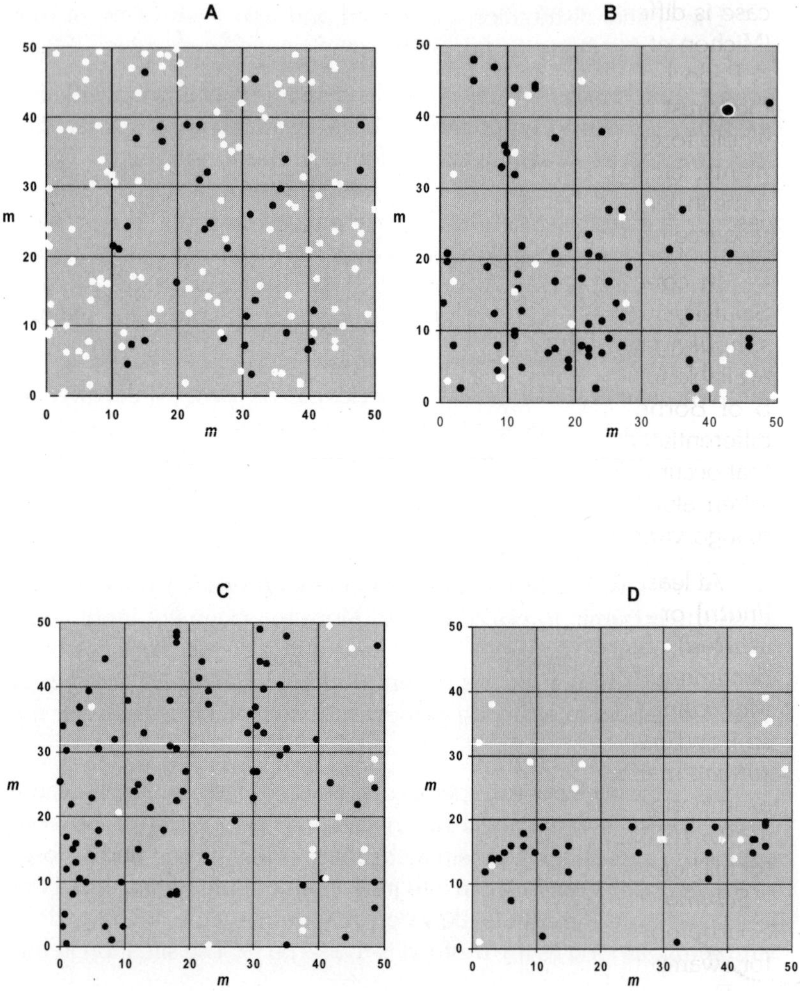

Note: Herbal plants and seedlings are not depicted!

***Fig.* 3.19: Distribution of planted (black) and wild (white) trees (DBH > 10 cm) in 4 plots containing *simpukng* of different age: 40 years (A), 10 years (B), 50 years (C, enriched with rubber trees ten years ago) and 15 years (D, only consisting of *Vitex pinnata*)**[104]

104. Data for *B*, *C* and *D* were gathered by Kori Basuki (1999 unpublished).

case is different from more intensively-used landscapes in Sumatra (Michon *et al.* 1986: 246-9) and West Kalimantan (Pinedo-Vasquez & Padoch 1996: 334), where many functions have to be covered by the forest garden. Around Lempunah, these are still covered by the whole forest landscape (e.g., supply of building material, medicinal plants, etc.). However, if the rate of land conversion remains the same in Jempang subdistrict, the importance of *simpukng* as a general resource-providing system will also increase in Lempunah.

In contrast to the market-oriented forest gardens studied by Salafsky in West Kalimantan (1994), the specific purpose of a *simpukng* in Lempunah is to have fruit trees or *tanyut* [*luatn*] trees available for food production. Among the most valued fruit trees are 5 of Borneo's 18 *Durio* species (durian), as well as 18 locally-differentiated *Mangifera* taxa (at least 8 of the 16 mango species that occur in Borneo). The fruit are mainly for personal consumption (often along the path), although in mass-fruiting years durian and mango varieties are also sold.[105]

At least ten tall-growing tree species are known locally as *tanyut* [*luatn*] or 'honey' trees: *Aput* (*Dipterocarpus* sp.); *Bilaas* (*Ficus albifila*); *Butakng Metapm* (*Shorea* sp.); *Lomuuq* (*Canarium decumanum*); *Lutukng* (*Alstonia* sp.); *Marlangat* (*Anisoptera* sp.); *Merjaakng* (*Sindora* sp.); *Puti* (*Koompassia excelsa*); *Tae* (*Canarium* sp.); and *Tempudau* (*Dipterocarpus* sp.). The blossoms of rice (*Oryza sativa*), maize (*Zea mays*) and at least another 12 plants are known as important for bees (mainly *Apis dorsata*[106] see Lahjie & Seibert 1990: 153, Koeniger *et al.* 1998: 24). Six plant species are reported for hill honey (*waniiq saikng*: *Lempukng Akas* — *Shorea* sp.; *Nagaaq* - *Schima wallachii*, *Ngoiiq* — *Dryobalanops* sp.; *Pengeraya* — *Spatholobus percicinus*; and *Puti* — *Koompassia excelsa*), and six for swamp honey (*waniiq lerap*: *Jelomaaq* — *Eugenia* sp.; *Juaaq* — *Daemonorops halleriana*, *Kedemaaq* — *Adina minutiflora*, *Prupuq* — *Barringtonia* sp.; and *Putat* — *Barringtonia* sp.). Only one species — *Koompassia excelsa* — offers blossoms and the site for honeycombs. *Koompassia excelsa* is also the most important and

105. Between 1996 and early 2000, no mass-fruiting occurred. Hence, I have no good data on the economic importance of traded fruits, which most people ranked rather low.

106. Two more species (one stingless) are known locally but so far remain unidentified.

revered *tanyut* tree, which can grow up to 84 m (MacKinnon *et al.* 1996: 179). It is the female ritual equivalent to ironwood (*Eusideroxylon zwageri*), and it is said to originate from the heart of a human being.

Collecting honey depends on the season, which is related to the flowering of the plants listed above. In order to climb the tall *tanyut* trees, hard pegs (about 3 cm thick and 25-30 cm long, see Lahjie & Seibert 1990: 155) usually made of ironwood (*Eusideroxylon zwageri*) or bamboo are knocked into the tree, which will be overgrown by the tree's callus tissue and bark and produce a kind of stairway in due course. Alternatively, the *tanyut* tree is climbed from a neighbouring smaller tree by casting a thin nylon rope (*tali jau*), weighed down with a stone or piece of wood (*bontakng*), around a branch of the taller tree. A thin rattan rope (*luyatn*) is tied to the nylon rope and pulled over the branch. At the end of the *luyatn*, a ladder made of rattan is fixed (*kerapai*) by which the *tanyut* tree can now be accessed. Fuming torches are used to dispel the stinging bees, while the honeycombs are let down in baskets to the ground (often with the help of wooden counter-weights, see Lahjie & Seibert 1990: 156), where the honey is squeezed and stored in plastic cans. Old trees can have up to 60 honeycombs,[107] each containing 5-25 litre of honey. The tangy-tasting honey is partially consumed by the family, and partially sold at local market prices between 5,000 Rp (1996-7) and 10,000 to 15,000 Rp (1998-9) per litre. Assuming an average annual production of 200 litres,[108] a mature *tanyut* tree can provide several million Rupiah of income. However, climbing *tanyut* trees is dangerous, and the job is frequently compared with the women's hazard during childbirth. When a climber who assists the owner of a *tanyut* tree falls to his death, the ownership of that tree is transferred to his bereaved family.

Another sweet produce from *simpukng* is *gula meaq*, or red palm sugar, derived from the *tuak* (Ind. *aren*) palm (*Arenga pinnata*). This tree does not have to be planted as its seeds are dispersed by the faeces of civet cats (*Viverridae*) in forest clearings. A saccharose-containing sap is gained from tapping the inflorescence stalks. In order to enhance the sap flow, the peduncle of the inflorescence is

---

107. Tingek in Koeniger *et al.* (1998: 29) reports 50-100 combs per tree, Lahjie & Seibert (1990: 155) speak of 50 combs.

108. Lahjie & Seibert report a range of 50 to 300 litres per year (*ibid.*).

swung and beaten for about two weeks[109] in an individual rhythm (e.g., 3 days swinging — *ngupi kami tuak* — 'shaking the hands of the tuak palm', 1 day of soft-beating with a wooden hammer — *ngentur*). Then the inflorescence is cut twice a day with a sharp knife (*ngetus*), and a bamboo tube is fixed to the end to collect the sap. The sap is evaporated over fire. When the sugar turns dark red it is poured into wooden moulds and later wrapped in palm leaves to packages of approximately 1 kg each. A single tree is said to produce 25-40 litre per day[110] (the unit is a *bane* — a bamboo internode of approximately 2 litres), which yield up to 5 kg of sugar.[111] The produce is used for sweetening rice cakes (during large religious festivals such as *kwangkai* or *guguq tautn*, but also for general sweets), *keloq* rice or snacks (e.g., fried cassava). It is traded locally at prices between 1,000 Rp (1996) and 4,000 Rp (1999-2000). Further, the palm juice is savoured as a refreshing beverage. In Lempunah, it is not generally fermented to make palm wine as it is in other areas in Borneo.

Mixed forest gardens are found all over Borneo (East Kalimantan: Sardjono 1990, Lahjie 1996; West Kalimantan: Salafsky 1993, 1994, Lawrence *et al.* 1995, Momberg 1993, Padoch & Peters 1993, Padoch & Pinedo-Vasquez 1996, Peluso & Padoch 1996, Pinedo-Vasquez & Padoch 1996; Sarawak: Harrison 1962), as well as in other parts of the tropics (West Sumatra: Michon *et al.* 1986, Michon & Mary 1990; Central Sumatra: Werner 1997; West Java: Christanty *et al.* 1986; Peru: Boster 1983). Their commercial value depends on their integration into the markets of the respective sites, ranging from mere subsistence (e.g., most of the time in Lempunah) to almost cash crop status (e.g., some forest gardens in West Kalimantan, see Salafsky 1994).

Most of these forest gardens originate from fruit gardens around former settlements and farm houses which have been abandoned (e.g., Pinedo-Vasquez & Padoch 1996: 335), although forest gardens

---

109. There is a great regional variation in the length of this period, between a few days and several weeks (Smits in Flach & Rumawas (eds.) 1996: 57).

110. Smits (*ibid.*) reports 60 litres per day for large palms. In areas specialised in palm sugar production, such as in North Sulawesi, 25 t of sugar are yielded annually per hectare (*ibid.*).

111. The sap contains 5-21 per cent sugar (*ibid.*: 55).

may also be established far from any settlement (see this study). However, in many cases, there is a continuous transition from house or home gardens to forest gardens, which is also observed by Salafsky, who sees these two garden forms along a gradient (1994b: 264); while Sardjono (undated a: 122) differentiates between house gardens,[112] and forest gardens depending on location. Due to their origin, forest gardens like *simpukng* and *mawa'n* are scattered over often large areas, forming a patchy landscape that bears the traces of former dwellings and swiddens (see sub-section 'Spatial Patterns' under chapter 4).

Rattan gardens

RATTAN CULTIVATION IN LEMPUNAH

The cane of rattan palms[113] ranks among the most important NTFPs found in Borneo (see Godoy 1990: 164, Weinstock 1983b: 59-60, Peluso 1992: 115-16, Weidelt 1990: 26). It has been traded between Borneo and China for some 800 years[114] (Weidelt 1990: 26), until a wider international trade started in the mid-ninteenth century (Dransfield & Manokaran 1994: 16). Rattan became increasingly important as a source of financial income in East Kalimantan during the 1970s and 1980s, when a strong demand from the world market provided high farmgate prices (Peluso 1992: 119-23, Godoy & Feaw

---

112. Home gardens, which are well-studied in Java (Soemarwoto 1985a, 1985b, Abdoellah 1990, Christanty 1990), are of little importance in Lempunah. Due to common floodings, only a few families cultivate crops around their houses, while the nearby forests (closer than 1 km) are completely converted to permanent forest gardens (mainly rubber and rattan). However, some *simpukng* might historically have evolved out of home gardens, as Salafsky suspects for forest gardens in West Kalimantan (1994: 265). Yet, the home gardens of Lempunah were established around former longhouses, as well as around farm houses. Where the latter were used for several subsequent years, large *simpukng* were often the result. These remained within the regrowing forest, while new gardens were opened in other places.

113. Rattans are spiny climbing palms occurring in the Old World's tropics and subtropics. The 13 known genera (approximately 600 species) belong to the tribe *Calameae* in the subfamily *Calamoideae* of the *Palmae* family (Dransfield & Manokaran 1994: 13-15,24-5).

114. According to Hall (1985, cited in Peluso 1992: 115), NTFPs like tree resins, camphor, edible birds' nests, and incense woods were extracted and traded from the interior of Borneo at least as early as the second or third century AD.

1991, Safran & Godoy 1993: 294).[115] Since then, policy implications and regional economic impacts have led to a decrease of rattan prices (see Haury & Saragih 1997).

While many wild-growing rattans are extracted from the forest, *Sokaq* (Ind. *Rotan Sega* — *Calamus caesius*) — has also been cultivated in special forest gardens for more than two hundred years (Fried 1995: 93). The most famous rattan gardens of East Kalimantan are found in the districts of Pasir and Kutai (Bentian Besar, Damai, and Jempang), while the gardens of Central Kalimantan are located around Sampit, as well as in the Barito Basin.[116] In Lempunah two of the 28 locally-used rattan taxa are frequently cultivated, another four are planted occasionally.[117]

Table 3.17: Cultivated rattan species in Lempunah

Benuaq	*Indonesian*	*Scientific Name*	*Cultivation*
Sokaq	Sega	*Calamus caesius*	common
Jepukng	Pulut Merah	*Daemonorops crinita*	common
Jehap	Jahab, Irit	*Calamus trachycoleus*	occasional
Ngono	Manau	*Calamus manan*	occasional
Si'it	Sega c.f.	*Calamus* c.f. *balingensis* or *Daemonorops grandis*	occasional
Ue Merangui	Sega c.f.	unidentified	occasional

Most families in Lempunah own several (1-20) rattan gardens, mainly consisting of *Sokaq* or *Jepukng*,[118] and averaging 0.25 ha in

115. In the late 1980s, the combined annual export value of rattan from Indonesia, Malaysia, Thailand and the Philippines reached US$ 400 millions (Dransfield & Manokaran 1994: 17).

116. These gardens are said to have existed for at least 150 years (Shim & Tan 1994: 76). They also consist of *Jahab* or *Irit* (*Calamus trachycoleus*), which is planted on some 12,000 ha (*ibid.* and Godoy & Feaw 1991: 29).

117. *Calamus trachycoleus* is only planted rarely in Lempunah. It has similar properties as *Calamus caesius*, but grows in a more branched (*stoloniferous*) way (Shim & Tan 1994: 76). The processing steps are similar. In 1996 it was only traded within the subdistrict. *Calamus manan*, a solitary species that develops only one stem, is also occasionally planted, while *Si'it* and *Ue Merangui* are locally regarded as *Sokaq* sub-species and sometimes planted together with *Calamus caesius*.

118. Since these two species have different ecological demands, a garden generally consists of only one of them.

size (n=15). Rattan gardens are usually established on swiddens or as enrichment plantings in the forest. Sites are selected fitting the ecological requirements of the respective species.[119] The gardens are individually owned and inherited from parents. Map 8 illustrates the scattered distribution of rattan gardens, which reflects the spatial pattern of former activities, such as swidden cultivation or temporary settlements. This pattern is further discussed in the sub-section concerning 'Spatial Patterns' under chapter 4.

The seeds of *Sokaq* can be planted in 2-3 cm depth before a swidden site is burnt (see also Soetarso & Amblani 1988: 63 for Bentian farmers). The burning heat probably cracks the skin of the seed and enables the plant to shoot, before weeds are too abundant.[120] Another technique is to peel off the skin and to wash the seed before planting it after burning (also reported in Tan & Shim 1994: 44). It is important that the seeds are dried well after the washing step in order to protect them from ants. In contrast to rubber, the percentage of households planting new *Sokaq* does not depend on the current farmgate price. The decision might depend rather on the availability of seeds, as well as the suitability of the respective swidden site for cultivating rattan.

Gardens are usually made close to water for transportation reasons (see also Sasaki 1997: 6), but not on wet soils. Planting distances vary individually but should be at least 5× 5 m, fitting Weidelt's findings from another Benuaq village (1990: 33).[121] At first, the young seedlings need some shadow. Once they become bigger, the garden has to be weeded and trees are sometimes girdled in order to increase light supply.[122] *Sokaq* grows in clusters of 20-60 stems (Tan & Shim

---

119. A detailed study on the ecological properties of rattan gardens is currently being conducted by Paulus Matius from UNMUL.

120. Banana layers are also generally planted before burning.

121. The recommendation of Kanwil Kehutanan is 10 × 10m (100 palms/ha), while Tan & Shim (1994: 45) use growth and yield data from commercial plantations with 500 palms per ha. Soetarso & Amblani (1988: 64) report 500-800 seedlings (or 1,500-2,000 seeds) per ha for Bentian farmers.

122. After girdling (cutting the phloem) the tree loses its leaves but remains standing for support (also reported by Sasaki 1997: 5). Godoy and Feaw (1991: 30-1) report that *Lagerstroemia* sp. is planted in Central Kalimantan for support and shade. As *Lagerstroemia* winters annually, more sunlight reaches the ground compared to other supporting trees.

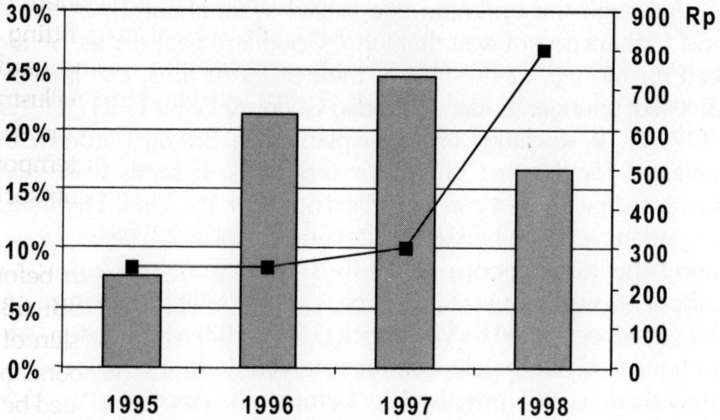

The black line indicates the average farmgate price for 1 kg of wet *Sokaq*

Fig. 3.20: Percentage of households who planted new *Sokaq*

1994: 44),[123] which can reach 20-30 metres after 12 years (Sasaki 1997: 5), and weighing more than 100 kg, although some of my informants reported smaller figures with only 10 kg per cluster after 10 years, which might only later increase to 40 or 50 kg.

On average, *Sokaq* gardens consist of 50-150 clusters yielding 2-7.5 tonnes after 15 years, depending on site conditions.[124] This figure is in the same range as the one reported by Weidelt (1990: 35) with 10 tonnes for a 10-year old garden (no size was reported). Assuming a conservative density of 400 clusters per ha with 50 kg each,[125] one hectare of *Sokaq* garden could reach a yield of 20 tonnes after 12-15 years. This equals an average growth rate of about 1.7 tonnes per hectare per year.[126] Godoy & Feaw (1991: 30) report 3.5 tonnes per hectare per year, after year 12-14 for *Calamus trachycoleus*; Soetarso & Amblani (1988: 64) speak of 3 tonnes per hectare every 2 years; while Tan and Shim (1994: 45) report 1.5 tonnes per hectare per year for commercial plantations in year 12, and thereafter.

---

123. If seeds are planted, a cluster only grows 20-30 stems (reaching 50-100 kg after 12 years) according to local informants.

124. No fertilisers are used. Local rattan farmers stated that the use of fertilisers would be counter-productive, as the stems would be too thick resulting in reduced prices.

125. Local farmers stated that some clusters can reach up to 200 kg.

126. Growth is non-linear.

Although the optimum age is said to be about 15-20 years,[127] most farmers do not wait that long. Good farmgate prices, an urgent need for money, or the fear of theft or forest fires, can lead to the harvest of younger gardens (see also Godoy & Feaw 1991: 31, Sasaki 1997: 6). If seedlings are transplanted, a *Sokaq* garden can be harvested for the first time after 6-8 years. If seeds were planted directly, a first harvest can be carried out after 10 years. Theoretically, the garden can be re-harvested after an interval of 2-5 years. However, during the rattan boom of 1986-8, all *Sokaq* in the gardens of Lempunah was harvested at once, even including immature canes. The system described by Weinstock (1983b: 63) where rattan gardens are harvested alternately from year-to-year before a new swidden is established, is not practised in Lempunah. According to Belcher (1997: 49), this mode could also not be confirmed from other case studies carried out in East Kalimantan. The interdependencies related to rattan harvesting are depicted in *fig.* 3.21.

Sokaq is collected by men who often spend several weeks in the forest until a certain area is completely harvested. On average, one man can harvest 50 kg of wet *Sokaq* per day.[128] The rattan cane is torn down from the canopy and the siliceous epidermis is removed with a mandau bush knife (see also Weidelt 1990: 34). If the cane gets stuck, the collector has to climb the tree to loosen it again (see Bayrischer Rundfunk 2000).

The harvest is then brought to the village in bundles of 70-100 kg on foot or by boat. The still 'wet' rattan is sold directly to traders,[129] or further processed to increase the value-added. Processing includes washing and polishing (generally done by women and children), and sometimes, depending on prices and demand, sulphurising and drying.[130] After drying and sulphurising, the *Sokaq* bundles are

---

127. If older, some plants might become long and precious, but others decline in quality, or even die.

128. This figure is also reported by Godoy and Feaw (1991: 31) for *Calamus trachycoleus*.

129. Rattan can also be sold directly in the forest to village middlemen, who provide transportation by boat or vehicles.

130. The cleaned rattan is sun dried. In order to preserve it against fungi and to further bleach it, bundles of *Sokaq*, covered with tight plastics, are fumigated with burnt sulphur for 1-3 days.

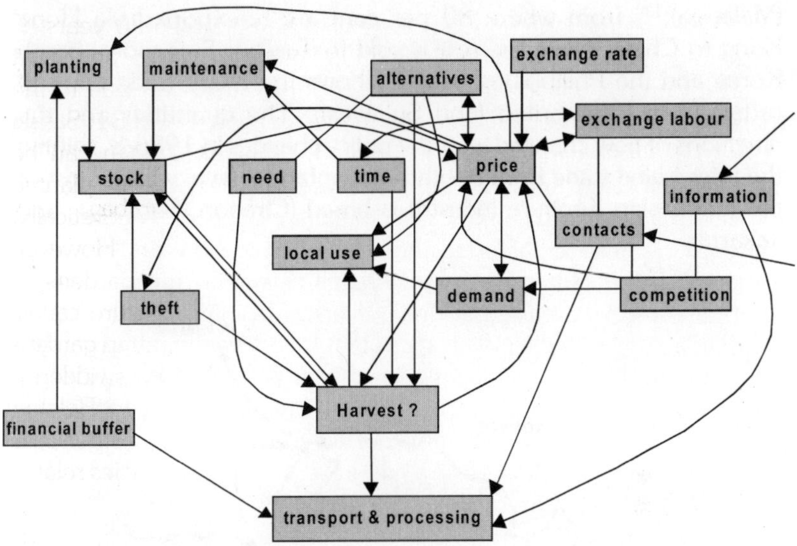

***Fig.* 3.21: Interdependencies related to rattan harvesting**

transported to Samarinda or Banjarmasin on trucks or by boat. In most cases, the transportation is done by middlemen who sell the freight to traders. Only occasionally, and in cases of good contacts, can rattan collectors bypass these middlemen and sell directly to Samarinda.[131]

Until the late 1980s, rattan used to be exported from South Kalimantan. After the virtual export ban, rattan had to be sold at much cheaper prices to the local processing industries in Java. However, an estimated minimum of 30 per cent of rattan harvested in Indonesia appears to be illegally exported to Tawau in Sabah

131. It was reported that collectors, who wanted to sell their yield directly, often received unprofitable prices in Samarinda, or even returned to their villages with an unsold freight. It appears that the Samarinda-based, mainly Chinese, buyers co-operate in order to maintain a more rigid market chain, maybe as a response to the breakdown of an earlier monopoly, where the interior of Kalimantan was less accessible and buyers could still set the price (see also Peluso 1992: 117-18).

(Malaysia),[132] from where 80 per cent are re-exported via Hong Kong to China, while the rest is sold to Taiwan, Singapore, South Korea and the Philippines. Map 5 shows the major trade flows of rattan from Kalimantan (and Sulawesi). The quantities and the directions of flow changed after the policy changes in 1986-8, shifting the inter-island trade from South Kalimantan to Java, where most of the Indonesian furniture industry is based (Cirebon, Surabaya, and Jakarta).

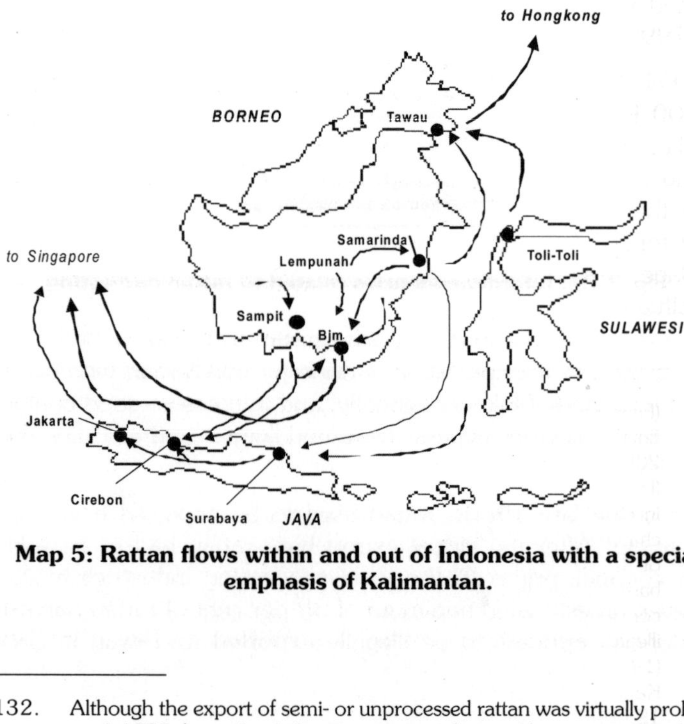

Map 5: Rattan flows within and out of Indonesia with a special emphasis of Kalimantan.

---

132. Although the export of semi- or unprocessed rattan was virtually prohibited until 1998 from the Indonesian point of view (the export tax charged from May 1992 onwards was US$ 15/kg for raw rattan and US$ 10/kg for semi-finished rattan, which equalled 250 per cent to 2,300 per cent of would-be export prices), it was allowed as barter trade from the Malaysian side. A Malaysian customs officer estimated the monthly average of 20 ships, delivering on average 70 tonnes of sulphurised rattan arriving from Kalimantan and Sulawesi. Official Malaysian data (1994-6 cited in Haury & Saragih 1997: 20), as well as unauthorisised data (from October 1997 to January 1998, my own data) show an increasing annual import of 15,000-25,000 tonnes. However, my own observations and interviews →

PROCESSING STEPS, VALUE-ADDED AND PRICE DEVELOPMENT

Although most farmers sell wet *Sokaq* directly to local middlemen, some carry out further processing steps, including washing, drying or sulphurising. Each step increases the value-added, although the risk of fluctuating prices counteracts these marginal profits. Table 3.18 illustrates the processing and transportation steps for one tonne of dry rattan (app. 2 tonnes of wet *Sokaq*). Transportation fees (SAK B/O) and taxes (IHH[133]), which further reduced profits, were officially abolished in 1998, and are only included in brackets. Prices are from early 1999.[134]

In February 1999, the profit of a local middleman reached about 200,000 Rp per tonne in cases where all processing steps were carried out by others, and no fees were paid. In early 2000, only the washing and polishing steps were carried out by wage workers. Hence, the middleman, who bears a rather high risk, earned 350,000 Rp per tonne of dry rattan at that time. By processing raw rattan in the village, the value-added can reach 1.7 to 2, depending on the price situation.[135]

→ (February 1998) of an important trader in Tawau suggest a much higher figure between 30,000 and 60,000 t (see also Haury & Saragih 1997: 20), which would be as much as 30-60 per cent of the officially exported (finished) rattan. Assuming an annual raw rattan production of 10-15,000 t in East Kalimantan (the official maximum was 13,500 t before the policy changes in 1986-8, see Haury & Saragih 1997: 13), and a production of 40-50,000 t from Sulawesi, as well as the estimation of a Tawau-based trader that similar amounts arrive from both islands, it must be concluded that most of the rattan harvested in East Kalimantan was illegally exported during the ban period! According to Haury & Saragih (1997: 15), no more than 4,000-5,000 t were sold annually to South Kalimantan-based rattan processing industries, compared with 10-12,000 t in 1987-8.

133. Iuran Hasil Hutan: forest product tax, generally imposed on all commercial forest products, although rattan derived from gardens should by definition not be included in this category (see critique in Haury & Saragih 1997: 7,20; as well as decrees cited *ibid*.: 41-2; see also Belcher 1997: 137).

134. Minister of Forestry's Decree No. 402/Kpts-IV/90, cited in Haury & Saragih 1997: 45.

135. If dry and sulphurised rattan is further processed, the value-added increases to 3.8 (for peel or core), 11.2 (for webbing and mats), up to 15.6 -18 (for furniture; see Haury & Saragih 1997: 55).

Table 3.18: Processing and trading steps for *Calamus caesius* from the forest to Samarinda (prices February 1999, the price is adjusted to dry rattan)

Processing step	*Working days*	*Costs*	*Quantity*	*Price (Rp)*
collecting	40 working days		2 tonnes of wet *Sokaq*	
buying price in the forest				1,000,000
transportation to Lempunah	usually by boat	200,000 Rp		1,200,000
buying price in Lempunah				
washing & polishing	20 working days	150,000 Rp		
drying	3-7 days	37,500 Rp	1 tonne of dry *Sokaq*	
sulphurising	1-2 days	11,000 Rp		
transportation to Samarinda	2 days	100,000 Rp		
(IHH royalties		65,000 Rp)		
(SAK B/O		50,000 Rp)		
sum of costs including fees		613,500 Rp		
sum of costs without fees		498,500 Rp		
buying price in Samarinda		1,700,000 Rp		

Between 1988 and 1999, farmgate prices fluctuated substantially in Lempunah. A first boom occurred between 1986 and 1988, when farmgate prices of unprocessed *Sokaq* reached 750 Rp per kg. At that time, this was equivalent to almost 2 kg of rice. The price dropped in 1989 to less than 400 Rp, and remained low until 1997, when one kg of *Sokaq* only equalled 250 g of rice. Mainly induced by the devaluation of the Rupiah and lowered export restrictions,[136] farmgate prices started to increase again with a temporary maximum of 800-

136. In 1998 the export tax was reduced to 30 per cent for all rattan species as part of an economic deregulation agreement with the IMF. A reduction of export and administrational fees was also promoted by the GTZ-SFMP (see Haury & Saragih 1997), and Natural Resource Management (NRM) project of USAID.

1,000 Rp per kg in October 1998 without, however, increasing the purchasing power as one kg was only sufficient to buy 300 g of rice. Since then, prices fell again to 500 Rp (equalling 200 g of rice), probably caused by a re-strengthening Rupiah (see *fig.* 3.22).

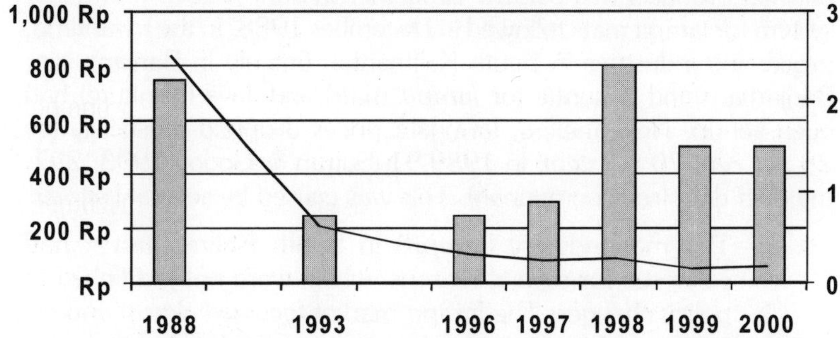

The black line indicates the ratio between rice and rattan prices per kg

***Fig.* 3.22: Price development for *Sokaq* (*Calamus caesius*) in Lempunah**

THE RATTAN CRISIS 1989-98

Until 1989, Indonesian rattan farmers and collectors profited from a strong demand for exports, especially after competing countries like Malaysia, Thailand and the Philippines had banned the export of unprocessed rattan in order to increase downstream processing. Although the Indonesian government discussed a similar step for many years, export of raw material was still possible until 1986, while the export of unwashed and unsulphurised rattan had already been prohibited in October 1979.[137] This led to a high income at the farmgate, but also to overexploitation and the invasion of external collectors who did not recognise traditional land rights (see Peluso 1992: 120).

Then in October 1986, a ban was imposed by the Indonesian government on the export of washed and sulphurised rattan in order to encourage investments in rattan industries for an increase in added value (see Nasendi 1994: 21).[138] Subsidies were given to processing

137. Minister of Trade and Cooperatives Decree No. 492/Kp/7/79 (cited in Haury & Saragih 1997: 43).

138. Minister of Trade's Decree No. 274/Kp/XI/86, and Bank Indonesia's Circular No. 19/37/ULN/1986 (cited in Haury & Saragih 1997: 43).

industries (furniture) which developed in Java. At the same time, the export ban of semi-finished products (polished poles, rattan core and peels), an export duty of 20 per cent charged from 1979 onward, was increased to 30 per cent in 1986, before the export of semi-finished products was banned altogether in June 1988.[139] A quota system for lampit mats followed in December 1988. In the meantime, processing industries in South Kalimantan (mainly in Banjarmasin, Banjarbaru and Amuntai for *lampit* mats) and Java (furniture) had been set-up. Nevertheless, farmgate prices dropped drastically (by 28 per cent-70 per cent) in 1989-91 (Safran & Godoy 1993: 297, my own data from Lempunah). This was caused by several factors:

- The mat industry (*lampit*) in South Kalimantan[140] had collapsed for several reasons, which were not just linked to policy changes. The *lampit* market focussed almost entirely on Japan (90 per cent), where rattan mats had been sold for low prices between 1986 and 1989, probably because of rather high competition amongst exporters. Japanese buyers had stock-piled *lampit* until the demand decreased[141] owing to low quality standards, and a decline in the Japanese economy (Sasaki 1997, Yudhi pers. comm.), as well as a partial substitution by cheaper bamboo mats from China (Belcher, pers. comm.). In order to increase quality standards, and (probably) to control exports, the Indonesian government released a quota system for the export of *lampit* which restricted the previously free export from South Kalimantan.[142] Only 24 out of more than 200 companies were given export permits in Banjarmasin in 1990-1. Thus, the *lampit* industry broke down only a few years after it had started booming. In South Kalimantan this effect was called *bom lampit*, the *lampit* bomb.

---

139. The ban was implemented on 1 July 1988, and extended on 1 September to the export of webbing.

140. Lampit was 'the bulk of the exports' from 1986-8 (Menon 1989: 29), when approximately 35 per cent of the rattan exported from Indonesia left the country via Banjarmasin (*ibid*.: 31).

141. Stocks were also built up abroad for semi-finished products before the ban came into effect (Menon 1989: 29).

142. Minister of Trade's Decree No. 410/Kp/XII/88, cited in Haury & Saragih (1997: 44).

- Another factor was the collapse of the 'webbing' market. Since the ban for webbing exports came unannounced two months after the original ban of semi-finished products (until then webbing was considered to be a finished product), Indonesian furniture industries were not prepared to take over the supply of webbing, which is used mainly for chairs and decoration (or they were at least not willing to pay the previous price). This added to the drop-off in prices in Central and East Kalimantan, the main suppliers of raw material.
- In addition, over-harvesting had reduced rattan stocks in many parts of East Kalimantan. In 1989, people in Lempunah said that their rattan resources had been finished due to the big demand in the previous years. However, in general, rattan supply was still higher than demand.[143] So over-exploited areas could no longer compete, especially since the quality of raw material had declined (plants which were not mature had been harvested).

Since East Kalimantan had sold most of its rattan to South Kalimantan-based *lampit* and webbing industries (>85 per cent), the breakdown hit the farmers severely. The prohibitive economic climate, with only limited market competition, left the farmers in a weak bargaining position.[144] Locally (like in Lempunah), the effect was further exacerbated because of overharvesting and a decline in quality standards. In 1989, *Sokaq* therefore ceased to be of great cash importance for Lempunah for almost ten years. During this time, the once exploited stocks recovered and would have been plentiful, if the devastating forest fires had not destroyed more than 80 per cent of the village's rattan gardens in 1997-8 (see Gönner 1999a).

The second frequently-cultivated rattan species in Lempunah is *Jepukng* (Ind. *Pulut Merah* — *Daemonorops crinita*). *Jepukng* is a highly-valued and expensive species that is only cultivated in the Middle Mahakam area.[145] Although *Jepukng* was already traded with Chinese

---

143. Although the number of factories for finished products increased substantially between 1986 and 1988, with an installed capacity of 438,960 tonnes per year, the actual utilisation was believed to be much less (Menon 1989: 20).

144. Without the illegal export to Tawau, many villages would have been even more deprived of their most important source of income.

145. *Daemonorops crinita* also occurs in South Sumatra, where it is not cultivated (Dransfield & Manokaran 1994: 107).

merchants during the colonial time, the cultivation history in the Jempang sub-district is rather new. Until 1975, the traditional chief of Mancong,[146] a neighbouring village of Lempunah, had the sole right to collect *Jepukng* in his village's forest. The annual yield at that time was about 50-100 t.[147] Then, a dispute about the collecting rights arose between the traditional chief (Ind. *kepala adat*) and the new (administrative) village chief (Ind. *kepala desa*), which escalated into a forest fire that destroyed most of Mancong's *Jepukng* stands. After the dispute, people started to transfer wild *Jepukng* into their own forest gardens, where they were tended. Nevertheless, because of its high value, seedlings are frequently stolen from other people's gardens, or gardens are burnt out of envy or as revenge, which makes the investment in *Jepukng* a risky business.

In order to establish a *Jepukng* garden, most people look for wild clusters of seedlings (3-10 stems), which are transferred to their gardens.[148] These clusters can be divided in up to four parts, and can be replanted separately to increase the yield. Some people plant seeds, or tend seedlings in polybags before planting.[149] Planting distances are about 3 × 3 metres,[150] and individual gardens can consist of 100-500 clusters. *Jepukng* should be planted 2-3 months before the annual floodings in humid habitats. Because of their high value, *Jepukng* is generally cultivated close to the village or to the river, where it can be regularly controlled. The management of *Jepukng* gardens requires further weeding and, similar to the *Sokaq* gardens, the girdling of trees.[151] Occasionally, *Jepukng* is intercropped with

---

146. *Jepukng* gardens are more common downstream of Lempunah in Mancong and Perigiq, where suitable habitats are more abundant. Gardens also appear to be larger in these two villages compared to Lempunah.

147. Haury and Saragih estimate the total Indonesian consumption of *Jepukng* at 3-5,000 tonnes per year (1997: 14). Besides, *Jepukng* was also found to be exported illegally to Tawau (my own observations).

148. Occasionally, clusters of seedlings were sold at 500 Rp each in 1996.

149. This was done recently by people in Mancong and Perigiq, where *Jepukng* is of much greater importance than in Lempunah. Fertiliser was not yet used, however.

150. The rattan section of Kanwil Kehutanan plants *Jepukng* in a 3×5m pattern.

151. Since *Jepukng* grows much more bushy than *Sokaq*, it is not as dependent on supporting trees.

rubber, although its spiny nature makes tapping rubber much more difficult.

Like in the case of *Sokaq*, there is no obvious dependence between the percentage of households planting *Jepukng*, and the respective farmgate price. Between 1996 and 1998, 35-9 per cent of all households planted *Jepukng*, while the farmgate price fluctuated between 1,000 Rp and more than 3,500 Rp (see *fig.* 3.23). If *Jepukng* gardens are made by planting clusters of seedlings, the yields given in Table 3.19 can be expected. In cases where seeds are planted, the first harvest is possible after 6-8 years, depending on the soil.

Table 3.19: Harvest and yield of *Jepukng* gardens, estimated by key-informants

1. harvest	after 3-4 years	5 kg per cluster
2. harvest	after 4-6 years	6-7 kg per cluster
3. harvest	after 6-10 years	10-15 kg per cluster
continuing	after 10 years	20-35 kg per cluster

The harvest of *Jepukng* (cut into 6 m pieces[152]) is arduous because of the innumerable spines. It is done by men and women, who use gloves and the backside of their *mandau*'s blade to rip off

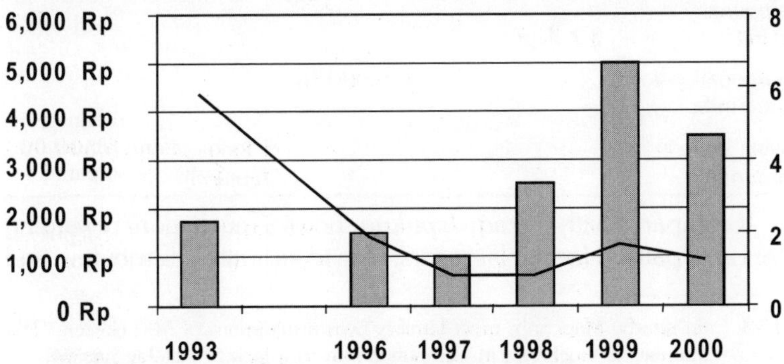

The black line indicates the ratio between rice and rattan prices per kg

***Fig.* 3.23: Price development for *Jepukng* (*Daemonorops crinita*) in Lempunah**

152. In 1997-8, 1-1.5 m sticks were also sold, but at a lower price.

the spiny skin. During one working day, about 30 kg of wet *Jepukng* can be harvested. If a density of 300 clusters is assumed per hectare,[153] a conservatively-estimated yield of 3 tonnes per year (one harvest every two years) per hectare seem possible. Given the excellent price (see *fig*. 3.23), the cultivation of *Jepukng* was one of the most rewarding land use modes of Dayak Benuaq.

The rationale for harvesting *Jepukng* is similar to the one described for *Sokaq*. In late 1997, when forest fires threatened Lempunah's *Jepukng* gardens, many people harvested their stocks despite a low price of only 1,000 Rp per kg. Because of the fire danger even wage workers were employed to harvest the threatened gardens, who were paid 25 per cent of the yield. Usually, *Jepukng* is sold to middlemen, who dry the harvest and sell it in Samarinda, from where it is partially traded to the furniture industry in Java or, illegally, to Tawau and further on to Singapore, Europe or to the United States.[154]

Table 3.20: Processing and trading steps for *Daemonorops crinita* from the forest to Samarinda (prices April 1998, the price is adjusted to dry rattan)

Processing step	*Working days*	*Costs*	*Quantity*	*Price (Rp)*
Collecting	100 working days		3 tonnes of wet *Jepukng*	
buying price in Lempunah				4,500,000
Drying	3-7 days			
transportation to Samarinda		100,000 Rp		
buying price in Samarinda			1 tonne of dry *Jepukng*	5,500,000

If compared with *Sokaq*, *Jepukng* shows a much more rewarding economic pattern for the last years. Due to its limited distribution and

153. In nearby Mancong, most families own a minimum of 500 clusters. The number is much less in Lempunah due to a lack of suitable habitats.

154. According to a rattan trader in Tawau, *Jepukng* is not re-exported to Hong Kong, Taiwan and South Korea like *Sokaq*, but sold directly to western countries, where it is used for café furniture (Haury, pers. comm.).

Jepukng can also be dried and sulphurised (uncommon). Depending on the age, the weight is reduced by 25-50 per cent. This working step is usually carried out by middlemen, who sell the harvest to traders in Samarinda, following the same chains as for *Sokaq*.

a constant demand from abroad, prices ranged from between 1,000 and more than 3,000 Rp/kg (equalling 0.5-1 kg of rice). After the fires had destroyed most of the gardens, and the value of the Indonesian Rupiah had fallen in 1998, farmgate prices increased to more than 5,000 Rp/kg (equalling 2 kg of rice) in early 1999.[155] However, at that time, most farmers in Lempunah had no more *Jepukng* left. In 2000, several families joined a new project developed by a local NGO to establish new *Jepukng* gardens in order to secure future financial income.

Rubber gardens

Rubber (*Hevea brasiliensis*) was introduced to (West) Kalimantan in 1909 (Uljee 1925: 74, cited in King 1988: 237) after seeds had been smuggled from Brazil to Singapore in 1876 (Tremeer 1964, cited in Dove 1993b: 137), from where it spread all over South-East Asia. Today, Indonesia is the world's second largest rubber producer (Dove 1993b: 136), with about 73 per cent of its rubber production derived from smallholders' gardens (Penot 1995: 11). Rubber trees were introduced in Lempunah in the 1930s. It remained a rather unusual crop until the late 1950s, when small-scale monocropping started.[156]

The clones used in Lempunah are still derived from the original seeds, despite the effort of the agricultural extension service to introduce improved clones.[157] According to local farmers, these old trees became even more productive the older they were.[158] Most

155. At that time, prices in Tawau were reported to be about 60,000 Rp per kg of dry *Jepukng*. In December 1999, dry *Jepukng* was sold in Samarinda at 13,750 Rp/kg.

156. A good example for the previously intercropped planting pattern is *simpukng A* in *fig.* 3.19, which was established in the 1950s when rubber trees were planted like any other cultivated tree species in a non-monocultural way.

157. The introduction of grafted high-yield varieties in early 1996 failed as the seedlings arrived at exactly the time of the rice harvest, when nobody had time to plant. Besides, the transportation between the grafting centre and the village had already taken too long to keep the seedlings viable.

158. This contradicts the findings from plantations, which are generally renewed after 20-35 years due to a decline of productivity (Rehm & Espig 1984: 339). However, rubber trees in Lempunah are tapped much less frequently than those in a plantation, which could result in a different productivity pattern.

families own a few (1-8) rubber gardens with an average size of 0.5 ha per garden (n = 21). The gardens generally consist of 300-500 trees (i.e., 600-1,000 trees/ha) planted with close distances in a rather random order (see *fig*. 3.24). In contrast, the planting distances in industrial plantations are much wider (150-400 trees/ha depending on the system, Rehm & Espig 1984: 339).

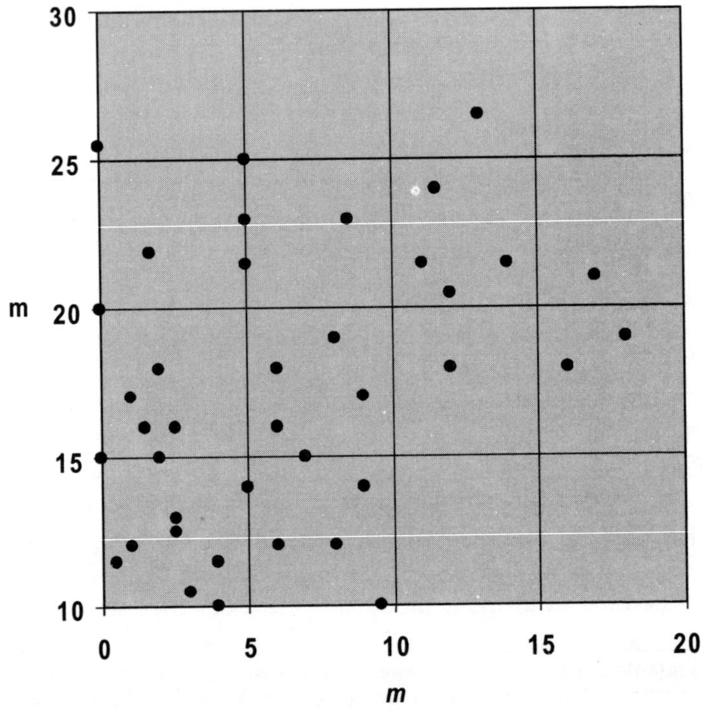

***Fig.* 3.24: Distribution of rubber trees in a *simpukng* enriched with rubber (black spots)**

Rubber can be planted as seeds or as seedlings. While seeds are perceived to result in more productive trees, seedlings show a greater survival rate against predation by bearded pigs.[159] As young trees are further threatened by deer (*Muntiacus* spp., *Tragulus* spp.), which feed on the bark, some farmers fence in their gardens, or set-up traps. Most rubber gardens are established on swiddens together with rice, or after the harvest. The decision to plant new rubber trees seems to correlate with good rubber prices (see *fig*. 3.25).

159. Bearded pigs (*Sus barbatus*) frequently visit rubber gardens in search of seeds.

After 8-10 years, depending on the respective soil fertility, the trees can be tapped. Tapping depends on farmgate prices, need for cash, rain-fall, available time (limited by other agricultural activities or important rituals) and alternative sources of income (see *fig*. 3.26).

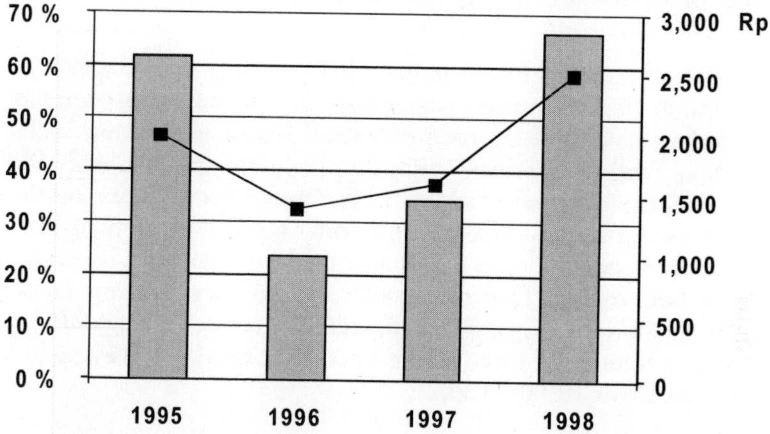

The black line indicates average rubber price during the planting season
Fig. 3.25: Percentage of households who planted rubber trees

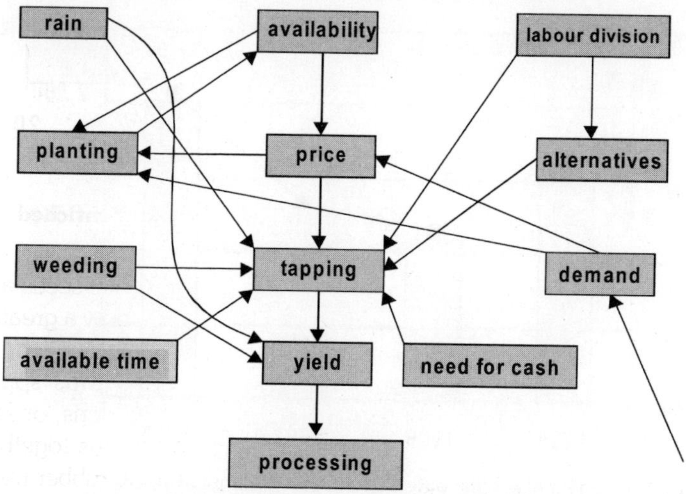

***Fig.* 3.26: Interdependencies related to the decision whether to tap rubber or not**

During the study period, the threshold for tapping was about 1,000 Rp. When prices fell below this mark in 1997, most people stopped tapping rubber, stating it was not even paying for their cigarettes any more. This contrasts with the inverse supply curve described for other regions in Borneo, where Dayak farmers increased their production in times of low prices *vice versa* (see discussion in Dove 1993b: 143).

The intensity of rubber tapping follows the price curve with the exception of 1997 when wage work on the oil palm plantation (including paid land clearing) distracted labour away from rubber tapping. Further, the rubber price dropped temporarily in mid-1997 to 1,000 Rp (not marked in *fig.* 3.27). Similar to the Kantu' of West Kalimantan, farmers in Lempunah only tap a part of their trees, sometimes alternating on a daily basis between different gardens to let the trees recover. Even during intensive use, most trees are tapped no more than 20 days per month, and, on average, most gardens at least rest during the more labour intensive periods of the rice cycle (also see Dove 1993b: 139).

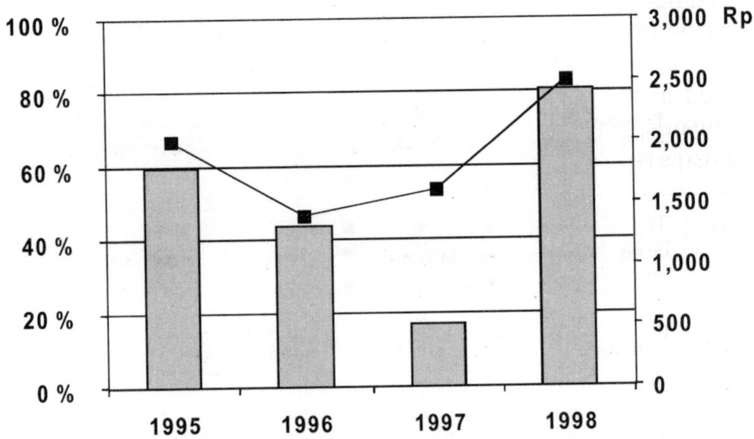

The black line indicates the average rubber price

***Fig.* 3.27: Percentage of households which tapped rubber**

The trees are usually tapped in the early morning hours when the hydrostatic pressure in the latex vessels is greatest due to a relatively low evapo-transpiration (Rehm & Espig 1984: 341). The bark is cut horizontally with the hollow blade of the *suloq* knife following the previous cut.[160] The latex flows along a vertical groove over a piece of bamboo and drops into a bamboo tube, or a plastic/metal can. After two or three hours, the white latex is collected and brought to the farm house, or to a temporary hut, where it is poured into a wooden trough and mixed with formic acid (app. 100 ml diluted 1: 5 with water for 10-12 l of latex). The mixture is stirred until the latex coagulates. 10-12 litres of latex yield a thick humid sheet of approximately 3-4 kg, which is only flattened with a bottle, but not pressed or smoked any more.[161]

The rubber sheets are stored and sold to middlemen if prices are reasonable, or if there is an urgent demand for money. The market chain leads from Lempunah via Tanjung Isuy to Samarinda, from where the raw rubber is further transported to Banjarmasin, where ribbed and smoked sheets (RSS, see Rehm & Espig 1984: 341) are produced and exported to Singapore.[162] In contrast to Amazonia (Romanoff 1992), the market chain is not fixed by a patronage system, but consists of a lose web of traders.

Although rubber tapping is in actual fact carried out by both men and women, it is considered to be women's work while men harvest rattan or extract ironwood far from the village. Since the trees are tapped in the early morning hours, other work can still be done afterwards, which makes rubber a suitable integrational part in the Benuaq's resource system. The gardens — usually close to the village

---

160. The first cut is usually done at a height of 50 cm to 1 m. Large trees can be cut at up to four different places. It is important that the cambium is not hurt (see Rehm & Espig 1984: 340), while the cutting direction is said to be free.

161. Formerly, rubber sheets had to be pressed with a mechanical roller and partially smoked until the sheets were completely dry. Nowadays, humid sheets are also bought by traders at insignificantly lower prices. According to Rehm & Espig (1984: 341), the rubber industry has developed new ways to use rubber coagulated in an uncontrolled way. Hence, the demand for a high quality raw rubber might have decreased. One local buyer complained that storing the humid sheets leads to a loss of weight in due course due to evaporation (others did not share this view).

162. Recently, a vulcanisation factory opened in Balikpapan, which might change the rubber flows in future (Yadi, pers. comm.).

(on average less than 4 km) — provide 4-5 kg of semi-dried rubber per day,[163] which is in the same range as the data provided by Dove for Kantu' rubber farmers (1993b: 139), who produce 2-7 kg/d of dry rubber per garden.

As rubber production is only one part of the Benuaq's resource system, which is used irregularly depending on various factors (see *fig*. 3.26), it is of little help to estimate annual production figures or yields per hectare. Given a reasonable price compared with rice, rubber can temporarily become a dominant source of income with up to 20,000 Rp per day (5-20 kg of rice). However, farmgate prices were very far from being stable during the research period, and ranged between 1,000 and 3,500 Rp per kg of semi-dried rubber (equalling 0.3-1 kg of rice, see *fig*. 3.28).

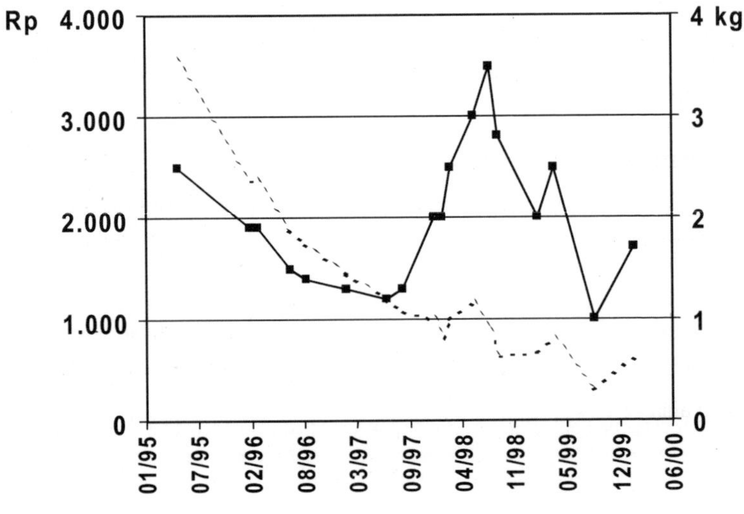

***Fig*. 3.28: Price development of semi-dried rubber sheets (per kg) in Lempunah**

The dotted line indicates the equivalence in rice for 1 kg of rubber

163. Estimated by 64 farmers (RSD = 37.6 per cent).

Functions of the forest 'in-between'

GENERAL ASPECTS

The forest landscape around Lempunah consists of a patchwork of forest gardens, swiddens, fallow bushland and fallow forests of different ages, as well as a small part of old secondary, or even primary *bengkar* forest. Although some animal and plant species are confined to specific habitat structures, all of the forest area is utilised according to aspects of access and practicability (distance and effort), but not at the same time, and not with the same intensity. For instance, a wild boar might be hunted in a 50 year-old *kerengkakng* forest, or in a new rubber garden; a ritual plant might be looked for in a *simpukng*, as well as in a *uraaq* fallow. Hence, it is necessary to explain the use of non-cultivated forest areas, which are sometimes referred to as 'empty forest' or *hutan kosong*, an unfortunate expression when it comes to land rights disputes between local communities and companies or government institutions. This 'forest in-between' is anything but empty. The forest landscape, including the forest gardens, provides Lempunah with a wide range of extracted forest products, such as medicinal and ritual plants, rattans, bamboos, timber, fish, game, fruits or construction wood. Table 3.21 summarises the number of locally-differentiated taxa that are used.

Table 3.21: Number of used plant and animal taxa

used plant taxa[164]: 402 including:		
	114	used for food
	111	used for building-material
	97	ritual plants
	70	medicinal plants
used animal taxa: > 104 including:		
	40	fish species
	5	turtle species
	2	snake species
	2	monitor lizards
	>33	bird species
	>22	mammal species
total number of taxa: > 506		

164. Taxa means here locally-classified species. Biologically, these taxa can be equivalent to species, sub-species or varieties.

Additional functions range from fresh water supply (river and wells) to religious aspects (former longhouses, sacrificial sites, graveyards, caves, rocks, hills and trees, inhabited by spirits). Furthermore, the uncultivated forest is an important buffer for future landuse, as well as in cases of natural disasters. After the drought of 1997-8, the swamp forest which was of limited use until then, provided villagers with fish and turtles, while parts of it were used in 1998 for cultivating swamp rice. Although only a few resources are used commercially, there is a substantial subsistence value.[165] Among the used plant species, the following families are the most common ones in Lempunah:

Table 3.22: Most abundant woody plant families

Plant family	*Number*	*Percentage*
Palmae	43	13.4 %
Euphorbiaceae	24	7.5 %
Anacardiaceae	22	6.9 %
Moraceae	22	6.9 %
Dipterocarpaceae	17	5.3 %
Lauraceae	14	4.4 %

Note: Among the *Palmae* are 28 local taxa of rattans.

FOOD FROM THE FOREST

At least 114 plant taxa are extracted for nutritional purposes from the forest (see Table 3.21). They include 78 fruit and nut tree species (including 18 *Anacardiaceae*, 12 *Moraceae*, 10 *Sapindaceae*, 7 *Euphorbiaceae*, 5 *Bombacaceae*, and 5 *Burseraceae*); 21 species related to honey (including 7 *Dipterocarpaceae*); as well as 6 palm species (*Palmae*) providing palm heart (*ur*). While several tree species are cultivated or maintained in *simpukng*, others grow in different stages of the fallow succession. Most fruits are used for direct consumption, gathered as a snack along the way, a few are traded, while some are known to attract animals (e.g., hill mynas — *Gracula religiosa*, hornbills — *Bucerotidae*, wild boar — *Sus barbatus*) which are then hunted close to these trees.

165. Estimating subsistence values in monetary figures is extremely difficult, as most estimates work with potential rather than actual market prices and conditions (see Peters *et al*. 1989), or neglect health and religious aspects which are even harder to evaluate.

The flesh of the edible arils of durian fruits (*Durio* spp.) is rich in carbohydrates, proteins, fats and minerals (Subhadrabandhu *et al.* 1992: 158). In good fruiting years, the different durian species and varieties temporarily become the major part of the diet in the village.[166] During these peak seasons, fruit-gathering and consumption can dominate village life in a way that most other activities come to a rest.[167] The fruits' importance is further stressed, as the durian harvest often coincides with the decline of rice stocks at the end of the agricultural cycle (December to March).[168]

Palm hearts (*ur* — shoots) are a necessary side dish for the final meals of rites including the sacrifice of a water buffalo (e.g., *kwangkai*, *guguq tautn*). The *ur* valued the highest is the heart of the *Niwukng* palm (*Oncosperma tigillarum*), but also rattans (e.g., *Juaaq* — *Plectocomiopsis geminiflora*), and cultivated palms (*Arenga pinnata*, *Elaeis guineensis*) are used, although in the everyday cuisine palm hearts are still regarded as a vegetable of second choice or 'forest food'. Data from other areas of East Kalimantan suggest a high nutritional importance of these forest snacks (Colfer 1997: 62-5). Although no quantitative diet studies were carried out in Lempunah, my impression is that, especially during the stay in the farm house, forest relishes contributed substantially to the nutrition[169] of the Benuaq.

While plant relishes add to the Benuaq's diet, meat and fish from the forests, rivers and swamps are the major sources of protein. The

---

166. I only witnessed a rich durian harvest in March 1991 when I visited the village for a couple of days. No mast-fruiting occurred between 1996 and 2000.

167. From other parts of Indonesia, it is even reported that the rice harvest suffers if it coincides with the durian harvest (Subhadrabandhu *et al.* 1992: 157).

168. The fermentation of fruits for liquor is reported to have stopped several decades ago. The reason, however, remains unclear. Drinking alcohol is not prohibited by the Benuaq's belief system, but they generally drink very little alcohol, and it was commonly stated that they do not like feeling dizzy. This voluntary abstinence might be affected by neighbouring Islamic groups, such as the Kutai or Banjarese.

169. My host family often stated that the meals eaten in the farm house tasted much better than those in the village. This perception might be biased by the exhausting physical labour in the field and a greater resulting appetite, but meals in the *ukop* were generally richer in side-dishes derived from the field crops, as well as from forest relishes.

game that is appreciated most (because of its high fat (*dawaaq*) content), is the Bearded Pig (*Sus barbatus*). Second to it are various deer species, such as the Sambar Deer (*Cervus unicolor*), two muntiac species (*Muntiacus muntjak*, *M. atherodes*) and two mouse-deer species (*Tragulus javanicus*, *T. napu*). But also porcupines (*Hystricidae*), pangolins (*Manis javanica*) and monitor lizards (*Varanus* spp.), as well as numerous bird species are hunted and eaten. Generally, all animals that cause damage to humans are culturally allowed to be killed.[170] Domestic animals are usually only eaten after religious sacrifices (including side-activities during these festivities such as cock-fighting), or in cases of a sudden death of an animal.[171]

As in most other areas on Borneo, game was traditionally hunted with spears, traps and blowpipes (*botatn*). The more than 2 metre-long blowpipes are made of ironwood (*Eusideroxylon zwageri*), *Puti* (*Koompassia excelsa*), *Daraq* (*Artocarpus dadah*) or *Kepuatn* (*Artocarpus anisophyllus*). Today, they are made with an industrial drill fixed to a boat engine; traditionally, they were burnt out. The darts are made from *Anau* (*Pholidocarpus majadum*) and *Belaakng* (*Borassodendron borneensis*) with filling corks at the end made of *Nanga* (*Palmae*). Blowpipes also play a ritual role in *belian* curing rites, where they (and the darts) get special ritual names. The major poison is derived from the *Ipu* tree (*Antiaris toxicaria*). It is individually mixed with other ingredients such as *Wakaai Sinaq* (unidentified). Blowpipes are used mainly for hunting smaller prey such as monkeys, birds or mouse deer, as larger mammals are still strong enough to run for a considerable distance before they collapse, making the search for them too arduous.[172] Today, however, they are rarely used,[173] but rather sold to souvenir traders. Spears (*bujak*) are still used for hunting pigs and deer. Their shaft is made from *Temias*,

---

170. This definition depends on the individual interpretation, but langurs (*Presbytis* spp.) and proboscis monkeys (*Nasalis larvatus*) are not killed, while macaques (*Macaca* spp.) — a notorious rice pest — are.

171. A chicken that had died because of poisoning by fertiliser was eaten the same day by my host family.

172. The Benuaq acknowledge that other indigenous groups such as the Punan are more skilled in the hunt with blowpipes, since they are even able to hunt wild boar with poisoned darts.

173. Blowpipes are still brought along in conflicts. This was also the case during the seizure of the oil palm company's base-camps in 1998.

which is as hard as ironwood but does not break as easily. The spears are straightened over a fire, before an iron blade is fixed to the tip.

Hunting can be done during daytime (*kasuq*) or at night (*tuyutn*). A hunter can operate alone or together with a pack of dogs. The second technique is mainly applied during the day. By hunting alone or in a small group, the hunters hide close to fruiting (as well as rubber[174]) trees (e.g., *Pipit Pare — Lithocarpus bennetti*, *Taman Laba — Elateriospermum tapos*, or *Cerikng — Archidendron jiringa*), or move slowly through the forest in search of the prey, while in the second case the dogs track the animals down. Alternatively to the spear, a self-made rifle can be used. The bullets are made of cut steel bars, the powder is derived from the heads of matches, and the trigger is a simple rubber mechanism. According to the hunters, a pig can be killed from a distance of about ten metres. Regarding the hazard of fighting a bleeding wild boar, the rifle is often preferred against the traditional spear, especially in dense forests, where a spear cannot be thrown from the hip.

Hunting techniques are often individual, and all of Lempunah's hunters prefer their own strategies. These include the careful observation of other animals, such as the movements of white-fronted langurs (*Presbytis frontata*), which are followed by bearded pigs, as these fructi- and herbivorous monkeys occasionally drop fruits. This strategy resembles a Penan technique, called *nedok*, which mimics the calls and movements of monkeys (in that case pig-tailed macaques — *Macaca nemestrina*) in order to attract pigs (Puri 1995: 33).

The amount of game caught was not assessed,[175] but according to my informants, the most successful hunter killed some 150-200 pigs in 1996. Regarding my own observations, this appears to be too high for an annual average, which would rather be around 100 pigs per year. Four other hunters, who hunt less regularly, might add another 100, depending on the migration patterns of the bearded pig. Deer is caught much less due to its relative scarcity. Two hunters estimated their average bag at 3 Sambar Deer (*Cervus unicolor*) and 10 muntiacs (*Muntiacus* spp.) per month. Apart from pork, wild

---

174. During the early drought of 1997-8, rubber gardens were a favourite hunting site, as many bearded pigs were attracted by the seeds.

175. As three of the hunters were often absent from the village, I had to rely on their own estimations.

pigs' fat (*dawaaq*) is most prised and preferred over commercial palm oil. It is melted in the forest, filled into bottles or plastic cans, and brought to the village where it is used for frying food (especially cassava). Animals can also be caught with traps. The most common kinds of traps are listed in Table 3.23.

Table 3.23: Different kinds of traps used in Lempunah

potiiq	spear trap made of bamboo
oyoot	snare trap for large animals
pelora	snare trap for small animals and birds
sentangoq	snare trap around the neck of large animals
goaaq	pit trap, including spears
tongkoop	pit trap with a lid
kahap	step trap with hidden spearheads made of bamboo
lidih	lime twigs for birds

These traps, especially the *potiiq* spear traps[176] (made from *Sangulai* wood (*Timonius lasianthoides*) with bamboo spearheads made of *Schizostachyum blumei*, and *Tana Gendikng* branches to guide the animals into the right direction) are scattered around swiddens, where they are an effective redress against predation. *Pelora* snare traps are often used to catch mouse deer (*Tragulus* spp.) or pheasants and partridges (*Phasianidae*).[177] The meat is partly consumed by the hunter's family, and partly sold in Lempunah or to traders in Tanjung Isuy. Occasionally, a piece is also given to the *kepala adat* (*mantiiq*). The meat of bearded pigs was sold at prices between 2,000 Rp and 3,500 Rp per kg, depending on the availability and on demand. Deer meat was sold for 2,500 Rp to 6,000 Rp per kg (Sambar Deer and muntiacs).

Fish is regularly caught with traps, or rod and line, from the Ohong river, small creeks and swampy forest parts. It is generally used as a daily dish (often dried and salted), but it became a traded commodity in 1998 when large amounts of catfish (*Siluriformes*) were caught, sometimes by applying electric shocks with car or

176. A demonstration of this trap is given in the film 'World Courier — Borneo' (Bayrischer Rundfunk 2000).

177. Occasionally, larger animals also get trapped. In a village on the Belayan river (also in Kutai), a rare Clouded Leopard (*Neofelis nebulosa*) was caught in a snare trap set-up for mouse deer.

motorbike batteries.[178] A daily catch was sold between 10,000 and 20,000 Rp (equalling 5-10 kg of rice), but yields already began declining in late April 1999. During the dry season, fish is also caught by poisoning the water with the *Twaq* vine (Ind. *Tuba — Derris elliptica*) or *Keroat*[179] (*Barringtonia pendula*). A piece of vine is beaten with a wooden stick, depending on the desired concentration.[180] The more shallow the water, the higher the concentration of the poison, and the more effective the catch. Fish traps made of rattan, as well as rattan fences, are set-up downstream, and soon the first dizzy or unconscious fish are collected from the surface. Two fish species are occasionally bred in wooden cages (*Ngkookng — Ophiocephalus striatus*, *Betutu — Oxyeleotris marmorata*) and achieve prices of 1,500 Rp/kg (*Ngkookng*) to 25,000 Rp/kg (*Betutu*).

When game became rare at the end of the drought in 1998, many people (especially children) caught small birds (*Passeriformes*) with lime twigs (*lidih*). The glue is derived from the bark of the *Pekalukng* tree (*Artocarpus elasticus*) and mixed with oil, while the sticks are made from the ribs of palm leaves. Several dozen *lidih* are stuck into the soil, or fixed to other twigs around forest wells, where birds come to bathe and drink. Within one hour, 54 small birds (11 species) were caught by this technique in late March 1998 by my host family.

TRADED ANIMALS AND PETS

Lidih lime twigs are also used to catch hill mynas (*Gracula religiosa*), which are sold as pets to traders.[181] Decoy birds are tied in the canopy

---

178. Electro-fishing was introduced to Lempunah by a Javanese teacher. It is demonstrated in a film shot in Lempunah in February 2000 ('World Courier — Borneo', Bayrischer Rundfunk 2000).

179. This second poisonous plant was only mentioned once. I never saw it applied. Another plant — *Lajaaq* (*Alpinia galanga*) was reported to be added to the Twaq vine.

180. For a 5 metre wide and 100 m long part of a small forest river, a vine of 2-3 metre in length was required. However, heavy rain partially spoilt the catch (mainly small fish, such as Boyut and Sepat — *Trichogaster* sp.).

181. Hill mynas (especially young birds) can imitate perfectly all kinds of sounds including the human voice. They are sought by rich town people who often pay several hundred thousand Rupiah for a young bird. The specialisation on hill mynas was introduced to Lempunah in the late 1980s by a Tonyoi teacher. It is more common in the area of Tonyoi (Tunjung) Dayak (see Jepson et al. 1998).

of a fruiting tree (e.g., *Keramuuq Soni — Dacryodes rostrata*), and several lime twigs are fixed around them. When the decoy birds call, other hill mynas are attracted and caught with the *lidih*. In 1995-6, 7 bird-catchers caught 151 hill mynas during the fruiting season. Most of these birds were sold at prices between 15,000 and 60,000 Rp. The same men only caught 22 birds in 1996-7. Their explanation was that the birds could not be fooled any more by the decoys. After the forest fires and the forest clearing of the oil palm company, catches declined further, and a trader in Tanjung Isuy estimated that the total number of hill mynas caught in Jempang subdistrict dropped to almost zero, while it used to be a few thousand birds per season (see also Jepson *et al.* 1998).

Many other bird species that are caught are kept as pets. The most favoured ones are the Blue-crowned Hanging Parrot (*Loriculus galgulus*); the Blue-rumped Parrot (*Psittinus cyanurus*); the Long-tailed Parakeet (*Psittacula longicauda*); the Spotted Dove (*Streptopelia chinensis*); and the Emerald Dove (*Chalcophaps indica*). But juvenile Black Hornbills (*Anthracoceros malayanus*) and a White-breasted Waterhen (*Amaurornis phoenicurus*) were also kept as pets. Mammals are also occasionally caught for sale (including skulls and skins) or pet-keeping (e.g., Sambar Deer — *Cervus unicolor*, Sun Bear — *Helarctos malayanus*, Otter — *Lutra* sp.), although at a relatively small-scale.

A new market for captured animals developed in late 1997, when Banjarese traders bought freshwater turtles (*Chelonii*) at high prices, and sold them to Samarinda and Banjarmasin, from where they were exported to Singapore, Hong Kong and Taiwan (see Momberg *et al.* 1998). The turtles achieved prices between 400 Rp and 25,000 Rp per kg, depending on the species and its size.[182] During the drought of 1997-8, an estimated minimum of 1,500 animals, covering at least 5 species (Malayan Giant Terrapin — *Orlitia*

182. In June 1998, *Kodoq Anau* (*Siebenrockiella crassicollis*) was sold at 4,000-5,000 Rp/kg, *Kodoq Katuq* (*Cuora amboinensis*) at 5,000-6,500 Rp/kg, and *Biukuu* (*Orlitia borneensis*) at 400 Rp/kg. The price for the soft-shelled *Kentawakng* (*Amyda cartilaginea*) depended on the individual weight: 1-1.5 kg were sold at 21,000-25,000 Rp, 1.5-5 kg at 19,000 Rp, 5-10 kg at 10,000 Rp, 10-20 kg at 5,000 Rp, and more than 20 kg (up to 50 kg or more) were sold at 4,000 Rp per kg. The price peak was in April 1998, while prices dropped slightly in 1999, despite a much reduced supply.

borneensis, Black Terrapin — *Siebenrockiella crassicollis*, Asian Box Turtle — *Cuora amboinensis*, Hillstream Soft-shelled Turtle — *Dogania subplana*, and South-East Asian Soft-shelled Turtle — *Amyda cartilaginea*), were extracted from swamp forests around Lempunah, providing an important additional income during a stressful time of failed harvests and increased living costs. The local trader in Tanjung Isuy reported that he traded about 10 tonnes of turtles in 1998, mainly derived from the swamps along the Ohong river.

CONSTRUCTION MATERIAL

To date, all construction materials used for house-building are derived from the forests around Lempunah.[183] At least 111 taxa are used for construction purposes, including hardwoods of the *Dipterocarpaceae* family (17 taxa, including *Shorea* spp.,

Table 3.24: Plant species used for the construction of farmhouses (*ukop*)

Roof	*Anau*	*Pholidocarpus majadum*
	Biangan	*Castanopsis javanica*
	Sunjuukng	not identified
	Tempuro	*Dillenia* sp.
Walls	*Lempukng*	*Shorea sp*
	Jangkau	*Xylopia altissima*
	Kumpat Layukng	*Castanopsis megacarpa*
	Deraya	*Horsfieldia* sp.
	Bencomang	*Litsea machilfolia*
floor	*Pokeeq*	not identified
	Tolakng Morakng	*Schizostachyum longispiculatum*
	Si'it	*Calamus sp.* or *Daemonorops grandis*
stilts	*Teluyaatn*	*Eusideroxylon zwageri*
	Bernipaq	*Diplospora singularis*
	Keliwatn	*Baccaurea pyriformis*
	Bekangin	*Commersonia bartramia*
rice store	*Nancakng*	*Macaranga triloba*
	Gemah	*Prunus arborea*
	Mermukng Puluuq	*Shorea ovalis*
	Pekalukng	*Artocarpus elasticus*
	Lempukng	*Shorea* sp.
fixing material	*Lalutn*	*Korthalsia scaphigera*

183. This is different in Benuaq-Tonyoi villages around Melak/Barong Tongkok (app. 70 km north-west from Lempunah), where timber has to be purchased upriver or replaced with bricks.

Dipterocarpus spp. and *Dryobalanops* spp.) and of the *Lauraceae* (14 taxa, including *Litsea* spp., *Cinnamomum partenoxylon*, and ironwood — *Eusideroxylon zwageri*). But also *Euphorbiaceae* and bamboos (*Bambusaceae*, *Poaceae*) are commonly used.

Supplementary to the local use of building material, several timbers are also commercially extracted and sold to entrepreneurs operating illegally in Tanjung Isuy or Gunung Bayan (Muara Pahu subdistrict). The major species traded are ironwood (*Teluyatn*, Ind. *Ulin* — *Eusideroxylon zwageri*), *Meranti* (*Shorea* spp.), *Ngoiiq* (Ind. *Kapur* — *Dryobalanops* sp.), and — since 1999 — *Itir* (*Intsia palembanica*). The price development is shown in Table 3.25.

Table 3.25: Some prices for timber beams at the forest gate (L) and in Tanjung Isuy (TI) per m³

Transportation costs are 50,000 Rp from the forest to Lempunah, and another 50-70,000 Rp per m³ from Lempunah to Tanjung Isuy (1996-98)[184]

Species	*Year*	*Beam in L*	*Beam in TI*	*Shingles in L*
Ulin	1996	100,000 Rp	175-185,000 Rp	4,000-4,500 Rp
	1997	100,000 Rp	200-225,000 Rp	4,000-5,000 Rp
	1998	100,000 Rp	200-250,000 Rp	5,000-6,000 Rp
	1999	150-200,000 Rp	400,000 Rp	6,000-9,000 Rp
Meranti	1997	35,000 Rp	200,000 Rp	
	1998	50,000 Rp	200,000 Rp	
Kapur	1997	40,000 Rp	200-225,000 Rp	
	1998	50-80,000 Rp	?	

The extraction of ironwood (*Eusideroxylon zwageri*) is an especially important source of income in Lempunah. The trees are felled with chainsaws and cut into 4 m beams (10 × 10 cm). This work, which is done exclusively by men who often spend several days or weeks in the forest, can yield between 100,000 and 200,000 Rp per day (equalling 30-80 kg of rice), while shingling (done with a *mandau* bush knife) achieves some 18,000 to 30,000 Rp per day (equalling 5-10 kg of rice).

184. The doubling of the timber prices between 1996 and 1999 was influenced by a general price increase following the Indonesian financial crisis of 1997-8. It only partially reflects the decrease in timber stocks.

In the meantime, ironwood has become increasingly scarce, and villagers have to travel at least 20-30 km to find remaining stocks. The produce is sold to merchants in Tanjung Isuy, who provide transportation by truck, and trade beams and shingles to Muara Muntai or Samarinda, where it is used locally or traded in Java and Sabah (Malaysia). During the financial crisis in 1997-8, these merchants built-up debt-bonds with the local extractors who were provided with basic food (rice, sugar, cigarettes, cooking oil) and chainsaw fuel. In due course, the extractors had to repay their debts with timber.[185]

Dug-out canoes can be made from several tree species such as ironwood (*Teluyatn — Eusideroxylon zwageri*), *Perowali* (*Cinnamomum partenoxylon*), *Bungur* (*Lagerstroemia speciosa*), *Kepapaaq* (*Vitex pubescens*), *Miyadukng* (*Pithecellobium splendens*) and *Seranai* (*Dactylocladus stenostachys*). Several bamboo and rattan species are also used for construction purposes, for fish traps, fences, floors, mats, baskets, tubes or ritual items.

FOREST MEDICINE

Despite the frequent and generally preferred use of modern medication, all interviewed households still apply traditional medicinal plants. The knowledge of medicinal (and ritual) plants is, however, not evenly distributed. Although most people have a certain basic knowledge (women usually more than men), more specific knowledge remains with the traditional *pembeliatn* healers. Table 3.26 summarises the major applications of medicinal plants used in Lempunah.[186]

---

185. In at least one case, the extractor did not feel comfortable with this system and broke out as soon as he had repaid the debts. He even preferred to tap rubber at a much lower revenue to keep his independence.

186. Although I describe many other aspects of local resource use in this study, I hesitate in this respect. As long as the question of intellectual property rights of indigenous knowledge (including an acknowledged compensation system) is not solved, I will not publish the names of plants for which a commercial application seems likely.

Table 3.26: Application fields for locally-used medicinal plant species

Application	n
hygiene (skin, hair, mouth)	20
digestive tract (against diarrhoea, vomitting, stomach-ache)	12
gynaecology (pregnancy, birth)	8
colds and cough	7
tonic	5
wounds	4
fever (including malaria)	4
mental (including attacks)	4
bones	2

A more obvious use than the application of medicinal plants is the one of ritual plants, which are found in religious ceremonies. At least 97 plant taxa are used in the different rituals, including 59 (covering 32 plant families) used in *belian* curing rites. Most species are ritually prescribed, such as young *Teluyatn* trees (*Eusideroxylon zwageri*) and *Lomuuq* trees (*Canarium decumanum*, but also *Lomuuq Potukng* — *Evodia alba* — and *L. Nancakng* — *Macaranga triloba*), which are necessary *ramuan* (Ind. ingredients) in the *belian*.[187]

Several bamboo (*Bambusaceae*, *Poaceae*) and wood species (e.g., *Kayutn Arakng* — *Diospyros* sp., *Nancakng* — *Macaranga triloba*, *Kelebahuq* — *Glochidion obscurum*, *Potukng* — *Evodia alba*) are also used for constructing the various ritual items, including wooden figures made from *Pesaaq* (*Fordia* sp.); *Nunuq Singah* (*Ficus* sp.); and *Deraya Sepatukng* (*Horsfieldia grandis*). Most ritual plants are found close to the village. However, trees like *Eusideroxylon zwageri* have already become scarce around other villages like Tanjung Isuy and must be sought as far away as 10-20 km from the village.

OTHER USEFUL RESOURCES FROM THE FOREST

At least 33 tree species are known as suitable fire-wood. Among these, *Kepapaaq* (*Vitex pubescens*) and *Pipit* (*Lithocarpus elegans*)

187. *Teluyatn* trees (the 'male' tree in the *beliatn* sometimes referred to as *Lomuuq Teluyatn*) are set with the canopy upwards, while the canopy of the other *Lomuuq* trees points to the floor. These trees are used to call the Kelelungan souls for help.

are the most favoured ones due to their high burning efficiency.[188] The charcoal of three hardwood species (*Teluyatn* — *Eusideroxylon zwageri*, *Kahooi* — *Shorea balangeran*, and *Kepahu*) is used by the local blacksmiths for heating the hearth.

Several plants were used for producing clothes in past times, including the leaf fibres of *Doyo* (*Curculigo* spp.) and pineapple (*Ananas comosus*), as well as the bast of *Ayaq* (*Ficus variegata*), *Ipu* (*Antiaris toxicaria*) and *Pekalukng* (*Artocarpus elasticus*). Today, bast clothes and woven *Doyo* fabrics (*ulap doyo*) are mainly produced for sale. Especially the production of *ulap doyo*, woven on a loom, provides a substantial income for women. The leaves are collected, washed, dried and segregated into fibres, which are then knotted to threads. These are put on a wooden frame, and motifs are wrapped with plastic. The unwrapped threads are then dyed with traditional dyes (see above) or chemical ones (more commonly), while the wrapped part remains blank (*ikat* technique). After that, the threads are put onto the loom and woven into an *ulap doyo*, which is usually bought by traders at prices between 7,000 Rp (1996) and 12,500 Rp (1999) for a small one, and 12,000 Rp (1996) and 25,000 Rp (1999) for a big one.

The fibres of two more species, *Kapoq* (*Ceiba pentandra*, cultivated) and *Padakng* (*Imperata cylindrica*, a common weed) are used for filling mattresses and pillows.

In past times, wild rubber and resins were traded between the interior of Borneo and itinerant merchants selling these forest products as far away as China or Arabia (see summary in Dove 1994: 383-5, citing also Wolters 1967 and von Heine-Geldern 1945). Among the wild rubbers traded were several *Sapotaceae* such as *Ketiau* (*Palaquium* sp.); *Malau* (*Palaquium* sp.), which is still used for fixing *mandau* blades to the handle; *Natu Beneeq* (*Palaquium* sp.); *Natu Tunyukng* (*Madhuca* sp.); as well as two more species from other families, *Kayutn Uraatn* (*Dyera costulata*, *Apocynaceae*), and *Wakaai Letatn* (*Willughbeia* sp., *Logantaceae*). Following Dove's typology of three categories for Bornean latexes (1994: 384-5), these species can be aggregated as in Table 3.27:

---

188. One informant told me that different wood species are used for specific dishes due to their different flame temperatures. However, in most cases, the temperature was regulated by the size of the fire.

Table 3.27: Categories of wild latexes, see Dove 1994

	Taxa given by Dove	*in Lempunah*
caoutchouc	*Ficus elastica*	
	Willughbeia spp.	*Wakaai Letatn*
gutta percha	*Palaquium* spp.	*Ketiau, Malau, Natu Beneeq*
	Payena spp.	
gutta jelutong	*Dyera* spp.	*Kayutn Uraatn*

Resins of at least 11 tree species are used as incense in rituals (*Jerapiq* — *Calophyllum soullatri*, *Kelaneh*, *Sengongong*), or as glue (*Bekalukng*, *Putaakng* — *Shorea* sp., *Butakng Metapm* — *Shorea* sp., *Lomuuq* — *Canarium decumanum*, *melasio* — *Shorea* sp., *Tebukng* — *Vatica* sp., and *Telaatn*), while the oleo-resin of *Mermukng Lemit* (*Shorea smithiana*) was formerly exported as *damar*. *Gaharu*, the highly-valued fragrant heartwood of fungus-infected *Alaas* trees (*Aquilaria* spp., mainly *A. malaccensis*), was also traded but appears to be rather rare around Lempunah.[189] Several plants are used as dye (especially for *Doyo* threads), including:

Table 3.28: Dye plants. * also mentioned in Lemmens & Wulijarni-Soetjipto (eds.) 1992

red	*Gelinapm*	*Bixa orellana*	fruits	*Doyo*
	Mepooq	*Ixonanthes* sp.*	bark	wood
brown	*Kalaakng*	*Durio zibethinus* *	bark	*Doyo*
	Kekereq	*Archidendron microcarpum*	bark	*Doyo*
green	*Puput*	*Jasminum sambac*	leaves	*Doyo*
black	*Sopaakng Piaq*	*Archidendron* sp.*	leaves	*Doyo*, rattan

The resin of *Wai Meaq* (*Eugenia fumida*), *Wai Pulut* (*Eugenia palembanica**), and the leaves of *Laliiq* (*Ficus quocarpa*) are used as wood varnish, while leaves of *Embagai* and *Kembang Sepatu* (*Hibiscus rosa-sinensis*) are added as fixers in the colouring of Doyo threads.

Among the 28 locally-differentiated rattan taxa are also several of commercial importance. Between 1996 and 1999 the following wild-growing species were traded: [190]

189. It appears to be more common in the interior of East Kalimantan, where Gaharu temporarily became the most important local NTFP (see Momberg *et al.* 1994 about the over-exploitation by outsiders).

190. A few data from earlier visits and reliable informants are included.

Table 3.29: Non-cultivated rattan species traded. Markets and prices do not exist for each species in every year

Local name	*Scientific name*	*Year*	*Rp / kg (wet rattan)*	*equivalent in kg of rice*
Beleh	*Calamus penicillatus*	1992-3	500-750 Rp	app. 1.5 kg
		1996	750 Rp	app. 1 kg
		1998	300 Rp	app. 0.1 kg
		1999	1,000 Rp	app. 0.3 kg
Boyukng	*Calamus optimus*	1997	150 Rp	app. 0.1 kg
Keheq	*Calamus muricatus*	1996	400 Rp	app. 0.5 kg
		1998	300 Rp	app. 0.1 kg
		1999	600 Rp	app. 0.2 kg
Inai	*Ceratolobus subangulatus*	1993-4	500 Rp	app. 1.2 kg
		1998	300 Rp	app. 0.1 kg
Jehap	*Calamus trachycoleus*	1996	150-250 Rp	app. 0.3 kg
Kotoq	*Daemonorops angustifolia*	1994-5	50-75 Rp	app. 0.2 kg
		1998	100-200 Rp	app. 0.1 kg
		1999	150-300 Rp	app. 0.1 kg
Lalutn	*Korthalsia scaphigera*	1992-3	350-450 Rp	app. 1 kg
		1996	400 Rp	app. 0.6 kg
		1997	400-600 Rp	app. 0.4 kg
		1998	400-2,500 Rp	app. 0.5 kg
		1999	1,000 Rp	app. 0.3 kg
Ngono	*Calamus manan*	1982	350 Rp	app. 1 kg
		1993-6	150-350 Rp	app. 0.6 kg
		1997	150 Rp	app. 0.1 kg
		1998	250-400 Rp	app. 0.1 kg
		1999	250-600 Rp	app. 0.2 kg
Sekolaq	*Calamus ornatus*	1998	200 Rp	app. 0.1 kg
		1999	250 Rp	app. 0.1 kg
Tuu'	*Calamus scipionum*	1984	25 Rp	app. 0.2 kg
		1991-96	100-150 Rp	app. 0.4 kg
		1998	200-250 Rp	app. 0.1 kg
		1999	150-250 Rp	app. 0.1 kg

In Lempunah, most of these species are only collected and sold directly to traders from Pentat or Tanjung Isuy, who further process the rattans. Several species are boiled in diesel for preservation (*Calamus manan, C. scipionum*, *Daemonorops angustifolia*), the others are dried and transported downriver to Samarinda.

In addition to rattan, some additional NTFPs are extracted for commercial reasons, such as *Inas* (*Bambusa* sp.), which was bought by the oil palm company for marking planting holes at 15-20 Rp per 2-metre stick. *Malau* (resin of *Palaquium* sp.) was traded at 1,000 Rp per piece (up to 10 cm), and the dried bark of *Kayu Lem* (*Litsea* sp. c.f.) was sold for 200-300 Rp per kg.

4

Socio-economy, Patterns and Strategies of Resource Use

Socio-economy

EXTENDED SUBSISTENCE

Livelihood in Lempunah is secured by an extended subsistence economy (see Gönner & Seeland forthcoming) with swidden agriculture, forest gardening and the extraction of NTFPs providing subsistence produce, and a broad range of other activities generating financial income. Such a combined strategy, based on a subsistence pattern, while also reaching deep into a market economy, is not an exception, but rather the rule in Borneo (see Dove 1993b: 137, Weinstock 1983b: 63-5; Colfer 1997: 3; Grossmann 1997: 7-8), which has been part of a wide trading network stretching over Asia since many centuries. In contrast to some remote areas of the island, where barter trade still prevails (see Inoue & Lahjie 1990), Lempunah has been well embedded into a monetary economy for several decades.[1] However, the border between subsistence resources and commercially—relevant ones is a floating one, depending on the current price situation and on local demand (see *fig.* 4.1).

Cash is required for supplementing food shortages, for health care, education, clothes, boat engines, chainsaws, motorbikes, TVs as well as for expensive rituals. Although most households still maintain a high level of subsistence, cash demand became an important factor influencing the decision-making of resource activities in the village.

---

1. The *kepala adat* of Lempunah still remembers resource prices (in cent or *sen*, which is also the Benuaq word for 'money') during the Dutch colonial period.

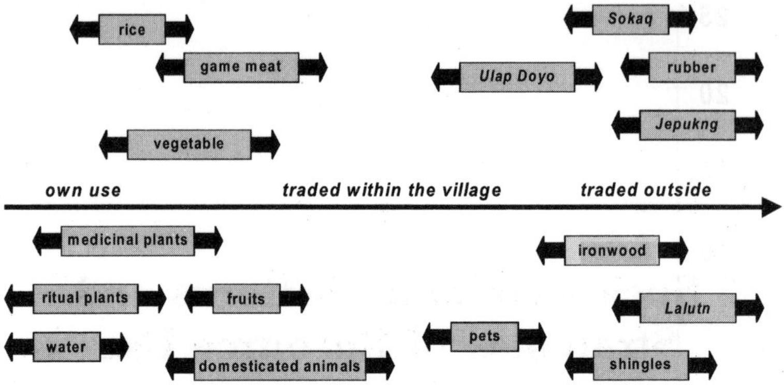

Sokaq (*Calamus caesius*), *Jepukng* (*Daemonorops crinita*) and *Lalutn* (*Korthalsia scaphigera*) are local rattan species

***Fig.* 4.1: 'Sledge model' of resources along a gradient from subsistence to commerce**

Especially during periods of low rice supply and high living costs (e.g., during the 1997-8 drought and during the Indonesian financial crisis) the demand for cash even increased, becoming a major driving force in economic activities.

Yet, while most families struggled to make ends meet, some better-off households managed to achieve added value that allowed investments, both in farm activities (e.g., by paying *konookng* wage workers, or, more recently, by buying pesticides and fertiliser) as well as in off-farm sectors (e.g., rattan seedlings for new rattan gardens, *Doyo* palm fibres).[2] Whether this development leads to an increased inequality remains to be seen. So far, income opportunities are rather equally distributed among the villagers with the exception of a few households that own small shops, or are in privileged positions with access to money from outside the village. In addition, a rather high proportion of the income is invested socio-religiously into large rituals. Although these investments are meant primarily in a religious way, they show an important social function by confirming the organiser's status within his or her social net.

INCOME SOURCES

Only a few people practice a regular income-generating profession

2. When the oil palm company offered land clearing jobs, several people bought chainsaws, occasionally even on credit, in order to use this opportunity.

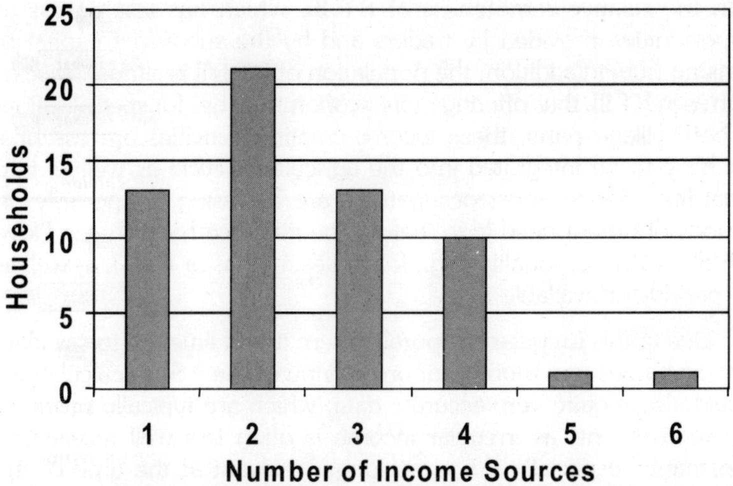

***Fig.* 4.2: Distribution of multiple income sources per household in RT I/II (1995-6). Some income sources, such as different rattan species are pooled into one category**

in Lempunah. These are the three teachers, one Protestant missionary, the school's caretaker, two carpenters, one woodcarver and two blacksmiths. But even those households prepare additional swiddens for ensuring their own subsistence. The rest of Lempunah supplements subsistence with a broad variety of different occupations, which often have to be combined to meet cash demands.

Less than 25 per cent of all households were able to live from only one source of income. The vast majority had to rely on at least two different occupations in addition to the swidden work. This diversifying strategy will be discussed later (under sub-section 'Diversification and Risk Minimisation' of this chapter).

A comparison of both village parts shows that the variety of income sources is larger in RT I/II (15 major categories), compared to the smaller and remote RT III (11 categories).[3] This finding correlates

3. The categories were: *belian* rituals, *Doyo* weaving, selling vegetables, help by others, trade, crafting, paid jobs, rubber, work for the oil palm plantation, other wage work, rattan, selling rice, animal husbandry, ironwood, other extracted plants, extracted animals. Among the sample of RT I/II (1996-8, *n*=18) only 'selling of vegetables' was missing, while the sample of RT III (1996-8, *n*=18) lacked 'trade', 'crafting', 'paid jobs', 'animal husbandry' and 'other extracted plants'.

with the relative remoteness of RT III, which has less access to opportunities provided by traders and by the subdistrict capital of Tanjung Isuy. In addition, the population of RT I/II is almost twice as high as in RT III, thus offering more economic niches for specialisation. In both village parts, these income-creating activities are essential but have to be integrated into the agricultural cycle as well as into ritual life. Hence, most occupations are focussing temporarily on periods of urgent need (e.g,. before the new rice harvest, see Dove 1993b: 142), seasonality (e.g., for turtles, mynas or fruits), as well as on periods of available time.[4]

Due to this irregular temporal pattern it is of little use to calculate income figures on a monthly or on an annual base.[5] Such calculations would also require very accurate data, which are typically prone to severe concerns, as irregular income is often less well recalled by informants, especially if it is no longer relevant at the time of the interview (see Ellis 1998: 9). Instead, the income for typical working periods are compiled in Table 4.1, and several case studies are given.

Table 4.1: Examples for financial income derived from household interviews (1996 and 1998)

Source	*Income*	*Period*	*Price range*	*Unit*
Jepukng	50,000-2,1 Mio. Rp	1-30 days	1,500-3,500 Rp/kg	50-700 kg
Sokaq	90,000-300,000 Rp	1-8 weeks	300-1,000 Rp/kg	app. 300 kg
Lalutn	160,000-12 Mio. Rp	1-8 weeks	1,600-2,000 Rp/kg	100-600 kg
Manau	60,000-315,000 Rp	2-30 days	350-400 Rp/kg	150-900 kg
Kotok	30,000-150,000 Rp	2-30 days	100-200 Rp/kg	300-1,000 kg
Inas	5,000-10,000 Rp	1 day	15-20 Rp/stick	250-500 sticks
rubber	4,000-15,000 Rp	1 day	1,000-3,000 Rp/kg	4-5 kg

4. Income is also used to get back into the optimal agricultural cycle in cases where money is spent for *konookng* work (e.g., felling or weeding) in order to ensure a sufficient harvest. Thus, in times of good prices, a family might be tapping rubber, while someone else prepares their swidden.

5. The distribution of estimated average monthly income figures (see *fig*.4.7) is only meant to illustrate the relative inequality among the households of Lempunah.

souvenir blowpipes	9,000-50,000 Rp	1 day	2,500-5,000 Rp/piece	3-25 pieces
souvenir figures	25,000-100,000 Rp	1-3 days	25,000-100,000 Rp/piece	1 piece
wooden table	25,000 Rp	3 days	25,000 Rp/piece	1 piece
wooden chair	15,500 Rp	3 days	15,500 Rp/piece	1 piece
souvenir *Mandau*	70,000-100,000 Rp	1 week	70,000-100,000 Rp/piece	1 piece
blacksmith	400,000 Rp	1 month		
construction work	12,000 Rp	1 day		
small *Ulap Doyo*	7,000-12,500 Rp	3 days	7,000-12,500 Rp/piece	1 piece
large *Ulap Doyo*	12,000-25,000 Rp	5 days	12,000-25,000 Rp/piece	1 piece
Lampit mat	25,000 Rp	10 days	25,000 Rp/piece	1 piece
rattan baskets	7,500-12,500 Rp	2-5 days	7,500-12,500 Rp/piece	1 piece
shingles	12,000-18,000	1 day	4,000-6,000 Rp/100 pcs.	200-300 pieces
ironwood	50,000-200,000 Rp	1 day	100-200,000 Rp/m^3	0.5-1 m^3
Itir wood	300,000 Rp	1 day	300,000 Rp/m^3	
construction wood	25,000-50,000 Rp	1 day	25,000-50,000 Rp	per day
hunting	40,000-100,000 Rp	1 day	2,000-4,000 Rp/kg	1 animal
turtles	100,000-500,000 Rp	1-3 months	1,000-25,000 Rp/kg	20-100 kg
mynas	125,000-500,000 Rp	1-3 months	15,000-30,000 Rp/bird	5-50 birds
fish	7,500-45,000 Rp	1 day	2,000-3,000 Rp/kg	5-30 kg
motorbike	5,000-10,000 Rp	1 hour	5,000-10,000 Rp	Lemp.-Tj.Isuy
belian service	5,000-10,000 Rp	1 night	+ paying in kind	
warung	10,000-15,000 Rp	1 day	10,000-15,000 Rp	per day
shop	> 2,000 Rp	1 day	> 2,000 Rp	per day
daily rice demand	1,600-7,500 Rp	1 day	per family	1.5 kg

The following case studies are taken from my extended host family.

Case studies

In 1995-6, the family's father (the village chief) and his wife tapped rubber for two months after he and his sons-in-law had extracted ironwood for three months, while his wife weaved *Ulap Doyo* fabrics, which were sold to a trading woman from Tanjung Isuy. The family further sold a few animals (pigs, ducks, chicken) and caught some hill mynas (*Gracula religiosa*) as well as monitor lizards (*Varanus salvator*), which were also sold locally. Additional income came from a few souvenir blowpipes made by the village chief himself.

His elder son (married, one child) also tapped rubber in the respective year. Apart from that, he caught 6 hill mynas, extracted approximately 6 cubic metres of ironwood and produced 2-3 packs of ironwood shingles per day over several weeks.

The oldest daughter and her husband (married, no children) lived on a combination of *Ulap Doyo* weaving, rubber tapping (for two months), shingling (120 packs within one month) and some extracted rattan (*Sokaq* — *Calamus caesius*, *Lalutn* — *Korthalsia scaphigera*); while the family of the younger daughter (married, one child) relied mainly on *Ulap Doyo* weaving, the extraction of ironwood (approximately half a cubic metre per day over several weeks) and shingling.

The 90 year-old *kepala adat* and his wife (the village chief's parents-in-law) earned some money and payments in kind by performing rituals and by selling pigs.

A nephew of the village chief's wife (married, two children) earned his family's livelihood with the local sale of woven baskets, rattan extraction, wage work on other's swiddens, shingling and with the bark of *Kayu Lem* (*Litsea* sp. c.f.).

Another nephew (married, three children) killed 13 bearded pigs (*Sus barbatus*) and 6 deer (*Muntiacus* spp., *Cervus unicolor*), which he sold partly in the village. He also caught 5 hill mynas and produced more than 130 packs of ironwood shingles in the same year. In addition, he earned some money and payments in kinds for performing *belian* curing rites.

While these examples show a rather high diversity of income sources, some families had to rely on less means, depending on the number and availability of their family members, as well as on an affordable investment (e.g., a chainsaw required for ironwood extraction) and the possibility to leave the village temporarily (e.g., for producing shingles, or for extracting rattan in remote parts of the forest). Most of these families lived from rubber tapping at that time.

As 1995-6 was a year with a large number of swiddens, following a meagre harvest in early 1995, all income-related activities had to fit into the temporal frame set by the agricultural cycle. Hence, most of these income sources were only of temporary use in-between the prioritised swidden activities. Additional income was provided by a government-sponsored poverty programme designed to facilitate investments into small-scale industries such as chicken-breeding or handicraft production (see above). However, most of the 100,000-500,000 Rp distributed per family was used for buying rice after the failed harvest.

Most of the financial income is used for daily consumption, but some is also spent for irregular expenses (see below), including investment at different levels (see above). While saving money in bank accounts is still uncommon (possible in Muara Muntai or in Tenggarong, which are almost one day away), surplus money is often invested in gold jewellery, which is bought and sold by Bugis traders, who frequently visit the Dayak villages.

Due to the generally temporary and unreliable character of income sources in Lempunah, it is not surprising to find great variation between different years. The figure on the following page illustrates these dynamics by comparing the ascribed importance of several categories

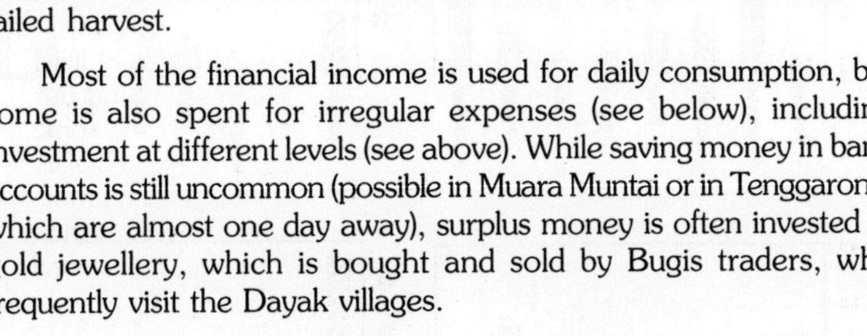

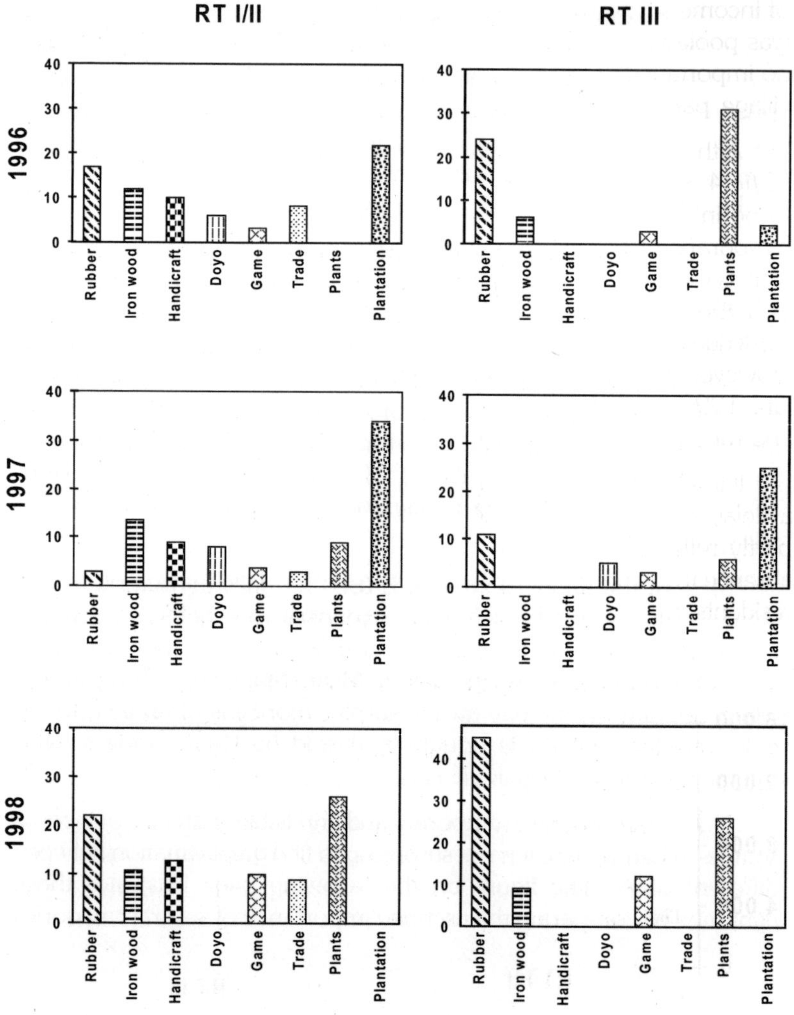

***Fig.* 4.3: Ascribed importance of income sources. The values on the ordinate are relative weights of importance ranging between 0 and 3 per household (*n*=18)**

of income sources over four years. The importance of each category was pooled based on weighted household interview data (from 0 = no importance, to 3 = great importance; *n* = 18 households in each village part).

Although the major strategic considerations behind the pattern of *fig*.4.3 will be discussed later, a few rather obvious findings have to be interpreted. The most prominent patterns in *fig*.4.3 are the temporary importance of wage work on the oil palm plantation,[6] as well as the fluctuation of rubber and extracted plants (mainly rattans). In 1996-7, many villagers switched from rubber tapping to wage work due to this new income opportunity and decreasing rubber prices. However, when the oil palm company stopped its field operation in late 1997/early 1998,[7] the same people switched back to rubber and rattan, which showed a partial price recovery at the time.

It is also noteworthy how RT III follows RT I/II in its dynamics, with a delay of several months regarding plantation labour. This delay partly reflects the remoteness of RT III which required temporary absence from the settlement in order to work on the plantation, while residents of RT I/II were picked up every morning by the company.

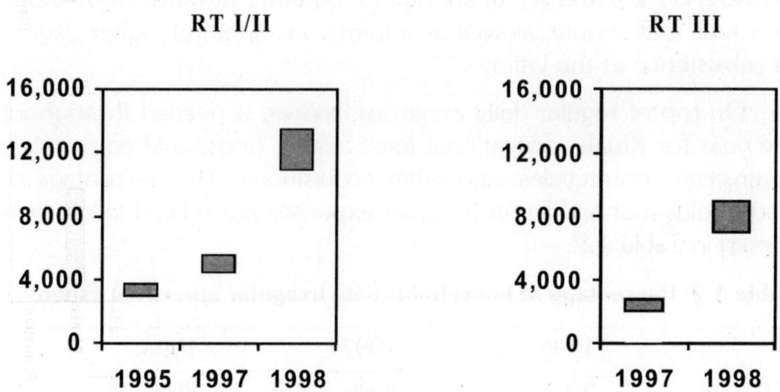

***Fig.* 4.4: Ranges of average daily household expenses. No interviews were carried in 1996, as living costs did not differ from 1995 (no data for RT III)**

6. This includes forest clearing, weeding, planting, and maintenance work in the nursery.
7. The oil palm company had to stop its operation due to financial problems, the drought, and a severe conflict with local people from nine villages.

Yet, as income chances declined in 1997 due to decreasing rubber prices, several people decided to leave RT III for a while to join the company. In general, the changing importance of these income sources depends mainly on market prices (e.g.,rubber, rattan, game), availability (rattan, game, *Doyo* fibres) and new opportunities (e.g., plantation work, a new market for turtles in 1998).

EXPENSES

The major daily expenses covered additional rice, cooking oil, sugar, cigarettes, onions, salt, gas, soap and tooth paste. The figures were de-quantified to ranges (illustrated in *fig*.4.4) despite exact quantitative answers, in order to avoid an overall impression that is more exact than the dynamic situation of real life (see sub-section 'Household Interviews and Socio-economic Surveys' under chapter 1).

There are two major findings: first, daily household expenses increased over the investigated four years; and second, expenses in RT I/II are significantly higher than in RT III. While the increase from 1997 to 1998 was caused by the Indonesian monetary crisis, and a failed harvest because of the El Niño-related drought, the differences between RT I/II and RT III are due to a greater distance from shops (6-8 km), less supply, as well as a (partly involuntary) higher degree of subsistence in the latter.

On top of regular daily expenses, money is needed throughout the year for rituals, educational fees, health, household equipment, chainsaws, motorcycles, and other acquisitions. The percentage of households that had larger irregular expenses not related to rituals is shown in Table 4.2.

Table 4.2: Percentage of households with irregular non-ritual expenses

	1996	1997	1998
RT I/II	39%	33%	89%
RT III	28%	16%	none

The average and maximum annual non-ritual expenses (of households with this kind of expenses) are illustrated in *fig*. 4.5.

While the mean expenses in RT I/II are rather constant over the three years, the figures of RT III show a strong increase from 1996 to 1997, and no such expenses at all in 1998. The increase was caused by three households who purchased chainsaws in order to find wage work at the oil palm company, during a time when most of RT III's households could not afford to spend much money outside their daily needs. In 1998, the financial crisis and the failed harvest did not allow any extraordinary expenses.

Households in RT I/II, which are generally better-off than their neighbours in RT III, overcame the crisis with the sale of gold at good prices that enabled many households to get connected to the electric grid (costs per household 400,000-500,000 Rp). [8] The 1998 column would have been even further beyond the scale of *fig.* 4.5, if the two richest households were included who bought a new house and a new expensive motorcycle. The higher percentage of households able to afford these extraordinary expenses, as well as higher absolute expenses in RT I/II as compared to RT III, reflects the higher economic standard of living in the main village, due to better infrastructure and market access, and a larger population size offering more niches for occupations. This difference, as well as inequalities between different

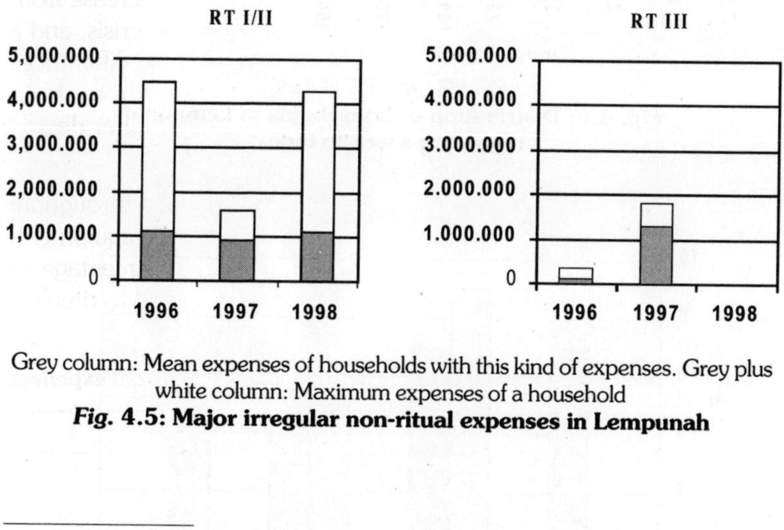

Grey column: Mean expenses of households with this kind of expenses. Grey plus white column: Maximum expenses of a household

***Fig.* 4.5: Major irregular non-ritual expenses in Lempunah**

---

8. Due to the devaluation of the Indonesian Rupiah, the gold price increased during 1998 from 25,000 Rp to more than 100,000 Rp per gram. Hence, many people decided to sell their gold savings. According to a gold trader in Tanjung Isuy, most households in RT I/II sold between 10 and 300 g of gold at an average price of 100,000 Rp/g. Although many families suffered from a failed rice harvest and devastating forest fires, only little money derived from the sale of the gold was used for supplementing food.

households becomes apparent in *fig.*4.6, where the visible wealth of households[9] is compared by applying an index based on the weighted number of several wealth indicators.

This pattern is also found in the distribution of households regarding the average monthly income estimated from socio-economic interviews.

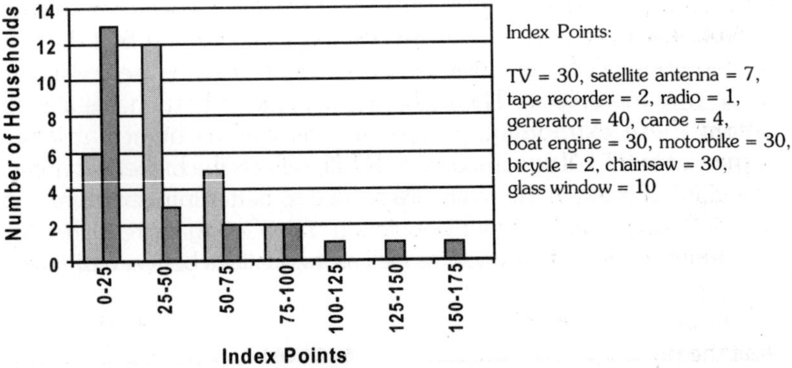

(RT I/II grey, RT III dark)

***Fig.* 4.6: Distribution of households in Lempunah regarding a wealth index**

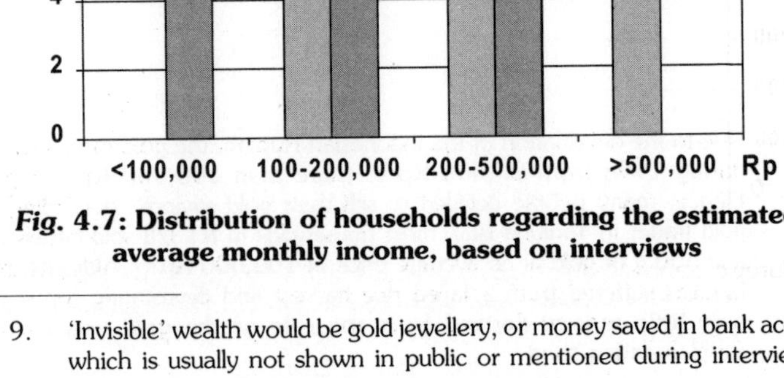

***Fig.* 4.7: Distribution of households regarding the estimated average monthly income, based on interviews**

9. 'Invisible' wealth would be gold jewellery, or money saved in bank accounts, which is usually not shown in public or mentioned during interviews.

Besides major expenses for material items, a rather large amount of money and resources (rice, chickens, and pigs) is spent each year for rituals (mainly *belian* and *bekeleeu* curing rites, a few also for *kwangkai* funerary rites). In most cases, people join a relative or a friend who organises a ceremony. Many of these rituals last up to several weeks. During this time, guests have to be hosted, and a large amount of drinks (tea and coffee) and food is spent. The percentage of households with such expenses is shown in Table 4.3.

Table 4.3: Percentage of households with irregular ritual expenses

	1996	1997	1998
RT I/II	50%	39%	67%
RT III	72%	44%	67%

The average ritual expenses are shown in *fig.* 4.8.

Much in contrast to the findings of non-ritual expenses, average sums spent for rituals (calculated as local shadow prices) show no significant difference between the two village parts, with the exception that the percentage of households with these expenses is even higher in RT III than in the main village. A comparison between ritual and non-ritual expenses shows further that households in RT III spend almost the triple the amount of money and resources on rituals than on material items (if the three chainsaws of 1997 are omitted), while material expenses exceed rituals in RT I/II by twice (if the new house and the new motorbike of 1998 are omitted). Nevertheless, rituals still play a similar role in both village parts. It is just that people of RT I/II can *also* afford to buy additional things.

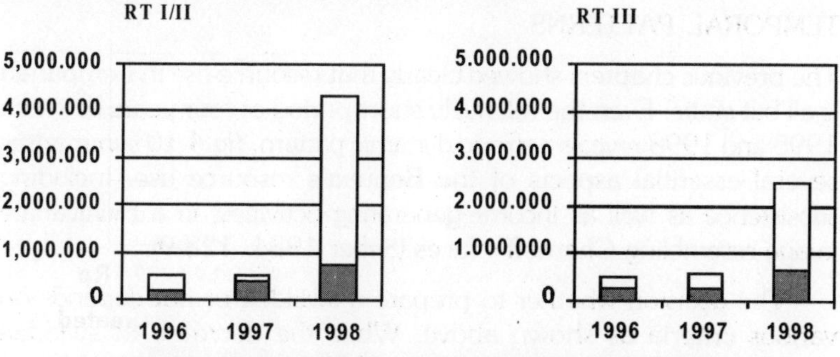

Grey column: Mean expenses of households with this kind of expenses.
Grey plus white column: Maximum expenses of a household.

***Fig.* 4.8: Major irregular ritual expenses in Lempunah applying shadow prices**[10]

Regarding the difficult economic situation of RT III in 1997-8, the question is: how do the people manage to afford these expensive rituals? One strategy is to divide the costs among often far extended families. Yet, equally importantly, is that these costs are not monetary costs, but contributions of sacrificial animals (chickens and pigs) and rice, which is all produced in RT III. The alternative to sell their farm produce was in most cases non-existent, as rituals are generally promised to the spirits long before they can be afforded. Selling an animal promised to be sacrified would however anger the spirits and bring sickness and misfortune to the respective person. Furthermore, these rituals are perceived as essential elements for securing a livelihood that includes economic aspects, but also surpasses them.

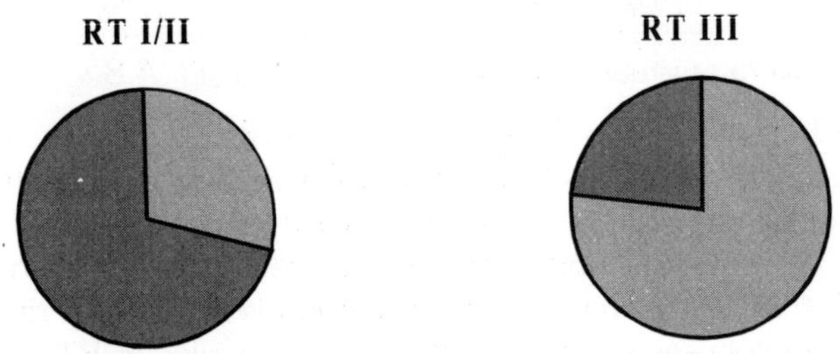

***Fig. 4.9*: Comparison of ritual (grey) and non-ritual (dark) expenses in Lempunah**

Patterns of resource use

TEMPORAL PATTERNS

The previous chapters showed clearly that resource use in Lempunah is all but static. Even the relatively short period of four years between 1995 and 1998 reveals a strong dynamic pattern. *fig.*4.10 summarises several essential aspects of the Benuaq's resource use, including subsistence as well as income-generating activities, in a multivariate image resembling Chernoff's faces (Seber 1984: 128-9).

The decision whether to prepare a swidden or not depends on various criteria as shown above. While the decrease of swidden numbers in 1996, as compared to 1995, was mainly caused by a good harvest and sufficient rice supply throughout 1996, allowing alternative work (e.g., wage work for the oil palm company), the

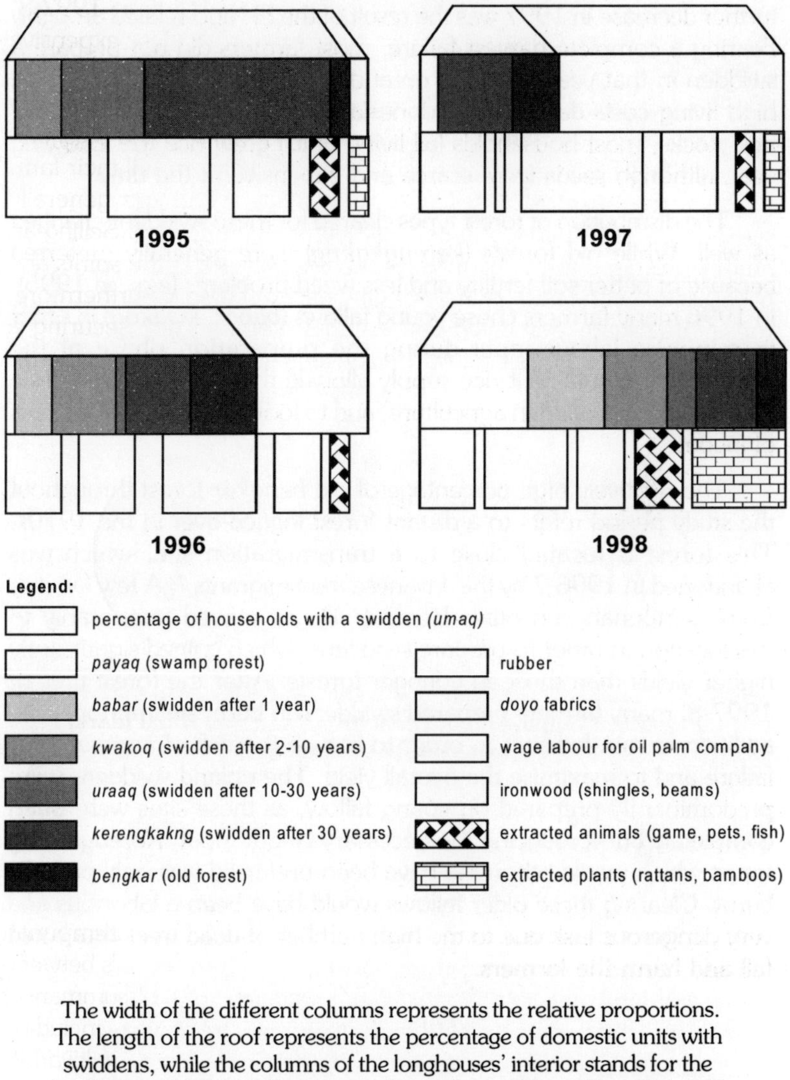

The width of the different columns represents the relative proportions. The length of the roof represents the percentage of domestic units with swiddens, while the columns of the longhouses' interior stands for the distribution of different forest types cleared for swiddens. The stilts' width represents the relative importance of income sources ascribed by interviewed households/ domestic units (n=18)

***Fig.* 4.10: Multivariate illustration of resource dynamics**

further decrease in 1997 was the result of the El Niño-related drought. Fearing a complete harvest failure, most farmers did not prepare a swidden in that year despite a great demand of rice. Suffering from high living costs due to the Indonesian financial crisis and depleted rice stocks, most households (all living units) grew rice the following year, although seeds were scarce and expensive at the time.

The distribution of forest types cleared for these swiddens changed as well. While old forests (*kerengkakng*) were generally preferred because of better soil fertility and less weed problems (e.g., in 1995), in 1996 many farmers chose young fallows (*babar*, *kwakoq*) in order to minimise labour input during the preparation phase of the swiddens.[11] A sufficient rice supply allowed them to invest less time and labour into swidden agriculture, and to look for additional sources of income.

The relatively high percentage of old *bengkar* forest throughout the study period refers to a distant forest logged-over in the 1970s. This forest is located close to a transmigration site, which was abandoned in 1996-7 by the Javanese transmigrants.[12] A few families from Lempunah and other Benuaq villages moved temporarily to this location in order to prepare swiddens, which gained significantly higher yields than those in younger forests. After the forest fires of 1997-8, many farmers prepared swiddens in burnt swamp forests in addition to rain-fed sites in order to reduce the risk of another crop failure and to maximise the overall yield. The upland swiddens were predominantly prepared on young fallow, as these sites were often completely burnt reducing the necessary labour input. *Kerengkakng* forest which would otherwise have been preferred was only partially burnt. Clearing these older fallows would have been a laborious and very dangerous task due to the high number of dead trees that could fall and harm the farmers.

---

10. Local prices for rice, chickens and pigs increased in 1998 by between 100-300 per cent.

11. Labour is only saved during the slashing and felling phase. Later, swiddens on young fallow require additional labour input due to an increased weed problem compared with older fallows.

12. Many transmigrants returned to Java as there were no nearby markets for selling their farm produce and no alternative working opportunities.

The variation of the ascribed importance of income sources[13] is caused mainly by price fluctuations (rubber, rattan); the occurrence of new markets (turtles, one bamboo species); and temporary job opportunities offered by the oil palm company. The rationale for the swift changes between different income sources will be further discussed in the following chapter. However, in order to understand the dynamics of resource activities, the integrated annual patterns of *fig.*4.10 must be regarded with a greater temporal resolution. If a single year (1998) is examined (*fig.*4.11), a substantial temporal overlap and change of resource activities becomes apparent. The pattern is shaped by temporally, rather than fixed subsistence activities, as well as by changing opportunities for generating financial income through extraction from the forest (ironwood, turtles, wild-growing rattans), or from forest gardens (rubber, cultivated rattans).

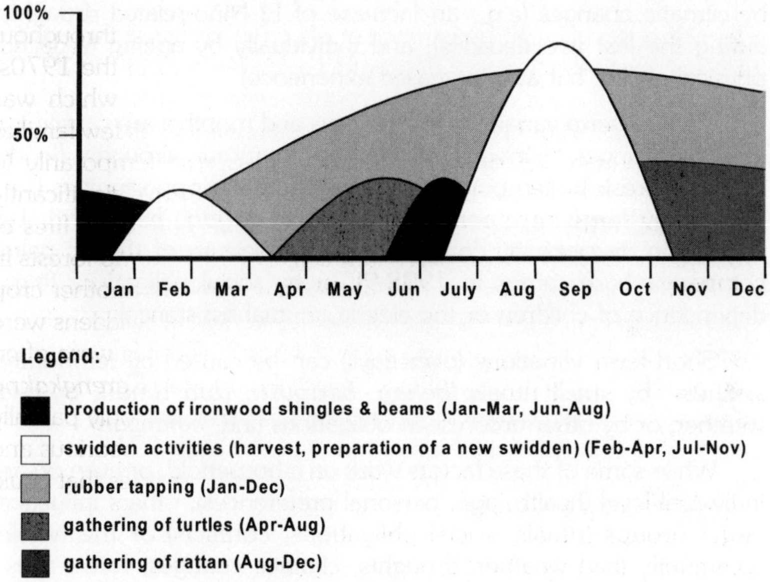

The height represents the proportion of households engaged in the respective activity.

***Fig.* 4.11: Major resource activities in Lempunah over 1998**

13. The relative importance does not necessarily reflect the amount of money earned by the respective activity, but only refers to the activities in any one given year in a relative way (3 points for the most important source of income, to 0 for no importance).

By integrating individual activities over time, illustrations like *fig*.4.10 or *fig*.4.11 might suggest that the village is the acting (systemic) entity. This is certainly not the case. Resource related interactions in Lempunah occur along a temporal and a social gradient, with the general temporal frame set by the annual swidden cycle. But this frame is modulated by a broad range of impact factors shaping the observed variable patterns.

Long-term changes (over years and decades) might be caused by policy impacts (e.g., government-induced land use changes, resettlement programmes); by a general shift of the socio-economic setting (e.g., transformation of mere subsistence to extended subsistence (see Gönner & Seeland forthcoming); or by replacement of extensive resource systems with plantations and mining); by shifts of socio-cultural values (e.g., preference of a more modern lifestyle); by climatic changes (e.g., an increase of El Niño-related droughts during the last two decades); and individually by ageing (reduced physical ability, but also increased experience).

Medium-term variations (over weeks and months) are caused by seasonal changes, by irregular events (e.g., temporary droughts, floods or forest fires); by temporary income generating opportunities (see above); by large ceremonies (*kwangkai*, *guguq*, *bekeleeu*); by continuing diseases; by conflicts (e.g., the seizure of the oil palm company's base camps in 1998-9); or by social obligations (e.g., dependence of children or the elderly, mutual assistance).

Short-term variations (over days) can be caused by temporary sickness, by small rituals (*belian*, *beriputn*, *tota timui*), by bad weather, or by other unforeseen obligations (Ind. *halangan*).

While some of these factors work on a household, or even on an individual level (health, age, personal preferences), others influence larger groups (rituals, social obligations, conflicts) or the whole community (bad weather, droughts, climatic changes, forest fires, resource prices, policy, national economics). Hence, the observed patterns depend very much on the temporal and on the social scale of reflection.[14]

---

14. These modulating factors are dynamic in themselves. Policies and prices change as much as do the performance of rituals or the necessities of social obligations.

	Short term	medium term	long term
community	weather	resource prices seasons droughts & floods forest fires	climatic changes socio-cultural change change of land use macro-economics policy
formal/ informal groups	small rituals social obligations	large rituals conflicts social obligations	alliances
household	sickness *halangan* obligations	diseases cash demand	age diseases marriages

***Fig*.4.12: Parameters modulating the chronology of resource use along a social and temporal gradient. The boundaries of these categories are floating**

These findings contrast with the often overly static descriptions of so-called traditional resource systems. This has strong implications on a practical policy level, as well as on the research level. If local resource systems can be that dynamic, short-term investigations bear the danger of producing biased interpretations. Although interviews about past resource use can reveal some dynamic aspects, others will certainly be overlooked if there is not a special focus on the issue, since past resources are often no longer relevant for the people interviewed.[15] Nevertheless, the awareness that these resource systems can be extremely dynamic should prevent researchers from omitting diachronical aspects of resource use.

SPATIAL PATTERNS

Looking at Lempunah's forest from a utilitarian point of view reveals two major patterns: one is the extractive use of the 'forest in-between', which is characterised by a high degree of fluctuation due to the structural dynamics of the fallow forest (e.g., Map 7, Map 8); the second pattern is more obvious, as it is defined by clearly demarcated swiddens and perennial forest gardens, which are scattered all over

15. It took me almost three years until I learned that the use of a certain tree bark (*Kayu Lem — Litsea sp.* c.f.) was of major importance in 1994-5. As the trees were completely exploited in 1996, no one mentioned the resource any more. A similar bias against the recalling of irregular and intermittent income sources is recognised by Ellis (1998: 9).

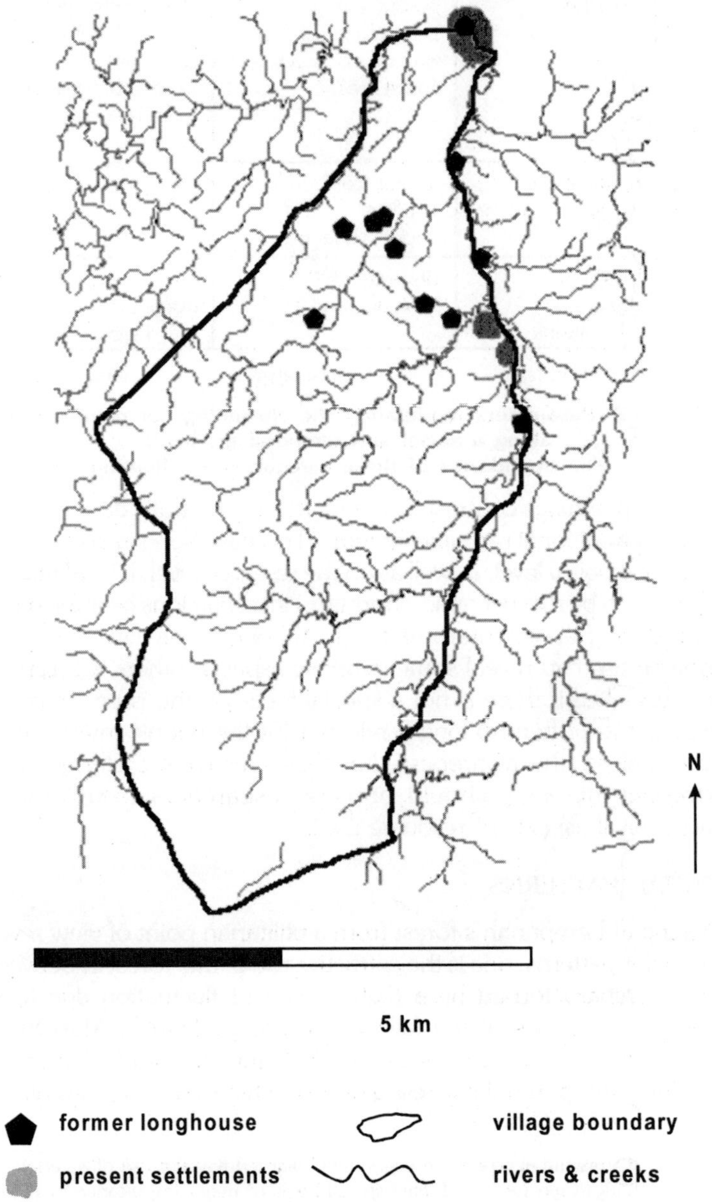

Map 6: Lempunah with Village Bondaries, Former Longhouses, and Rivers

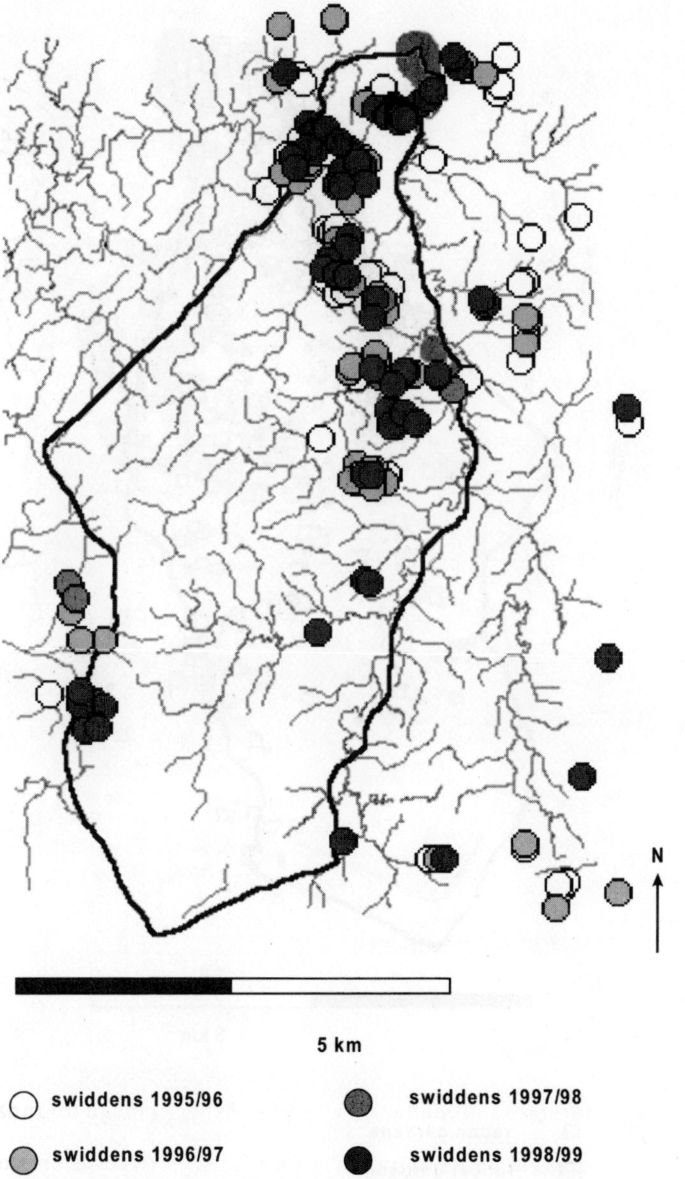

Map 7: Swiddens between 1995/96 and 1998/99

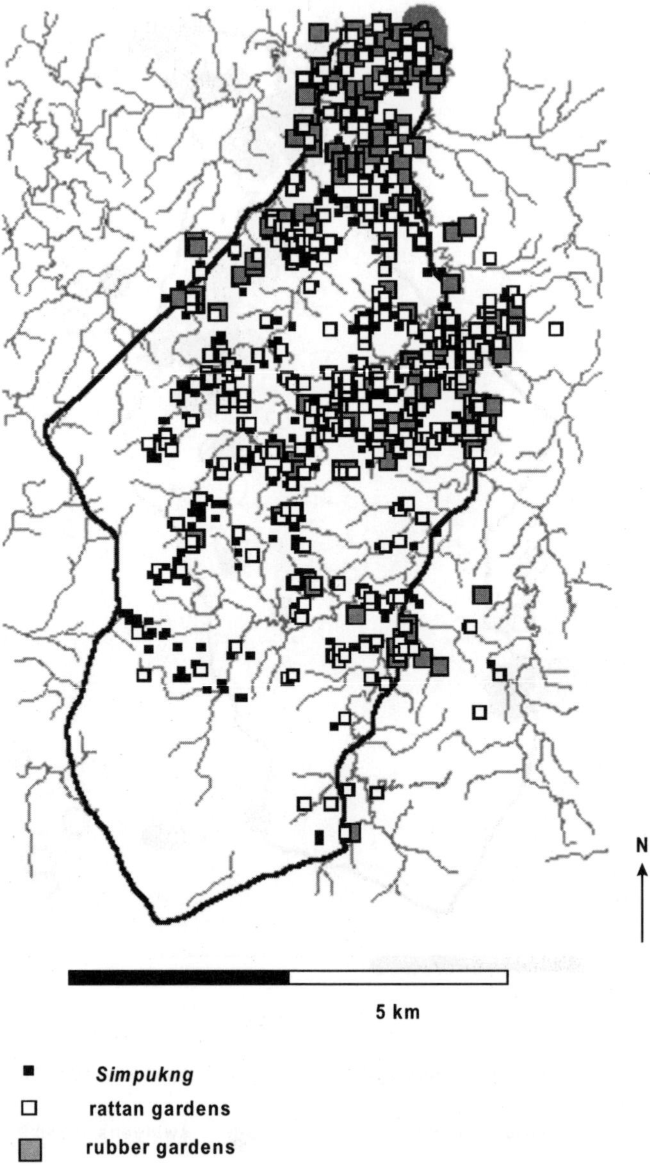

Map 8: Forest Gardens

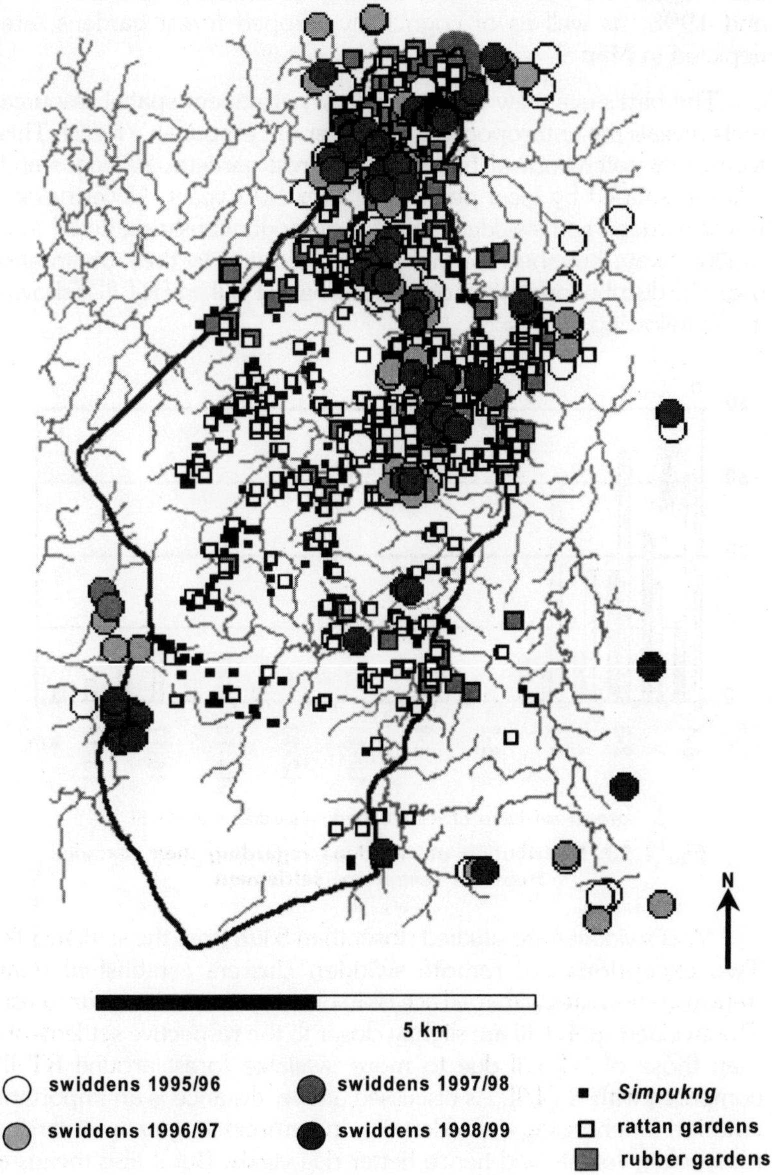

Map 9: Swiddens and forest gardens

the village's forest area. The distribution of swiddens between 1995 and 1998, as well as of cognitively-mapped forest gardens, are depicted in Map 9.

The bird's-eye view of these rather permanent spatial resource units reveals the anthropogenic character of Lempunah's forest. This forest is a patchwork of hundreds of forest gardens, swiddens and fallows, shaped by local people for over 300 years. Nevertheless, forest gardens and swiddens are not homogeneously scattered in a random way, but show certain patterns related to their origin and use. The distribution of their distances from RT I/II and RT III is shown in the following figures:

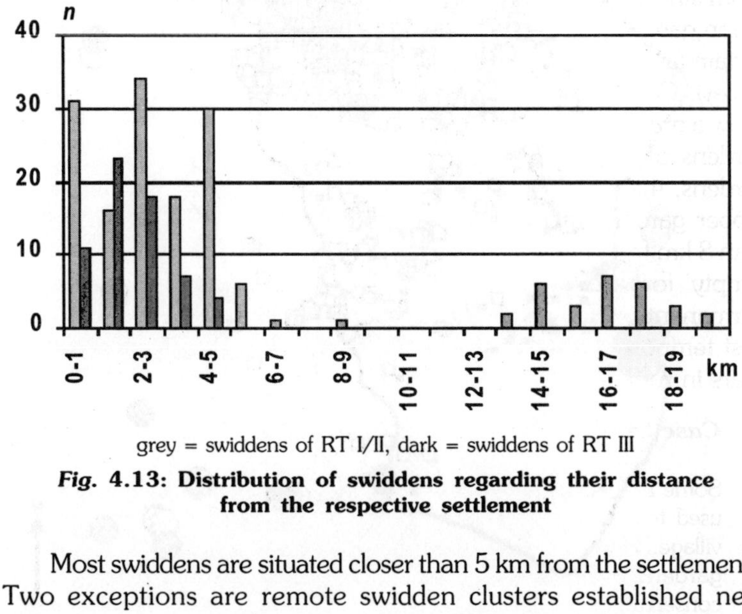

grey = swiddens of RT I/II, dark = swiddens of RT III

***Fig.* 4.13: Distribution of swiddens regarding their distance from the respective settlement**

Most swiddens are situated closer than 5 km from the settlements. Two exceptions are remote swidden clusters established near transmigration sites with road access in old logged-over *bengkar* forest. The swiddens of RT III are slightly closer to the respective settlements than those of RT I/II due to more available forest around RT III compared with RT I/II. As discussed above, distance is an important criterion for choosing a swidden site. In Lempunah, greater distances mean older forests and hence better rice yields. But it also means a greater time demand, and usually more pest problems due to less frequent controls, whereas a walking distance of 4-5 km (1-1.5 hours) allows daily visits. Swiddens that are too remote (especially without river or road access) also complicate the transportation of the harvest.[16]

Compared with recent swiddens, *simpukng* and rattan gardens[17] are more homogeneously distributed over the village area as they also reflect former swidden sites, going partly back to former longhouses or other distant settlements. Rubber gardens, on the other hand, are established closer to the village in order to keep the time demand for access and transportation of the produce at a reasonable level. The same principle holds for highly valued *Jepukng* gardens, which need to be controlled frequently because of the risk of theft and arson.

Distance is less relevant for cultivated resources such as fruits (from *simpukng*) or rattan (i.e., *Sokaq — Calamus caesius* — from rattan gardens) that are not used continuously, but only harvested at certain favourable times (e.g., during mast-fruiting, or at high market prices). Comparing the two village parts, forest gardens of RT I/II show a greater distance from the village than those of RT III. While all gardens of RT III are closer than 8 km, 44 per cent of all rattan gardens, 43 per cent of all *simpukng,* and even 17 per cent of all rubber gardens, belonging to households from RT I/II are further than 8 km from the main village. This is caused partly by less available 'empty' forest close to RT I/II, due to the village area's shape as a permanent settlement dating back almost a century; but it also reflects past temporary dwellings of villagers, who sometimes spent several years in remote parts of the forest.

Case Study

Some 50 years ago, the *kepala adat* of Lempunah and his family used to live in a part of the forest 10 km away from the main village. Here, he established many rattan and *simpukng* forest gardens over the years, which have now become part of a conservation area set-up by his son-in-law and by himself. Close to this area, are many other gardens which were created by his former neighbours who now also live in the main village. Nowadays, this kind of temporary settlement is rare due to the school system, public health care and access to markets.

---

16. A harvest of 1 tonne of unhusked rice needs approximately 30 walks from the field back to the village.

17. Rattan appears to be more confined to areas close to rivers for transportation reasons and — at least in the case of *Jepukng* (*Daemonorops crinita*) — also because of more suitable soils.

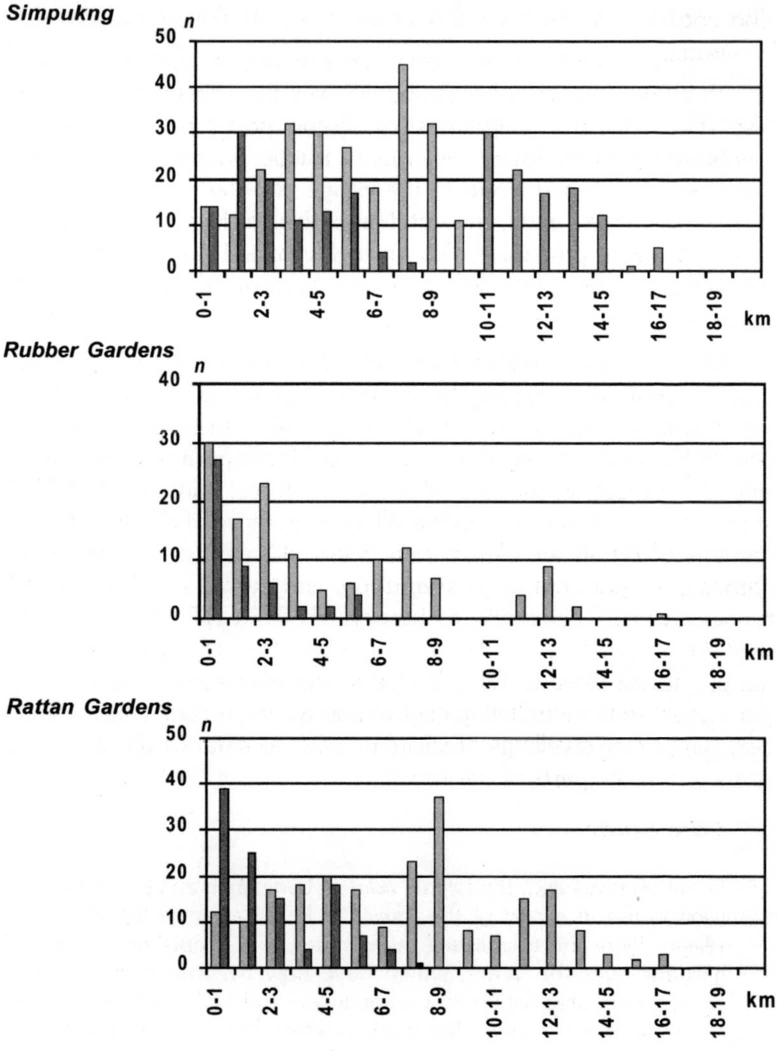

grey = gardens of RT I/II, dark = gardens of RT III.

***Fig.* 4.14: Distribution of forest gardens regarding their distance from the respective settlement**

The cognitively-mapped gardens represent about 80 per cent of Lempunah's households. The remaining 20 per cent cover another 200 to 300 gardens,[18] while approximately 30 per cent of all existing gardens were probably forgotten in the mapping process.

Table 4.4: Number of mapped forest gardens and estimated totals

Garden type	*Mapped*	*Unmapped gardens*	*Forgotten gardens*	*Total*
Simpukng	461	app. 100-130	app. 90-100	app. 650-690
Rattan	339	app. 80-90	app. 60-70	app. 480-500
Rubber	189	app. 30-40	app. 30-40	app. 250-270
total	989	app. 210-260	app. 180-230	app. 1,380-1,460

Assuming an average size of *simpukng* around 0.1 ha, rattan gardens around 0.25 ha, rubber gardens around 0.5 ha, and swiddens at 1.5 ha; the total area under cultivation, including recent swidden fallows, is around 3,400-3,500 ha (see Table 4.5):

Table 4.5: Area distribution of different land uses and forest types

Land Use	*Area in ha (app.)*	*in %*
present swiddens	120	1.3
recent swidden fallows (0-25 years)	3,000	32.6
old swidden fallows (>25 years)	5,258	57.1
simpukng	67	0.7
rattan gardens	125	1.4
rubber gardens	130	1.4
bengkar (very old secondary) forest	200	2.2
swamp forest	300	3.3
total area	9,200	100

As shown in *fig*. 4.14, and with a higher spatial resolution in *fig*. 4.15, the various cultivation units and fallow stages constitute a rich mosaic of anthropogenic forest. So far, examples of larger forest areas transformed by indigenous people in Borneo into partially-cultivated forests appear to be rare. Examples of forest gardens have been discussed above, but only few of these studies refer to larger areas (e.g., Padoch & Peters 1993). In most cases, only

18. This number is the sum of average garden numbers weighted by the village chief.

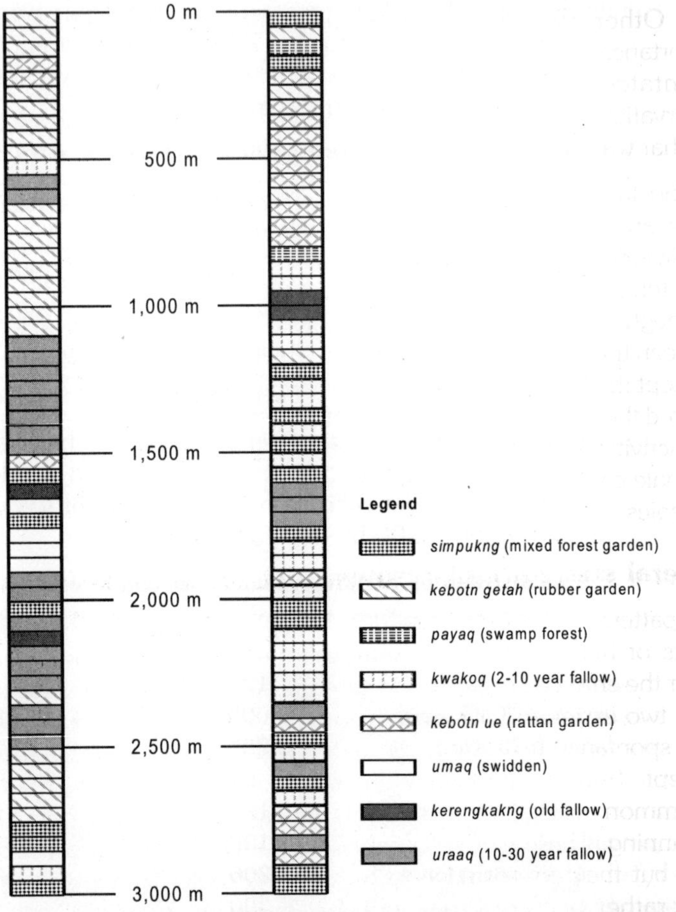

***Fig.* 4.15: Spatial distribution of resource units and forest types along two 3 km transects**

agroforests or forest gardens that are close to villages are described without a special focus on landscape aspects and history (e.g., Sardjono 1990, Salafsky 1994, Lawrence *et al.*1998). This phenomenon is, however, well-known for Brazilian Amazonia where at least 12 per cent of the *terra firme* forests appears to have been shaped by anthropogenic influence (Balée 1989, 1993).

The recognition of patterns always depends on perspectives and perceptions. Hence, to segregate temporal and spatial patterns is only one analytical means to emphasise several aspects of resource use. Other aspects such as cultural meaning, socio-economic importance or ecological implications are not included in this observer-orientated image. An image that resembles the behavioural observations of a natural scientist, still needs a deeper interpretation of what was observed.

So far, the described temporal and spatial patterns show that there are continuous processes shaping the environment into a patchwork of useful spaces (e.g., swiddens, forest gardens) overlayed with temporary activities that leave little traces in the landscape. Although it is fascinating to see how a co-evolution-type relation between the people of Lempunah and their surrounding environment has kept the forest in a dynamically changing state — which obviously secured the livelihood of the village for so long — the rationale behind the activities leading to these patterns still remains unclear. This rationale can only be understood, however, by examining the actual strategies of resource use in Lempunah.

General strategies of resource use

The patterns of resource use described in earlier chapters are the results of human activities, some rationally planned, others being rather the enforced responses to external events. The border between these two extreme forms of activities is a shifting one, and even the most spontaneous reaction can be part of a more general strategic concept. 'Strategy' is meant in this context in the rather broad sense of common activity patterns, which appear to include a certain kind of planning. These patterns might be reflected locally at a conscious level, but they do not have to be. In fact, some 'strategies' might work rather unconsciously, possibly based on previous 'cultural learning' processes, which have led to unreflected habituation. By applying this definition, the resource management strategies observed in Lempunah can be aggregated into several major patterns:

- Manipulation of the environment
- Conservation of resources
- Temporal fitting, self-dynamics and flexible responses
- Diversification and risk minimisation
- Socially and religiously-embedded strategies

MANIPULATION OF THE ENVIRONMENT

This phrase bears the underlying assumption that human behaviour is usually intentional and active (see Balée 1989: 2). It does not mean, however, that human action is unidirectional, originating out of itself. In most cases, people react with regards to external impact parameters. By reacting, these parameters are themselves influenced and might respond again in a different way, leading to new reactions. Hence, human beings are regarded here as parts of a dynamically-changing causal net. Their actions cannot be understood without looking at the net's general structure and behaviour. A certain action might look like a severe manipulation of the environment, but this environment always includes the actor him- or herself. Nevertheless, some actions, which are here referred to as 'strategies', alter the environment more than others. Among these strategies are those activities that change the species composition of the environment towards an easier or more secure resource supply. This can be done by switching from an extractive use of resources to domestication or cultivation (see Homma 1996: 66-73; Sasaki 1997: 7; Weinstock 1983b: 63-4). Recent examples in Lempunah are rattan gardens (see their history) and *simpukng* forest gardens.[19]

Such transitions from extraction to cultivation do not only depend on direct economic incentives (see Homma 1996: 66), but also on expectations and on the socio-cultural frame. In addition, long-term prospects and the often-stated perception of forest gardens as a future security for children and grandchildren, play an important role. However, this perception refers directly to the traditional land tenure system, and might change in due course with the declining external acknowledgement of traditional land rights. The development in Lempunah towards cultivated resources and an increasing management intensity are generally in line with Homma's transformation model (*ibid.*). Cultivating fruit trees in *simpukng* gardens probably started centuries ago. Even though it is unclear what originally caused the transition to forest gardens, subsistence

---

19. Dating much further back is the domestication of other food crops such as rice, cassava, or sweet potatoes (see Köhler & Seitz 1993: 566-569, Hutterer 1984).

needs and improved labour efficiency most probably played an important role.[20]

We also find the transition from an extracted resource to a cultivated one in the case of rattan. Economic demand was, however, also only one among several factors triggering this transition. While the history of *Sokaq* (*Calamus caesius*) cultivation is unclear, the development of *Jepukng* (*Daemonorops crinita*) gardens was induced mainly by social conflicts regarding access and property rights (see above), although a strong economic demand and a limited local supply were certainly also important for this innovation. The case of rubber gardens is slightly different, as *Hevea brasiliensis* is not autochthonous to South-East Asia. As described above, *Hevea* rubber was introduced to Lempunah in the 1930s. Until the early 1950s, rubber trees were planted in a similar way to fruit trees, in rather scattered patterns mixed with many other cultigens. Since then, the cultivation has become increasingly intensive,[21] and today rubber gardens consist mainly of only one planted tree species.

Beyond the enrichment of the forest with desired plant species, its opposite, the removal of unwanted species through weeding, burning and other kinds of pest control, is also an important manipulation strategy. Other strategies, such as gradual intensification and the management of cultivations (e.g., by burning for fertilisation, selection of seeds, protection of cultigens, harvesting techniques; see Sasaki 1997: 7; McCay 1978: 410-11, 415-17; Anderson & Ioris 1992: 364) follow these initial manipulations.

However, some changes of the environment that turn out to be benefitial for local people are positive side-effects, rather than due to intentional strategies. Most farmers would not state that they grow rice in order to hunt pigs on their swidden, although these pigs substantially contribute to their diet (see Dove 1985a: 239).[22] In a

---

20. In a case study from West Kalimantan, Lawrence *et al.* (1995) clearly show a strong preference by local people for durian fruits derived from forest gardens compared with those growing in primary forest. This is not surprising as the collecting efficiency is much higher in a forest garden, with a greater fruit tree density than in a primary forest.
21. In some areas, genetically-improved high yield varieties are used.
22. According to Brown and Marten (1986: 242), agricultural pests are tolerated by local communities because they are agricultural products, which can be consumed or otherwise used.

similar vein, plants which are confined to certain succession stages of the forest fallow (e.g., many ritual and medicinal plants) are maintained by the cyclical swidden system without being its major purpose. Although these examples are side-effects of the main strategies, they show that an integrated system can have many simultaneous advantages.

CONSERVATION OF RESOURCES

Conservation as a conscious strategy, as reported by Anderson and Ioris (1992: 364) for the Amazon estuary, is not very obvious in Lempunah. Although no large mammal species, possibly with the exception of the Sumatran Rhinoceros (*Dicerorhinus sumatrensis*),[23] has become extinct so far, there are no explicit strategies to conserve certain animals. All animals that harm people can be hunted, and there are no general food taboos in contrast with other areas in Borneo at the beginning of the twentieth century, when Krohn wrote:

> So tame are the deer in Central Borneo that they enter the villages without fear. Unless the garden plots of Dutch officers at the outposts are palisaded with high, pointed, closely-driven stakes, they are devastated by deer on their forays. I found no Dyaks who would eat deer meat.
>
> — 1991 [1927]: 162

Food and other taboos (*buyatn*) do exist, however, during pregnancy. Until the child's birth, no mammal, bird or reptile may be killed by the parents, and the consumption of the meat of snakes, turtles, certain fishes and pheasants (Great Argus — *Argusianus argus*, Crested Fireback — *Lophura ignita*) is not permitted. The prohibitions referring to the Great Argus remain valid until the child is able to say '*Jue*', the bird's name in Benuaq. Since this may take almost two-and-a-half years (including the pregnancy), this taboo provides a certain conservation status, although maybe only as a side-effect, as the rationale behind it is a cultural analogy.[24]

---

23. One killed animal was reported for the early 1980s close to Lempunah, but it is unclear whether the rhinoceros ever occurred as a resident in the area during the last centuries.

24. The taboos referring to pheasants and fishes is related to ocelli patterns (eye-spots) on feathers and on the back of certain fish species. An offence against these taboos might make the baby faint frequently. If a fish's eyes →

Due to relatively high hunting pressure around the settlements (and despite the counter-acting effects of the *buyatn* taboos), several bird and reptile species have become increasingly rare (e.g., hornbills — *Bucerotidae*, pheasants and partridges — *Phasianidae*, mynas — *Gracula religiosa*, crocodiles[25] and, more recently, freshwater turtles; see also Jepson *et al.* 1998, Momberg *et al.* 1998). High market prices also lead to a severe decline of ironwood trees (*Eusideroxylon zwageri*) and another tree species (*Kayu Lem — Litesa sp.* c.f.) that was commonly extracted in 1994-5.

During the drought of 1997-8, when the extraction of turtles temporarily became the most important source of income, there were also no regulative forces to prevent over-harvesting (see also Nietschmann 1973: 65 for the market induced over-harvesting of turtles among Miskito Indians in eastern Nicaragua). The only chance for a recovery of the population was new rain-fall that filled the swamps once again and made them inaccessible, at least for a certain period of time.

Yet, the view that there are no extinct large mammal or bird species so far, *only* because of a lack of means to hunt them more effectively, is certainly exaggerated, as several people in Lempunah are (at least nowadays) concerned about endangered species. Recently, the village chief initiated a 2,500 ha hunting reserve, where timber extraction and swidden agriculture are also prohibited. Since 1996, another 300 ha consisting of several scattered old forest patches, have been protected locally as a *hutan wisata*, a forest demarcated for eco-tourism.[26] Due to the small number of people using the remote

→ are taken out by one of the parents, this might lead to blindness of the child. The prohibition on reptiles refers to their ability to withdraw their head. It is believed that the killing or the consumption of a reptile may cause the baby to retreat into the womb.

There is also a wide range of individually-inherited taboos referring to the use of certain animal and plant species. One farmer, for example, is not allowed to keep gibbons (*Hylobates muelleri*) as pets, based on the close relation of one of his ancestors with a gibbon who saved his life during a head hunting raid.

25. One hunter explained the decline of mynas by the increasing experience of the birds that would not be as easily fooled by decoy birds. The recent lack of crocodiles is explained by a tale about a shaman who turned into a crocodile a few kilometers downriver, and now prevents other crocodiles from swimming upriver.

26. This concern is also influenced by contacts with environmental groups and myself.

old-growth forests (including the local conservation forest), these areas function well as reserves for rare animals and tree species, and thus contribute to conservation.

TEMPORAL FITTING, SELF-DYNAMICS AND FLEXIBLE RESPONSE

The adaptation of resource activities to temporal patterns of the environment, such as seasonal changes (e.g., rice cultivation, optimised planting time for cultigens); pseudo-periodic phenomena (e.g., mast-fruiting and the migrations of bearded pigs, see Caldecott 1991: 58, and Dove 1993c: 115-16); or even rather stochastic events (e.g., sudden market opportunities such as responses to boom-and-bust cycles, see Vayda 1996: 21, McCay 1978: 410, 416) is certainly not confined to the Benuaq, but figures as one of their most important strategies in living within their environment. By moulding their resource activities around the natural pace of their surrounding, the Benuaq use a high degree of the forest's self-dynamics. This was already shown for the *simpukng* forest gardens which only require a minimum of labour input to enhance the productivity of a particular forest patch, while relying on natural succession. The same holds for cultivated rattans, which are regarded as 'bank accounts' with interests assured by natural growth.

Apart from the adaptation to rather regular temporal patterns, which set the general frame for agricultural activities, the Benuaq also show a permanent readiness and flexibility for sudden opportunities rising out of irregular and unforeseen events, such as price fluctuations (e.g., rattan and rubber); new markets (e.g., freshwater turtles in 1998, *Kayu Lem* (*Lisea* sp. c.f.) in 1994-5, or *Itir* wood (*Intsia palembanica*) in 2000); new income opportunities (e.g., wage work for the oil palm plantation in 1996 and 1997[27]); policy changes (e.g., rattan); or climatic phenomena like the El Niño-related drought of 1997-8 (e.g., use of dry swamp forests). The common pattern, shown in *figs.*4.3 and 4.10, was to switch between these different opportunities. The underlying economic reference was thereby the amount of Rupiah earned or the equivalence in rice. Nevertheless, the decisions are not solely profit-maximising. Usually, besides the economic factors, a trade-off is made considering social, religious and emotional aspects.

---

27. A similar massive shift from farming to commercial fishing is described by McGrath *et al*. for the lower Amazon floodplain (1993: 180).

Case studies

In early 1998, several men worked for an illegally-operating timber entrepreneur from Tanjung Isuy. They were provided with fuel and basic food, which was expensive at that time due to the Indonesian financial crisis and a failed rice harvest. The food and the fuel were counted as a credit, which was to be repaid with timber; and additional wages were paid irregularly per cubic metre. On average, one worker could earn up to 100,000 Rp per day, equalling approximately 40 kg of rice. However, two men stopped after a couple of weeks and switched to rubber tapping despite a price of only 2,500 Rp per kg, which allowed a daily income of about 10,000 Rp or 4 kg of rice. Their rationale for stopping the more lucrative timber work was the irregular payment and the strong dependency on the local timber baron. Hence, they decided to stop and to earn some money with rubber which they wanted to invest into fuel for their chainsaws to work more independently.

Several women stopped working on the oil palm plantation as they did not feel '*tahan*' anymore, i.e., they could not stand the working conditions ('too hot'). They preferred to return to a combined work of rubber tapping and *Doyo* weaving that earned them a comparable income (*ca.* 6,000 Rp per day or 2-2.5 kg of rice).

Should these responses be called strategic, or are they mere passive reactions to external forces? The respective resource activities can indeed hardly be called strategies since they cannot be planned due to the very nature of the causative events. Yet, these events (including rain-fall and fruiting seasons, as well as price fluctuations) are perceived as unpredictable by the local farmers. Hence, they rarely rely on deceptive prognoses,[28] but prefer to maintain a certain level of readiness that allows them to react swiftly.[29] This readiness to switch

28. There are several indicators for droughts (e.g., flowering fruit trees and certain types of animal behaviour), but none for future price developments. None the less, some people considered political decisions such as the planned ASEAN free market (once scheduled for 2003), or peridodic shortages in the Samarinda rubber stocks, for their own resource decisions.

29. In order to seize these chances in time, most people try to get as much information as possible about new income opportunities or general price developments. Some prices are reported regularly by radio, other developments are broadcast on TV. Most information, however, is exchanged personally.

between different resources must, however, be regarded as a central strategy, as it is a prevailing pattern in Lempunah. There is certainly no lack of 'willingness to change', as Colfer also states for Kenyah farmers (1983: 84). As long as local people see an advantage in a new opportunity, they will try it.[30] This openness is also reflected in the Benuaq's attitude to try new rice varieties or new kinds of fruits. Hence, the stereotypical image of conservative, 'traditional' forest dwellers who are 'resistant to change' (*ibid.*) has to be dismissed.

Nevertheless, the range within the Benuaq can switch is mainly set by the eco-cultural environment, which is *per se* more diverse than, for example, in a Central Asian steppe. Yet, the maintenance and the management of such a diversity that allows a variation of practices according to the respective demands (see Brookfield & Padoch 1990: 9) is a strategy in itself.

DIVERSIFICATION AND RISK MINIMISATION

Closely linked to the concept of flexibility, are diversification strategies. The 'construction of a diverse portfolio' (Ellis 1998: 4) of activities occurs along the whole gradient of the Benuaq's extended subsistence economy, extending from crop diversification through to the diversification of income sources. Not only are species and activities diversified, however, but also their settings in time and space, as well as their management regarding social aspects. The scattered distribution of forest gardens, the chronology of different resource activities, the organisation of labour; all of this shows a diversified character suited to fit into the dynamic opportunities of life in Lempunah.

Although livelihood diversification is 'an infinitely heterogeneous social and economic process' that needs to be regarded in its respective local contexts (*ibid.*: 29), it is a common phenomenon,[31] including both deliberate and planned *ex ante* strategies with a risk avertion tendency (*ibid.*: 13); as well as involuntary *ex post* coping activities, following disasters or unforeseen events (*ibid.*). While the first kind of

---

30. One recent example was the production of charcoal out of burnt trees, after the fires, which was planned by a Chinese businessman. Several people in Lempunah were ready to participate in this new business, but the project never started due to financial problems of the entrepreneur.

31. Livelihood diversification is not restricted to rural areas or development countries, but occurs worldwide in different contexts (Ellis 1998: 3).

activities are strategies in the sense defined above, the latter would rather be coping mechanisms, embedded in a form of strategic readiness.

Among the *ex ante* strategies is the diversification of crops, both for subsistence and for commerce. Crop diversification is known all over the tropics as a risk avertion strategy mitigating environmental hazards, price fluctuations and other unpredictable events (e.g., Anderson & Ioris 1992: 364 for fishermen in the Amazon estuary; Schelhas 1996: 298 for cattle farmers in Costa Rica; Dove 1985a: 159-99 for the Kantu' rice farmers of West Kalimantan; Godoy & Feaw 1991: 34-7 for rattan farmers in South Kalimantan; Godoy & Bennett 1991: 83-4 for coconut cropping systems in Indonesia). According to Schelhas (1996: 299) crop diversification has several advantages including: (1) exploitation of environmental differences (including climate and fertility); (2) better use of household labour throughout the year; (3) risk reduction of crop failure due to pests, or from market instability; (4) advantages of synergies of labour, nutrients, micro-climate and plant associations; (5) overcoming the declining returns of labour by switching to, or adding, high-value cash crops; and (6) meeting the full range of household needs for products (including building materials, fencing, and foods with different nutritional values).

Most of these rationales also hold for Lempunah's farmers, who use a wide range of different crops as shown above. For example, the combination of rice, maize, sweet potatoes and cassava, reduces the risk of a complete crop failure, as the maturing periods, and often the locations, of these cultigens are different, thus diluting pest predation or the impacts of temporary droughts. Hence, after the failed rice harvest in 1998, cassava became an important staple food, which reinforced its reputation as a 'famine food'.[32] The combination of swamp rice and hill rice varieties, as well as the intercropping of varieties with different maturing times, also appears to be useful in less extreme years to mitigate losses due to pests, floods, or a temporary lack of rain. However, this intra-species diversity of more than 100 local rice varieties is not explicitly maintained in order to minimise risk, but rather owing to individual preferences. In fact, during the drought of 1997-8, all rice varieties failed; and in 1999 and 2000, all were equally affected by locusts, rats and mice.

---

32. Dove (1993c: 117) mentions the importance of forest fruits during periods of rice shortage, especially before the new rice harvest.

Crop diversification certainly does not reduce these risks all by itself, as it always depends on the interaction between the different crops, as well as on the kind and amount of edible plant material and pests (see Brown & Marten 1986: 252). All the same, if different crop species are further diversified regarding temporal and spatial aspects (*ibid.* 259-60), the risk due to pests and climatic hazards should at least be partially buffered.

Another labour extensive strategy is the great diversity of different forest garden locations. These gardens are easily established and require little management until they are used. Left more-or-less to natural succession, they become reservoirs of future resources. Their management and their importance depend on the availability of fruits, rattans, and other products, as well as on their respective location. As they are scattered over the whole forest area, some forest gardens are always in reach of a swidden, which is of special importance during mast-fruiting periods when fruits from *simpukng* gardens become open access for personal consumption. Further, the sheer number of gardens is a strategy in itself, as it increases the chances that at least some will become useful in the future.[33]

A high diversity is also found among income-generating activities (see also job diversification in Newfoundland described by McCay 1978: 403-10, 415-17, and household strategies compiled by Ellis 1998), which buffer unpredictable price fluctuations or market instabilities. According to Ellis (1998: 17), the diversification of income sources may occur on three levels to: (1) 'reduce the risk of income failure overall'; (2) 'to reduce the risk of intra-year income variability'; and (3) 'to reduce the risk of inter-year income variability'. Some of these rationales are met in Lempunah, including the diversification of commercially-used forest gardens (rattan, rubber), as well as gender-related labour division. Yet, the majority of diversified income sources is the result of opportunistic switching integrated over time.

33. The strategy of producing large numbers of possible survivors is also known from ecology. For instance, many pioneer plants in Bornean rain forests produce large numbers of small seeds (MacKinnon *et al.* 1996: 188). The same strategy is applied in the cultivation of side-crops. Despite a high number of sweet potatoes, cucumbers, bananas, sugar-cane, etc., only a small amount is harvested due to pests and crop failure. However, the time and labour invested into these crops is rather little compared to rice. So any harvest of these additional cultigens must be regarded as a success.

Occasionally, these switches must be regarded as rather involuntary coping reactions (e.g., after the forest fires or during the drought), while responses to temporary resource availability and market opportunities are chosen deliberately among different alternatives.

However, the diversification of temporary resource activities is not only risk avertion, but also an expression of a culturally-favoured way of life. In fact, mono-specific occupations with tight schedules and a high degree of dependence (e.g., through debt-bonds) are perceived as unfavourable in Lempunah, and only very few young people choose to work permanently off-farm. The majority would not rely on specialised work without the security of a swidden, or at least a full rice store. A permanent job would further exclude longer periods of spare time, which are used for ritual and social life. Given the priority of a secure subsistence and the necessary rituals, additional income sources must fit into a fragmented time frame. Hence, diversification is almost an inevitable result of cultural values and economic opportunities.

SOCIALLY AND RELIGIOUSLY-EMBEDDED STRATEGIES

The mutual acknowledgement of individual ownership of resources or resource areas (swiddens, fallows, forest gardens) is an indispensible precondition for perpetual resource use (see also Peluso & Padoch 1996: 126-8, and Lawrence 1997: 9). Violations against the traditional *adat* law are punished with symbolic and material fines imposed by an assembly of elders which is generally led by the *kepala adat*.[34] The respective ownership of individual forest gardens is usually known by many people, who can function as witnesses in these disputes.[35] This social stratification which played an important role in the past in the control and management of resources, including partial contributions of the harvest to the *mantiiq* (noblemen), shows very

---

34. These fines are generally expressed in terms of traditional currency. However, more important than the financial aspects, is the social re-integration of a punished person. One of my key-informants, who was sentenced to pay a certain amount of money for rattan theft, paid the fine despite his different view of the situation, in order to again be regarded as a respectable man.

35. This traditional land tenure system is, however, currently being eroded by the conflict with the nearby oil palm company (see Gönner 1999a). As the company and the Indonesian state only partially acknowledge traditional land rights, this conflict has escalated in 1998-9.

little direct impact today. Only occasionally, the *kepala adat* receives parts of a killed animal, while assisting with work on the *mantiiq's* swiddens no longer occurs.

Forest gardens and swiddens, including their fallows, are individually owned, but they are generally managed in a co-operative way by groups linked either by close family ties or by friendship. These social groups also co-operate in rituals, during conflicts, and in cases of sickness or need.[36] Social networks like in *fig.* 4.16 also limit the autonomy of decisions for individual households,[37] as resource activities are often organised regarding the structure of formal and informal social groups with a special emphasis on the extended family.

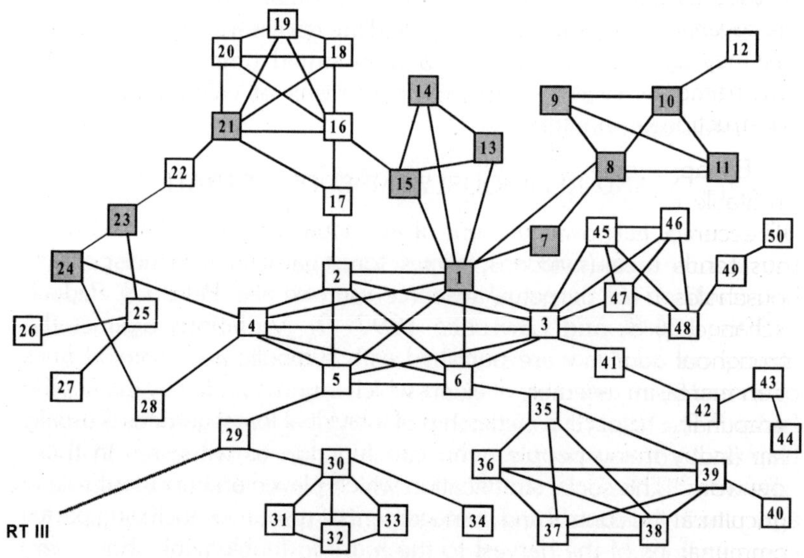

The grey boxes indicate households that were directly involved in the conflict with the oil palm company. Household No. 29 is related to households in RT III.

***Fig.* 4.16: Social net of households in RT I/II related via parental and sibling bonds**

36. Social nets do not always redress misfortune, however, as shown by Godoy *et al.* (1998a: 67) for Tsimane' indians in Bolivia.

37. This calls into question the concept of the household as the decision-making unit (see critique in Ellis 1998: 6-7).

Hence, the activities of socially (and often also politically and economically) more dependent households are restricted due to social obligations towards more powerful households. On the other hand, they profit from an increased security provided by the more influential partners of this social network.

Social co-operation is a general feature of resource activities in Borneo (e.g., Dove 1985a: 305-7, Freeman 1992: 234-238). Apart from the social obligations mentioned already, labour exchange, labour division and wage work are the most common patterns (see also Dove 1985a: 307-14, and Freeman 1992: 238-40). By dividing labour, whether on an exchange basis or for cash, several tasks can be performed simultaneously. Hence, additional income sources may be used temporarily, while routine tasks, such as swidden activities, are covered by helpers. Other tasks might be of such a large dimension that they cannot be covered by a single household within a reasonable time-frame, and thus require social co-operation (e.g., large rituals, construction work, group swiddens).

By applying *konookng* wage work, an added value (due to profitable off-farm activities) can be achieved, while subsistence is still secured. However, this strategy requires access to capital, and thus tends to enhance inequalities between well-off and poor households. The observation by Thandee (1986: 162) that labour exchange, which predominates over traditional agricultural production throughout South-East Asia, shifts to paid contractual labour in cases of an increasing agricultural commercialisation, can be confirmed in Lempunah. An often-stated complaint of village elders is that mutual help (Ind. *gotong-royong*) is vanishing, as the villagers would only now work if they are paid. While labour exchange is still frequent in agricultural (subsistence) activities (*plou*), this statement holds for communal work such as construction work, or the maintenance of forest trails, as well as for commercial activities like rattan extraction. Wage work is common in many fields of resource use, ranging from swidden activities (*konookng*, during all steps of the swidden cycle), extractive use (e.g., rattan, timber), through to services such as construction work, rice-hulling, or rattan-processing, applying a daily wage of one *beleq* of rice (ca. 11 kg), or cash between 7,500 Rp and 50,000 Rp, depending on the job.

Labour division is found between age groups and between sexes. The kind of division depends mainly on physical abilities, although most tasks can be done by men and women and appear to be much less strictly divided than among the Iban (Freeman 1992: 227-31; Sutlive 1992: 75; but see Colfer for only lose labour division among the Kenyah sexes 1981: 78). Tasks usually covered by men include tree-felling, dibbling, hunting, shingling, extraction of timber, honey-gathering, extraction of remote rattans, blacksmith's work, construction work, and (strictly) the *pengewara* activities in *kwangkai* funerary rites; while women are usually responsible for the making of *Ulap Doyo* fabrics, for rice planting, knitting and embroidering, midwifery, and assistance of shamans (both male and female) during *belian* rituals. Yet, typical household tasks such as washing or cooking may be done by both sexes, although they are generally covered by women. During periods of equally important options, labour division becomes an important strategy as an alternative to wage work for households which are sufficiently large. This kind of labour splitting is also reported for Kantu', who might grow rice on a swidden at the same time as other family members tap rubber in another place (Dove 1985a: 64).

Case studies

When rattan prices increased in October 1998, about twenty farmers went to remote parts of the forest, where they stayed for several weeks in temporary camps, harvesting rattan from those gardens that were not burnt by the forest fires. However, as rice was short due to a failed harvest in early 1998, and living costs were still soaring after the Indonesian financial crisis, nobody dared to rely solely on rattan. Hence, the swiddens and swamp rice fields that were prepared between July and September, were now managed by women, children and by the elderly.

During the land clearing phase of the oil palm company (in 1996) many men found temporary work over several months, while their wives remained at home tapping rubber trees and weaving *Ulap Doyo*. One year later, the situation was vice versa, when women and children worked (temporarily) in the company's nursery or on the plantation (mainly weeding), and men tapped rubber.

Labour is also divided among age groups including children and elderly family members, who participate in many daily tasks in the household, on the farms, and in other kinds of resource use (including wage work), according to their skills and physical ability.

An important parameter concerning the availability and the management of resources is population density. Compared to other case studies,[38] population density in Lempunah is rather low (3.8 persons/km^2), but in a similar range as the figures given by Freeman (1992: 64) for the Iban (3.5 persons/km^2). It is well below the carrying capacity calculated for Bornean swidden systems (ca. 16 persons/km^2 for the Kantu', see Dove 1985a: 381; 2.5-6.7 families/km^2 for Kenyah villages, see Colfer n.d.: 72; equalling about 14-37 persons/km^2, see *ibid*.: 69), and does not seem to be limiting resource use in any way.

After a longhouse fission many decades ago, there was apparently some moderate migration out of Lempunah to Tenggarong and Samarinda, and according to the memory of village elders, the indigenous population has remained rather stable over the last 50 years. However, a low population density can only be called a strategy if it is actively maintained by birth control or migration. Otherwise, it would be a passive response by reduced fertility and increased mortality due to a limiting environment (see also Moran 1991: 367).

In Lempunah, several traditional techniques of birth control are still known, although most women practice modern contraception (mainly the pill) since the early 1970s. Yet, the controlled low population density is counteracted by governmental transmigration projects, and by the immigration of labour forces organised by the various companies.[39] Another set of strategies is based on the traditional religion, such as the *buyatn* food taboos during pregnancy, and other ritual elements which show an impact on the local resource use. As explained in the chapter about swidden agriculture, the interpretation of omens can lead to a certain randomisation of the site selection which redresses suggestive, but uncertain, prognoses such as the rain-fall prediction based on the previous year (see Dove 1993a: 158). Occasionally, small individual rites are carried out in the swidden in order to ensure a successful maturing of the crops, and to protect them from pests.

---

38. Dove (1985: 381) reports 11.5 persons/km^2 for the Kantu', Conklin (1957: 146) speaks of 24.2 persons/km^2 for the Hanunóo.

39. During recent years, hundreds of temporary oil palm workers arrived from other parts of Indonesia without an official registration by the company (hence, no reliable data are available). Further, two new transmigration sites with approximately 300-500 Javanese families were established between 1997 and 1998, enhancing the pressure on the available forest.

Other religiously-motivated strategies are large collective rituals (*guguq tautn*, *bekeleeu*) performed for a fertile new year with prosperous harvests of rice, other swidden crops, game, fish, and honey; as well as rituals that are believed to end droughts and other natural disasters (*nular*, *melas tautn*). During these rituals, which are often performed after the harvest (but directed towards the new annual cycle), a substantial amount of rice is distributed amongst the guests. Since these rituals are only possible after a good harvest, they are also a strategy to mitigate individual harvest losses. On a smaller scale, hunters perform individual rituals to receive spiritual protection on their way through the forest (see also Hopes 1997: 115-20), while the good fortune of envied persons is believed to have been influenced by black magic (mainly by spells, *ibid*.: 109-14).

Closing remarks

The livelihood of Lempunah is based on a combination of cyclical swidden agriculture and irregular income-generating activities, resulting in an extended subsistence economy (Gönner & Seeland forthcoming). The vulnerability of this combination to environmental hazards (e.g., pests, droughts, fires, floods) and market instabilities is mitigated by a broad range of risk avertion strategies, including diversification, social co-operation, and flexible responses. In addition, existing forces and processes are used in a highly efficient way. Natural processes are manipulated at certain sensitive steps (e.g., after removing competing vegetation, or at the beginning of the succession on a left swidden), and by adding some initial labour input to change the conditions in favour of the actor. The subsequent growth of the resource is then left to nature, with more (swiddens) or less (*simpukng*, rattan gardens) intensive management.

In an almost analogous way, existing economic forces, such as booming or emerging markets, are exploited by switching between different income sources, depending on the expected rate-of-return, available time or existing alternatives. This surfing on a wave of opportunities requires a permanent readiness for flexible reactions, although these responses are usually limited by more highly-valued subsistence activities and socio-religious obligations.

5

Conclusions

Prospects for resource use in Lempunah

THE extended subsistence system of Lempunah, based on a self-sufficient food supply, a flexible adaptation to new opportunities and a labour-efficient use of natural dynamics, has persisted so far through continuous adaptation processes. Although the observed resource management strategies are not explicitly sustainable,[1] in a purposive sense, resource use in Lempunah shows a 'genuine sustainability' (Gönner & Seeland forthcoming). Instead of keeping an 'equilibrium' in balance, local people use the forest in the flexible way described above. This can include temporary intensive exploitation (e.g., rattan during the boom between 1986 and 1988; turtles in 1998) along with long periods of non-use (see section 'Rattan Gardens' under chapter 3). Under favourable conditions (i.e., sufficiently large buffer areas and enough time for a recovery of animal or plant populations), this could lead to a cyclical approach towards sustainability (see also Bennett 1976: 137).

---

1. Despite a wide and public discussion about the necessity of sustainability and a common but vague understanding of what sustainability means, it is methodologically impossible to prove that a certain way of resource management is sustainable. Such a proof would require a comprehensive but non-existing knowledge reaching well into the future, as sustainability can only be evaluated along a temporal axis. What can be proved is only the falsification, i.e., if a certain resource management is not sustainable. This is comparable to the impossibility of proving truth. Instead, Popper (1993: 376-382) suggests using closeness to truth ('Wahrheitsnähe'). Hence, it might be more suitable to speak of the closeness to sustainability by considering ecological, socio-economic, religious, and cognitive aspects. Taking these aspects into account, one can conclude whether a certain resource use is more likely to be sustainable than another.

The managed forest of Lempunah maintains a high level of biodiversity. Transect counts and species richness simulations revealed no significant difference in the number of bird species (as a practical example for biodiversity) between an old part of Lempunah's forest, which was probably never used for swidden cultivation, and a typical part consisting of forest gardens and swidden fallows. While 102 species were counted along a transect of 1,500 m cutting across the first, 101 were counted in the latter. The simulation even put the managed forest at 108 species, against 106 in the old forest (see Gönner 1999b, 2000a). This is contrary to findings from Sumatra (Thiollay 1995), where avian species richness was 41-62 per cent less in traditional agroforests compared with primary forest.[2] Due to the different forest structure, as well as less hunting pressure, the species composition differed slightly between the two sites in Lempunah with a Sørensen's index of similarity of 68 per cent.

Hunting puts a high pressure on several species such as wild boar (*Sus barbatus*); deer (*Tragulus spp.*, *Muntiacus spp.*, *Cervus unicolor*); sun bear (*Helarctos malayanus*); hornbills (*Bucerotidae*); pheasants (*Phasianidae*); Hill Myna (*Gracula religiosa*); or most recently, freshwater turtles (*Chelonii*). Mainly due to remote and less accessible parts of the forest, all hunted species have survived so far. However, exceptional events such as the drought and the fires of 1997-8, increase the danger of local extinction, as hundreds of deer were reported to have fled the fires right into the waiting arms of hunters.[3] More than 1,500 freshwater turtles were collected in the dry swamp forests around Lempunah, and during the fruiting season of 1995-6 more than 150 Hill Mynas were caught with lime twigs.

Since large-scale overexploitation of resources happens in Lempunah only irregularly, much depends on the time between these phases, as well as on sufficiently large buffer areas. Further to these ecological considerations, this 'genuine sustainability' also addresses social and cognitive aspects. If compared to recent plantation projects

---

2. The old forest studied in Lempunah contains both patches of forest probably never used for swiddening, as well as old forest gardens (older than 50 years). Hence, it is not a 'true' primary forest, but its avian species composition is the same as in a so-called 'primary' forest (based on my own studies from various sites in Borneo).

3. So far, only self-made fire arms with a very limited range are in use. But if the legal restriction of fire arms is loosened (as currently discussed), hunting might soon become very far from sustainable.

(oil palms, timber) the traditional ways of resource use were also socially sustainable. Extreme inequality was buffered by social networks, mutual labour exchange, and by resource re-distribution during ceremonies. The individual disposal of land and forest gardens, however, is now eroding this social sustainability. New, unbuffered inequilities and envy created by an inequal financial compensation of forest gardens converted by the oil palm company has led to severe conflicts, both within the communities and between local people and the company (see Gönner 1998a, 1999a). While conflicts were traditionally solved by *adat* law, those induced by land rights problems and a strong dependence on a monocropped resource, such as oil palm or rubber, often persist for many years (see King 1999: 52-9, Dove 1985b, 1986).

Another aspect of sustainability refers to knowledge. So far, traditional knowledge of resource management as well as ritual knowledge was passed down from generation to generation. Traditional medicinal plants are still used, but the detailed knowledge remains with elderly people and the healers, while modern medication increasingly predominates. Responding to the accelerated change of lifestyle, traditional knowledge[4] is being substituted with knowledge that is perceived as more relevant to surviving in the present world.[5]

This last observation, especially, emphasises the difficulty in evaluating dynamic processes like socio-cultural change in terms of sustainability.[6] Sustainability has to be differentiated from preserving

4. The expression 'traditional' is meant as opposed to new sorts of knowledge, such as the use of mass media, computers or western medicine. Traditional knowledge in the sense of a rigid and unchanging canon has probably never existed.
5. Due to a general socio-cultural change that influences social values, as well as individual goals, money is nowadays only rarely spent on the expensive and long apprenticeship of a *pembeliatn* or a *pengewara*.
6. King (1999: 129-31) also explores 'the difficulties in determining sustainability'. He lists 'ecological soundness and environmental protection, the importance of the welfare and quality of life of human beings, and local-level participation and bottom-up community-based strategies', as well as indigenous knowledge and the sustaining of livelihoods for future generations, quoting Braganza (1996: 312). However, this set of criteria only refers to development projects, assuming the given sustainability of local resource use. None the less, King admits that 'many local people are themselves currently involved in environmental exploitation because of poverty, marginality, and the perceived need to secure some of the benefits of natural resources use before these are realised by outsiders.' (ibid.).

a certain status quo. The idea of sustainability is related to the concept of a balanced equilibrium, which might work as long as the setting or the frame of a system is constant. It gets more complex once the system starts to shift and equilibria turn into steady states. Then, one has to decide which variates should be kept constant (i.e., 'sustainable'), and which are allowed to float and become dynamic. Hence, if the present resource management in Lempunah is regarded, much depends on the individual perspective. A more conservation-oriented person might regret the loss of traditional knowledge and values, while a process-oriented researcher will appreciate people's ability to adapt to new circumstances (Gönner 2000a).

Regarding the long persistence of resource use in Lempunah, the major question is: what are the chances for this resource system to further adapt and survive into the future? Before this question can be addressed, some basic preconditions of Lempunah's extended subsistence have to be examined. The combination of rather conservative, safety-oriented subsistence agriculture with an extraordinaryly dynamic and flexible use of additional resources was shown to be the key to securing a livelihood in Lempunah. However, both complementary parts require certain conditions in order to work successfully, such as: (1) decision autonomy; (2) security of land rights and usufruct; (3) individual flexibility to react to fluctuations; (4) maintenance of a high level of biodiversity; and (5) reliability of the social and religious frame.

These preconditions are influenced by various internal and external parameters, which connect Lempunah via trade relations, politics, information and conflicts to the outside world. In order to represent the local situation in a comprehensive way, the most relevant aspects and parameters, as well as the interconnecting links between them, are aggregated into a causal net. The causal validity of each link is based on observations and interview data. Nevertheless, this analytical step reflects an expert-like position, on which the selection of variates and the aggregation itself depend. In order to minimise the subjective arbitrariness, the aggregated variates have to cover the relevant areas of life, the relevant physical entities (matter, energy, information), as well as the dynamic aspects of the local situation. Several check-lists are available to ensure a perspective as comprehensive as possible (e.g., Seeland n.d., Vester 1999: 189-92). In the case of Lempunah, a set of 20 aggregated variates was chosen (by me) to represent the most relevant aspects of resource use:

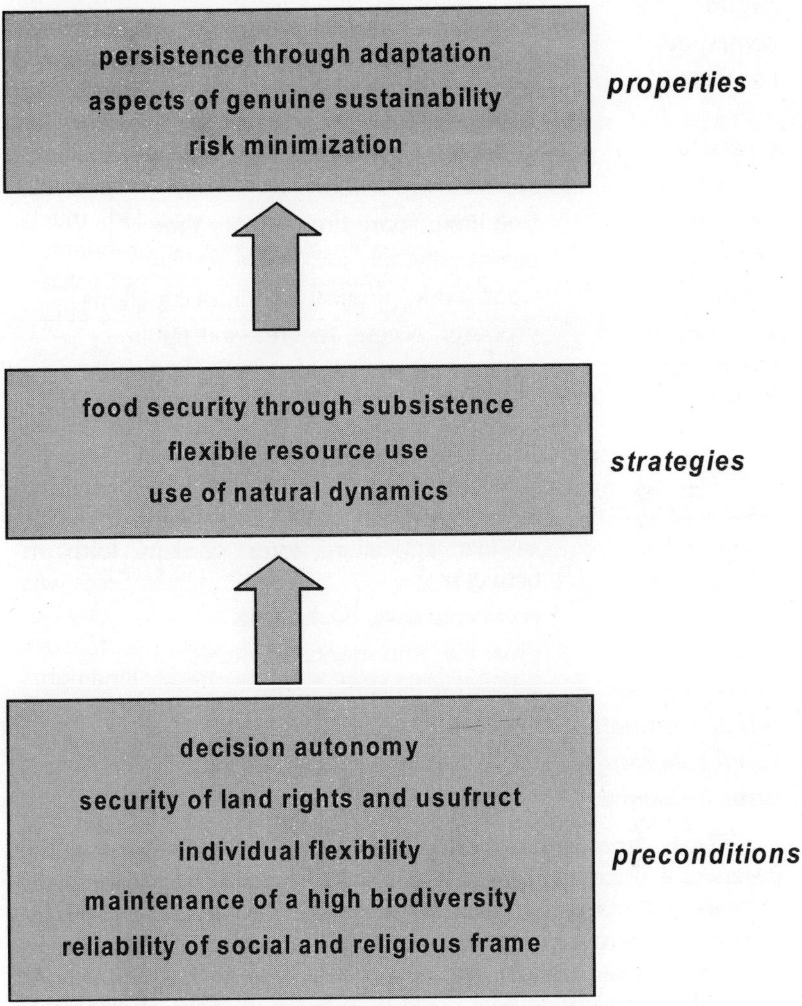

***Fig.5.1*: Preconditions, major strategies and properties of extended subsistence in Lempunah**

capital:	money, commodities, land
companies:	economic benefit of companies
conflicts:	internal social conflicts, conflicts between villagers and others
diversity:	crops and biodiversity, job diversity
education:	schools, high schools
free time:	free time, spare time, leisure time
environment:	biodiversity, air, soil, water, fertility
labour:	wage work, physical labour, occupations
land tenure:	property, access, tenure, land rights
livelihood:	subsistence security, food supply, health
mobility:	permanent or temporary migration to and from the area
prices:	resource prices, commodity prices
quality of life:	subjective feelings, nutrition, health, welfare
resource use:	swidden agriculture, forest gardens, forest in-between
risk:	economic risks, health risks
rituals:	ritual life, importance of rituals
safety feeling:	subjective feelings
self-determination:	freedom of decision-making
social cohesion:	social life, mutual help, social security
state influence:	policy, extension-work

These variates show a high degree of interdependency. For instance, a price increase of a particular resource could lead to an increase of mobility, as some people could move to a remote part of the forest, where the respective resource is abundant. The temporary absence of these people, however, could have various impacts on social life. Family members could be missing in cases of disease or conflicts. Interdependent relations of this kind are depicted in *fig.* 5.2. All causal links are derived from field data collected between 1988 and 2000. Due to the obvious complexity, the practical use of *fig*.5.2 is somewhat limited. The picture is meant rather to visually depict this complexity and interdependency, rather than to follow individual causal links.

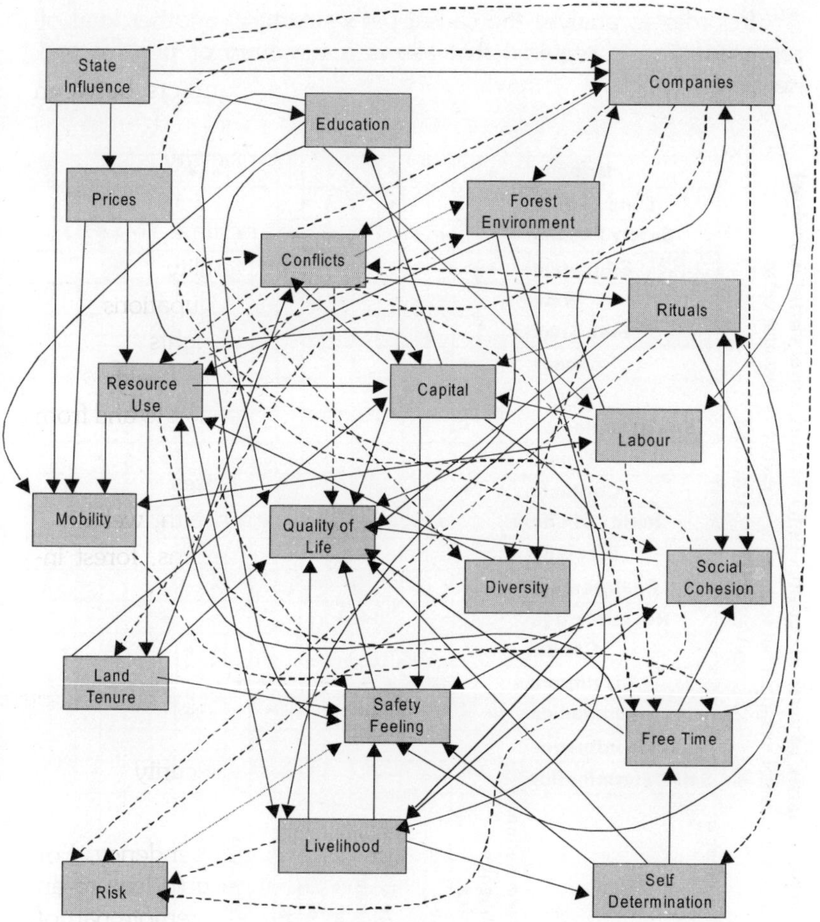

Positive interrelations (i.e., an increase of the first variate induces an increase of the second) are symbolised by plain lines, negative interrelations (i.e., an increase of the first variate induces a decrease of the second[7]) are symbolised by dotted lines

***Fig. 5.2*: Causal net of variates related to resource use in Lempunah**

7. Due to the high degree of aggregation, the variates themselves do not necessarily increase, but the overall aspects integrated into them do. Hence, just as the profits of a company might increase, the company itself might not grow.

In order to analyse the causal net's structure, another kind of representation is required that allows a summary of positive and negative impacts:

Table 5.1: Impact matrix of vertical variates (left) on horizontal variates (below)
The impacts are not weighted but reduced to a positive or negative value.
Modified from Vester (1999:196-200)

	Self-Determination	State Influence	Companies	Livelihood	Capital	Resource Use	Environment	Diversity	Quality of Life	Conflicts	Rituals	Social Cohesion	Prices	Labour	Free Time	Risk	Education	Safety Feeling	Land Tenure	Mobility
Mobility		+				+							+	+			+			
Land Tenure			-			+														
Safety Feeling	+			+	+					-	+	+				-	+		+	
Education		+			+															
Risk				-				-			-	-								
Free Time	+					-				-				-						
Labour			+														+			+
Prices		+																		
Social Cohesion			-								+				+					-
Rituals												+			+					
Conflicts			+		+						-	-							+	
Quality of Life	+			+	+		+			-	+	+			+		+	+	+	
Diversity			-				+													
Environment			-			-				-			-							
Resource Use							+	+		-			+		+					
Capital						+					-		+	+			-		+	
Livelihood					+	+	+				+	+								
Companies		+					+			-			-	+						
State Influence																				
Self-Determination		-		+																

Each variate influences other variates and is influenced by others. The sum of active influences is called 'active sum', while the sum of passive influences is called 'passive sum' (see Vester 1999: 199). The relation between the active and the passive sum of a variate indicates its allocated role within the whole set. The relative activity of a variate is expressed by the ratio between its active and its passive sum, reaching from active to reactive variates. The degree of a variate's participation (from critical to buffering) can be derived from the product of its active and its passive sum (*ibid*.: 200-1). In *fig*.5.3, all 20 variates are ordered referring to their active and to their passive sums. The four corners of the figure indicate the different qualities 'active', 'reactive', 'critical' and 'buffering'.

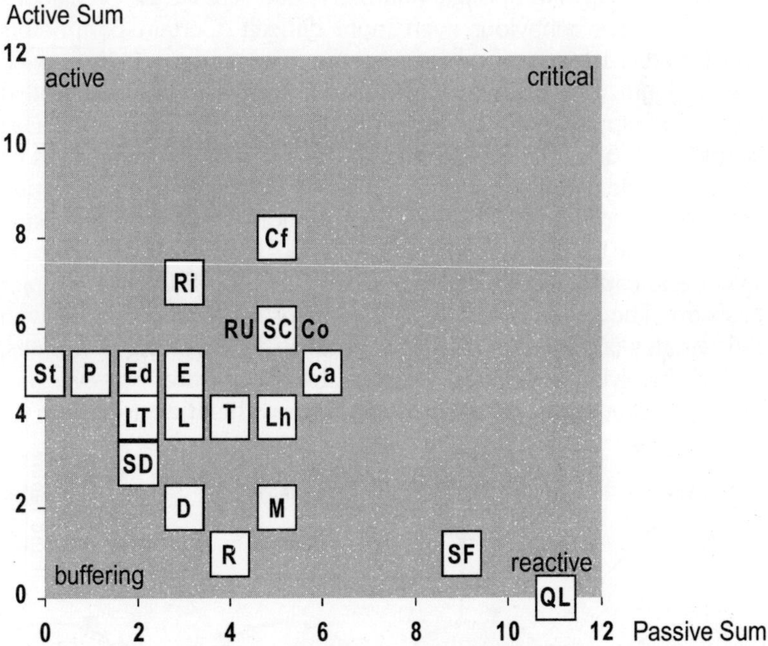

Abbreviations: **Ca**pital, **Co**mpanies, **C**on**f**licts, **D**iversity, **Ed**ucation, **E**nvironment, **L**abour, **L**and **T**enure, **L**iveli**h**ood, **M**obility, **P**rices, **Q**uality of **L**ife, **R**esource **U**se, **R**isk, **Ri**tuals, **S**afety **F**eeling, **S**elf-**D**etermination, **S**ocial **C**ohesion, **St**ate Influence, Free **T**ime.[8]

***Fig.* 5.3: Role allocation of variates (see Vester 1999:204-208)**

8. Three variates (RU, SC, Co) have the same active and passive sums.

Extremely reactive variates are 'Safety Feeling' and 'Quality of Life'. These two variates are influenced by many others without significant active (direct) influence. Both would be suitable as indicators for the general state of this causal net (Vester 1999: 205). In contrast, 'Rituals' and 'Conflicts' are the most active variates, being involved in many relations. 'Diversity' and 'Self-Determinism' can be regarded as buffering variates, without much direct participation in the network. However, both variates belong to the preconditions for securing livelihood in Lempunah, although the connectings between 'Diversity' and 'Livelihood' as well as between 'Self-Determination' and 'Livelihood' are not direct, but run via other variates, such as 'Resource Use' or 'Free Time'.

These kinds of temporally-retarded relations make the predictions of a network's behaviour even more difficult. Certain parameters could even reach critical values, apparently without prior signs. Such events might thus behave in a threshold-style, i.e., nothing at first seems to happen until a critical threshold is suddenly passed (see Bennett 1976: 250). For instance, a decline in biodiversity could be without visible consequences for livelihood security over a rather long time. But then, all of a sudden, the situation comes to a head and redressing the balance is too late. Analytically, such unknown threshold values and causal feed-back loops (e.g., Co-D-RU-E-Co) are a major problem. The causal net of *fig*.5.2 contains 44 feedback loops with 2-4 variates (23 loops involving 4 variates, 11 involving 3 variates, and 10 involving 2 variates). Most of these loops are, however, not only cyclical but also contain cross-relations within them (see *fig*.5.4).

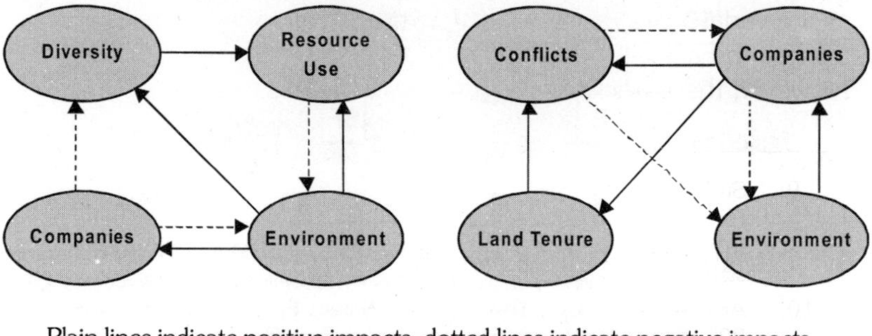

Plain lines indicate positive impacts, dotted lines indicate negative impacts.
***Fig.* 5.4: Feedback loops between different variates**

The number of feedback loops in which the individual variates are involved is given in Table 5.2:

Table 5.2: Number of feedback loops per variate. Only 5 variates (State Influence, Prices, Quality of Life, Safety Feeling, and Risk) are not involved in feed-back relations

	2 variates	*3 variates*	*4 variates*	*Sum*
Conflicts	3	9	17	29
Resource Use	2	3	12	17
Free Time	1	2	10	13
Companies	3	3	7	13
Social Cohesion	2	3	7	12
Capital	1	3	7	11
Rituals	2	3	6	11
Environment	2	2	6	10
Land Tenure	0	2	5	7
Labour	2	1	2	5
Mobility	1	0	3	4
Education	1	1	1	3
Self-Determination	0	0	3	3
Livelihood	0	0	3	3
Diversity	0	1	1	2

Feedback loops are well-known from cybernetics, where negative feedback relations (i.e., an increase in the first variate is counteracted by the impacts re-addressing itself) are important regulative forces. Due to the cross-relations within the feedback loops, it is not always possible to differentiate negative from positive feedbacks, especially as the variates are further affected by other parameters.[9] In order to analyse the actual impacts, the temporal dynamics must be known. However, these are only given for very specific cases.[10]

9. Such a differentiation could only be done after a mathematical simulation. However, although the preconditions for such a simulation do not exist in this case, a simulation can be useful in relatively simple contexts with stable structures.

10. At this step, classical systems analysis (and partly also Vester, see *ibid.*: 225-33) would apply computer-based simulations in order to predict the network's (or the system's) temporal behaviour. Although Vester restricts his method to the analysis of reduced 'if-then' scenarios applying fuzzy logic, even such rather isolated simulations are based on at least weighted semi-quantitative assumptions. However, given the great dynamic change →

So, if a clear analysis appears to be impossible for a causal net as complex as the one in *fig.* 5.2, what can be said about the future prospects for resource use in Lempunah beyond the trivial answer that it is complex? On the one hand, the qualitative analysis illustrated in *fig.* 5.3 shows which variates are rather active or critical, and which might be buffering. Even if the impact of a given variate changes in time (e.g., conflicts), its qualitative role remains similar as long as there are no new causal relation. The general impression one gets from *fig.* 5.4 is that most variates show a buffering character. Even though many hidden dangers, such as threshold effects, should not be underestimated, the high degree of interdependency and non-enhancing feedback loops suggests a certain elasticity and flexibility of the whole net. Hence, many influences from outside are probably buffered without any serious consequences.

But how far can this buffering capacity secure a livelihood? In order to estimate this capacity, we have to examine the two most critical and active compounds, 'Conflicts' and 'Rituals'. Both variates are involved in a broad variety of regulative connections. While the first finding is of little surprise given the high social explosiveness of land rights disputes all over Borneo, the latter appears to be rather site-specific, as ritual life is still very vivid among the Benuaq compared with many other ethnic groups on the island.

The combined role of rituals and conflicts became most apparent in early 1999, when several families from Lempunah, together with people from neighbouring villages, celebrated a *melas tautn* ceremony in the base camp of the oil palm company which they had seized a few months before. This large ritual complex was meant to purify the clear-cut forest, to appease the spirits, and to pray for a peaceful and adequate solution to the conflict. However, in May 1999, the *melas tautn* was ended violently by police forces and mercenaries hired by the oil palm company. Several people were arrested[11] and the ritual setting was destroyed. The violent disturbance of the

→ of the relative importance of different aspects of resource use, economic opportunities, or the political frame, as well as the unpredictable occurrence of 'events', such a simulation would not be very sound, but rather give the impression of a mechanistic 'system'. The reliability of predictions based on such a qualitative model would be extremely weak and of very little practical use.

11. In October 1999, as mentioned before, all arrested villagers were found non-guilty, and it became public that the company had operated illegally.

ceremony, especially, was perceived as a great shock, as ritual life had always been sacredly respected by state authorities.

Due to the high degree of interdependence of conflicts, it is impossible to foresee future developments. Yet, the critical role of conflicts is most apparent and might decide the chances for Lempunah's inhabitants to secure their livelihood in the future. But this predominant role should not distract from the less obvious and indirect impacts, which changes in the degree of self-determinism and (bio)diversity might cause (see above). If we examine once again the essential pre-conditions of Lempunah's extended subsistence, we find three of the five criteria directly linked to 'Self-Determination': (1) decision autonomy: (2) security of land rights and usufruct; and (3) individual flexibility. All three pre-conditions are currently endangered all over Borneo by the replacement of the existing land use with logging, plantations, transmigration projects and mining.

Self-determination and the freedom of decision-making are necessary in order to react fast enough to external fluctuations such as market prices. If this flexibility is restricted, for example, by focussing on single crop species, such as rubber or oil palms, individual livelihoods will be exposed more directly to these fluctuations. Drop-offs in farmgate prices cannot be mitigated by switching to other income sources, and misfortune cannot be effectively coped with any more. These restrictions leave local people in the dependence of large companies or the state depriving them of their proven livelihood strategies. Hence, it is not surprising if reduced incomes lead to frustration and violence, this is often re-addressed to the companies themselves.

Apart from affecting the self-determination of local communities, the replacement of existing forms of landuse also erodes the other two pre-conditions of the extended subsistence: (4) the maintenance of a high biodiversity, and (5) the reliability of the social and religious frame. While biodiversity is directly reduced by several kinds of new landuse practices (e.g., plantations and mining),[12] social and religious life is affected more indirectly. For example, the rigid time-frame of plantation or mining work severely restricts the flexible time budget

12. A relatively high level of biodiversity can be maintained in logging operations, only if several environmental criteria are met (see Gönner 1998b).

required for rituals, and conflicts triggered by new inequities (through unequal distribution of jobs, income or financial compensation, see Gönner 1999a) further threaten the social cohesion.

Given the complex interdependencies between economic, political, social, religious, emotional and environmental parameters, a profound prediction is certainly unrealistic, but a few aspects can be discussed regarding possible solutions. As resource use in Lempunah was never isolated, but was rather shaped by demands from often far-away markets, transitions, adaptations and changes are not new to Benuaq farmers. However, most of the economic responses and strategies observed so far in Lempunah have occurred without state intervention, or the dominance of large-scale agroindustries. This situation has changed over the last few decades (see sub-section 'Chronology of Events' under chapter 2). Suddenly, traditional *adat* law that was accepted by state authorities, as long as it did not interfere with state law, was neglected, and a conflict of competing interests between the state, commercial enterprises and local communities emerged.

It is thus less a question whether local communities can adapt to these changes, than whether they will be given the chance to adapt. If the farmers maintain their freedom of decision-making, many of them will integrate new crops into their resource sets as long as they expect an advantage from these innovations. They will also experiment with new combinations of wage work, resource use and other opportunities. But all of these adaptations require the pre-conditions discussed above. Regarding their rates-of-return, these locally-adapted resource patterns could survive, gradually adjusting to a changing world. They might even coexist in a complementary way with large-scale plantations (see Gönner & Seeland forthcoming), if they are politically and legally given a real chance.[13]

Final reflections

Any investigation of a culture can only be a preliminary one. Yet, many ethnographies give the impression that they *are* complete. As this is usually not the case (not for my own study) I would like to discuss three final questions:

---

13. The specific future of Lempunah depends mainly on the possible occurrence of coal. If the deposits are as large as estimated, the land use described in this study will be entirely replaced by a coal mine.

(1) *Is it possible to describe patterns of resource use in an 'objective' way?*

(2) *How can the actions of people in their environment be described and analysed in a comprehensive way?*

(3) *Which epistemological base should be considered for such studies?*

(1) *Is it possible to describe patterns of resource use in an 'objective' way?*

The goal of this study was to describe local systems of resource use in a comprehensive way and to analyse them regarding the plausibility of the respective decision-making processes and acting strategies. However, it must be questioned whether such contexts can be sensibly depicted at all. At least since the post-modern and interpretative critique of ethnology there is little doubt that different realities cannot be comprehended in an objective way (Stellrecht 1993: 45). An ethnography is only 'the interpretation of an interpretation of an interpretation' (*ibid*.: 53). The written result of this study has also passed various intersubjective (and intercultural) filters.

Already, the initial questions of an ethnologist are not free of context (i.e., without intention). Their exact formulation is always based on preliminary interpretations. The same holds for the informant's answer. Depending on the person, he or she tries to explain, or to blur, the requested information.[14] Again, information is interpreted

14. This kind of intentionality can be shown by several examples from this study. The damages of forest gardens in RT III caused by forest fires were estimated to be two to three times higher immediately after the fires, than compared with one year later. As there was no difference between the two estimates among inhabitants of RT I/II, it seems likely that the higher damage estimates of RT III were related to an (also outspoken) hope that I could help looking for mitigation. It could well be that the people of RT I/II knew more realistically about my limited possibilities as they knew me much better due to my permanent stay. The immediate material and psychological consternation after the fires was similar in both village parts and does not count for the different estimations (see Gönner 1999a).

Another example was observed during the investigation of irregular expenses. Although most families bought gold in the respective year, no one mentioned this as an 'expense'. Some people regarded the buying of gold not as an 'expense', but as the exchange into a different kind of →

and filtered. The informant's answer is even preceded by another interpretative level on which a certain context or phenomenon is interpreted by the informant for him- or herself. The transferred answer is then interpreted by the ethnologist, who will later integrate the informant's answer together with information derived from other people and from literature to another interpreted picture. Such a repeatedly-filtered ethnography appears smooth and complete (*ibid.*: 49-50,53),[15] and it is left to the critical reader to accept or to reject this picture.

Hence, the representation by the ethnologist can only be a subjective image of a phenomenon, which would most likely be drawn in a different way by a different researcher.[16]

This subjective character of an ethnography is further enhanced by the common restriction to a few key-informants, who stand for *the* Benuaq, *the* Iban or *the* Kenyah. In order to avoid an authoritative, expert-like smoothness, post-modern ethnology asks for the polyphonic transparency of an ethnography (see Schweizer 1996: 61). A similar approach is attempted by cognitive ethnology contrasting the inner ('emic') perspective as opposed to the outer, expert-like ('etic') perception of cultural phenomena (see Dougherty 1985: 5 ff.). By using an indigenous terminology, this approach avoids one of the intercultural translation problems, but the intersubjective filters shown in *fig.* 5.5 and, thus, the subjective character of the representation remain valid to their full extent.

Although I tried to follow some of the demands of post-modern ethnology in my study,[17] I have to accept the accusation of an expert-

---

→ value; while others did not like such a personal question, as wealth is generally not shown in public. Both cases led to a different interpretation from what professional gold sellers from Tanjung Isuy told me about Lempunah.

15. A detailed discussion of intercultural translations is given in Marcus & Fischer (1986: 29-31). The authors also show how interpretative ethnology, and later the post-modern ethnology, evolved out of 'the crisis of representation in the human sciences' (*ibid.*: vii,7-16).

16. This problem was widely discussed during the Mead-Freeman debate of the 1980s (see Marcus & Fischer 1986: 3-4).

17. This refers to the analysis of the political and historical perspective of my research context, the polyphony expressed in individual case studies, and to these final reflections.

like perspective at least in some respects, especially regarding the synopsis of the last chapter. On the other hand, there are some good reasons for such a perspective, as it is based completely on the (generally cross-checked) explanations of my informants, on my own observations, and on comparable data of other authors. However, it is not possible to tell whether all the rationalities explained to me were of relevance for practical decisions (see sub-section 'Decision-making processes before establishing a swidden' under chapter 3 for a critical discussion of the selection of a swidden site). Hence, it would be more appropriate to speak of plausibilities instead of rationalities. These plausibilities can be regarded as valid until they are replaced by a more convincing explanatory pattern.

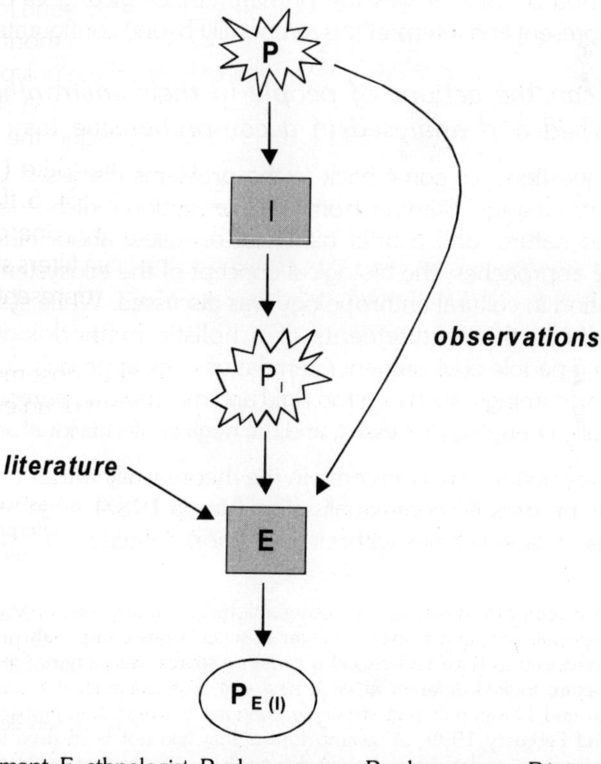

I: informant, E: ethnologist, P: phenomenon, P_I: phenomenon P interpreted and translated by I, $P_{E(I)}$: phenomenon P_I interpreted and translated by E

Fig. 5.5: Levels of depiction and translation of a phenomenon

By proceeding in this iterative Popperian way, scientific progress appears to be possible also by discussing subjective representations in a critical sense. By neglecting the problem of intercultural representation, any 'truth' would anyway be of a merely pseudo-objective quality.

Thus, the initial question whether an 'objective' description of resource use patterns is possible, does not really make sense. If one follows the argumentation of the ontological constructivism (e.g., Krieger 1996: 163) the conclusion would be: *The* resource use of the Benuaq does not exist, at least not outside its communicatively-constructed context. I would like to modify this argument slightly by regarding resource use in Lempunah as the totality of aspects related to resource use that were reported to me, or observed by me over a certain period of time. It was the primary ethnological goal of my study to represent and interpret this temporally-bound configuration.[18]

(2) *How can the actions of people in their environment be described and analysed in a comprehensive way?*

With this question, we come back to the problems discussed in the introductory chapter. Starting from the conventional dichotomy of culture and nature, and a brief historical overview about different theoretical approaches, the biological concept of the ecosystem and its application in cultural anthropology was discussed. While systems theory sufficed the requirements of a holistic methodology for investigating people-environment interrelations, the approach showed several shortcomings, such as a too rigid and mechanistic perspective of temporally-changing processes, and the neglect of individual action.

Both restrictions are overcome in the theoretically rather prosaic concept of 'progressive contextualisation' (Vayda 1983), which allows an analysis of causal chains without an *a priori* definition of research

---

18. The temporal dimension of observations and interpretations became especially apparent after a longer absence from Lempunah. If I was convinced to have understood a certain resource use pattern, the whole picture looked different at each new visit. For example, the landscape around Lempunah had strikingly changed between September 1998 and February 1999, as swamp forests that had not been used for rice cultivation so far were slashed due to fire damages that facilitated the clearing. Hence, it took several years to notice the general dynamics of the local resource use, which cannot be described in an adequate way without considering its temporal dimension.

boundaries. However, the result of following these causal chains is not linear, but leads to a complex net of many interconnections. Due to the high number of feedback relations,[19] the direction of cause and effect is unclear. Hence, many phenomena can only be explained in a multi-causal way *ex post*, while predictions also become theoretically unreliable.

But are such causal nets suitable to follow interrelated impacts and dependencies between people and their environment? From a purist's point of view, this appears incommensurable. Crop failures are explained by incestuous marriages, as well as by the sub-optimal selection of a swidden site. Thus, subjective culturally-bound explanations are interwoven in the same net with physical findings. However, the accusation of incommensurability leads us back to the categorical rigidity of segregating social systems from ecological systems. In order to overcome this segregation, combining apparently incompatible aspects could well be a first step. Regarding the local rationality of decision-making, such a combination seems to be not only legitimate, but suitable. If incest is regarded as an explanation for a natural disaster, this perception cannot be neglected. Neither would the rejection of a statistically-proven relation between forest age, soil fertility and rice yield be reasonable. By disregarding either the local or the positivist scientific explanation, one side of the medal is inevitably lost.

This unifying approach even integrates different individual explanatory patterns (plausibilities) within the same causal net. The integration of individual case studies constitutes the causal space of a research question (see section 'Theoretical Frame' under chapter 1). As the various acting persons also interact, the reduction to a single explanation is not sufficient.[20] Three criteria were applied throughout this study in order to construct a causal net: (1) a causal relation should be reported by at least two different informants; (2) a causal relation could be observed or measured by myself; and (3) a causal relation was reported by other authors under similar circumstances[21].

---

19. This is similar to Rappaport's term 'coherence' (1984: 227-8).
20. In some respects, this also refers to the post-modern call for polyphony.
21. This criterion refers to Benuaq cosmovision, since there are only very few studies of Benuaq resource use.

Hence, the suggested approach is a synthesis of various elements of analytical ethnology (see Schweizer 1993), ethnographic realism (Marcus & Fischer 1986: 23), interpretative and post-modern ethnology[22] (Stellrecht 1993, Marcus & Fischer 1986), and progressive contextualisation (Vayda 1983). Such an integrated methodology in respect to the current theoretical discussion, seems at least suitable for studying people-environment relations.[23]

(3) *Which epistemological base should be considered for such studies?*

This question is generally neglected by most authors. Among Bornean studies of resource use, there are cultural-materialistic approaches (Dove 1985a, see comments in King 1999: 125), eclectic investigations including interpretative elements (the studies of Colfer) as well as descriptions in the sense of ethnographic realism (Freeman 1992). My own study lacks a defined ontological base. Regarding its basic assumptions there is a certain closeness to Edmund Husserl's phenomenology (Husserl 1996). At least, I agree with Irmtraud Stellrecht, who says referring to Husserl, Heidegger and Gadamer:

> The phenomena of the world are not given by themselves and there is no privileged perspective. It is rather man who perceives and addresses phenomena, and who guides his perspective during this process of perception according to his own preconception, motivation et cetera. He interprets the phenomena of the world and by doing so he adds meaning to them, *his* meaning. The phenomenon, the perception of the phenomenon, i.e. the interpretation, and the conditions

---

22. A purely interpretative or post-modern approach was rejected as I share Schweizer's critique (1996: 64-9), including: (1) the overemphasis of subjective feelings and a language full of jargon; (2) a neglect of thorough, or quantitative field data; (3) an underestimation of culturally-shaped patterns; (4) over-emphasis on the different quality of different cultures; (5) neglect of ecological, economic and social conditions; as well as (6) neglect of alternative research approaches, such as cognitive anthropology.

23. In a similar vein, Marcus and Fischer ask for an eclectic transition between periods of 'settled, paradigm-dominated styles of research', which would allow a certain experimental open-ness and innovation (*ibid.*: x). Researching against methodological rules is also propagated by Paul Feyerabend (e.g., 1988: 14-32) as a suitable means for epistemological progress.

> that guide the perception coincide. Phenomena, far from the observer, cannot exist.'
>
> — Stellrecht 1993: 38, a.t.

The approach starting from observable and communicable phenomena which are filtered by subjective interpretations constitutes the practical base for this study. The metaphysical questioning of the reality of these phenomena is, however, left aside. It would lead too far to discuss whether the observed phenomena are social constructions (Berger & Luckmann 1980), a world constructed through communication (Krieger 1996: 163), or yet another ontological category. These considerations are only meant to encourage others to search for an ontological base for these kinds of studies. A base without which any analysis and interpretation remains doubtful after all.

Annex-1
Benuaq Word List

This list is based on Swadesh (1971:283). Terms specific to Benuaq culture are additionally included.[1]

alive	*bolupm*	bone	*tulakng*
all	*oreekng*	to breathe	*ngasakng*
already	*epuuq*	bridge	*apar*
and	*dan* (Ind.)	to burn	*nyuru*
animal	*esaaq*	cat	*meong*
apartment	*orook*	child	*anak*
ash	*bonur*	close to	*totoq*
back (body)	*tutuq*	clothes	*pakayatn*
bad	*daat*	cloud	*jautn, mang*
to bark	*kolit kayuq*	cold	*jelap*
to beat	*menaq*	to come	*mpat*
big, fat (person)	*bogol*	commoner	*merentika*
to bind	*ngikat*	to cook	*ngeaaq*
bird	*kepuluuq*	to count	*ngareken*
to bite	*ngikit*	to cry	*nangih*
black	*metapm*	to cut	*motaq*
blood	*daya*	to dance	*ngaraq*
to blow	*nyiup*	day	*olo*
boiled rice	*nahi*	dead	*mate*

1. Throughout this study I followed the orthography of my informants, as there is no official spelling for Benuaq. The orthography resembles the spelling rules for Bahasa Indonesian (see Nothofer & Pampus 1988:xiii-xv; for mythical expressions and remarks referring to Benuaq orthography, see also Hopes 1997:163). Exceptions are: (1) long vowels, which are doubled, and glottal stops that are expressed by *q* or (in slightly more audible cases) by *k* (see Hopes *ibid.*). The spelling of Benuaq expressions used in this study was cross-checked by my informants and, in the case of plant names, by a Benuaq botanist of Mulawarman University (Samarinda).

dibbling stick	asaq	heavy	*oyatn*
different, other	*laitn*	here	*bohoq*
to dig	*ngaliiq*	hill rice	*pare*
dirty	*omoq*	to hold	*gap*
dog	*koko*	how?	*kelameq?*
to drink	*misap*	hulled rice	*boyas*
to drive	*gelampokng*	to hunt	*kasuq*
dry	*koteeq*	husband	*sawaq*
dull	*loput*	I	*aap*
dust	*bonur*	in	*pede*
ear	*kelingaq*	intestine	*tenaiq*
earth	*tana*	to kill	*pekate*
to eat	*maan*	to know	*tahu*
egg	*toli*	ladder	*tukar*
eye	*mataq*	lake	*kenohan* (Kutai)
to fall	*lotuq*	large	*solai*
far	*oroq*	to laugh	*kokah*
fat	*dawaaq*	leaf	*bete*
father (ref.)	*taman*	left	*bila sei*
feather	*buluuq*	leg	*kenekng*
to fight	*bulo*	lever	*ate*
fire	*api*	to lie down	*lokuq*
fish	*kinas*	little, small	*kediq*
flower	*bungaq*	long	*mooq*
to fly	*tilikng*	longhouse	*louu*
fog	*kenelukup*	louse	*kutuq*
foot	*kenekng*	man	*sookng*
forest	*roboot*	many	*deooq*
fruit	*buah*	meat	*dagiq*
to give	*nyieeq*	mother (ref.)	*tinan*
glutinous rice	*pulut*	mountain	*saikng*
to go	*manan*	mouth	*molot*
gong	*genikng*	name	*nai*
good	*buatn, bueeq*	narrow	*solot*
grain of rice	*tunutn*	neck	*tinga*
grass	*jikut*	new	*bayu*
green	*jerau*	night	*malapm*
hair	*balooq*	no (subjects)	*aba*
hand	*kami*	no, not	*beau*
he, she, it	*ulutn*	nobleman	*mantiiq*
head	*puaq*	nose	*urukng*
to hear	*nempaning*	not yet	*male*
heart	*lempusu*	old	*tuhaq*

on	*pede*
path	*lalaaq*
person	*senarikng*
to plant	*ngulaq*
to play	*gao*
to pull	*nepook*
to push	*nejuk*
rain	*osaaq*
red	*meaaq*
right	*bila sanan*
right	*tumung*
river	*sungei*
rotten	*botooq*
root	*wakaai*
rope	*taliiq*
to rub	*ngisuk*
salt	*dangiiq*
sand	*oneeq*
to say	*paner*
to scratch	*ngelatar*
to see	*kitaq*
seed (of rice)	*bini*
seedling	*tokok*
to sew	*nyarut*
sharp	*terap*
to shoot (blow pipe)	*nyipat*
short	*bodaq*
sibling (older)	*tukatn*
sibling (younger)	*taritn*
side-dish (no rice!)	*kaluq*
to sing	*bedodoi*
to sit	*tuat*
skin	*kolit*
sky, heaven	*langit*
slave	*ripatn*
to sleep	*turi*
slim	*maih*
to smell	*ngeooq*
to smoke	*asutn*
snake	*nipaq*
soft	*kediq*
to sow rice	*moyaas*
to spit	*tempus*

to split wood	*mokak*
to squash	*menyet*
to stand	*jakar*
star	*bintakng*
to stay over night	*senturi*
stick	*derai*
to sting	*ninak*
stomach, belly	*butukng*
stone	*batuq*
to suck	*ncuuq*
sun	*mataq olo*
swamp rice	*pare payaq*
to swell	*kemukng*
swidden	*umaq*
to swim	*serangui*
tail	*ikui*
that	*iro*
there	*pede doq*
they	*ulutn*
to think	*nyeranat*
this	*ohoq*
this person	*ohaq*
threshed rice	*oikng*
to throw	*nikapm*
tongue	*lola*
tooth	*kukut*
tree	*poutn*
to turn around	*pusing*
to vomit	*nuta*
warm	*berakng*
to wash	*bedepas*
water	*danum*
we (excl.)	*kaitn*
we (incl.)	*taka*
wet	*bisooq*
what?	*otn?, on?*
where?	*pede meq?*
white	*bura*
who?	*njeq?*
wide	*solai*
wife	*sawaq*
wind	*dolaq*
wing	*ekap*

to wipe	*nyapuq*	year	*tautn*
with	*ngkaq*	yellow	*lemit*
woman	*bawe*	yes	*oi*
wood	*kayuq*	you (sg.)	*iko*
to work	*ngamuh*	you (pl.)	*iko, ika*
worm	*keremeq*		

Kinship

mother	*tinan*	nephew	*anak nakatn*
father	*taman*	grandmother	*itaaq*
child	*anak, anaaq*	grandfather	*kakah*
younger sister/brother	*taritn*	great-grandparents	*alau*
older sister/brother	*tukaatn*	great-grandchildren	*inggikng*
cousin	*piariiq, piaritn*	parents-in-law	*tuputn*
first degree	*warsinai*	son/daughter-in-law	*anak nantutn*
second degree	*warduaq*	uncle/aunt of spouse	*tuputn ngantai*
third degree	*wartolu*	sister/brother-in-law	*ayuuq*
uncle	*tuaaq*	spouse of sister/ brother-in-law	*ruai*
aunt	*tere*		
niece	*anak nakatn*		

Numbers

1	*erai*	10	*sepuluh*
2	*duaq*	11	*sebeleh*
3	*tolu*	12	*duabeleh*
4	*opat*	13	*tolubeleh*
5	*limaq*	20	*duapuluh*
6	*jawatn*	30	*tolupuluh*
7	*turu*	100	*seratur*
8	*walo*	300	*toluratus*
9	*sie*	1,000	*seribu*
		3,000	*toluribu*

Annex-2

Extracted Plants

All the plants were identified by local informants. The scientific confirmation was kindly provided by Ir. Paulus Matius, MSc from UNMUL. Medicinal plants are not included because of unresolved property rights.

Abbreviations: **C**onstruction, **D**ye **P**lants, **Fa**bric, **Fo**od, **Fu**el, **H**ousehold, **F**ertility **I**ndicators, **P**oison, **R**ituals, **T**rade

Family	Scientific name	Author	Benuaq name	Use
Amaranthaceae	*Amaranthus hybridus*	L.	Bayam	Fo
Amaranthaceae	*Celosia cristata*	L.	Bungaq Gerungakng	
Amaryllidaceae	*Curculigo sp.*		Doyo	T Fa
Amaryllidaceae	*Curculigo silvestris*		Lingan	Fo
Anacardiaceae	*Mangifera quadrifida*	Jack.	Kelaauq	Fo
Anacardiaceae	*Mangifera odorata*	Griff.	Kuini	C Fu Fo T
Anacardiaceae	*Mangifera indica*	L.	Mempelam	C Fu
Anacardiaceae	*Mangifera sp.*		Ncapm	C Fu
Anacardiaceae	*Mangifera sp.*		Ncapm Bakatn	Fo
Anacardiaceae	*Mangifera sp.*		Ncapm Bokut	Fo
Anacardiaceae	*Mangifera macrocarpa*	Bl.	Ncapm Bucur	Fo
Anacardiaceae	*Mangifera similis*	Bl.	Ncapm Bulaau	Fo
Anacardiaceae	*Mangifera sp.*		Ncapm Buyukng	Fo

Family	Scientific name	Author	Benuaq name	Use
Anacardiaceae	*Mangifera quadrifida*	Jack.	Ncapm Kelauu	Fo
Anacardiaceae	*Mangifera sp.*		Ncapm Palung	Fo
Anacardiaceae	*Mangifera sp.*		Ncapm Payaakng Pelanuk	Fo
Anacardiaceae	*Mangifera pajang*	Kosterm.	Ncapm Payaakng Solaai	Fo
Anacardiaceae	*Mangifera sp.*		Ncapm Raas	Fo
Anacardiaceae	*Mangifera sp.*		Ncapm Rawa	Fo
Anacardiaceae	*Mangifera caesia*	Jack.	Ncapm Wanyi	Fo
Anacardiaceae	*Pentaspadon motleyi*	Hook. f.	Pelaro	Fo
Anacardiaceae	*Gluta renghas*	L.	Rengas	R Fu C
Anacardiaceae	*Mangifera sp.*		Repeeh	C Fo Fu
Anacardiaceae	*Campnosperma auriculata*	(non Hook. f.) King	Sentakng Leso	
Anacardiaceae	*Campnosperma sp.*		Tentaakng Lesooq	C Fu
Anacardiaceae	*Mangifera decandra*	Ding Hou	Wantan	Fo
Annonaceae	*Popowia pisocarpa*		Bemaai	
Annonaceae	*Polyalthia sp.*		Dendang Dara	R
Annonaceae	*Xylopia altissima*		Jangkau	C
Annonaceae	*Xylopia malayana*		Kojeekng	Fu
Annonaceae	*Mezzettia parviflora*		Ncapm Uneeq	Fo C
Annonaceae	*Friesodielsia sp.*		Wakaai Munookng Puti	H
Apocynaceae	*Dyera costulata*	(Miq.) Hook.	Kayutn Uraatn	R H
Apocynaceae	*Alstonia sp.*		Lutukng	C T Fo
Apocynaceae	*Ervatamia macrocarpa*		Lutukng Tukak	R
Aquifoliaceae	*Ilex cissoides*		Bengkarau	C R Fu
Aquifoliaceae	*Ilex sp.*		Penyempur Namis	R

Araceae	*Colocasia esculenta*	(L.) Schott	Dompuq	
Araceae	*Colocasia sp.*		Jompuq	Fo
Aspleniaceae	*Asplenium sp.*		Ngkapaaq Beleekng	*R*
Asteraceae	*Blumea balsamifera*	(L.) D.C.	Mukng	R
Balsaminaceae	*Impatiens sp.*		Pasar	
Bambusaceae	*Dendrocalamus asper*		Betukng	H R
Bambusaceae	*Bambusa sp.*		Buluuq	C
Bambusaceae	*Bambusa sp.*		Inas	T
Bambusaceae	*Dendrocalamus sp.*		Perikng	C
Bambusaceae	*Bambusa vulgaris*		Tolakng Bulaau	R
Bambusaceae	*Dendrocalamus sp.*		Tolakng Inas	C
Bambusaceae	*Bambusa sp.*		Tolakng Solooq	C R
Bixaceae	*Bixa orellana*	L.	Gelinapm	D
Blechnaceae	*Stenochlaena sp.*		Pakuq	Fo R
Bombacaceae	*Durio zibethinus*	Murr.	Kalaakng	Fo T D
Bombacaceae	*Ceiba pentandra*	(L.) Gaertn.	Kapoq	Fa T
Bombacaceae	*Durio wyatt-smithii*		Kelenceekng	Fo
Bombacaceae	*Durio oxleyanus*	Griff.	Ketungan	C T Fo
Bombacaceae	*Durio kutejensis*	Becc.	Laai	Fo
Bombacaceae	*Durio dulchis*		Layukng	Fo
Burseraceae	*Dacryodes rostrata*	(Bl.) H.J. Lam.	Keramuuq Botatn	Fo
Burseraceae	*Dacryodes rostrata*	(Bl.) H.J. Lam.	Keramuuq Soni	Fo H
Burseraceae	*Canarium decumanum*	Gaertn.	Lomuuq	Fo T R
Burseraceae	*Dacryodes sp.*		Ncapm Uraakng	Fo
Burseraceae	*Canarium sp.*		Tae	Fo
Caesalpiniaceae	*Cassia alata*	L.	Gerengaakng	

Family	Scientific name	Author	Benuaq name	Use
Caesalpiniaceae	*Koompassia excelsa*	(Becc.) Taub.	Puti	R Fo T H
Caesalpiniaceae	*Caesalpinia sappan*		Sopaakng	R
Callitrichaceae	*Ocimum basilicum*	L.	Ngeraseh	R
Cannaceae	*Canna edulis*		Raja Keaau	R
Caricaceae	*Carica papaya*		Gadakng Biasa	Fo T
Caricaceae	*Carica papaya*		Gadakng Ramai	Fo T
Celastraceae	*Lophopetalum sp.*		Derenyakng	C
Celastraceae	*Lophopetalum multinervium*	Ridl.	Lipaaq	C
Celastraceae	*Lophopetalum sp.*		Prupuq	C Fu Fo
Crypteroniaceae	*Dactylocladus stenostachys*	Oliv.	Seranai	C
Cucurbitaceae	*Momordica charantia*	L.	Periaq	Fo T
Cucurbitaceae c.f.	*Macropanax dispermus*	Bl.	Beramboyut	H I
Cyperaceae	*Cyperus spp.*		Sempirikng	R
Dianellaceae	*Dianella sp.*		Luak Jekari	R Fu
Dianellaceae	*Dianella sp.*		Luak Usar	R
Dilleniaceae	*Dillenia excelsa*	(Jack.) Gilg.	Gaharaq	Fu R
Dilleniaceae	*Tetracera asiatica*	(Lour.) Hoogl.	Koyur	H
Dilleniaceae	*Dillenia excelsa*	(Jack.) Gilg.	Segaraq	Fu
Dilleniaceae	*Dillenia sp.*		Tempuro	C
IDioscoreaceae	*Dioscorea sp.*		Gadukng	Fo
Dioscoreaceae	*Dioscorea alata*	L.	Uiiq	Fo
Dipterocarpaceae	*Dipterocarpus sp.*		Aput	T Fo
Dipterocarpaceae	*Shorea laevis*	Ridl.	Bengkirai	C
Dipterocarpaceae	*Shorea sp.*		Butakng Metapm	Fo

Dipterocarpaceae	*Shorea balangeran*	(Korth.) Burck.	Kahooi	C
Dipterocarpaceae	*Shorea spp.*		Lempukng Akas	Fo C
Dipterocarpaceae	*Shorea spp.*		Lempukng Kunit	C
Dipterocarpaceae	*Shorea sp.*		Lempukng Seru	R
Dipterocarpaceae	*Anisoptera sp.*		Marlangat	C T Fo
Dipterocarpaceae	*Shorea sp.*		Melasio	H
Dipterocarpaceae	*Shorea smithiana*	Sym.	Mermukng Lemit	H
Dipterocarpaceae	*Shorea ovalis*	(Korth.) Bl.	Mermukng Puluuq	C H
Dipterocarpaceae	*Dryobalanops sp.*		Ngoiiq	C Fo
Dipterocarpaceae	*Shorea sp.*		Nyerakat	C
Dipterocarpaceae	*Shorea spp.*		Orai	Fo H C
Dipterocarpaceae	*Shorea sp.*		Putaakng	C
Dipterocarpaceae	*Vatica sp.*		Tebukng	C Fu H
Dipterocarpaceae	*Dipterocarpus sp.*		Tempudau	C T Fo
Ebenaceae	*Diospyros sp.*		Kayutn Arakng	R
Elaeocarpaceae	*Elaeocarpus sp.*		Ngkodooi	Fu
Euphorbiaceae	*Trigonopleura malayana*	Hook. f.	Amih	R
Euphorbiaceae	*Macaranga gigantea*		Bengkuukng	C
Euphorbiaceae	*Aleurites moluccana*	(L.) Willd.	Geriiq	Fo
Euphorbiaceae	*Hevea brasiliensis*	(H.B.K.) Muell. Arg.	Getah	T Fu
Euphorbiaceae	*Manihot esculenta*	Crantz	Jabau Pasar	
Euphorbiaceae	*Manihot sp.*		Jabau Pikur	R
Euphorbiaceae	*Adina minutiflora*		Kedemaaq	Fo
Euphorbiaceae	*Glochidion obscurum*		Kelebahuq	R
Euphorbiaceae	*Baccaurea pyriformis*		Keliwatn	C

Family	Scientific name	Author	Benuaq name	Use
Euphorbiaceae	*Codiaeum variegatum*		Komaat (Siraakng)	R
Euphorbiaceae	*Baccaurea lamponga*		Lemposu	Fo
Euphorbiaceae	*Macaranga trichocarpa*	(Rchb. f. & Zoll.)	Lunai	R
Euphorbiaceae	*Mallotus paniculatus*		Mawaah	
Euphorbiaceae	*Baccaurea puberula*		Mawooi	Fo
Euphorbiaceae	*Baccaurea stipulata*		Mengkuning	R
Euphorbiaceae	*Macaranga triloba*	(Bl.) M.A.	Nancakng	R C
Euphorbiaceae	*Macaranga hulletti*		Ncakng Sisit	
Euphorbiaceae	*Endospermum diadenum*		Ngkebor	
Euphorbiaceae	*Macaranga sp.*		Ngkuukng	C I
Euphorbiaceae	*Elateriospermum tapos*	Bl.	Pahaaq	C Fu Fo
Euphorbiaceae	*Baccaurea griffithii*		Pasi	Fo
Euphorbiaceae	*Baccaurea edulis*	Merr.	Ruiiq	Fo
Euphorbiaceae	*Codiaeum variegatum*		Serendenapm	R
Euphorbiaceae	*Aporosa lunata*		Tulang Bekaraaq	
Fabaceae	*Sindora sp.*		Merjaakng/Angi	H Fo T
Fabaceae	*Spatholobus percicinus*	Ridl.	Pengeraya	Fo
Fabaceae	*Fordia sp.*		Pesaaq	R I
Fabaceae	*Derris elliptica*		Twaq	P
Fabaceae	*Spatholobus sp.*		Wakaai Pengeraya	
Fagaceae	*Castanopsis javanica*	(Bl.) A.D.C.	Biangan	C Fu
Fagaceae	*Castanopsis megacarpa*	Gamble	Kumpat Layukng	C
Fagaceae	*Castanopsis javanica*	(Bl.) A.D.C.	Limaat	Fu C
Fagaceae	*Lithocarpus elegans*	(Bl.) Hatus. ex S.	Pipit	Fu C I

Fagaceae	*Lithocarpus bennetti*	(Miq.) Rehd.	Pipit Pare	C H
Flacourtiaceae	*Flacourtia sp.*		Erat	C
Gleicheniaceae	*Gleichuria linearis*	Clarke	Jangaang	H R
Guttiferae	*Garcinia sp.*		Bonah	Fo
Guttiferae	*Garcinia dioica*	Bl.	Empana	C
Guttiferae	*Calophyllum soullatri*	Burm. f.	Jerapiq	
Guttiferae	*Garcinia cowa*	Roxb.	Keni	Fo
Hypericaceae	*Cratoxylum formosum*	(Jack.) Dyer	Bentalekng	R
Hypericaceae	*Cratoxylum sp.*		Gerungakng	Fo C R
Hypericaceae	*Cratoxylum glaucum*	Korth.	Mera Sipaq	Fu C
Ixonanthaceae	*Ixonanthes sp.*		Mepooq	C Fu
Lauraceae	*Litsea sp.*		Ayaau	C
Lauraceae	Litsea firma	(Bl.) Hook. f.	Ayau Bulau	C
Lauraceae	*Litsea brachystachys*	Boerl.	Ayau Bura	C
Lauraceae	*Litsea sp.*		Ayau Meaq	C
Lauraceae	*Litsea odorifera*	Valeton	Ayau Piawaq	C
Lauraceae	*Litsea sp.*		Ayau Sabeq	C
Lauraceae	*Litsea machilfolia*	Gamble	Bencomang	C
Lauraceae	*Litsea sp. c.f.*		Kayu Lem	T
Lauraceae	*Litsea sp.*		Lalatn	C
Lauraceae	*Dehaasia incrassata*		Lalatn Kunyit	C
Lauraceae	*Litsea augulata*		Lalatn Lego	C
Lauraceae	*Litsea resimosa*		Mara Besiq	H
Lauraceae	*Litsea sp.*		Medakng	C Fo
Lauraceae	*Cinnamomum partenoxylon*	Meissn.	Perowal/Perauwali	C R

Family	Scientific name	Author	Benuaq name	Use
Lauraceae	*Eusideroxylon zwageri*	T. et B.	Teluyatn	R C T
Lecythidaceae	*Barringtonia pendula*		Keroat	P
Lecythidaceae	*Barringtonia sp.*		Putat	Fo
Leguminosae	*Intsia palembanica*	Miq.	Itir	C T
Liliaceae	*Cordyline sp.*		Biowo Beneeq	R
Liliaceae	*Cordyline sp.*		Biowo Kodoq	R
Liliaceae	*Cordyline sp.*		Biowo Nayuuq	R
Logantaceae	*Willughbeia sp.*		Wakaai Letatn	T
Lythraceae	*Lagerstroemia speciosa*		Bungur	C Fo
Malvaceae	*Hibiscus rosa-sinensis*		Kembang Sepatu	R H
Malvaceae	*Hibiscus schizopetalus*		Kepilaaq	R
Marantaceae	*Donax canniformis*	K. Schum.	Bemaatn	
Marantaceae	*Stachypterinum jagorianum*	Butootn	I	
Maranthaceae	*Cominsia gigantea*		Isaaq Ngkookng	H I
Melastomataceae	*Melastoma malabathricum*	L.	Bekakakng	Fo
Melastomataceae	*Pternandra coerulescens*	Mencemooq	Fu	
Meliaceae	*Lansium domesticum*	Correa	Lisaat	Fu Fo
Mimosaceae	*Adenanthera pavonina*	L.	Bewai	
Mimosaceae	*Archidendron jiringa*	(Jack.) Nielsen	Cerikng	H
Mimosaceae	*Mimosa pigra*	L.	Jepun	R
Mimosaceae	*Archidendron microcarpum*	(Benth.) Nielsen	Kekereq	
Mimosaceae	*Pithecellobium splendens*	(Miq.) Corner	Miyadukng	C
Mimosaceae	*Paraserianthes falcataria*	(L.) Nielsen	Sengon	CT
Mimosaceae	*Archidendron sp.*		Sopaakng Piaq	D

Moraceae	*Ficus sp.*		Araaq Ulau Lemit	R
Moraceae	*Ficus sp.*		Araaq Ulau Meaaq	R
Moraceae	*Ficus variegata*		Ayaq	Fa
Moraceae	*Artocarpus odoratissimus*		Benturukng	*Fo*
Moraceae	*Ficus albifila*		Bilaas	Fo
Moraceae	*Artocarpus dadah*		Daraq	Fo R C
Moraceae	*Artocarpus kemando*		Daraq Kumar	
Moraceae	*Antiaris toxicaria*	(Pers.) Lesch.	Ipu	Fa P
Moraceae	*Artocarpus anisophyllus*	Miq.	Kepuatn	C Fo
Moraceae	*Ficus quocarpa*		Laliiq	R H
Moraceae	*Artocarpus integer*		Nakatn	Fo C
Moraceae	*Artocarpus heterophyllusLamk.*	NakatnJawaq	Fo	
Moraceae	*Artocarpus sp.*		Nakatn Lati	Fo C
Moraceae	*Ficus sp.*		Nunuq Singah	R
Moraceae	*Artocarpus lanceifolius*	Roxb.	Obeeq	Fo
Moraceae	*Artocarpus elasticus*		Pekalukng	Fa C
Moraceae	*Artocarpus anisophyllus*	Miq.	Pepuatn Beneeq	Fo
Moraceae	*Artocarpus sp.*		Pepuatn Daya	Fo
Moraceae	*Artocarpus kemando*	Miq.	Puduuq	Fo H
Moraceae	*Morus sp.*		Sura	
Moraceae	*Artocarpus teysmanii*	Miq.	Todaq	
Moraceae	*Artocarpus elasticus*		Toyop	Fo
Musaceae	*Musa sp.*		Jelooq Saba	R
Myristicaceae	*Horsfieldia grandis*		Deraya Sepatukng	R C Fu
Myrsinaceae	*Maesa sp.*		Lemonuuq	Fo

Family	Scientific name	Author	Benuaq name	Use
Myrtaceae	*Eugenia kunstleri*	(King) Bahadur & G.	Bengkulat	Fu
Myrtaceae	*Psidium guajava*	L.	Jamuuq	Fo
Myrtaceae	*Eugenia sp.*		Jelomaaq	Fu Fo
Myrtaceae	*Eugenia spicata*	Lamk.	Kebetiq	
Myrtaceae	*Rhodamnia cinerea*	Jack.	Kemuncikng	C Fu
Myrtaceae	*Eugenia fumida*		Wai Meaq	D
Myrtaceae	*Eugenia palembanica*		Wai Pulut	C D
Nepenthaceae	*Nepenthes sp. c.f.*		Sengongong	R
Nephrolepidaceae	*Nephrolepis bisserata*	(Sw.) Schott	Pakuq Parapm	R
Oleaceae	*Jasminum sambac*	(L.) Ait.	Puput	D
Palmae	*Pholidocarpus majadum*	Becc.	Anau	C
Palmae	*Borassodendron borneensis*	Belaakng		Fo C
Palmae	*Licuala valida*	Becc.	Biruq	C R
Palmae	*Metroxylon sagu*	Rottb.	Jemiaq	
Palmae	*Daemonorops halleriana*	Juaaq	Fo	
Palmae	*Elaeis guineensis*	Jacq.	Kelapa Sawit	T
Palmae			Nanga	C Fo
Palmae	*Oncosperma tigillarum*	(Jack.) Ridl.	Niwukng	Fo
Palmae	*Cocos nucifera*	L.	Nyui Gadikng	Fo T R H
Palmae	*Cocos nucifera*	L.	Nyui Sopaakng	R H
Palmae	*Licuala sp.*		Paleh/Palas	R
Palmae	*Calamus scipionum*		Pesiakng	Fo, T
Palmae	*Areca catechu*	L.	Sepootn	R
Palmae	*Areca sp.*		Sepootn Sendawar	R

Palmae	*Arenga pinnata*	(Wurmb.) Merr.	Tuak	T Fo R
Palmae	*Caryota mitis*		Ukor	R C
Pandanaceae	*Pandanus tectornes*		Kajakng	
Pandanaceae	*Pandanus sp.*		Pudaq	R Fo
Passifloraceae	*Passiflora foetida*	L.	Kelepos	R Fo
Piperaceae	*Piper betle*	L.	Laur	Fo
Poaceae	*Gigantochloa hasskarliana*	(Kurz) Back. ex Hey.	Baloq	C
Poaceae	*Schizostachyum blumei*		Bawatn	H
Poaceae	*Dinochloea sp.*		Buluuq Rindu	H
Poaceae	*Coix lacryma-jobi*	L.	Lore	R Fo
Poaceae	*Imperata cylindrica*	(L.) Beav.	Padakng	R H
Poaceae	*Chrysopogon aciculatus*		Sengkeruput	R
Poaceae	*Cymbopogon nardus*	(L.) Rendle	Serai Munteeq	R
Poaceae	*Schizostachyum sp.*		Temiang	R H
Poaceae	*Gigantochloa atter*		Tolakng Kwayatn Beneeq	R
Poaceae	*Gigantochloa sp.*		Tolakng Kwayatn Bulaau	R
Poaceae	*Schizostachyum longispiculatum*		TolakngMorakng	C
Poaceae	*Saccharum officinarum*		Touq Meaq	R Fo
Poaceae	*Saccharum spontaneum*	L.	Touq Salah	R
Polygalaceae	*Xanthophyllum affine*	Korth. ex Miq.	Meloyaq	H
Rhamnaceae	*Zyzyphus sp.*		Sengkeromet	H
Rosaceae	*Prunus arboreum*	(Bl.) Bl.	Gemah	H
Rubiaceae	*Diplospora singularis*		Bernipaq	C
Rubiaceae	*Gardenia augusta*		Kemang Piring	R
Rubiaceae	*Tarrena sp.*		Mardangiiq/Sentang iiq	R

Family	Scientific name	Author	Benuaq name	Use
Rubiaceae	*Morindra citrifolia*	L.	Ngkuduuq	R
Rubiaceae	*Timonius lasianthoides*		Sangkulai	H
Rubiaceae	*Tricalysia sp.*		Wakaai Lempekeeq	R
Rutaceae	*Citrus sp.*		Muntee	R Fo
Rutaceae	*Evodia alba*		Potukng	R
Sapindaceae	*Dimocarpus longan c.f.*		Bukuuq	Fu Fo T
Sapindaceae	*Dimocarpus c.f. longan*		Ihaau	Fu Fo T
Sapindaceae	*Guioa diplopetala*	(Hassk.) Radlk.	Kecimpi	
Sapindaceae	*Nephelium lappaceum*	L.	Kopeq/Kopekaan	Fo T
Sapindaceae	*Nephelium cuspidatum*	Bl.	Lempukat	Fo
Sapindaceae	*Nephelium sp.*		Ngkaraai	Fo
Sapindaceae	*Nephelium maingayi*	Hiern.	Ridatn	Fo
Sapindaceae	*Nephelium sp.*		Rupaai	Fo Fu
Sapindaceae	*Nephelium mutabile*	Bl.	Semayaap	Fo
Sapindaceae	*Nephelium sp.*		Siwo	Fo
Sapindaceae	*Nephelium cuspidatum*	Bl.	Torookng	Fo
Sapotaceae	*Palaquium sp.*		Ketiau	C T
Sapotaceae	*Palaquium sp.*		Malau	H
Sapotaceae	*Madhuen sericea*		Meradikng	C
Sapotaceae	*Palaquium sp.*		Natu Beneeq	H
Sapotaceae	*Madhuca sp.*		Natu Tunyukng	H
Sonneratiaceae	*Duabanga moluccana*	Bl.	Benuaang	C
Sterculiaceae	*Pterospermum diversifolium*	Bl.	Bayur	
Sterculiaceae	*Theobroma cacao*	L.	Kakau	R

Styracaceae	*Styrax benzoin*	Dryand.	Minyin	R
Theaceae	*Schima wallichii*	(D.C.) Korth.	Nagaaq	Fo I
Thymelaeaceae	*Aquilaria malaccensis*	Lamk.	Alaas	T R
Ulmaceae	*Gironniera nervosa*	Planch.	Mparee	C
Verbenaceae	*Clerodendron sp.*		Bungaq Pangir Bura	R
Verbenaceae	*Clerodendron sp.*		Bungaq Pangir Meaaq	R
Verbenaceae	*Vitex pinnata*	L.	Kelapapa	D
Verbenaceae	*Vitex pubescens*	Vahl	Kepapaaq	C Fu
Verbenaceae	*Peronema canescens*	Jack.	Sungkai	Fo C
Zingiberaceae	*Nicolaia solaris*	Horan.	Bowooi	R
Zingiberaceae	*Alpinia galanga*		Lajaaq	R
Zingiberaceae	*Catimbium muticum*		Tengkelimas	Fo
Zingiberaceae	*Amomum sp.*		Teniiq	R
Zingiberaceae	*Costus sp.*		Touq Tawaai	R
			Akar Pandai	R
			Bangkatn	C H
			Banyum	Fo
			Bekalukng	R I
	Commersonia bartramia		Bekangin	C
			Belau	H
			Belonge	R
			Benuaang Rangka	R
			Beramanun	C
			Beteteq	I
			Bilapm	R

Family	Scientific name	Author	Benuaq name	Use
			Blunge	Fo
			Bungaq Mekaau	
	Dracontomelon dao	(Blanco) Merr. & Ro.	Dahuuq	Fo
	Planchonia valida		Dut	C
			Embagai	
			Jayatn	R
	Coniogrammea fraxinea		Jiee	C
			Karawat	R
			Kelaneh	R
			Longaq	R
			Mantotor	
			Mburaatn	C
			Nintuuq	R
			Petakaq	H
			Pokeeq	C
			Sahap	Fo
			Sekur	R
			Sempuli Wakaai	R
			Serkoop	Fo
			Sincikng Sipat	Fo
			Sunjuukng	C
	Elateriospermum tapos	Bl.	Taman Laba	H
			Tana Gendikng	R

Tawar Seribu	
Telaatn	H
Temias	H
Topus Tongau	
Turutn Luikng	R
Wakaai Besaq	R
Wakaai Sinaq	P

76 FAMILIES WITH 336 LOCALLY-DIFFERENTIATED SPECIES

Rattans (Calameae)

Benuaq name	Scientific name	Author
Beleh	*Calamus penicillatus*	Roxb.
Beleh Belatn	*Calamus penicillatus c.f.*	Roxb.
Beleh Jautn	*Calamus penicillatus Roxb.c.f.*	
Biungan	*Daemonorops sabut oder*	Becc.
	Calamus polystachys	Becc.
Boyukng Bura	*Calamus optimus c.f.*	Becc.
Boyukng Meaaq	*Calamus optimus c.f.*	Becc.
Danan	*Korthalsia rigida*	Bl.

Danan Dakutn	*Calamus tomentosus*	Becc.
Danan Lentokng	*Korthalsia ferox*	Bl.
Danan Solai	*Korthalsia rigida*	Bl.
Emporooq	*Korthalsia sp.*	
Inai	*Ceratolobus subangulatus*	
Jehap	*Calamus trachycoleus*	Becc.
Jepukng	*Daemonorops crinita*	(Miq.) Bl.
Juaaq	*Plectocomiopsis geminiflora*	(Griff.) Becc.
Keheh	*Calamus muricatus*	Becc.
Kotoq	*Daemonorops angustifolia*	(Griff.) Mart.
Kotoq Boga	*Daemonorops fissa*	(Miq.) Bl.
Lalutn	*Korthalsia scaphigera*	Griff. ex Mart.
Lulu	*Calamus sp.*	
Ngono	*Calamus manan*	Miq.
Sekolaq/Pesiakng	*Calamus ornatus*	Bl.
Si'it	*Calamus* c.f. *balingensis oder* *Daemonorops grandis*	(Griff.) Mart.
Sokaq	*Calamus caesius*	Bl.
Tuuq	*Calamus scipionum*	Lour.
Ue Meaq	*Korthalsia echinometra*	Becc.
Ue Merangui	unidentified	
Ue Pakuq	*Calamus exilis*	Griff.
Ue Rooq	possibly identical to Emporooq	

Annex-3
Cultivated plants

The plants listed here are not botanically confirmed. They were identified by my informants according to local systematics. It is possible that the list contains species or varieties with different names, which are botanically indistinguishable. Scientific names follow Rehm & Espig (1984) and Afriastini (1992). Tree species, as well as cultivated bamboos and rattans, are listed in Annex-2. Rice varieties are listed in the main text.

Cassava varieties	**Sweet potato varieties**	**Sugar-cane varieties**
(*Manihot esculenta Crantz*)	(*Ipomoea batatas* (*L.*) *Poir.*)	(*Saccharum spp.*)
Abang	Ayaàq Bokut	Touq Baukng
Balooq	Ayaaq Bungkar	Touq Berau
Bulau	Ayaaq Gaben	Touq Beteteq
Gerungokng	Ayaaq Kapar	Touq Bongkunung Biakng Biakng
Kapoq	Ayaaq Kentang	Touq Jawa
Lutukng	Ayaaq Kepapaq	Touq Lampatn/Rampatn
Pasar	Ayaaq Lai	Touq Lomuq
Putih	Ayaaq Mentega	Touq Loyaq
Sawah	Ayaaq Naga	Touq Meaq
Semarang	Ayaaq Ongkong	Touq Moruq
Bakoq	Ayaaq Ramại	Touq Nayuq
Berowari	Ayaaq Semangka	Touq Pentih
Gaben	Ayaaq Sungkai	Touq Tokolokng
Idaq	Ayaaq Tola	Touq Toliiq
Kilip	Ayaaq Toliiq	Touq Ungul
Mentega		Touq Wakai
Pikur		Touq Waniiq
Sanukng		
Seloakng		
Terabeeq		

Cucumber varieties
(*Cucumis sativus L.*)
Timun Api
Timun Baukng
Timun Belongkaq
Timun Bulatn
Timun Lomuq
Timun Poruuq
Timun Tanuq
Timun Telaus
Timun Tintiq

Ginger varieties
(*Zingiber officinale Rosc.*)
Loyaq Benuang
Loyaq Cina
Loyaq Pare
Loyaq Uraakng

Chilli varieties
(*Capsicum spp.*)
Sabeq Bura
Sabeq Keriting
Sabeq Lai
Sabeq Poq
Sabeq Rawit
Sabeq Semat
Sabeq Taji
Sabeq Tajuq
Sabeq Temperesa
Sabeq Tiokng
Sabeq Wakai

Banana varieties *(Musa x paradisiaca L.)*

Ambon	*Gergoq*	*Kerakng*	*Nakatn*	*Ruta*	*Ulukng*
Anduq	*Iratn*	*Korau*	*Obouuq*	*Saba*	
Bugis	*Jelmoq*	*Lempeko*	*Okor*	*Sebet*	
Bujak	*Kampar*	*Manoq Ur*	*Puneq*	*Susuq*	
Emas	*Kapas/Kapeh*	*Moliq*	*Rajah*	*Ue*	

Other cultivated vegetables

Bawang Balooq	chives	*Allium sp.*
Bawang Bura	garlic	*Allium sativum* L.
Bawang Doyo	allium	*Allium sp.*
Bawang Lagena	allium	*Allium sp.*
Bawang Meaq	onion	*Allium cepa* L. *Var. ascalonicum*
Botokng		
Dawaq		
Gandum	sorghum	*Sorghum vulgare Pers.*
Jagokng	maize	*Zea mays* L.
Jagokng Boyas	Mais	*Zea mays* L.
Jagokng Ketepe	maize	*Zea mays* L.
Kacang Hijau	green gram	*Phaseolus radiatus* L. c.f.
Kacang Minyak		
Kacang Panjang	French bean	*Phaseolus vulgaris* (L.)
Kacang Tanah	peanut	*Arachis hypogaea* L.
Kangkukng	water spinach	*Ipomoea aquatica* Forak.
Kenas Beneeq	pineapple	*Ananas comosus* (L.) Merr.
Kenas Meaq	pineapple	*Ananas comosus* (L.) Merr.
Kunyit Api	curcuma	*Curcuma domestica* Val.
Kunyit Katemu	curcuma	*Curcuma domestica* Val.
Kunyit Kerewau	curcuma	*Curcuma domestica* Val.
Kunyit Lepo	curcuma	*Curcuma domestica* Val.
Kunyit Makar	curcuma	*Curcuma domestica* Val.

Labu Jawa	pumpkin	*Cucurbita pepo c.f.*
Lajaq		
Lempekng Pera		
Longaq		
Loreeq	Job's tears	*Coix lacryma-jobi* L.
Periaq Beneeq		*Momordica charantia* L.
Periaq Penganan		*Momordica charantia* L.
Semangka	water melon	*Citrullus lanatus* (Thunb) Matsum. et Nakai
Sekur		
Serai Beneeq	citronella grass	*Cymbopogon nardus* (L.) Rendle
Serai Jengan	citronella grass	*Cymbopogon nardus* (L.) Rendle
Serai Munteeq	citronella grass	*Cymbopogon nardus* (L.) Rendle
Timun Belanda		
Tomat	tomato	*Lycopersicon lycopersicum* (L.) Farw.
Tonai	taro	*Colocasia esculenta* (L.) Schotc.f.
Tenaian Beneeq	taro	*Sagittaria sinensis Sims. c.f.*
Tenaian Tungkur	taro	
Toyukng Bulatn	eggplant	*Solanum sp.*
Toyukng Kanap	eggplant	*Solanum sp.*
Toyukng Minjapm	eggplant	*Solanum sp.*
Toyukng Puluuq	eggplant	*Solanum sp.*
Toyukng Ulapm	Eggplant	*Solanum melongena* L.
Twaq	tuba root	*Derris elliptica* Benth.

Annex-4

Bird species

Until May 1999, 184 bird species have been recorded in the forests of Lempunah. Many records were taken along two 1,500 m transects. The transects were used for a comparison of cultivated forest (including swidden fallows and forest gardens) and old secondary forest. Each of the transects represents about 60 per cent of the local avifauna (not including nocturnal and arial-feeding species). For a more detailed study of the birds of the Middle Mahakam Area, see Gönner (2000b); for details of the applied methodology, see Gönner (1998b). The identification was based on my own experience and on the available literature (MacKinnon & Phillipps 1993, King *et al.* 1975, Davison & Chew 1996). Systematology mainly follows MacKinnon & Phillipps (1993). In a few cases, the nomenclature of King *et al.* (1975) is used. Local names were listed by my informants.

CW: observed along the transect through cultivated forest
SW: observed along the transect through old secondary forest

Benuaq name	English name	Scientific name	CW	SW
	Black Bittern	*Dupetor flavicollis*		
	Storm's Stork	*Ciconia stormi*		
	Crested Serpent-Eagle	*Spilornis cheela*		✓
	Changeable Hawk-Eagle	*Spizaetus cirrhatus*		
	Wallace's Hawk-Eagle	*Spizaetus nanus*		
Beniang	Brahminy Kite	*Haliastur indus*		
	Japanese Sparrowhawk	*Accipiter gularis*		

Benuaq name	English name	Scientific name	CW	SW
	Crested Goshawk	*Accipiter trivirgatus*	✓	
	Black-thighed Falconet	*Microhierax fringillarius*		
Lempeko	Blue-breasted Quail	*Coturnix chinensis*		
Rangkekng	Long-billed Partridge	*Rhizothera longirostris*		
Lesio	Crested Partridge	*Rollolus rouloul*	✓	
Sakatn	Crested Fireback	*Lophura ignita*		
Jue	Great Argus	*Argusianus argus*		
Senggerenak	White-breasted Waterhen	*Amaurornis phoenicurus*		
Puneeq Rosou	Pink-necked Green Pigeon	*Treron vernans*	✓	
Puneeq Ladu	Cinnamon-headed Green Pigeon	*Treron fulvicollis*		
	Large Green Pigeon	*Treron capellei*		
Puneeq Sulikng	Little Green Pigeon	*Treron olax*	✓	✓
Tuatn Gogok	Green Imperial-Pigeon	*Ducula aenea*	✓	✓
Bengkukur	Spotted Dove	*Streptopelia chinensis*	✓	
Jotukng	Emerald Dove	*Chalcophaps indica*	✓	
Teriap	Blue-crowned Hanging-Parrot	*Loriculus galgulus*	✓	✓
Tialikng	Blue-rumped Parrot	*Psittinus cyanurus*	✓	
Terabeeq	Long-tailed Parakeet	*Psittacula longicauda*	✓	✓
Kangkang Kapot	Indian Cuckoo	*Cuculus micropterus*		✓
	Oriental Cuckoo	*Cuculus saturatus*		
	Asian Koel	*Eudynamis scolopacea*		
Sentapit	Plaintive Cuckoo	*Cacomantis merulinus*	✓	
	Banded Bay Cuckoo	*Cacomantis sonneratii*	✓	✓

	Violet Cuckoo	*Chrysoccocycx xanthorhynchus*		
Nape	Chestnut-bellied Malkoha	*Phaenicophaeus sumatranus*	✓	✓
Nape	Raffles's Malkoha	*Phaenicophaeus chlorophaeus*		✓
Nape	Chestnut-breasted Malkoha	*Phaenicophaeus curvirostris*	✓	✓
Bumut Beneeq	Lesser Coucal	*Centropus bengalensis*	✓	
Bumut Lawaakng	Greater Coucal	*Centropus sinensis*	✓	✓
Toyup Toru	Sunda Ground-Cuckoo	*Carpococcyx radiceus c.f.*		
Ketupaq	Buffy Fish-Owl	*Ketupa ketupu*		
	Brown Hawk-Owl	*Ninox scutulata*	✓	✓
Beniak Buaq	Brown Wood-Owl	*Strix leptogrammica*		
Uruk Datu	Reddish Scops-Owl	*Otus rufescens*		
	Collared Scops-Owl	*Otus lempiji*		
Kaor	Gould's Frogmouth	*Batrachostomus stellatus*		
Kaor	Javan Frogmouth	*Batrachostomus javensis*		
Kaor	Large Frogmouth	*Batrachostomus auritus*		
Tak Taha	Malaysian Eared-Nightjar	*Eurostopodus temminckii*		
	Edible-nest Swiftlet	*Collocalia fuciphaga*		
	Little Swift	*Apus affinis*		
	Asian Palm-Swift	*Cypsiurus balasiensis*		
	Silver-rumped Swift	*Rhaphidura leucopygialis*		
	Grey-rumped Treeswift	*Hemiprocne longipennis*	✓	
Papou	Diard's Trogon	*Harpactes diardii*	✓	✓
Papou	Red-naped Trogon	*Harpactes kasumba*	✓	✓
Papou	Scarlet-rumped Trogon	*Harpactes duvaucelii*	✓	✓
Bekakaq	Stork-billed Kingfisher	*Pelargopsis capensis*	✓	

Benuaq name	English name	Scientific name	CW	SW
Selebinti	Blue-eared Kingfisher	*Alcedo meninting*		
	Banded Kingfisher	*Lacedo pulchella*	✓	✓
Selebinti	Rufous-backed Kingfisher	*Ceyx rufidorsa*	✓	✓
Selebinti	Black-backed Kingfisher	*Ceyx erithacus*		
Ngkurau	Blue-tailed Bee-Eater	*Merops philippinus*	✓	
	Blue-throated Bee-Eater	*Merops viridis*		
	Red-bearded Bee-Eater	*Nyctyornis amictus*		✓
Mendalukng	Dollarbird	*Eurystomus orientalis*	✓	✓
Terakuuq	Bushy-crested Hornbill	*Anorrhinus galeritus*		✓
Totoh	Wrinkled Hornbill	*Aceros corrugatus*	✓	✓
Mengkeeq	Oriental Pied Hornbill	*Anthracoceros albirostris*	✓	✓
Moeq	Asian Black Hornbill	*Anthracoceros malayanus*		✓
Tongau	Rhinoceros Hornbill	*Buceros rhinoceros*		✓
Batu Uluk	Helmeted Hornbill	*Buceros vigil*		
Soyu	Brown Barbet	*Calorhamphus fuliginosus*		✓
Teruaq	Red-throated Barbet	*Megalaima mystacophanos*		✓
Teruaq	Yellow-crowned Barbet	*Megalaima henricii*		✓
Teruaq	Gold-whiskered Barbet	*Megalaima chrysopogon*		
Teruaq	Blue-eared Barbet	*Megalaima australis*	✓	✓
Teruaq	Red-crowned Barbet	*Megalaima rafflesii*	✓	✓
	Rufous Pickulet	*Sasia abnormis*		✓
Tekalih	Crimson-winged Woodpecker	*Picus puniceus*	✓	✓
Tekalih	Checker-throated Woodpecker	*Picus mentalis*		✓

Tekalih	Banded Woodpecker	*Picus miniaceus*		
Tekalih	Rufous Woodpecker	*Celeus brachyurus*	✓	✓
Tekalih	Sunda Woodpecker	*Picoides moluccensis*	✓	
Tekalih	Buff-rumped Woodpecker	*Meiglyptes tristis*	✓	✓
Tekalih	Buff-necked Woodpecker	*Meiglyptes tukki*	✓	✓
Tekalih	Grey-and-buff Woodpecker	*Hemicircus concretus*	✓	
Tekalih	Olive-backed Woodpecker	*Dinopium rafflesi*		✓
Tekalih	White-bellied Woodpecker	*Dryocopus javanensis*	✓	
Tekalih	Great Slaty Woodpecker	*Mulleripicus pulverulentus*	✓	✓
Tekalih	Orange-backed Woodpecker	*Reinwardtipicus validus*		
Sanjalano	Black-and-red Broadbill	*Cymbirhynchus macrorhynchus*	✓	
Belowari	Black-and-yellow Broadbill	*Eurylaimus ochromalus*	✓	✓
Belowari	Banded Broadbill	*Eurylaimus javanicus*	✓	✓
	Dusky Broadbill	*Corydon sumatranus*		✓
Sentoa	Green Broadbill	*Calyptomena viridis*		✓
	Hooded Pitta	*Pitta sordida*	✓	✓
Piaq Pelanuq	Garnet Pitta	*Pitta granatina*		✓
	Blue-headed Pitta	*Pitta baudii*		✓
Keputukng	Barn Swallow	*Hirundo rustica*		
Keputukng	Pacific Swallow	*Hirundo tahitica*		
	Black-winged Flycatcher-Shrike	*Hemipus hirundinaceus*	✓	✓
	Lesser Cuckoo-Shrike	*Coracina fimbriata*	✓	✓
	Bar-bellied Cuckoo-Shrike	*Coracina striata*	✓	
	Fiery Minivet	*Pericrocotus igneus*	✓	
	Scarlet Minivet	*Pericrocotus flammeus*	✓	✓

Benuaq name	English name	Scientific name	CW	SW
	Green Iora	*Aegithina viridissima*	✓	✓
	Common Iora	*Aegithina tiphia*	✓	
Datu Da	Lesser Green Leafbird	*Chloropsis cyanopogon*	✓	✓
Datu Da	Greater Green Leafbird	*Chloropsis sonnerati*	✓	✓
Datu Da	Blue-winged Leafbird	*Chloropsis cochinchinensis*		✓
	Asian Fairy-Bluebird	*Irena puella*		✓
Nyeekng	Black-headed Bulbul	*Pycnonotus atriceps*	✓	✓
Biorooq	Grey-bellied Bulbul	*Pycnonotus cyaniventris*		
Biorooq	Yellow-vented Bulbul	*Pycnonotus goiavier*	✓	
Biorooq	Olive-winged Bulbul	*Pycnonotus plumosus*	✓	✓
Biorooq	Cream-vented Bulbul	*Pycnonotus simplex*	✓	✓
Biorooq	Spectacled Bulbul	*Pycnonotus erythrophtalmus*	✓	
Biorooq Bungkokng	Puff-backed Bulbul	*Pycnonotus eutilotus*	✓	✓
Biorooq	Red-eyed Bulbul	*Pycnonotus brunneus*	✓	✓
Biorooq Pentih	Grey-cheeked Bulbul	*Alophoixus bres*		✓
Biorooq	Yellow-bellied Bulbul	*Alophoixus phaeocephalus*		✓
Biorooq	Hairy-backed Bulbul	*Tricholestes criniger*		✓
Biorooq	Puff-vented Bulbul	*Iole olivacea*		
	Bronzed Drongo	*Dicrurus aeneus*		
	Crow-billed Drongo	*Dicrurus annectans*		✓
Ketiakng	Greater Racket-tailed Drongo	*Dicrurus paradiseus*	✓	✓
	Black Magpie	*Platysmurus leucopterus*	✓	✓
	Slender-billed Crow	*Corvus enca*	✓	✓

	Bornean Bristlehead	*Pityriasis gymnocephala*		✓
	Velvet-fronted Nuthatch	*Sitta frontalis*	✓	
	Black-capped Babbler	*Pellorneum capistratum*	✓	✓
	Short-tailed Babbler	*Trichastoma malaccense*	✓	✓
	White-chested Babbler	*Trichastoma rostratum*	✓	✓
	Ferruginous Babbler	*Trichastoma bicolor*	✓	✓
	Moustached Babbler	*Malacopteron magnirostre*	✓	✓
	Rufous-crowned Babbler	*Malacopteron magnum*	✓	✓
	Scaly-crowned Babbler	*Malacopteron cinereum*	✓	✓
	Sooty-capped Babbler	*Malacopteron affine*	✓	✓
	Chestnut-winged Babbler	*Stachyris erythroptera*	✓	✓
	Chestnut-rumped Babbler	*Stachyris maculata*	✓	✓
	Black-throated Babbler	*Stachyris nigricollis*	✓	✓
	Fluffy-backed Tit-Babbler	*Macronous ptilosus*	✓	✓
	Striped Tit-Babbler	*Macronous gularis*	✓	✓
	Brown Fulvetta	*Alcippe brunneicauda*	✓	
	Rufous-tailed Shama	*Trichixos pyrrhopygus*		✓
	Magpie Robin	*Copsychus saularis*		
	White-rumped Shama	*Copsychus malabaricus*	✓	✓
	Golden-bellied Gerygone	*Gerygone sulphurea*	✓	
	Arctic Warbler	*Phylloscopus borealis*		✓
Nene	Ashy Tailorbird	*Orthotomus ruficeps*	✓	✓
Nene	Dark-necked Tailorbird	*Orthotomus atrogularis*	✓	✓
Nene	Rufous-tailed Tailorbird	*Orthotomus sericeus*	✓	✓
	Yellow-bellied Prinia	*Prinia flaviventris*	✓	

Benuaq name	English name	Scientific name	CW	SW
	Asian Brown-Flycatcher	*Muscicapa dauurica*	✓	
	Malaysian Blue-Flycatcher	*Cyornis turcosus*	✓	
	Bornean Blue-Flycatcher	*Cyornis superbus*		
	Rufous-chested Flycatcher	*Ficedula dumetoria*		
	Grey-chested Jungle-Flycatcher	*Rhinomyias umbratilis*		✓
	Rufous-winged Philentoma	*Philentoma pyrhopterum*		✓
	Maroon-breasted Philentoma	*Philentoma velatum*		
	Black-naped Monarch	*Hypothymis azurea*	✓	✓
Burung Doyo	Asian Paradise-Flycatcher	*Terpsiphone paradisi*		✓
	Pied Fantail	*Rhipidura javanica*	✓	
	Spotted Fantail	*Rhipidura perlata*		✓
	Mangrove Whistler	*Pachycephala cinerea*	✓	
	White-breasted Wood-Swallow	*Artamus leucorhynchus*		
	Yellow Wagtail	*Motacilla flava*		
	Chestnut-cheeked Starling	*Sturnus philippensis*	✓	
Tiokng	Hill Myna	*Gracula religiosa*	✓	✓
	Plain-throated Sunbird	*Anthreptes malacensis*	✓	✓
	Ruby-cheeked Sunbird	*Anthreptes singalensis*	✓	✓
	Olive-backed Sunbird	*Nectarinia jugularis*		
	Purple-throated Sunbird	*Nectarinia sperata*	✓	✓
	Crimson Sunbird	*Aethopyga siparaja*	✓	
	Purple-naped Sunbird	*Hypogramma hypogrammicum*		✓
Seset	Little Spiderhunter	*Arachnothera longirostra*	✓	✓

Seset	Long-billed Spiderhunter	*Arachnothera robusta*		✓
Seset	Grey-breasted Spiderhunter	*Arachnothera affinis*		✓
Seset	Yellow-eared Spiderhunter	*Arachnothera chrysogenys*	✓	
Mentit	Crimson-breasted Flowerpecker	*Prionochilus percussus*	✓	✓
Mentit	Yellow-rumped Flowerpecker	*Prionochilus xanthopygius*	✓	✓
Mentit	Scarlet-backed Flowerpecker	*Dicaeum cruentatum*	✓	✓
Mentit	Orange-bellied Flowerpecker	*Dicaeum trigonostigma*	✓	✓
Mentit	Yellow-vented Flowerpecker	*Dicaeum chrysorrheum*	✓	
Burung Gereja	Eurasian Tree-Sparrow	*Passer montanus*		
Empit	Dusky Munia	*Lonchura fuscans*	✓	
Empit	Black-headed Munia	*Lonchura malacca*		
			101	102

Annex-5
Mammal species

During the case study, 42 mammal species were noted in the forests of Lempunah. This equals 42 per cent of the Bornean land mammals, not regarding *Muridae* (mice and rats), *Soricidae* (shrews) and *Chiroptera* (bats), which were not included in the study. Systematology follows Payne *et al.* (1985). The status of each species is noted in the right margin.

✓	seen by the author
c.f.	*cum fide*, believed to be this species (seen by the author)
w	reported by reliable witnesses (mainly hunters)
w✞	reported, but extinct in the area
s	confirmed by skin or skull
*	hunted, used

Benuaq	English name	Scientific name	status
Tupai	Common Treeshrew	*Tupaia glis*	✓
Tupai	Lesser Treeshrew / Slender Treeshrew	*Tupaia minor* / *Tupaia gracilis*	c.f.
Tupai	Painted Treeshrew	*Tupaia picta*	✓
Kuukng Batiq	Colugo	*Cynocephalus variegatus*	w
Bawikng	Large Flying Fox	*Pteropus vampyrus*	✓
Bekikiiq	Slow Loris	*Nycticebus coucang*	✓ *
Ukar	Western Tarsier	*Tarsius bancanus*	w *
Lutuukng	Maroon Langur	*Presbytis rubicunda*	w
Buus	White-fronted Langur	*Presbytis frontata*	✓ *
Bekaraq	Proboscis Monkey	*Nasalis larvatus*	✓
Kodeq	Long-tailed Macaque	*Macaca fascicularis*	✓ *
Boruq	Pig-tailed Macaque	*Macaca nemestrina*	✓ *
Kelawat	Bornean Gibbon	*Hylobates muelleri*	✓ *
Ayapm	Pangolin	*Manis javanica*	s *
Marau	Giant Squirrel	*Ratufa affinis*	✓
	Prevost's Squirrel	*Callosciurus prevostii*	✓

Pokakng	Plantain Squirrel	*Callosciurus notatus*	✓
Sentuku	Plain Pigmy Squirrel	*Exilisciurus exilis*	✓
	Red Giant Flying Squirrel	*Petaurista petaurista*	w
Titukng	Common Porcupine	*Hystrix brachyura*	s *
Pegeekng	Long-Tailed Porcupine	*Trichys fasciculata*	
Titukng	Thick-Spined Porcupine	*Thecurus crassispinis*	✓ *
Biakng	Sun Bear	*Helarctos malayanus*	✓ *
Dorooq	Yellow-Throated Marten	*Martes flavigula*	w
	Malay Weasel	*Mustela nudipes*	c.f.
Dongan	Hairy-Nosed Otter	*Lutra sumatrana*	✓ *
Dongan	Oriental Small-Clawed Otter	*Aonyx cinerea*	✓ *
Kuliiq Teniq	Malay Civet/Tangalung	*Viverra tangalunga*	s *
Munin Tuyutn	Bearcat/Binturong	*Arctitis binturong*	✓
Bosikng	Small-Toothed Palm Civet	*Arctogalidia trivirgata*	✓
Munin	Common Palm Civet	*Paradoxurus hermaphroditus*	s *
Munin Tuyutn	Masked Palm Civet	*Panguma larvata*	✓
Kalang Perahn	Banded Palm Civet	*Hemigalus derbyanus*	✓
Kalang Perahn	Banded Linsang	*Prionodon linsang*	w
Meong Mamar	Marbled Cat	*Felis marmorata*	s *
Badak	Sumatran Rhinoceros	*Dicerorhinus sumatrensis*	w✞
Bawi	Bearded Pig	*Sus barbatus*	✓ *
Pelanuk-Longkiikng	*Lesser Mouse-Deer*	*Tragulus javanicus*	✓ *
Pelanuk-Belongkaaq	*Greater Mouse-Deer*	*Tragulus napu*	✓ *
Telaus	Bornean Red Muntjac	Muntiacus muntjak	✓ *
Telaus	Bornean Yellow Muntjac	*Muntiacus atherodes*	✓ *
Tekayo	Sambar Deer	Cervus unicolor	✓ *
Lemui	Banteng	*Bos javanicus*	✓ *

Annex-6

Reptile and fish species

The following species were extracted mainly during the drought of 1997-8 from swamp forests. The identification of turtles was kindly done by C.L. Chan and Indraneil Das. The two extracted snake species and one of the two monitor lizards were identified based on Cox *et al.* (1998). Another 18 snake species were locally-differentiated, but remain unidentified so far.

Benuaq name	**English name**	**Scientific name**
Panganan	Reticulated Python	*Python reticularis*
Bersisiq	Elephant-trunk Snake	*Acrochordus javanicus*
Miaaq Merayo	Monitor Lizard	*Varanus salvator*
Miaaq Araakng		*Varanus sp.*
Kentawakng	Asian Softshell Turtle	*Amyda cartilaginea*
Kentawakng	Malayan Softshell Turtle	*Dogania subplana*
Biukuu	Malayan Giant Turtle	*Orlitia borneensis*
Kodoq Katuq	Malayan Box Turtle	*Cuora amboinensis*
Kodoq Anau	Black Pond Turtle	*Siebenrockiella crassicollis*

18 locally-differentiated snake species (*nipaq*):

Bantuukng	*Nipaq Ue*	*Suaiq*
Bumuiiq	*Nipaq Uot*	*Susuq Tana*
Dopukng	*Nipaq Yang*	*Tikang Nyuy*
Layun	*Oar*	*Toran Bulan*
Layun Natakng	*Panganan Laweq*	*Toran Jate*
Lomuyaq	*Pokuyo*	*Ular Lidi*

So far, the 40 locally-differentiated fish species (*kinas*) could not be identified. Hence, only local names are listed.

Baan	*Enjolong*	*Ketam*	*Puyau*
Baan Touq	*Eparang*	*Ketiung*	*Ruay*
Baukng	*Gesiliq*	*Kinas Buntal*	*Rungan*
Berukung	*Jalawat*	*Kosung*	*Salap*
Betutuq	*Jue Danum*	*Lais*	*Seluang*
Biawan	*Jukuq*	*Larang*	*Sopat Putih*
Bokaq	*Juling*	*Lindung*	*Sopat Siam*
Boneh	*Kapukng Sopa*	*Lopuq*	*Susur Batuq*
Boyot	*Kepar*	*Padiq*	*Tanggolosiq*
Ekong	*Kepuyuq*	*Penang*	*Uhing*

Glossary

babar: one year-old fallow used again as a swidden

bekeleeu: curing rite including the sacrifice of a pig

beleq: measure for rice, app. 11 kg (Ind. *kaleng*)

belian: common curing rite

bengkar: old forest, not yet used as a swidden

dempaq: flat area (in contrast to swamp or hill areas)

guguq: large ritual complex, usually including curing and purifying rites

intootn: legends, folk-tales

jaras: heath forest (Ind. *kerangas*)

kanwil kehutanan: provincial branch of the Ministry of Forestry

kayuq: wood/woods

kebotn: garden

kebotn getah: rubber garden

kebotn ue: rattan garden

kepala adat: traditional chief

kepala desa: administrative chief

kerengkakng: old fallow forest (generally older than 30 years)

konookng: wage work(er)

kwakoq: young (2-10 years) fallow used again as a swidden

kwangkai: death ceremony

ladang: swidden (Ind.)

louu: longhouse

mandau: bush knife

melas tautn: purifying ritual for the new year

nular: purifying ritual including the sacrifice of a pig (usually during droughts)

payaq: swamp (forest)

pembeliatn: shaman (specialist for curing rites)

pengewara: specialist for death ceremonies

plou: mutual help

roboot: forest (in contrast to village, fields or forest gardens)

sahu: taboo

saikng: hill, mountain

sawah: irrigated rice field (Ind.)

simpukng: mixed forest garden (mainly fruit trees)

temputn: myths

ukop: field house

umaq: swidden

uraa: 1. general expression for fallows

2. special expression for 10 to 30 year-old fallow

warung: food stall (Ind.)

Pl. I Longhouse in Mancong

Pl. II Longhouse in Lempunah

Pl. III House in Lempunah

Pl. IV Field hut

Pl. V Low water level near the village Lempunah

Pl. VI High water level near the village Lempunah

Pl. VII *Behempas* (traditional martial art) fight

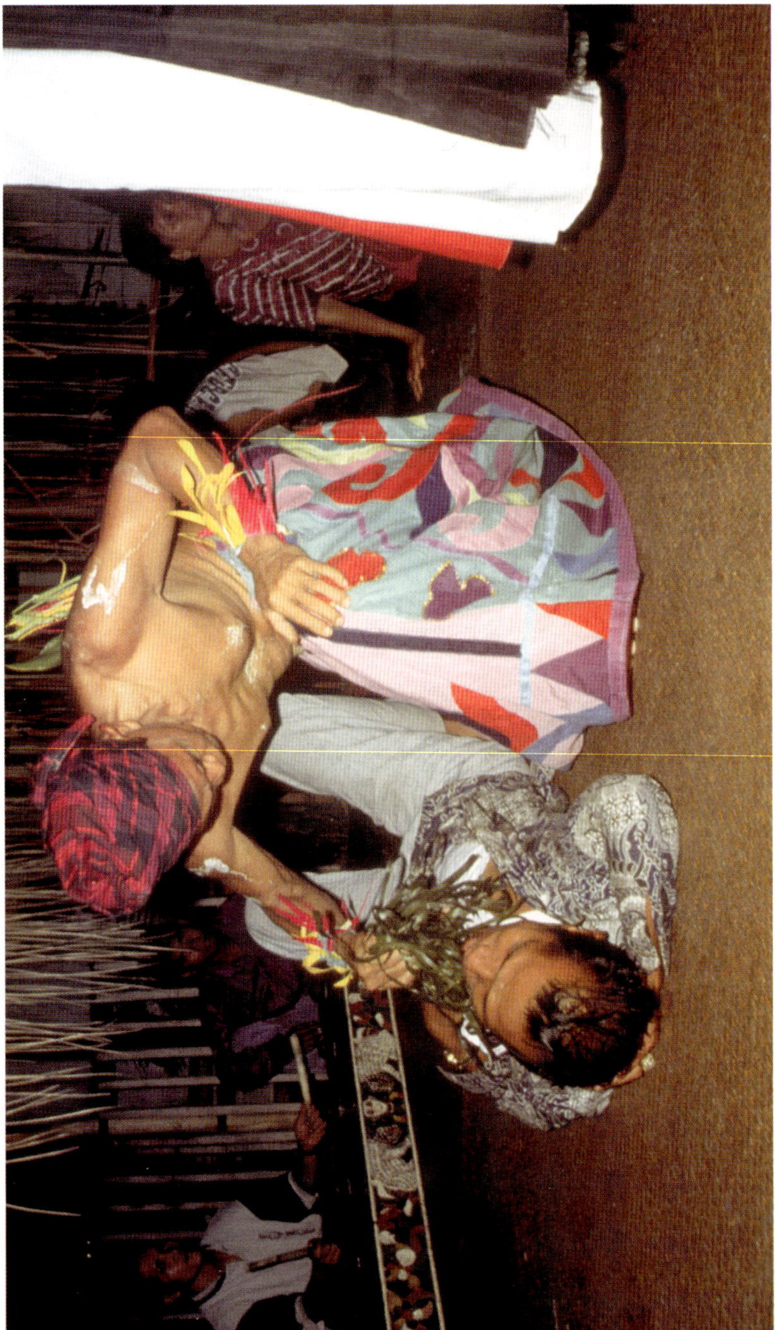

Pl. VIII *Pemeliatn* healer

Pl. IX Praying man performing a *kwangkai* ceremony

Pl. X Praying shaman

Pl. XI Funeral ceremony

Pl. XII Kepala Adat (traditional village chief) of Lempunah

Pl. XIII Ngerangkau dance

Pl. XIV Singing *Pemeliatn* healer

Pl. XV Rattan collectors

Pl. XVI Children watching TV

Pl. XVII A Benuaq lady weaving *Ulap Doyo*

Pl. XVIII Timber Company trucks for commercial logging

Pl. XIX Saw mill

Pl. XX Shingles made from iron wood (*Eusideroxylon zwageri*)

Pl. XXI Rubber processing equipment

Pl. XXII Villager using a casting net

Pl. XXIII Benuaq lady fishing with a rod

Pl. XXIV Children fishing in a water hole

Pl. XXV Jepukng bush with farmer

Pl. XXVI Plantation workers in an oil palm nursery

Pl. XXVII Benuag lady in the field

Pl. XXVIII *Belontakng* statue in a field

Pl. XXIX Cleaning the forest floor as fire-break (*ladakng*)

Pl. XXX Simple water pump in the forest — farmer sprays water on a fire-break line

Pl. XXXI Dry forest during the drought of 1997-8

Pl. XXXII A *ladakng* fire-break in a fire-prone landscape

Pl. XXXIII Rubber garden damaged by fire

Pl. XXXIV Burnt swidden site (close up)

Pl. XXXV Farmers dibbling in the freshly burnt swidden

Pl. XXXVI Green swidden

Pl. XXXVII Harvestings farmers with forest in the background

Pl. XXXVIII Modern oil palm plantation

Pl. XXXIX Access road to an oil palm plantation

Pl. XL Swidden with palms

Bibliography

Abdoellah, O.S., 1990, Home Gardens in Java and Their Future Development. In: Landauer, K. & M. Brazil (eds.): *Tropical Home Gardens*. United Nations:9-20.

Afriastini, J.J., 1992, *Daftar Nama Tanaman,* Penebar Swadaya, Jakarta.

Alexander, J., 1992, Must Ascribed Status Entail Inequality? Reproduction of Rank in Lahanan Society. *Oceania* 62:207-26.

Anderson, A.B./Ioris, E.M., 1992, Valuing the Rain-Forest-Economic Strategies by Small-scale Forest Extractivists in the Amazon Estuary. *Human Ecology* 20,8:337-69.

Ansyahari/Bower, R.P./Hoffmann, R./Nitsch, M./Poerwanto/Speller, D.R., 1984 *Land Capability Classification, Muara Muntai, Tanjung Isuy,* TAD, Samarinda.

Appell, G.N., 1986, Kayan Land Tenure and the Distribution of Devolvable Usufruct in Borneo. *Borneo Research Bulletin* 18,2:119-30.

Armstrong, R., 1992, The Cultural Construction of Hierarchy among the Kenyah Badeng. *Oceania* 62:194-206.

Avé, J.B., 1972, Kalimantan Dayaks. In: LeBar, F.M. (ed.): *Ethnic Groups of Insular Southeast Asia*, vol. I, Indonesia, Andaman Islands and Madagascar. New Haven.

Avé, J.B./King, V.T., 1986, Borneo: *The People of the Weeping Forest. Tradition and Change in Borneo*, Leiden.

Balée, W., 1989, The Culture of Amazonian Forests. *Advances in Economic Botany* 7:1-21.

———, 1993, Indigenous Transformations of Amazonian Forests — An Example from Maranhao, Brazil. *Homme* 33,2-4:231-54.

Bargatzky, T., 1986, *Einführung in die Kulturökologie. Umwelt, Kultur und Gesellschaft,* Dietrich Reimer Verlag, Berlin.

———, 1992, Kulturökologie. In: H. Fischer (ed.): *Ethnologie. Einführung und Überblick*, Dietrich Reimer Verlag, Berlin:383-406.

Barlett, P.F., 1980, Adaptive Strategies in Peasant Agricultural Production. *Annual Review of Anthropology* 9:545-73.

Basuki, K., 1999, *Simpukng structures*. Unpublished Data.

Bayrischer Rundfunk, 2000, *World Courier — Borneo*. Film.

Belcher, B.M., 1997, *Commercialisation of Forest Products As a Tool for Sustainable Development: Lessons from the Asian Rattan Sector*. PhD thesis, University of Minnesota.

Bennett, J.W., 1976, *The Ecological Transition: Cultural Anthropology and Human Adaptation*, Pergamon Press, New York.

Benyamin, 2000, *Tempuutn Adat*. Unpublished collection of 4 Benuaq Myths.

Berger, P.L./Luckmann, T., 1980, *Die gesellschaftliche Konstruktion der Wirklichkeit. Eine Theorie der Wissenssoziologie*. Fischer, Frankfurt am Main.

Blicher-Mathiesen, U., 1994, Borneo Illipe, a Fat Product from Different *Shorea* spp. (Dipterocarpaceae). *Economic Botany*, vol. 48, 3:231-42.

Bonoh, Y., 1985a, *Belian Bawo*. Departemen Pendidikan dan Kebudayaan Kantor Wilayah Propinsi Kalimantan Timur.

———, 1985b, *Lungun dan Upacara Adat*. Departemen Pendidikan dan Kebudayaan Kantor Wilayah Propinsi Kalimantan Timur.

Boserup, E., 1965, *The Conditions of Agricultural Growth. The Economics of Agrarian Change under Population Pressure*, Aldine, Chicago.

Bossel, H., 1989, *Simulation dynamischer Systeme*, Vieweg, Braunschweig.

Boster, J., 1983, A Comparison of the Diversity of Jivaroan Gardens with that of the Tropical Forest. *Human Ecology*, vol.11, No.1:47-68.

Boyce, D., 1986, *Kutai, East Kalimantan*. A Journal of Past and Present Glory. Kota Bangun, Indonesia.

Braganza, G.C., 1996, Philippine Community-based Forest Management. Options for Sustainable Development. In: Michael J.G. Parnwell & Raymond L. Bryant (eds.): *Environmental Change in South-East Asia: People, Politics and Sustainable Development*, Routledge, London:311-29.

Brookfield, H./Padoch, C., 1994, Appreciating Agrodiversity. A Look at the Dynamism and Diversity of Indigenous Farming Practices. In: *Environment,* vol. 36, no. 5:6-11, 37-43.

Brown, B.J. /Marten, G.G., 1986, The Ecology of Traditional Pest Management in Southeast Asia. In: G. Marten (ed.): *Traditional Agriculture in Southeast Asia*, East-West Center, Westview Press, Colorado,241-72.

Caldecott, J., 1991, Monographie des Bartschweins (*Sus barbatus*). *Bongo,* 18:54-68.

Campos, J.E.L. /Root, H.L., 1995, Markets, Norms, and Peasant Rebellions. *Rationality and Society*, 7,1:93-115.

Casimir, M.J., 1993, Gegenstandsbereiche der Kulturökologie. In: T. Schweizer, M. Schweizer, W. Kokot (eds.): *Handbuch der Ethnologie,* Dietrich Reimer Verlag, Berlin,215-39.

Christanty, L., 1986, Shifting Cultivation and Tropical Soils: Patterns, Problems, and Possible Improvements. In: G. Marten (ed.): *Traditional Agriculture in Southeast Asia*, East-West Center, Westview Press, Colorado,226-40.

———, 1990, Home Gardens in Tropical Asia, with Special Reference to Indonesia. In: Landauer, K. & M. Brazil (eds.): *Tropical Home Gardens,* United Nations,9-20.

Clarke, W.C., 1971, *Place and people: an ecology of a New Guinean community.*, University of California Press, Berkeley, Los Angeles.

Colfer, C.J.P., 1983, Change and Indigenous Agroforestry in East Kalimantan, *Borneo Research Bulletin* 15,1:70-87.

———, 1991, Indigenous Rice Production and the Subtleties of Cultural Change: An Example from Borneo. *Agriculture & Human Values,* 8, 1/2:67-84.

———, 1997, *Beyond Slash and Burn*. The New York Botanical Garden.

———, n.d., *Shifting Cultivators of Indonesia: Marauders or Managers of the Forest? Rice Production and Forest Use Among the Uma' Jalan of East Kalimantan,* FAO Community Forestry Case Study Series 6.

Colinvaux, P., 1986, *Ecology,* John Wiley & Sons, New York.

Conklin, H.C., 1957, *Hanuóo Agriculture. A Report on an Integral System of Shifting Cultivation in the Philippines,* FAO, Rome.

Cox, M.J./van Dijk, P.P./Nabhitabhata, J./Thirakhupt, K., 1998, *A Photographic Guide to Snakes and Other Reptiles of Peninsular Malaysia, Singapore and Thailand,* New Holland, London and Singapore.

Davison, G.W.H. /Chew, Y.F., 1996, *A Photographic Guide to Birds of Borneo,* New Holland, London.

Dawkins, R., 1989, [1976] *The selfish gene*. New edition. Oxford University Press, Oxford and New York.

di Castri, F., 1976, International interdisciplinary research in ecology: some problems of organisation and execution. The case of the Man and the Biosphere (MAB) Programme. *Human Ecology,* 4:235-46.

Dougherty, J.W. (ed.), 1985, *Directions in Cognitive Anthropology*, Urbana.

Dove, M.R., 1985a, *Swidden Agriculture in Indonesia. The Subsistence Strategies of the Kalimantan Kantu*', Berlin.

———, 1985b, Plantation Development in West Kalimantan. *Borneo Research Bulletin,* 17,2:95-105.

———, 1986, Plantation Development in West Kalimantan II: The Perspectives of the Indigenous Population. *Borneo Research Bulletin,* 18,1:3-27.

———, 1993a, A Revisionist View of Tropical Deforestation and Development. *Environmental Conservation,* 20,1:17-56.

———, 1993b, Smallholder Rubber and Swidden Agriculture in Borneo — A Sustainable Adaptation to the Ecology and Economy of the Tropical Forest. *Economic Botany,* 47,2:136-47.

———, 1993c, Uncertainty, Humility and Adaptation in the Tropical Forest — The Agricultural Augury of the Kantu. *Ethnology,* 32,2:145-67.

———, 1993d, The Responses of Dayak and Bearded Pig to Mast-Fruiting in Kalimantan: An Analysis of Nature-Culture Analogies. In: C.M. Hladik *et al.*: *Tropical Forests, People and Food: Biocultural Interactions and Applications to Development*, Paris/Carnforth: UNESCO, Man and Biosphere Series, 13:113-23.

———, 1994, Transition from Native Forest Rubber to *Hevea brasiliensis* (*Euphorbiaceae*) among Tribal Smallholders in Borneo. *Economic Botany*, vol.48, no.4:382-96.

———, 1997, The Political Ecology of Pepper in the Hikayat Banjar. The historiography of commodity production in a Bornean Kingdom. In: Boomgaard, P., F. Colombijn & D. Henley (eds.) *Paper Landscapes: Explorations in the environmental history of Indonesia,* KITLV Press, Leiden:341-77.

Dransfield, J./Manokaran, N., 1994, *Rattans. Plant Resources of South-East Asia,* no.6, Bogor.

Eliade, M., 1991 [1951], *Schamanismus und archaische Ekstasetechnik.* 7th edn., Suhrkamp Taschenbuch Wissenschaft, Frankfurt am Main.

Ellen, R., 1978, Problems and Progress in the Ethnographic Analysis of Small Scale Human Ecosystems. *Man,* 13:290-303.

———, 1982, *Environment, Subsistence, and System: the Ecology of Small Scale Social Formations,* Cambridge University Press, Cambridge.

———, 1990, Trade, Environment, and the Reproduction of Local Systems in the Moluccas. In: E.F. Moran (ed.): *The Ecosystem Approach in Anthropology. From Concept to Practice,* The University of Michigan Press, Ann Arbor:191-227.

Ellis, F., 1998, Household Strategies and Rural Livelihood Diversification. *The Journal of Development Studies,* vol. 35, no.1:1-38.

Engelberg, J./Boyarsky, L.L., 1979, The Noncybernetic Nature of Ecosystems. *The American Naturalist,* vol. 114, no. 3:317-24.

Evans, F.C., 1956, Ecosystems as the Basic Unit in Ecology. *Science,* vol. 123:1127-8.

Feyerabend, P., 1988, *Against Method*, rev.edn. Verso, London, New York.

Fischer, H., 1985, *Feldforschung. Berichte zur Einführung in Probleme und Methode,* Reimer, Berlin.

———, 1992, Feldforschung. In: H.Fischer (ed.): *Ethnologie*, Reimer, Berlin,79-99.

Foin, T.C./Davis, W.G., 1987, Equilibrium and Nonequilibrium Models in Ecological Anthropology: An Evaluation of “Stability” in Maring Ecosystems in New Guinea. *American Anthropologist* vol. 89, no. 1:9-31.

Frake, C.O., 1962, Cultural ecology and ethnography. *American Anthropologist*, 64:53-9.

Freeman, D., 1992 [1955] *The Iban of Borneo. Monographs on Social Anthropology,* Majeed & Co., Kuala Lumpur, Malaysia.

———, 1999, Iban Augury. In: B.E. Smythies: *The Birds of Borneo,*4th edn., Revised by G.W.H. Davison, Natural History Publications in association with The Sabah Society, Kota Kinabalu,103-21.

Fried, S.T., 1995, *Writing for Their Lives: Bentian Dayak Authors and Indonesian Development Discourse*, Dissertation, Cornell University.

Fried, S.T./Sardjono, M.A., 1992, *Social and Economic Aspects of Rattan Production Middle Mahakam Region*. A Preliminary Survey. GFG-Report No. 21, Samarinda.

Friedman, J., 1974, Marxism, Structuralism and Vulgar Materialism. *Man,* 9:444-69.

Geertz, C., 1963, *Agricultural Involution,* Univ. of California Press, Berkeley and Los Angeles.

Gleason, H.A., 1926, The Individualistic Concept of the Plant Association. *Bulletin of the Torrey Botanical Club* 53:7-26.

Godoy, R.A., 1990, The Economics of Traditional Rattan Cultivation. *Agroforestry*, 12:163-72.

Godoy, R.A./Bennett, C., 1991, Monocropped and Intercropped Coconuts in Indonesia: Project Goals which Conflict with Smallholder Interests. *Human Ecology,* 19:83-98.

Godoy, R.A./Feaw, T.C., 1991, Agricultural Diversification among Rattan Cultivators in Central Kalimantan, Indonesia. *Agroforestry Systems,* 13:27-40.

Godoy, R.A./Jacobson, M./Wilkie, D., 1998a, Strategies of Rain-Forest Dwellers Against Misfortunes: The Tsimane' Indians of Bolivia. *Ethnology,* vol. 37, no. 1:55-69.

Godoy, R.A.,/Jacobson, M./de Castro, J./Aliaga, V./Romero, J./Davis, A., 1998b, The Role of Tenure Security and Private Time Preference in Neotropical Deforestation. *Land Economics,* 74 (2):162-70.

Gönner, C., 1990, *Ethnologische und Zoologische Auswertung zweier Borneo-reisen*. Unpublished report for Studienstiftung des Deutschen Volkes.

———, 1991, *Avifaunistische Artendiversität im Sepilok Virgin Jungle Reserve (Sabah/Malaysia): Ein Methodenvergleich*. Unpublished diploma thesis, Universität Konstanz, Germany.

———, 1998a, *Conflicts and Fire Causes in a Sub-District of Kutai, East Kalimantan, Indonesia.* A field report for WWF Indonesia.

———, 1998b, *Assessing Biodiversity for Forest Certification — Different Approaches & Practical Experiences from a Case Study in East Kalimantan*. SFMP Document No. 13 (1998), Samarinda, Indonesia.

———, 1999a, *Causes and Effects of Forest Fires: A Case Study from a Sub-District in East Kalimantan, Indonesia*. Paper presented at the ICRAF workshop: "Environmental Services and Land Use

Change: Bridging the Gap between Policy and Research in Southeast Asia", Chiang Mai, 31 May to 2 June 1999.

———, 1999b, *Resource Diversification and Avian Diversity*. Poster presented at the International Centre for Research in Agroforestry (ICRAF) workshop: Environmental Services and Land Use Change: Bridging the Gap between Policy and Research in Southeast Asia", Chiang Mai, 31 May to 2 June 1999.

———, 2000a, *Resource Management in a Dayak Benuaq Village: Strategies, Dynamics & Prospects. A Case Study from East Kalimantan, Indo-nesia*. TÖB publication number TÖB FTWF-20e, Eschborn, Germany.

———, 2000b, Wetland Birds of Lake Jempang and the Middle Mahakam Area. *Kukila 11* (Bulletin of the Indonesian Ornithological Society).

Gönner, C./Seeland, K., forthcoming, A close-to-nature forest economy adapted to a wider world: A case study of local forest management strategies in East Kalimantan, Indonesia. Accepted by *Journal of Sustainable Forestry*.

Görlich, J., 1993, Die Theorie rationalen Handelns in der Wirtschaftsethnologie. In: T. Schweizer, M. Schweizer, W. Kokot (eds.): *Handbuch der Ethnologie*. Dietrich Reimer Verlag, Berlin:241-62.

Golley, F., 1993, *A History of the Ecosystem Concept in Ecology*, Yale University Press, New Haven and London.

Graham, P., 1987, *Iban Shamanism. An Analysis of the Ethnographic Literature.* Australian National University, Canberra.

Gross, D.R., 1990, Ecosystems and Methodological Problems in Ecological Anthropology. In: E.F. Moran (ed.): *The Ecosystem Approach in Anthropology. From Concept to Practice*, The University of Michigan Press, Ann Arbor: 309-19.

Grossmann, C.M., 1997, *Significance and Development Potential of Non-Wood Forest Products in Central East Kalimantan. A Case Study from PT. Limbang Ganeca, Long Lalang and Ritan Baru*. SFMP Document No. 13 (1997), Samarinda, Indonesia.

———, 2000, *Nichtholz-Waldprodukte in Ost-Kalimantan, Indonesien. Analyse der waldwirtschaftlichen und sozio-ökonomischen Aspekte ihrer Bede-utung und ihres Entwicklungspotentials für die Lokalbevölkerung in einem Holzkonzessionsgebiet*. PhD. dissertation, Universität Hamburg.

Grzimek, B. (ed.), 1988, *Grzimeks Enzyklopädie* — Säugetiere. 5 vols., Kindler, München.

GTZ-SFMP, 1997, *Forestry Highlights from the Indonesian Press*. June-July 1997. Samarinda.

Hagen, J. B., 1992, *An Entangled Bank. The Origin of Ecosystem Ecology,* Rutgers University Press, New Brunswick.

Hall, K.R., 1985, *Maritime Trade and State Development in Early Southeast Asia,* University of Hawaii Press, Honolulu.

Harris, M., 1968, *The rise of anthropological theory*, Routledge and Kegan Paul, London.

Harrison, T., 1962, *The Malays of South-West Sarawak before Malaysia: A Socio-Ecological Survey,* MacMillan, London.

Haury, H.D./Saragih, B., 1997, *Low Rattan Farmgate Prices in East Kalimantan. Causes and Implications*. SFMP Document 12 (1997), Samarinda.

Holling, C.S., 1973, Resilience and Stability of Ecological Systems. *Annual Reviews in Ecology and Systematics,* 4:1-23.

Homer-Dixon, T., 1996, Strategies for Studying Causation in Complex Ecological-Political Systems. *Journal of Environment and Development*, vol. 5, no. 2:132-48.

Homma, A.K.O., 1996, Modernisation and Technological Dualism in the Extractive Economy in Amazonia. In: Ruiz Pérez, M./Arnold, J.E.M. (eds.): *Current Issues in Non-Timber Forest Products Research*, Cifor, Bogor,:59-82.

Hopes, M./Madrah/Karaakng, 1997, *Temputn: Myths of the Benuaq and Tunjung Dayak*. Puspa Swara and Rio Tinto Foundation, Jakarta.

Hopes, M., 1997, *Ilmu: Magic and Divination amongst the Benuaq and Tunjung Dayak*. Puspa Swara and Rio Tinto Foundation, Jakarta.

Hudson, A. B., 1966, Death Ceremonies of the Maanyan Dayaks. *Sarawak Museum Journal*, vol. XIII, no. 27:341-416.

———, 1967, *Padju Epat: The Ethnography and Social Structure of a Ma'anjan Dajak Group in Southeastern Borneo*, Cornell Univ.

Hultkrantz, Å., 1973, A Definition of Shamanism. *Temenos,* 9:25-37.

Husserl, E., 1996, *Die Krisis der europäischen Wissenschaften und die transzendentale Phänomenologie*. Meiner, Hamburg (3rd edn.).

Hutterer, K.L., 1984, Ecology and Evolution of Agriculture in Southeast Asia. In: A.T. Rambo & P.E. Sajise (eds.): *An Introduction to Human Ecology Research on Agricultural Systems in Southeast Asia,* Univ. of the Philippines at Los Baños, Laguna,75-97.

Inger, R.F./Lian, T.F., 1996, *The Natural History of Amphibians and Reptiles in Sabah*. Natural History Publications (Borneo), Kota Kinabalu, Malaysia.

Inoue, M./Lahjie, A.M., 1990, Dynamics of swidden agriculture in East Kalimantan. *Agroforestry Systems,* 12, 269-84.

Jepson, P./Momberg, F./van Noord, H., 1998, *Trade in the Hill Myna Gracula religiosa From the Mahakam Lakes Region, East Kalimantan*. Technical Memorandum 4, WWF Indonesia.

Jessup, T./Peluso, N.L., 1986, Minor Forest Products as Common Property Resources in East Kalimantan, Indonesia. In: *Proceedings of the Conference on Common Property Resources*, National Academy of Sciences. n.pl.

Jessup, T.C., 1983, *Interactions between people and forests in the Apo Kayan*. Unpublished final report for the 1979-82 East Kalimantan Man and the Biosphere project, revised version.

Kartawinata, K./Vayda, A.P., 1984, Forest conversion in East Kalimantan, Indonesia: the activities and impact of timber companies, shifting cultivators, migrant pepper farmers, and others. In: F. di Castri, F.W.G. Baker & M. Hadley (eds.): *Ecology in Practice*, Part I. Tycooly, Dublin,98-126.

Kartawinata, K./Soedjito, H./Jessup, T./Vayda, A.P./Colfer, C.J.P., 1984, The impact of development on interactions between people and forests in East Kalimantan: a comparison of two areas of Kenyah Dayak settlement. In: J. Hanks (ed.): *Traditional Life-styles, Conservation and Rural Development*, International Union for the Conservation of Nature and Natural Resources (Commission on Ecology Papers No. 7), Gland, Switzerland,87-95.

Kemp, W.B., 1971, The flow of energy in a hunting society. *Scientific American,* 225 (3):105-15.

Kemper, T.D., 1993, Reason in Emotions or Emotions in Reason. *Rationality and Society,* 5,2:275-82.

King, V.T., 1985, *The Maloh of West Kalimantan: An Ethnographic Study of Social Inequality and Social Change among an Indonesian Borneo People*. Dordrecht: Verhandelingen van het Koninklijk Instituut voor Taal-, Land- en Volkenkunde (no. 108) Cinnaminson, USA:Foris.

———, 1993, *The Peoples of Borneo*, Blackwell, Oxford.

———, 1994, *World Within: The Ethnic Groups of Borneo,*Majeed & Co., Kuala Lumpur, Malaysia.

———, 1999, *Anthropology and Development in South-East Asia. Theory and Practice*, Oxford University Press, Oxford.

King, B./Woodcock, M./Dickinson, E.C., 1975, *A Field Guide to the Birds of South-East Asia,* Collins, London.

Knappert, S.C., 1905, Beschryving van de Onderafdeeling Koetai. In: *Bijdragen tot de Land-, Taal en Volkenkunde* 58:575-654.

Köhler, U./Seitz, S., 1993, Agrargesellschaften. In: T. Schweizer, M. Schweizer, W. Kokot (eds.): *Handbuch der Ethnologie*. Dietrich Reimer Verlag, Berlin:561-92.

Koeniger, N./Tingket, S./Koeniger, G./Gries, M./Kelitu, A., 1998, A Taste of Honey. Exploring the Centre of Honeybee Diversity. *Borneo*, vol. 4 no. 1/2:18-33.

Kokot, W., 1992, Kognitive Ethnologie. In: H. Fischer (ed.): *Ethnologie. Einführung und Überblick*, Dietrich Reimer Verlag, Berlin,367-81.

Krebs, C.J., 1985, *Ecology. The Experimental Analysis of Distribution and Abundance,*3rd edn., Harper & Row, New York.

Krieger, D.J., 1996, *Einführung in die allgemeine Systemtheorie*. Wilhelm Fink Verlag, München.

Kroeber, A.L., 1917, The superorganic. *American Anthropologist,* 19:163-213.

———, 1939, *Cultural and natural areas of native north America*, University of California Publications in American Archaeology and Ethnology 38. University of California Press, Berkeley.

Krohn, W.O., 1991 [1927], *In Borneo Jungles. Among the Dayak Headhunters,* Oxford University Press, Singapore, Oxford, New York.

Küppers, B.-O. (ed.), 1987, *Ordnung aus dem Chaos. Prinzipien der Selbst-organisation und Evolution des Lebens*. Piper, München and Zürich.

Lahjie, A.M., 1996, Traditional Land Use and Kenyah Dayak Farming Systems in East Kalimantan. In: C. Padoch/Peluso, N.L. (eds.): *Borneo in Transition,* Oxford University Press, Kuala Lumpur,150-61.

Lahjie, A.M./Seibert, B., 1990, Honey Gathering by People in the Interior of East Kalimantan. *Beeworld*, vol. 71,4:153-7.

Lang, H., 1981, Systemanalyse und Systemtheorie in der Ethnologie. *Zeitschrift für Ethnologie,* 106:3-22.

———, 1992, Die Untersuchung von Kultur als System. In: H. Fischer (ed.): *Ethnologie. Einführung und Überblick,* Dietrich Reimer Verlag, *Berlin*, 407-19.

———, 1993, Ethnodemographie. In: T. Schweizer, M. Schweizer & W. Kokot (eds.): *Handbuch der Ethnologie*, Dietrich Reimer Verlag, Berlin,117-44.

Langup, J., 1993, Hunting and Gathering: A View from Within. In: Vinson H. Sutlive, Jr. (ed.): *Change and Development in Borneo*, Borneo Research Council, Williamsburg,101-12.

Lawrence, D.C., 1996, Trade-offs between rubber production and maintenance of diversity: the structure of rubber gardens in West Kalimantan, Indonesia. *Agroforestry Systems,*34:83-100.

Lawrence, D.C./Leighton, M./Peart, D.R., 1995, Availability and Extraction of Forest Products in Managed and Primary Forests around a Dayak Village in West Kalimantan, Indonesia. *Conservation Biology,* 9,1:76-88.

Lawrence, D.C./Peart, D.R./Leighton, M., 1998, The impact of shifting cultivation on a rainforest landscape in West Kalimantan: spatial and temporal dynamics. *Landscape Ecology* 13:135-48.

Leach, E.R., 1950, *Social Science Research in Sarawak,* London.

Leaman, D.J., 1995, Malaria Remedies of the Kenyah of the Apo-Kayan, East Kalimantan, Indonesian Borneo — A Qualitative Assessment of Local Consensus as an Indicator of Biological Efficacy. *Journal of Ethnopharmacology*, vol. 46, 1:1-16.

Leaman, D.J./Yusuf, R./Sangat-Roemantyo, H./Arnason, J.T., 1996, The Contribution of Ethnobotanical Research to Socio-economic and Conservation Objectives: An Example from the Apo Kayan Kenyah. In: C. Padoch/Peluso, N.L. (eds.): *Borneo in Transition*, Oxford University Press, Kuala Lumpur, 245-55.

Lees, S.H./Bates, D.G., 1990, The Ecology of Cumulative Change. In: E.F. Moran (ed.): *The Ecosystem Approach in Anthropology. From Concept to Practice*, The University of Michigan Press, Ann Arbor, 247-77.

Lemmens, R.H.M.J./Wulijarni-Soetjipto, N. (eds.), 1992, *Dye and tannin-producing plants*. Plant Resources of South-East Asia, No.3, Bogor.

Lévi-Strauss, C., 1978 [1973], *Structural Anthropology* 2, Penguin Books, Hardmondsworth, England.

———, 1994 [1962], *Das Wilde Denken*. Suhrkamp Taschenbuch Wissenschaft, Frankfurt am Main.

Liat, B.L./Das, I., 1999, *Turtles of Borneo and Peninsular Malaysia*, Natural History Publications (Borneo). Kota Kinabalu.

Lindeman, R.L., 1941, Seasonal food-cycle dynamics in a senescent lake. *American Midland Naturalist,* 26:636-73.

Löffler, U., 1996, *Land Tenure Developments in Indonesia,* GTZ.

MacKinnon, J./Phillipps, K., 1993, *A Field Guide to the Birds of Borneo, Sumatra, Java and Bali*, Oxford University Press, Oxford.

MacKinnon, K./Hatta, G./Halim, H./Mangalik, A., 1996, *The Ecology of Kalimantan, Indonesian Borneo*. The Ecology of Indonesia Series Vol. III. Periplus Editions, Hongkong.

Mallinckrodt, J., 1927, De Stamindeeling van de Maanjan-Sioeng-Dajaks, der Zuider- en Oosterafdeeling van Borneo. *Bijdragen tot de Land-, Taal en Volkenkunde* vol.80.

Marcus, G.E./Fischer, M.M.J., 1986, *Anthropology as Cultural Critique: An Experimental Moment in the Human Sciences*, The University of Chicago Press, Chicago and London.

Marten, G.G./Saltman, D.M., 1986, The Human Ecology Perspective. In: G. Marten (ed.): *Traditional Agriculture in Southeast Asia*, East-West Center, Westview Press, Colorado.

Mason, O., 1895, Influence of environment upon human industries and arts. *Annual Report of the Smithsonian Institution*,639-65.

Massing, A.W., 1981, The Journey to Paradise: Funerary Rites of the Benuaq Dayak of East Kalimantan. *Borneo Research Bulletin,* 13:85-104.

———, 1982, Where Medicine Fails: Belian Disease Prevention and Curing Rituals among the Lawangan Dayak of East Kalimantan. *Borneo Research Bulletin,* 14,2:56-84.

May, R.M., 1973, *Stability and complexity in model ecosystems*. Princeton University Press, Princeton, N.J.

Mayer, J., 1989, *Socioeconomic Aspects of the Forest Fire 1982/83 and the Relation of Local Communities towards Forestry and Forest Management in East Kalimantan,* GTZ, FR-Report No.9.

McCay, B.J., 1978, Systems Ecology, People Ecology, and the Anthropology of Fishing Communities. *Human Ecology*, vol. 6, no. 4:397-422.

McGrath, D. G./de Castro, F./Futemma, C./de Amaral, B.D./Calabria, J., 1993, Fisheries and the Evolution of Resource Management on the Lower Amazon Floodplain. *Human Ecology,* 21,2:167-95.

Menon, K.D., 1989, *The Rattan Industry — Prospects for Development*. Direc-torate General of Forest Utilization, Ministry of Forestry & FAO, Jakarta.

Michon, G./Mary, F., 1990, Transforming Traditional Home Gardens and Related Systems in West Java (Bogor) and West Sumatra (Maninjau). In: K. Landauer & M.A.Brazil (eds.): *Tropical Home Gardens,* United Nations.

Michon, G./Mary, F./Bompard, J., 1986, Multistoreyed agroforestry garden systems in West Sumatra, Indonesia. *Agroforestry Systems,* 4:315-38.

Möbius, K., 1877, *Die Auster und die Austernwirthschaft*. Verlag von Wiegandt, Hempel und Parey, Berlin.

Momberg, F., 1993, *Indigenous Knowledge Systems: Potentials for Social Forestry Development — Resource Management of Land-Dayaks in West Kalimantan*, Technische Universität Berlin.

Momberg, F./Jessup, T./Puri, R., 1994, *Gaharu Collecting in the Kayan Mentarang Nature Reserve: Problems and Prospects for Sustainable Community-based Forest Management in East Kalimantan, Indonesia*. Unpublished report, WWF Indonesia Programme.

Momberg, F./Damus, D./Limberg, G./Padan, S., n.d. *Participatory Tools for Community — Forest Profiling and Zonation of Conservation Areas. Examples from the Kayan Mentarang Nature Reserve, East Kalimantan, Indonesia*. WWF Indonesia Programme.

Momberg, F./Jepson, P./van Noord, H., 1998, *Trade in Reptiles From the Middle Mahakam Lake Area, East Kalimantan Indonesia, With Evidence of a Causal Link to the Forest Fires*. Technical Memorandum 3, WWF Indonesia.

Moran, E.F., 1990a, Ecosystem Ecology in Biology and Anthropology: A Critical Assessment. In: E.F. Moran (ed.): *The Ecosystem Approach in Anthropology. From Concept to Practice*, The University of Michigan Press, Ann Arbor: 3-40.

———, 1990b, Levels of Analysis and Analytical Level Shifting: Examples from Amazonian Ecosystem Research. In: E.F. Moran (ed.): *The Ecosystem Approach in Anthropology. From Concept to Practice*, The University of Michigan Press, Ann Arbor: 279-308.

———, 1991, Human Adaptive Strategies in Amazonian Blackwater Ecosystems. *American Anthropologist,* 93. S.361-82.

Murdock, G.P., 1960, *Social Structure in Southeast Asia,* Edition Chicago.

Nasendi, B.D., 1994, *Socio-Economic Information on Rattan in Indonesia*, Ministry of Forestry, Jakarta.

Nash, M., 1967, The Social Context of Economic Choice in a Small Society. In: G. Dalton (ed.): *Tribal and Peasant Economies. Readings in Economic Anthropology*, Univ. of Texas Press, Austin and London, 524-38.

Netting, R.Mc.C., 1990, Links and Boundaries: Reconsidering the Alpine Village as Ecosystem. In: E.F. Moran (ed.): *The Ecosystem Approach in Anthropology. From Concept to Practice,* The University of Michigan Press, Ann Arbor: 229-45.

Ngo, T.H.G.M., 1996, A New Perspective on Property Rights: Examples from the Kayan of Kalimantan. In: C. Padoch/Peluso, N.L. (eds.): *Borneo in Transition,* Oxford University Press, Kuala Lumpur, 137-49.

Nietschmann, B., 1973, *Between land and water*, Seminar Press, New York.

Nothofer, B./Pampus, K.-H., 1988, *Bahasa Indonesia. Indonesisch für Deutsche Teil 1*. Julius Groos Verlag, Heidelberg.

Odum, E.P., 1953, *Fundamentals of Ecology,* Saunders, Philadelphia.

———, 1971, *Fundamentals of Ecology*, 3rd edn., Saunders, Philadelphia.

Orlove, B.S., 1980, Ecological Anthropology. *Annual Review of Anthropology,* 9:235-73.

Padoch, C., 1985, Labor Efficiency and Intensity of Land Use in Rice Production: An Example from Kalimantan. *Human Ecology,* 13,3:271-89.

———, 1986, Agricultural Site Selection among Permanent Field Farmers: An Example from East Kalimantan, Indonesia. *Journal of Ethnobiology,* 6,2:279-88.

Padoch, C./ Harwell, E./Susanto, A., 1998, Swidden, Sawah, and In-Between: Agricultural Transformation in Borneo. *Human Ecology*, vol.26, no.1:3-20.

Padoch, C./Peluso, N.L. (eds.), 1996, *Borneo in Transition*, Oxford University Press, Kuala Lumpur.

Padoch, C./Peters, C., 1993, Managed forest gardens in West Kalimantan, Indonesia. In: C.S. Potter *et al.* (eds.): *Perspectives on Biodiversity: Case Studies of Genetic Resource Conservation and Development,* Washington D.C.:167-76.

Padoch, C./Pinedo-Vasquez, M., 1996, Smallholder Forest Management: Looking Beyond Non-Timber Forest Products. In: Ruiz Pérez,

M./Arnold, J.E.M. (eds.): *Current Issues in Non-Timber Forest Products Research*, CIFOR, Bogor:103-18.

Park, R.E. /Burgess, E.W., 1924 [1921], *Introduction to the science of sociology,* Chicago University Press, Chicago.

Patten, B.C./Odum, E.P., 1981, The Cybernetic Nature of Ecosystems. *The American Naturalist,* 118:886-95.

Payne, J./Francis, C.M./Phillipps, K., 1985, *The Mammals of Borneo*, The Sabah Society, Kuala Lumpur.

Peluso, N.L., 1992, The Rattan Trade in East Kalimantan, Indonesia. *Advances in Economic Botany,* 9:115-27.

———, 1995a, *Extraction Interactions: Logging Tropical Timbers in West Kalimantan, Indonesia. East-West Center Occasional Papers*. Environment Series 19.

———, 1995b, Whose Woods are These? Counter-Mapping Forest Territories in Kalimantan, Indonesia. *Antipode,* vol. 27, 4:383-406.

Peluso, N.L./Padoch, C., 1996, Changing Resource Rights in Managed Forests of West Kalimantan. In: C. Padoch/Peluso, N.L. (eds.): *Borneo in Transition,* Oxford University Press, Kuala Lumpur, 121-36.

Penot, E., 1995, Taking the 'jungle' out of the rubber. Improving rubber in Indonesian agroforestry system. *Agroforestry Today,* July-December 1995:11-13.

Peters, C., 1996, Illipe Nuts (*Shorea* spp.) in West Kalimantan: Use, Ecology, and Management Potential of an Important Forest Resource. In: C. Padoch/Peluso, N.L. (eds.): *Borneo in Transition*, Oxford University Press, Kuala Lumpur, 230-44.

Peters, C./Gentry, A./Mendelsohn, R., 1989, Valuation of an Amazonian Rainforest. *Nature,*339:655-6.

Phillips, J., 1931, The biotic community. *Journal of Ecology,* 19:1-24.

———, 1934, Succession, development, the climax, and the complex organism: An analysis of concepts. Pt.1. *Journal of Ecology,* 22:554-71.

———, 1935a, Succession, development, the climax, and the complex organism: An analysis of concepts. Pt.2. Development and the climax. *Journal of Ecology,* 23:210-43.

———, 1935b, Succession, development, the climax, and the complex organism: An analysis of concepts. Pt.3. The complex organism: Conclusion. *Journal of Ecology,* 23:488-508.

Pinedo-Vasquez, M./Padoch, C., 1996, Managing Forest Remnants and Forest Gardens in Peru and Indonesia. In: J. Schelhas & R. Greenberg (eds.): *Forest Patches in Tropical Landscapes*, Island Press, Washington D.C.:327-342.

Poffenberger, M./McGean, B., 1993, *Communities and Forest Management in East Kalimantan: Pathway to Environmental Stability,* Center for Southeast Asia Studies, Berkeley.

Popper, K.R., 1993, *Objektive Erkenntnis. Ein evolutionärer Entwurf*, Hoffmann und Campe, Hamburg.

Primack, R.B./Hall, P., 1992, Biodiversity and Forest Change in Malaysian Borneo. *Bioscience*, vol. 42, no. 11:829-37.

Puri, R.K., 1995, *Penan Benalui Knowledge and Use of Tree Palms,* Draft. WWF.

Rambo, A.T., 1984, Human Ecology Research by Social Scientists on Tropical Agroecosystems. In: A.T. Rambo & P.E. Sajise (eds.): *An Introduction to Human Ecology Research on Agricultural Systems in Southeast Asia,* Univ. of the Philippines at Los Baños, Laguna:39-60.

Rappaport, R.A., 1968, *Pigs for the ancestors. Ritual in the ecology of a New Guinea people*, Yale University Press, New Haven.

———, 1984, *Pigs for the Ancestors. Ritual in the Ecology of a New Guinea People*, new, enlarged edition, Yale University Press, New Haven and London.

———, 1990, Ecosystems, Populations and People. In: E.F. Moran (ed.): *The Ecosystem Approach in Anthropology. From Concept to Practice,* The University of Michigan Press, Ann Arbor: 41-72.

Ratzel, F., 1882, *Anthropo-Geographie, oder Grundzüge der Anwendung der Erdkunde auf die Geschichte*. J. Engelhorn, Stuttgart.

Rehm, S./Espig, G., 1984, *Die Kulturpflanzen der Tropen und Subtropen*, Ulmer, Stuttgart.

Rigler, F.H., 1975, The concept of energy flow and nutrient flow between trophic levels. In: W.H. van Dobben & R.H. Lowe-McConnell (eds.): *Unifying Concepts in Ecology,* Dr. W. Junk B.V., The Hague,15-26.

Riwut, T., 1958, *Kalimantan Memanggil*. N.V. Pustaka, Jakarta, Indonesia.

Romanoff, S., 1992, Food and Debt among Rubber Tappers in the Bolivian Amazon. *Human Organisation,* 51,2:122-35.

Rousseau, J., 1990, *Central Borneo. Ethnic Identity and Social Life in a Stratified Society,* Oxford.

———, 1994, The Kayan. In: V.T. King (ed.): *The Ethnic Groups of Borneo, S.* Abdul Majeed & Co., Kuala Lumpur, Malaysia,101-19.

Rubin, E.L., 1998, Putting Rational Actors in Their Place: Economics and Phenomenology. *Vanderbilt Law Review,* 51,6:1705-27.

Ruiz Pérez M./Byron, N., n.d., A methodology to analyse divergent case studies of non-timber forest products and their development potential. Submitted to *Forest Science*.

Safran, E.B./Godoy, R.A., 1993, Effects of Government Policies on Smallholder Palm Cultivation — An Example from Borneo. *Human Organisation,* vol. 52,3:294-8.

Salafsky, N., 1993, Mammalian Use of a Buffer Zone Agroforestry System Bordering Gunung Palung National Park, West Kalimantan, Indonesia. *Conservation Biology,*7,4:928-33.

———, 1994, Forest Gardens in the Gunung Palung Region of West Kalimantan, Indonesia. Defining a Locally-developed, Market-oriented Agroforestry System. *Agroforestry Systems,*28,3:237-68.

Sardjono, M.A., 1990, *Die Lembo-Kultur in Ost-Kalimantan: Ein Modell für die Entwicklung agroforstlicher Landnutzung in den Feuchttropen*. Diss. Univ. Hamburg.

———, 1996, The Lembo System: A Model for Agroforestry in Dipterocarp Forest Ecosystems of East Kalimantan, Indonesia. In: A. Schulte/Schöne, D. (ed.): *Dipterocarp Forest Ecosystems,* World Scientific, Singapore,354-68.

———, n.d., *Soil conservation aspects of the traditional tree gardening in East Kalimantan.*

Sarwoto, Kertodopoero, 1963, *Kaharingan*, Sumur Bandung.

Sasaki, H., 1997, *Technical and Economic Innovations in Swidden-based Rattan Cultivation of Benuaq-Dayak People in the Middle Mahakam, East Kalimantan, Indonesia*. Paper for the ICRAF regional workshop on "Indigenous Strategies for Intensification of Shifting Cultivation in Southeast Asia", Bogor, Indonesia, June 23-8,1997.

Schelhas, J., 1996, Land Use Choice and Change: Intensification and Diversification in the Lowland Tropics of Costa Rica. *Human Organization*, vol. 55, No. 3:298-306.

Schönhuth, M./Kievelitz, U., 1994, *Participatory Learning Approaches. Rapid Rural Appraisal, Participatory Rural Appraisal*. Schriftenreihe der GTZ, No.248.

Schwaner, C.A.L.M., 1853, *Borneo*. vol. 1, P.N. van Kampen, Amsterdam.

Schweizer, T., 1993, Perspektiven der analytischen Ethnologie. In: T. Schweizer, M. Schweizer & W. Kokot (eds.): *Handbuch der Ethnologie*, Dietrich Reimer Verlag, Berlin,79-113.

———, 1996, *Muster sozialer Ordnung. Netzwerkanalyse als Fundament der Sozialethnologie,* Dietrich Reimer Verlag, Berlin.

Seber, G.A.F., 1984, *Multivariate Observations,* John Wiley & Sons, New York.

Seeland, K. (ed.), 1997, *Nature is Culture. Indigenous knowledge and socio-cultural aspects of trees and forests in non-European cultures,* IT Publications, London.

Seeland, K., n.d., *Entwurf einer kultur-ökologischen Checkliste*, ETH Zürich, unpublished.

Seitz, S., 1988a, Die Penan (Punan). In: H. Harrer (ed.): *Borneo*, Pinguin-Verlag, Innsbruck,163-91.

———, 1988b, Die Iban. In: H. Harrer (ed.): *Borneo*, Pinguin-Verlag, Innsbruck,192-206.

Setyawati, I., n.d.a, *Indigenous Knowledge and In Situ Crop Germplasm Conservation*. Draft.

———, n.d. b, *Environmental Variability and the Indigenous Knowledge and Use of Crop Varieties*. Draft.

Shelford, V.E., 1915, Principles and Problems of Ecology as Illustrated by Animals. *Journal of Ecology,* 3:1-23.

Shim, P.S./Tan, C.F., 1994, *Calamus trachycoleus* Beccari. In: J. Dransfield & N. Manokaran: *Rattans. Plant Resources of South-East Asia*, No.6, Bogor:75-9.

Sillander, K., 1995, Ethnicity among the Luangan and the Bentian. *Borneo Research Bulletin* vol. 26:69-95.

Simberloff, D., 1980, A Succession of Paradigms in Ecology: Essentialism to Materialism and Probabilism. *Synthese,* 43:3-39.

Sirait, M./Prasodjo, S./Podger, N./Flavelle, A., 1994, Mapping Customary Land in East Kalimantan, Indonesia: A Tool for Forest Management. *Ambio,* 23,7:411-17.

Smits, W.T.M., 1996, *Arenga pinnata* (Wurmb) Merrill. In: M. Flach & F. Rumawas (eds.): *Plants yielding non-seed carbohydrates*, Plant Resources of South-East Asia No. 9, Bogor, 53-9.

Smuts, J.C., 1926, *Holism and Evolution,* Macmillan, New York.

Smythies, B.E., 1981, *The Birds of Borneo,* The Sabah Society, Kuala Lumpur.

———, 1999, *The Birds of Borneo,* 4th edn., Revised by G.W.H. Davison, Natural History Publications in association with The Sabah Society, Kota Kinabalu.

Soemarwoto, O., 1985a, The Javanese Home-Garden as an Integrated Agroecosystem. *Food and Nutrition Bulletin,* 7,3, New Dehli:44-7.

———, 1985b, The Telun-Kebun: A Man-made Forest fitted to Family Needs. *Food and Nutrition Bulletin,* 7,3, New Dehli:48-51.

Soetarso, P./Amblani, 1988, Budidaya Rotan Sega (*Calamus caesius*) di Daerah Bentian Kalimantan Timur. *Wanatrop* vol. 3, no. 2:55-70.

Sokal, R.R./Rohlf, F.J., 1973, *Introduction to Biostatistics,* Freeman, San Francisco.

Southwell, C.H., 1959, The Kayans and Kenyahs. In: T. Harrison (ed.): *The Peoples of Sarawak*, Sarawak Museum, Kuching, Malaysia.

Spencer, J.E., 1966, *Shifting Cultivation in Southeastern Asia,* Univ. of California Press, Berkeley and Los Angeles.

Spradley, J.P., 1979, *The Ethnographic Interview*, New York.

———, 1980, *Participant Observation*, New York.

Stellrecht, I., 1993, Interpretative Ethnologie: Eine Orientierung. In: T. Schweizer, M. Schweizer & W. Kokot (eds.): *Handbuch der Ethnologie*, Dietrich Reimer Verlag, Berlin, 29-78.

Steward, J.H., 1955, *Theory of Culture Change*, Univ. of Illinois, Urbana.

Subhadrabandhu, S./Schneemann, J.M.P./Verheij, E.W.M., 1992, *Durio zibethinus* Murray. In: Verheij, E.W.M./Coronel, R.E. (eds.): *Edible fruits and nuts,* Plant Resources of South-East Asia, No.2, Bogor.

Sumual, K., 1998, Papatn Puti. An Eco-cultural Museum. *Borneo,* vol. 4, no.1/2:48-55.

Suryadiputra, N.N./Gönner, C./Wibowo, P./Ratnawati, E., 2000, *The Mahakam Lakes*. Paper presented at the Global Nature Fund Conference from June,16-17, 2000 at Hannover, Germany.

Sutlive, V.H., Jr., 1992, *The Iban of Sarawak. Chronicle of a vanishing world,* Majeed & Co., Kuala Lumpur, Malaysia.

Swadesh, M., 1971, *The Origin and Diversification of Language*, Aldine-Atherton, Chicago, Ill.

Tan, C.F./Shim,P.S,1994, *Calamus caesius* Blume. In: J. Dransfield & N. Manokaran: *Rattans*. Plant Resources of South-East Asia, No.6, Bogor, 43-6.

Tansley, A.G., 1935, The Use and Abuse of Vegetational Concepts and Terms. *Ecology*, vol. 16, no. 3:284-307.

Taylor, P./García-Barrios, R., 1995, The social analysis of ecological change: from systems to intersecting processes. *Social Science Information*, 34,1:5-30.

Thandee, D., 1986, Socioeconomic Factors and Small-scale Farmers in Southeast Asia. In: G. Marten (ed.): *Traditional Agriculture in Southeast Asia*, East-West Center, Westview Press, Colorado,159-70.

Thiel, J.F., 1984, *Religionsethnologie. Grundbegriffe der Religionen schriftloser Völker,* Dietrich Reimer Verlag, Berlin.

Thiollay, J.-M., 1995, The Role of Traditional Agroforests in the Conservation of Rain Forest Bird Diversity in Sumatra. *Conservation Biology,* vol. 9/2:335-53.

Tremeer, R.E., 1964, The early history of rubber planting in Sarawak, 1880-1910. *Sarawak Gazette,* 90:50-2.

Uljee, G.L., 1925, *Handboek voor de Residentie Westerafdeling van Borneo,* Visser, Weltevreden.

van Valkenburg, J.L.C.H., 1997, *Non-Timber Forest Products of East Kalimantan. Potentials for sustainable forest use*. Tropenbos series 16, Wageningen.

van Voris, P./O'Neill, R. V./Shugart, H.H./Emanuel, W.R., 1980, Functional complexity and ecosystem stability. *Ecology,* 61:1352-60.

Vargas, D.M., 1985, *The Interface of Customary and National Land Law in East Kalimantan, Indonesia,* Yale University.

Vayda, A.P., 1965, Anthropologists and ecological problems. In: A. Leeds, A.P. Vayda (eds.): *Man, culture and animals,* American Association for the Advancement of Science, Publication 78, Washington D.C.

———, 1983, Progressive Contextualization: Methods for Research in Human Ecology. *Human Ecology*, vol. 11, no. 3:265-81.

———, 1996, *Methods and Explanations in the Study of Human Actions and their Environmental Effects*. CIFOR/WWF Special Publication.

Vayda, A.P./Rappaport, R.A., 1968, Ecology, cultural and non-cultural.

In: J.A. Clifton (ed.): *Introduction to cultural anthropology: essays in the scope and methods of the science of man,* Houghton Mifflin, Boston.

Vayda, A.P./McCay, B.J., 1975, New Directions in Ecology and Ecological Anthropology. *Annual Review of Anthropology,* 4:293-306.

Vester, F., 1984, *Neuland des Denkens — vom technokratischen zum kybernetischen Zeitalter*. dtv München.

———, 1999, *Die Kunst vernetzt zu denken. Ideen und Werkzeuge für einen neuen Umgang mit Komplexität*. DVA Stuttgart.

von Bertalanffy, L., 1950, An outline of general systems theory. *British Journal of Philosophy Science,* 1:134-65.

———, 1968, *General System Theory. Foundations, Development, Applications,* George Braziller, New York.

von Heine-Geldern, R., 1945, *Prehistoric research in the Netherlands Indies,* Southeast Asia Institute, New York.

Waddell, E., 1972, *The mound builders: agicultural practices, environment and society in the central highlands of New Guinea*. American Ethnological Society Monograph 53. University of Washington Press, Seattle and London.

Weidelt, H.-J., 1990, Rattan Growing in South-East Asia — An Ecologically Well-Adapted Form of Land Use. *Plant Research & Development*, 31:26-37.

Weinstock, J.A., 1981, Kaharingan: Borneo's 'Old Religion' Becomes Indonesia's Newest Religion. *Borneo Research Bulletin*, vol. 13, no. 1:47-8.

———, 1983a, *Kaharingan and Luangan Dayaks. Religion and Identity in Central-East Borneo*. PhD-Thesis. Cornell University.

———, 1983b, Rattan: Ecological Balance in a Borneo Rainforest. *Economic Botany,* 37,1:58-68.

Werner, S., 1997, *The Development of Central Sumatran Traditional Fallow Systems in a Changing Environment — Draft*. Paper for the ICRAF regional workshop on "Indigenous Strategies for Intensification of Shifting Cultivation in Southeast Asia", Bogor, Indonesia, June 23-8, 1997.

White, L.A., 1949, *The science of culture: a study of man and civilization*, Grove Press, New York.

Whitmore, T.C., 1990, *An Introduction to Tropical Rain Forests*, Oxford University Press, Oxford.

Whittier, H.L., 1973, *Social Organization and Symbols of Social Differentiation. An Ethnographic Study of the Kenyah Dayak of East Kalimantan*. Dissertation, Michigan State University.

———, 1978, The Kenyah. In: V.T. King (ed.): *Essays on Borneo Societies*, Oxford, 92-122.

———, 1994, The Kenyah. In: V.T. King (ed.): *The Ethnic Groups of Borneo*, S. Abdul Majeed & Co., Kuala Lumpur, Malaysia,120-59.

Wilk, R./Miller, S., 1997, Some Methodological Issues in Counting Communities and Households. *Human Organization*, vol. 56, no. 1:64-70.

Winterhalder, B., 1984, Reconsidering the Ecosystem Concept. *Reviews in Anthropology,* 11 (4):301-30.

Wissler, C., 1917, *The American Indian: an introduction to the anthropology of the New World*, McMurtie, New York.

———, 1928, The Culture Area Concept as a Research Lead. *American Journal of Sociology,* 33,6:894-900.

Wolters, O., 1967, *Early Indonesian commerce*, Cornell University Press, Ithaca.

Index